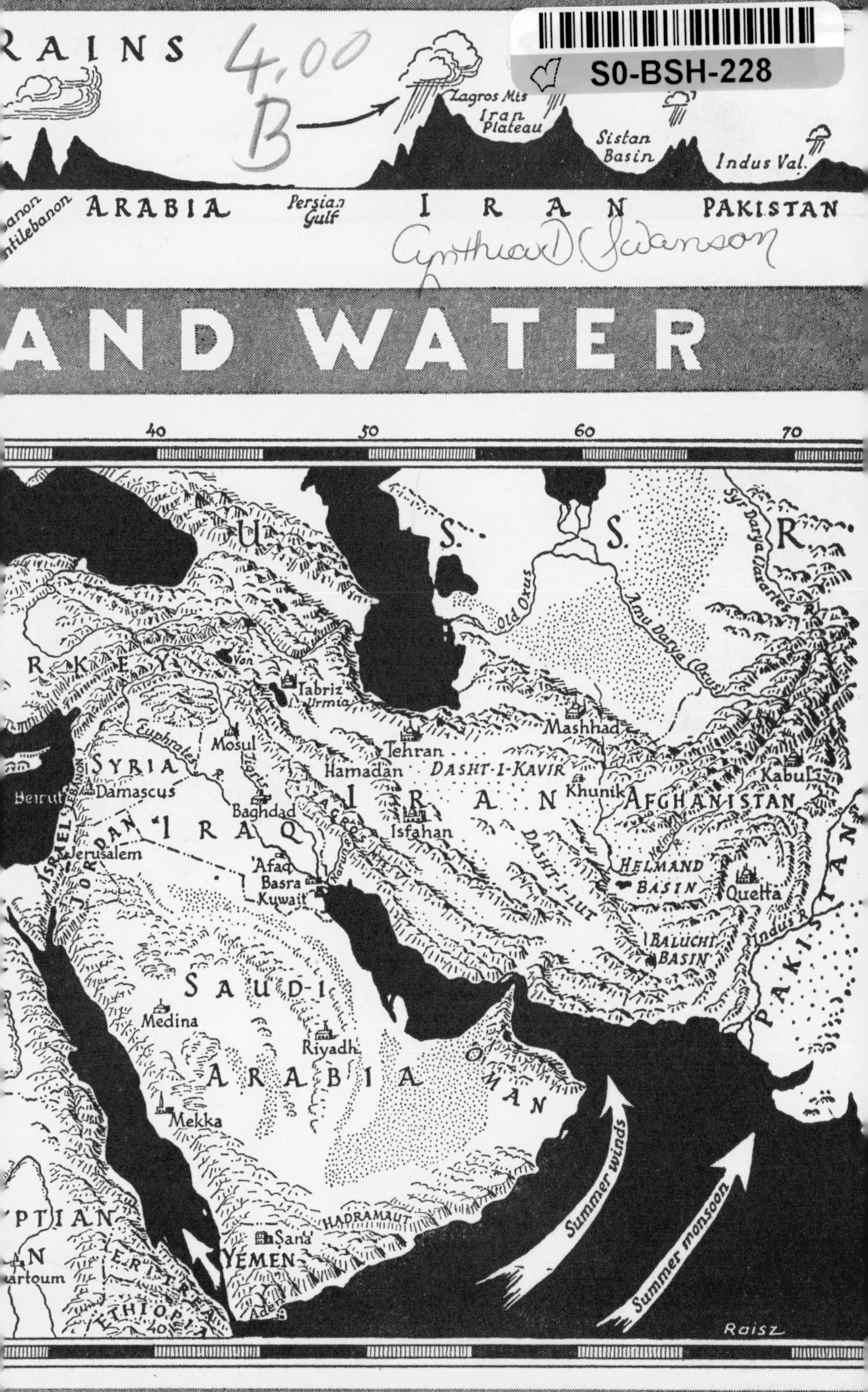

RAINS
Zagros Mts
Iran Plateau
Sistan Basin
Indus Val.
ARABIA
Persian Gulf
IRAN
PAKISTAN
AND WATER
40
50
60
70
U. S. S. R.
Old Oxus
Amu Darya (Oxus)
Syr Darya (Jaxartes)
Van
Tabriz
Urmia
Mashhad
Tehran
Hamadan
DASHT-I-KAVIR
Khunik
Mosul
Tigris
Euphrates
SYRIA
Beirut
LEBANON
Damascus
Baghdad
IRAQ
IRAN
AFGHANISTAN
Kabul
Isfahan
ZAGROS MTS.
Karun R.
DASHT-I-LUT
Helmand R.
HELMAND BASIN
Quetta
BALUCHI BASIN
Indus R.
PAKISTAN
ISRAEL
JORDAN
Jerusalem
Afaq
Basra
Kuwait
SAUDI ARABIA
Medina
Riyadh
OMAN
Mekka
HADRAMAUT
Sana
YEMEN
Aden
ERITREA
ETHIOPIA
Khartoum
Summer winds
Summer monsoon
Raisz

CARAVAN: THE STORY OF THE MIDDLE EAST

CARAVAN:

THE STORY OF THE MIDDLE EAST

REVISED EDITION

CARLETON S. COON

HOLT, RINEHART AND WINSTON
NEW YORK · CHICAGO · SAN FRANCISCO

In Canada, Holt, Rinehart and Winston of Canada, Limited

Library of Congress Catalog Card No. 58–13740

Revised Edition

3456 090 98765

ISBN: 0-03-005105-3

Printed in the United States of America

FOREWORD

No MAN COULD HOPE to draw together the various fields from which the materials of this book are derived if he were a scholar in any one of them. No one could feel less scholarly than I do. This becomes particularly evident when the subject of Arabic transliteration arises, as it always does in forewords to books on the Middle East. I have before me the handiwork of Hitti, Gibb, and Calverley, three men whose erudition and integrity are of the highest order, and yet I cannot find complete agreement among them. Take the word for judge. Hitti spells it *qāḍi,* Gibb *ḳāḍī,* and Calverley *qāḍī.* At this point the lay reader may exclaim, "So what?"—but the lay reader does not review these books. To the myopic dotter of i's and crosser of t's, a dot under a consonant or a macron over a vowel are matters of utmost importance. The presence or absence of a dot under the k will distinguish between the word for "heart" and that for "dog." Only a heartless dog would countenance such confusion.

To avoid it I sought the aid of a most kindly and scholarly gentleman who has much more to offer than spelling: Dr. E. E. Calverley of the Hartford Seminary Foundation, editor of the *Muslim World,* a man of profound erudition and wisdom, as well as long editorial experience. He read the manuscript from beginning to end. His polite but firmly expressed corrections appeared on many pages, and not one of them has been ignored. He has grasped my arm on the brink of many a pitfall, theological and historical as well as orthographic. If despite his efforts I may be shown to have fallen in here and there, please be assured that I have not drawn him with me. For a scholar of his stature to have had the grace to bother with this work places him beyond the level of possible contamination.

Three other readers from outside my immediate academic neighborhood have helped me. Sir Hamilton Gibb, the dean of British Islamicists, who read the manuscript after Dr. Calverley, picked up a number of remaining points about which he had special knowledge. Dr. George Cameron, chairman of the Department of Near Eastern Studies at the University of Michigan, read Chapters One through Five at an early stage and set me right on many a controversial point in ancient history and linguistics. His colorful comments appear in several footnotes. His colleague, Dr. George F. Hourani, concentrated on Chapter Four. His special knowledge of the history of navigation in the Indian Ocean and Persian Gulf helped me over a very high hurdle.

Within the range of local telephone calls or short excursions on foot, I have profited greatly from daily association and special handouts of information on the part of a number of my colleagues and associates, particularly Drs. Samuel N. Kramer, Francis Steele, Mahmūd al-Amīn, Schuyler van R. Cammann, Hermann Ranke, and Henry Hoenigswald. In Iran, my companion Mr. Habibullah Samadie performed the same service. Four of my students at the University of Pennsylvania and Harvard have also aided me greatly: Jane Goodale, David Hart, William D. Schorger, and Paul F. M. Schumacher. I only wish that I could also list the names of the hundreds of persons of many faiths and nationalities who have helped me in the field and at home during the last quarter of a century, to learn something useful about the Middle East.

Devon, Pennsylvania Carleton S. Coon

FOREWORD TO THE REVISED EDITION

Not long ago a request was received for permission to publish a Persian translation of *Caravan*. However, I felt that it first needed revision. Since the first writing I had spent many months working in Iran, Sa'udi Arabia, Afghanistan, and Syria, and had visited Pakistan, Baḥrain Island, Lebanon, and Cyprus. Also some excellent source books previously unavailable had appeared. With the help of D. W. Lockard, Edmund Gordon, and L. Cabot Briggs, I made hundreds of corrections and revisions for the naturally critical Persian audience. This new American edition contains all these changes. The book is as up to date as I can make it, in its original sense, that of a source book of Middle Eastern civilization. From the standpoint of contemporary politics no book on the Middle East can be up to date once the ink is dry. However, I have added a new chapter at the end to help point up the meaning of modern events as they continue to follow traditional channels.

West Gloucester, Massachusetts Carleton S. Coon

CONTENTS

MAPS

ILLUSTRATIONS

1 THE PICTURE AND ITS PIECES

In the name of God, the Compassionate, the Merciful

WHEN A MIDDLE EASTERNER begins an undertaking, including the telling of a tale, he is likely to call on the Divine Being for guidance and help, in either these very words or others which convey the same general meaning. Few undertakings in the literary field could require more help and guidance than this one, the picture of the civilization of the Middle East, with all its peoples, in space and time.

We have chosen to call this picture *Caravan,* because it is a moving picture in full color, with sound, smell, heat and cold, and the beating of windborne sand and rain; because the most visible element in Middle Eastern civilization is transport and the traffic in fine goods, many of which are made in Middle Eastern cities; because a caravan is a highly complex and finely organized institution, which again typifies the civilization of the Middle East; and because the greatest caravans in history have been those devoted to the movement of pious folk to holy places, and the Middle East is holy to many peoples.

From beginning to end this story is blinded by the dazzling light of too much history for easy assimilation, needled by emotion, and therefore fraught with controversy. One of the simplest of these controversies deals with the name of the region itself, and scholars who enjoy arguing about nonessentials are of two minds about the term *Middle East.* It seems to have been concocted during World War II to designate the Cairo command of the British Army. Before that people referred to the Near East, meaning in a general way the Arabic-speaking areas of the former Turkish Empire, from Egypt to ʿIraq and from Syria to the Arabian peninsula. Some still do.

The Middle East as generally but not universally understood today includes the predominantly Muslim[1] countries from Morocco to

[1] With two exceptions, Lebanon being in the majority Christian, Israel Jewish.

Afghanistan, incluring Morocco, Algeria, Tunisia, Libya, Egypt, Israel, Jordan, Lebanon, Syria, 'Iraq, Sa'udi Arabia, the Yemen, the Aden Protectorate, the Trucial sheikdoms, Oman, Muscat Kuwait, Baḥrain,[2] Turkey, Iran, and Afghanistan. One may, if one chooses, add Pakistan as well as the Sudan, although, like Turkey, each is transitional to another culture area.

People who think in terms of longitude reject the word "Middle" as inapplicable, since part of the territory lies west of Greenwich and closer to America than continental Europe. It is, however, "Middle" in latitude, and it is "Middle" also in a more important sense. It lies strategically between the richer and more populous subcontinents of the Eurasiatic land mass, China, India, and Europe, and is in contact by ship and caravan with Africa south of the Sahara. The Middle Easterners have long served as Middle Men for the goods and ideas of these mutually distant regions.

One can further justify the whole term "Middle East" in a cultural sense. As I hope to demonstrate, it is a culture area of its own, with a center and peripheries. The civilization which characterizes it, in various regional forms, is not only a unit, and not only intermediate between those of East and West, but in many essentials ancestral to both. It has served not only as a vehicle of transmission but also as a creator. From it we have received most of the plants and animals which and whose products we eat every day, the art of metallurgy, the lore of the scribe, and a religious way of life which, whether or not we attend divine services, regulates our everyday behavior. More than this one could not ask from a strip of landscape which appears singularly barren in contrast to the lush meadows and forests of the Western world.

To describe the civilization of the Middle East is just as formidable a task as to describe that of western Europe. In both areas one finds a variety of languages and cultural subdivisions which cannot be understood without excursions into history. Going back scarcely beyond the Romans, the history of western Europe is relatively brief, and the changes in European culture per unit of time are relatively great. The history of the Middle East goes back over five thousand years, and one can find people living today as they did in the time of Christ, or even of Abraham.

The most conspicuous fact about Middle Eastern civilization is that in each country the population consists of a mosaic of people. For

[2] Also claimed by Iran.

example, in the city of Baghdad one will find Muslim Arabs, Christian Arabs, Assyrians, Kurds, Jews, Turks, Persians, Armenians, and a number of other kinds of peoples. The Muslim Arabs will be divided into people from different tribes or villages living as separate entities, and into two main religious groups, Sunni and Shīʿa. Each of the dozen or more kinds of people living in a single community could have been distinguished, some forty or fifty years ago, by special costumes, special languages or dialects, special ways of treating the hair and beard, special diets, and special days of worship and of rest. Today many of them wear the drab raiment of the Western world and are less easy to tell apart.

If while in Baghdad you stop in one of the hotels which cater to Britons and Americans, you will find the proprietors and clerks to be Christian Arabs, while the servants are Assyrians. Across the street is an automobile agency run by a Jew. Two doors down, an Armenian conducts a profitable import-export business, while Kurdish porters carry boxes on their backs on the sidewalks, and in the street automobiles whiz by, driven by bearded Arabs in headcloths and turbans.

If you are an archaeologist, you will take to your dig a dozen or more trained pickmen, provided by the Department of Antiquities. These men can find and clean a skeleton without chipping a bone and excavate a glazed pot without a scratch. They are specialists. We call them Shergatis, from the village in which they live when not digging. Some archaeologist in the past excavated a site near their home and trained the men who presented themselves for work. These trained their sons, and now they have become a special people, a shiny stone in the mosaic of the Middle East. They have a monopoly in their work, which they do exceedingly well.

It was undoubtedly an accident that started off this chain of events and produced the specialists of Shergat. Other accidents in the past, less simple to trace, will explain the special role of the Armenians or will tell us why all the welldiggers in Morocco come from the land of the Draʿa, or why until recently most clerks in Egypt were Copts. However it happened, the peoples of the Middle East are organized into a complicated social system based on an ethnic division of labor. By spending much of their time together, by celebrating their holidays as separate communities, and by bringing up their children in the idea that they are to learn a special kind of work and learn it well, the members of each of these groups have been able to perfect some kind of technique, some consummate skill. The sum of all these skills is the civilization of the Middle East. How can they spin silk so finely? How can human hands produce such a rug? How did they ever get that ripple onto the dagger blade? How can that merchant in the bazaar work out the price of a bolt of cloth in dollars, in his head, faster than I can do it on paper? For a very simple reason. These people have been concentrating on special techniques not only for a lifetime but for generations.

Although this division of labor may have begun as a series of accidents, it was no accident that the system grew and perpetuated itself as each new stone in the mosaic fell into place. It was and is the most efficient way for people to live in a lean environment,—with settlements widely spaced and sources of raw materials even farther apart, at a metal-age level of hand-powered industry. From time to time the rise of new religions and the expansions of imperial powers have changed the design a bit, but the over-all picture tells the same story in only a slightly different way. The story cannot change as long as the environment remains the same and people still use the force of their own muscles as their primary source of industrial power. The goodness of fit between man and landscape has long ago reached its peak, and any change, short of the introduction of powered machinery, is likely to be no more vital than hanging a new kind of paper on a very old wall.

The mosaic system of Middle Eastern society is not unique. When Cortes conquered Mexico, the Aztecs, whose gory sacrifices he so rudely disturbed, had begun to be organized in much the same way. In India, it is carried to a world extreme, with thousands of endogamous castes, each devoted to a special technique, or even part of a technique. Even a medium-sized Indian village of 1,400 persons[3] includes members of twenty-six separate castes or subcastes, while individuals belonging to six other castes, resident outside, come into the village from time to time to render special services. The Middle Eastern and Indian systems differ in two principal ways. While occupations tend to be hereditary in the Middle East, no person is under strict obligation to follow his father's trade. The water carrier may become king. While marriages between religious groups are uncommon, families of the same religion, race and eco-

[3] M. Opler and R. D. Singh, "The Division of Labor in an Indian Village," in C. S. Coon, *A Reader in General Anthropology* (New York, 1948), pp. 464–496, chap. 17.

nomic level usually marry freely without reference to specific occupation. The mosaic system is not a caste system. Racial consciousness is not as marked in the Middle East as it is in India and Pakistan. Most of the peoples of the Middle East are members of a single race.

The test of the strength of a social system is to submit it to strain and see what happens. That experiment was performed for us ten years ago. In Pakistan more than five million Hindus have packed up their boxes and mattresses and pots and pans and carted them to India; while seven millions of Muslims have moved the other way.[4] This has meant the removal from each area, particularly from Pakistan, of many key specialists, before the remaining inhabitants of the country could have time to learn the skills needed to replace them.

In the Yemen, tens of thousands of Jews, whose colonies date back into prehistoric times, likewise said good-by to their ancient home and moved to Israel. The Jews of the Yemen have long had a virtual monopoly of that country's export-import trade, money-handling, retail marketing of textiles, stone masonry, and ironworking. With the traders and money-changers and textile merchants and masons and smiths gone, the Muslim Yeminis must be having a hard time readjusting. The departure of similarly useful Jews from 'Iraq and other Middle Eastern countries to join their European coreligionaries in Israel undoubtedly has disturbed the equilibrium of these nations, and whether or not the departing colonists take their capital with them is of minor importance compared to the loss of human competence. These two examples show clearly the strength of the mosaic system, through the disturbances created when an element is removed.

The old mosaic system and modern nationalism are clearly incompatible. Nationalism demands that every person living permanently in a country become a citizen and feel himself a member of the nation with rights and responsibilities equal to those of all other members. According to the mosaic system, if you are a Christian in a Muslim land you are a visitor, albeit you and your ancestors have been visiting for some hundreds or even thousands of years. Your loyalty is to your own private people or "nation," although the latter may at present have no national home.

How the mosaic system works can be shown quickly by a simple comparison. Let us say that you get up on a wintry morning, shake

[4] See *United Nations World* (November, 1950), pp. 50 f.

your furnace and stoke it, help your wife prepare breakfast, drive to the station, read the newspaper on the train, go to your office, do your business, come home late in the afternoon, and settle down for a cocktail before dinner. You may spend the evening building cabinets in the kitchen or rewiring a lamp. If it is summer you may work in the garden.

Your Middle Eastern opposite, a man of equal status and comparable income, would not think of touching a furnace or any other heating device. Nor would he cook food, drive his car, work in the garden, nor handle carpenters' tools and wire. He is a businessman, and his own special business is the only economically useful thing with which he will concern himself. He will not go to the store to buy a pound of meat on his afternoon off—he has a servant to do this who also cooks his breakfast; another man drives his car; still others cultivate his garden. Only a carpenter builds the cabinets, only an electrician handles wire. He can afford to maintain a stable of flunkies. A laboring man, if he is lucky, earns fifty cents a day; the cook may get fifteen to twenty dollars a month, plus gifts from the butchers and greengrocers whom he favors with his trade.

The official inspectors whom the Middle Eastern governments assign to us Americans to travel with us and handle our credentials are amazed and shocked at our behavior; they cannot understand why we insist on driving our own jeeps and trucks, why we go around in dirty, patched-up trousers, why we get down in the trench and do some of the excavating ourselves, and why we are always in such a rush. Mad emissaries of the inscrutable West.

One of the greatest differences lies in our concern for the value of time. We pay workmen by the hour; they pay by the job. A master coppersmith who manufactures tea trays comes to work when he pleases and quits when the spirit moves him. He has no regular hours, no sign on his door saying, "Out to lunch, will return in 15 minutes." When he has finished a first-class tray, he sells it and begins on another. He has no boss, no time clock. Nothing in the nature of his work requires a close synchronization between his efforts and those of other kinds of specialists, as in a Western factory.

The merchant sits in his shop reading a book or chatting with his neighbor in the next booth. The customer appears and asks the price of a pair of slippers. Merchant and customer may argue over this for as much as a half an hour. Friends and by-passers may even join in the sport. The customer pretends to go away, the merchant to put back his goods. Finally the customer buys the slippers, usually at a reasonable price. Why, asks the foreign visitor, do they go to all this trouble? Why not just tag the merchandise with a fixed price? Because the merchant likes to bargain with his customers. It is his job, and he enjoys it. From his point of view it is not a waste of time. Some day he will get a gullible customer and make a killing. But that is less important than the pleasure this kind of interaction gives him.

Your Middle Easterner asks a lot of personal questions: How much did you pay for this? How many children have you, and are they sons or daughters? He likes to deal with people on a personal basis, and his arguing of the price of goods is merely one aspect of this personal approach. Automatic vending machines leave him cold. He is not interested in labor-saving devices. Where he lives, labor is cheap. He is less interested in gadgets than in people, and if you are alert and well mannered and understanding he will like you, whatever your religion or language or race.

However, he may find it hard to understand why some of us Americans have English names, some German, some Italian, and others Slavic. How is it possible that although some of us are Protestants, others Catholics, and still others Jews, we all do the same jobs and live and work together without distinction? It is not that they are unused to a medley of peoples, nor that in their countries different people cannot live together side by side, as they have done for millenniums; what puzzles them is the degree to which we have become a single people.

At present one can find a few hundreds of individuals in each of the Middle Eastern countries who cease to be disturbed by these curious facets of our civilization. These men and women were trained in the West. Some of them, children of diplomats, were born there. As interpreters of our civilization to their countrymen, they are of incalculable value to us. But we must not let them carry the burden alone. If we learn something about their civilization, we can help them out. And time is against us. We must learn what we can, and quickly.

We cannot learn it very well, or very quickly, if we concentrate on the complexities of Rashid Street in Baghdad, or the Gezireh section of Cairo, or the Place de l'Horloge in Casablanca. We must get off the paved street with its honking automobiles and movie theaters and head for the depths of the bazaar, and even better, wander into a rural village away from the road, a tenting ground of shepherds in the high meadows, or a Bedawin camp. But even these have been affected to some extent. We must do more, we must go backward in time. A culture in transition is hard to describe and harder to understand; we must find some period of history when the culture was, relatively speaking, at rest. Then when we know the background we can bring in the automobiles and the movies and the parliaments and the radio broadcasts; and the presence of these bits of plastic and broken glass in our mosaic will no longer obscure the plan of the picture.

The civilization of the Middle East was at its height in the time of the ʿAbbasid Caliphate in Baghdad and the caliphate of Cordova in Spain.[5] That time, however, is too far back for our purpose and not closely enough related to the present. The rise of the Italian states, Spain, Portugal, the Netherlands, France, and England as maritime powers, their skill as deep-water sailors and cannoneers, threw the Middle Eastern countries into a period of reduced trade, wealth, and intercommunication. The invasion of Hulagu, grandson of Jenghiz Khan, wrought fearful destruction in Iran and ʿIraq. From this calamity these countries have never wholly recovered.

About the time when the Western nations were taking to salt water with Bibles and cannon and snatching the trade of the East from the Arabs and Persians, the countries with which we are here concerned, from Algeria eastward to and including ʿIraq, became parts of the Ottoman Empire, leaving only Morocco, Iran, and Afghanistan as independent nations. This political association under a Muslim power helped keep the civilization of the Middle East relatively constant and relatively homogeneous for another three or four centuries, varying locally, until the time when the Turks withdrew and the Westerners came in with their trains and trucks and oil-drilling machinery and new ideas about government and industry. Only then was the manpowered, metal-age culture of the East irrevocably shaken.

One can set the date of the impact of the industrial revolution in Egypt at 1805, with the rise to power of Muḥammad ʿAlī. In the Yemen it has only begun to strike. In other countries with which we are concerned, the time lies in between these periods.

The civilization described in this book, then, is the civilization of

[5] Described in detail by Philip Hitti in his *History of the Arabs* (4th ed., London, 1949).

these lands BEFORE that impact had been felt, whenever that time occurred in each particular place. Should a native of the Middle East come across this book, let him not say: "Professor Coon has drawn an incorrect and insulting picture of my country. We are much more modern than that!" I know you are. But if YOU would learn about US, you would do well to study the history of the United States and the culture of America at the time of the American Revolution. I have attempted only to pay your country the same courtesy.

2 LAND, WIND, AND WATER

BECAUSE GEOGRAPHY IS TAUGHT in grade schools along with spelling and arithmetic, most of us are likely to think of it as something very simple and rudimentary, something like "What is the capital of Afghanistan?" or "Bound Iowa." Few of us realize that it is the prince of disciplines, combining the fruits of geology, meteorology, anthropology, sociology, economics, and dozens of other specialties. The good geographer is a philosopher.

The medieval Arabs, who wrote some of the finest geographical treatises ever penned, knew this. They knew that the culture of a people bears an intimate relationship to the landscape on which they live. They knew that the geography of a region shapes the way of life of its inhabitants, as the bones and muscles of a healthy man shape his skin. Scholars like Ibn Baṭṭūṭa, al-Idrīsi, and Ibn Khaldūn realized that if one is to understand the civilization of a people, one must start with the geography of the land they inhabit.

Geologically speaking, the world's oldest civilizations arose in some of the world's youngest lands. During Mesozoic and early Cenozoic times, most of North Africa, Arabia, Palestine, Syria, ʿIraq, Iran, and Afghanistan were under water. When these lands finally rose to the surface they were covered with sea-deposited layers of sandstone and limestone. Sandstone and limestone are easily worked and make excellent building material. Limestone also can be converted into slaked-lime and used for mortar. Marble is a rare form of limestone, excellent for statuary. Flint is a common impurity in limestone and makes excellent cutting tools for primitive men.

Sandstone and limestone, however, do not contain metallic ores or such useful materials as jade and soapstone. In the Middle Eastern countries it is only where the mountains have folded and faulted, exposing older layers, that these desirable minerals are to be found. Hence the iron mines of the Atlas Mountains, the copper of Sinai, the copper and iron of Armenia, the copper of the Zagros in Iran, the silver of the Taurus, and the iron and silver of Afghanistan. The scarcity of these substances and the long distances between known deposits have kept Middle Eastern peoples on the move since the dawn of the age of metal; the need for Armenian obsidian and Turkestan jade for cutting tools made trade over long distances imperative even earlier.

Like young mountains everywhere the young mountains of the Middle East are steep and craggy. The Atlas, running diagonally across Morocco and Algeria into Tunisia from southwest to northeast, is divided into three principal ridges, with high valleys between. At the western end the rich valley of the Sus, lying between the Anti-Atlas and Grand Atlas, forms an isolated geographical area, and this isolation is reflected in its retention of an early cultural pattern, as we shall see later. At the other end three fingers of mountains trail into the Gulf of Gabès where the coast line has shifted to a north-south axis. This forms the two wide valleys which hold the bulk of the population of Tunisia. North of the Atlas, in Morocco, the Riffian coastal range curves around to form, with the Spanish Sierra Nevada, a broken circle. The Taza Gap, lying between the Rif and the Middle Atlas, has felt the sharp impact of hoofs and the crush of tank treads from ʿUqba down to Patton.

Between Taza and Ujda the Atlas chains sink for a space, letting the Sahara thrust an arm to the sea at the mouth of the Muluwiya River and tying up the transatlean world of the Mediterranean seacoast with the oasis of Tafilelt, once famous for its desert port Sijilmāsa and the routes to the Sudan. Another and more effective Saharan encroachment divides the highlands in back of Tripoli from the lofty head of Cyrenaica; these low-lying zones of desert divide North Africa, including Egypt, into three compartments, known to the Arabs as al-Miṣr, Ifrīqiya, and al-Maghrib al-Akṣā, or Egypt, Africa in the Roman sense, and the Extreme West.

In Egypt itself the river has cut through sandstone and underlying igneous rocks to form cliffs, from which building materials have been quarried since the days of the Pharaohs. Sinai again is mountainous. Palestine, Lebanon, and the Syrian coast form a double chain bordering the sea and merging on the north with the limestone mountains of Anatolia. Although generally flat, the Arabian peninsula lies slantwise like a playing card propped on one side, with its southwestern corner, the Yemen, highest. On the other side, facing the Persian, Jabal Akhḍar, the Green Mountain, curves like a stray member of the Zagros pack trying to rejoin its fellows.

Up in the northwest corner of Iran, and in adjoining parts of Turkey and Transcaspian Russia, thrusts the knot of the Armenian highlands, reaching its peak at Mount Ararat. This knot divides into two ropes, one running southeast and bordering the Indian Ocean. This is the Zagros. The second goes almost due east, to the borders of Turkestan and Afghanistan. This is the Elburz. Between Zagros and Elburz stands the bleak Iranian plateau. The major tectonic feature of Afghanistan is the Hindu Kush range, the western spur of the Himalayas; another range to the south and east, the Sulaimaniya Mountains, cuts it off from Pakistan and ends the plateau.

Some of these mountains are high, although none reaches the 20,000-foot level of the Himalayas and Pamirs, just beyond the northeastern border of Afghanistan. The highest mountain in our area is Demavend, in the Elburz within sight of Tehran. Attaining 18,934 feet, it is taller than any mountain you will find as you move westward around the globe, in the northern hemisphere, until you reach Orizaba in Mexico, which tops it by a mere 234 feet; passing Orizaba you will not find its equal again until you come to Mount Logan and Mount McKinley. Seen from the Caspian shore, some 85 feet below sea level, the snow-capped cone of Demavend is as regal as Fujiyama, and nearly half again as high.

Shah Fuladi in Afghanistan reaches 16,870 feet, and Ararat, forming the other shoulder of Demavend, 16,946 feet. Moving westward, we find the mountains lower. Mount Lebanon attains 10,049 feet, the highest point of the Yemen escarpment is said to reach over 12,000 feet,[1] and the Moroccan Atlas achieves 13,771 feet at its highest point. It must be remembered that although most of the mountains in the Middle East are under 10,000 feet they are still not easy to cross. The rugged Riffian chain, the highest peak of which is only 8,105 feet tall, and most of which lies below 6,000 feet, is a most effective barrier and has been so throughout history, making this window over the busy Strait of Gibraltar a human refuge area.

Mountains, then, are to be found in every Middle Eastern state except Kuwait, and in every state they perform the dual function of hindering travel and sheltering rebels and refugees. They also perform a third and much more vital function; they gather clouds and rake the moisture out of the winds. The moisture which they lift from the winds was earlier drawn from the sea. Hence the seas and the winds deserve our attention.

[1] Hugh Scott, *In the High Yemen* (London, 1942, rev. ed., 1947), p. 3.

The Middle East is bounded by seven bodies of water: two oceans, the Atlantic and Indian; four seas, the Mediterranean, Black, Caspian, and Red; and one gulf, the Persian. Most of the water that reaches the countries of the Middle East comes, as one would expect, from the two oceans, and of the two the Atlantic furnishes by far the greater volume. Of the seas, the Mediterranean and Caspian are the greatest contributors.

During the winter months westerly winds blow off the Atlantic. They carry masses of water eastward. Most of it follows the northern path, and much of it comes to earth in the Alps and Carpathians. Hence the Rhône, Rhine, Po, Danube, Elbe, and most of the other great rivers of Europe. Europe is a well-watered subcontinent. Some of the westerlies break into the Mediterranean trough across Provence. Others drive in below Gibraltar, losing loads of snow and rain in the Atlas and Riffian mountains on the way. From here on, the Cyrenaican massif takes its share, and Mount Lebanon more. What is left floats on to the east, to come to rest on the Green Mountain of Muscat, the Zagros, the Elburz, and the mountains of Afghanistan. The farther east one goes, the thinner the harvest; if the mountains did not grow higher as the westerlies blew eastward, most of Iran and Afghanistan would be uninhabited.

The westerlies are fickle winds in this latitude. In some years they unload much more rain than in others. Whatever the total rainfall, ranging from zero to fifty-five inches in their belt, the annual variability is much greater. A spot on the desert that has had no rain in a dozen years may be washed out by a downpour that brings flash floods and swamps the caravan men in their tents. A field that has yielded wheat for several millenniums, off and on, will produce none on the year when the rainfall is one inch instead of the usual twenty. The ancients knew this, and built granaries to provide for it.

There is nothing fickle, however, about the monsoons from the Indian Ocean. They arrive like clockwork and are as steady as the Hudson River. They water, unfortunately, only a small part of the lands with which we are concerned. Coming up from the East African coast in summer, they ride over the southern point of the Arabian peninsula until they drop their load on two high places: the Qara Mountains rimming Dhufar on the southern coast and the Yemen escarpment. At the same time, farther west, they strike the highlands of Ethiopia, filling Lake Tsana to overflowing. This water, with that from Uganda, supplies the Nile. Thus Egypt, situated on the Mediterranean, uses Indian Ocean water, and like all water from that source, it is constant from year to year, and rises in the summer.

Black Sea water, carried by the westerlies to the southern slopes of the Caucasus and the Transcaspian divide, plus Atlantic cloud-loads, are responsible for the lush forests of the Batum area, where Jason sought the golden fleece and his shipmates felled timber for masts. Caspian water, blowing from the north, along with moisture from the Black Sea and the Atlantic, strikes the northern slope of the Elburz a mighty blow, and the Caspian provinces of Iran are exotically wet. This rainfall is also relatively constant, for we are now on the edge of the northern storm belt.

Except for the Yemen, Dhufar, and the sources of the Nile, none of the Middle Eastern lands receive summer rain in any quantity. I have seen it fall in Tangier in July, but Tangier has a freak climate, related more to that of Portugal than to the regular Mediterranean variety. I have witnessed thunderstorms in the foothills west of Lake Urmiya in the same month, and it is on the record that Rasht receives some precipitation every month of the year, though the summer season is the least wet in that lush *jangal* (whence our word "jungle"). In the summer months the predominant winds blow off the land, and coming from deserts they are hot and sometimes gritty.

Egypt and the Levant states have a famous horror called the *ḳhamsīn,* or fifty, from the number of days of its alleged duration. In Morocco it is called the *sharqi,* meaning easterly. The sharqi can blow for a week at a time; while it is on the rampage no motorless sailing ship can enter the Strait of Gibraltar from the Atlantic. Visitors to the famous Caves of Hercules, home of Neanderthal man in the days before Hercules had strangled his first lion, often notice the covey of ships anchored in the lee of the cliffs, two masts or more in height, in which the watergods hewed the caves. Travelers unwise or unfortunate enough to be caught in Baghdad during the summer seal the doors and windows of their bedrooms in a vain attempt to keep out the fuller's-earth-fine dust that the southerly winds bring to plague the city. And so it goes. Each country has its diabolical summer winds to try the faith of the godly.

Nearly everywhere in the Middle East, except in the mountains, it is hot in summer. This heat varies from one hundred and twenty degrees and more in the Persian Gulf and Red Sea countries and in parts of ʿIraq, to the seventies in Tangier and also in Hamadan, the ancient summer capital of Darius. The deserts are hot everywhere in summer, but they have one advantage over the humid Tihāma of the Red Sea coast, Oman, Kuwait, and the Shaṭṭ-al-ʿArab: the air is dry, and except for a few difficult weeks it cools rapidly at night.

It is characteristic of Mediterranean climates, and of the continental climates which depend on winter rains, that the heat ends abruptly, and summer changes to winter without the interposition of what we in our forest climes know as the fall. In winter temperatures in the various parts of the Middle East differ widely. Along the Mediterranean coast of North Africa, in Egypt, riverine ʿIraq, coastal Lebanon, and the southern shore of the Caspian, and a few other favored spots, the temperature never or hardly ever goes below freezing. It is wet and brisk and invigorating. Farmers choose this time to do their plowing. Oranges ripen in January, and shortly after this the rain slacks off, the grain grows tall, wild flowers cover the landscape which in September looked like a desert, and spring has arrived, with its cool crisp air, bright sun, fleeting clouds, a general feeling of exhilaration and gaiety. This is the season for carnival among all Mediterranean peoples regardless of their formal religious affiliation. Up on the Iranian plateau the succession of seasons is the same, but the temperature changes much more. The early rains of winter are often followed by snow, depending on the altitude and the caprice of the year. This snow fills the mountain passes and hinders travel. Poor man's manure, it lies over the fields, to melt in the spring. Plowing comes either earlier or later, or both; the crops ripen later. But the Persian *No Ruz,* or New Year's Day, is just as happy and gay as the carnival feasts of the Mediterranean.

In the high mountains, Atlas, Zagros, Elburz, and Hindu Kush, winter snow is so inhibiting that most of the people who summer in the high, lush pastures with their flocks move for the winter to the drier and warmer regions below. In the Yemen, however, a different situation obtains. The winter is cold and dry; the countrymen huddle in their sheepskin coats as they walk the windy roads. Now and then a thin shell of ice forms on the masonry tanks in which they store some of the summer water with which they flood their fields to simulate the conditions of the lands to the north.

Jidda, the Tihāma, Aden, coastal Oman, Kuwait, and the oil ports of Iran have summer temperatures the year round. In January, 1934,

I landed at Mukalla on the Ḥaḍramaut coast, to be greeted by the port physician, an Indian Muslim, shivering in a woolen overcoat. "Everyone here is suffering from the cold," he said. The temperature was in the eighties. This coastal strip bounding Arabia on three sides is a special environmental province bearing little resemblance to the rest of the Middle East with which we are concerned. It has developed special people and special ways of life.

The distribution of mean annual rainfall is shown on Map 1; hence it needs no detailed description here. It will be noted that only in a few favored spots does the total reach the forty- and fifty-inch level, characteristic of the eastern United States, western Europe, India, and China. Each of these areas has some balancing disadvantage. In Morocco the wettest spot lies in the Middle Atlas Mountains, at an altitude of nearly ten thousand feet, in a lush forest of cedar. Aside from its lumber potential, this land is too cold for year-round occupation at the cultural level of Middle Eastern peoples, whose style of living is geared to warmer and drier regions. Its forest glades are knee high in snow in the winter, too deep for sheep. Hence the tribesmen (who owned this pasture before the French turned it into a skiing and trout-fishing paradise) had to move to lower altitudes each fall, to return in the early summer when the grass down below had begun to wither.

Next to the east is the rainy coastal region of Tabarka, Cape Blanco, and Cap Serrat, in Tunisia. I share a personal knowledge of this area with others who fought through the dense cork and live oak forest during World War II. This country supports vast herds of wild boar and a few miserable Arabic-speaking householders who still cook in Neolithic-style pottery. They make their living by grazing goats and cattle on the leaves; the soil is too sandy for serious agriculture.

One must jump all the way to Lebanon to find other landscapes of this greenness. Here the mountain is steep and the coastal plain narrow. The ruggedness of the terrain has made this a prime refuge area for members of unorthodox or unwanted religious sects, and the chief stronghold of pre-Islamic Christianity in the whole Middle East. Every inch of the western slope of the mountain is terraced. The country is populous and prosperous. From this small nation hundreds of thousands of people have migrated overseas. Their remittances, sent to their relatives, are partly responsible for

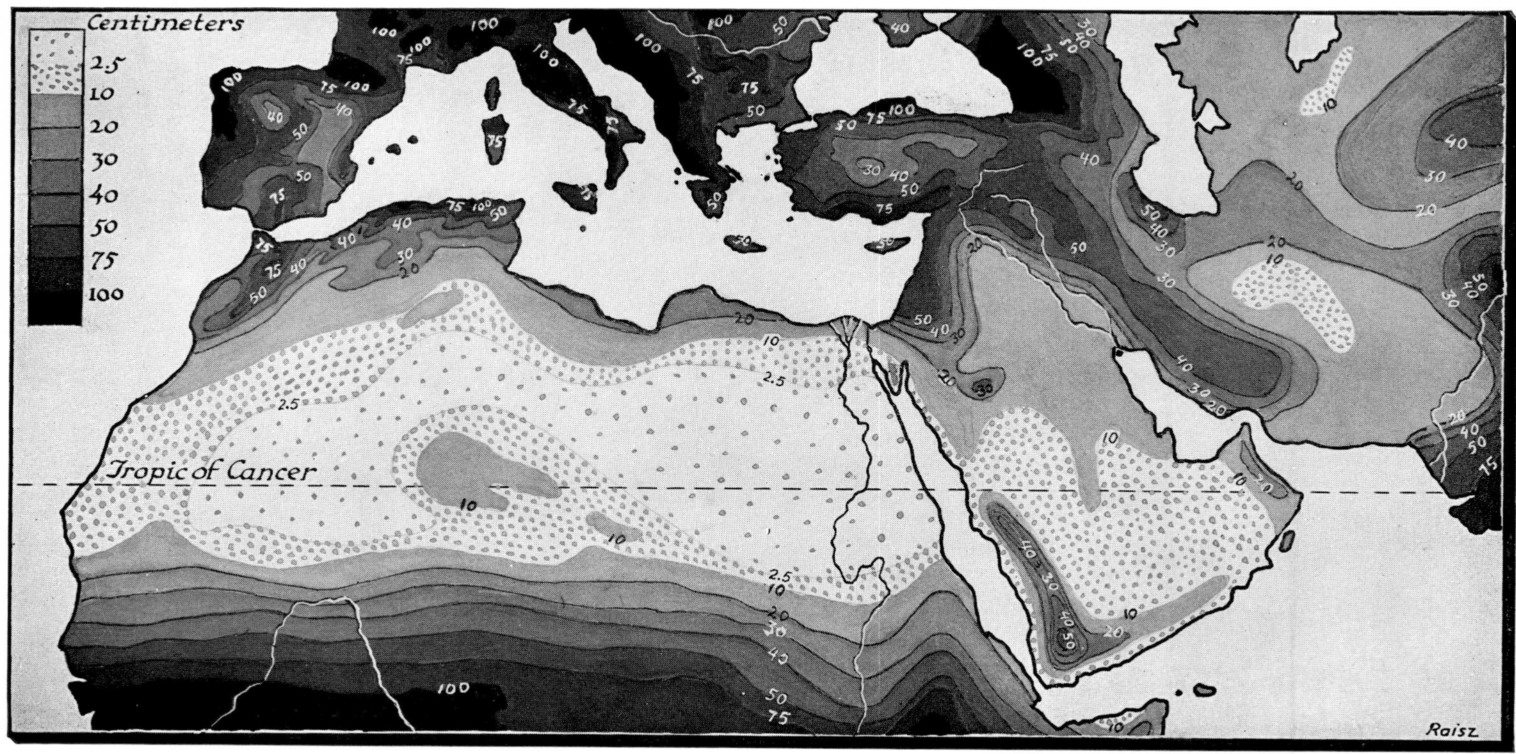

Map 1: *Mean Annual Rainfall*

the standard of living of Lebanon which at present is quite high.

Moving ever eastward we come to the jangal of the Caspian shore, the home of the fabulous White Monster of Mazandaran whom Rustem slew in the folklore of Firdusi's epic. This too is a favored spot, not only a source of excellent hardwoods and charcoal but also capable of intensive cultivation, nowadays of rice, tea, silkworm fodder (mulberry leaves), cotton, tobacco, and citrus fruits. Although the most populous in Iran, this region has its drawback—malaria. DDT however, is rapidly overcoming the disease.

Little is known about the rainfall in the remote Hindu Kush, but it must be great because its slopes are heavily forested—or were. Here again we find a refuge area, inhabited by the famous wine-drinking, idol-worshiping Kafirs, converted to Islam by the sword some half century past by a nonanthropologically-minded Amir, ʿAbd ur-Raḥmān Khan.

It is evident, then, that the regions of high rainfall in the Middle East are not comparable to London, Philadelphia, Calcutta, or Shanghai. In the Middle East there is something wrong with each region—too cold, too steep, too sandy, or too swampy and hence unhealthy. These are not the centers in which the characteristic civilization of the area developed.

The centers are located in regions where the water supply is constant and abundant, where although the summer heat may be uncomfortable, the winters are not too cold for barefooted and loosely clad people, where the soil is always rich and transportation of crops, building materials, and other heavy goods easy. These centers are the exotic river valleys: the lands along the banks of the Nile, Tigris-Euphrates, lower Karun, Helmand, and Indus. All of them have perennial water which can be used for irrigation. Thus the farmers of these valleys can grow their crops whether or not it rains. These waters, flowing from mountains and fed by seasonal freshets, carry fertilizing silt. They are all navigable, permitting extensive use of small boats both in their beds and in canals. In Egypt the prevailing northerly wind permits boatmen to sail upstream and float down again with the current.

High civilizations have a habit of arising in such places. The Aztecs had an advantage over the other Indians of Mexico in being located on a lake; they brought their goods to markets in boats

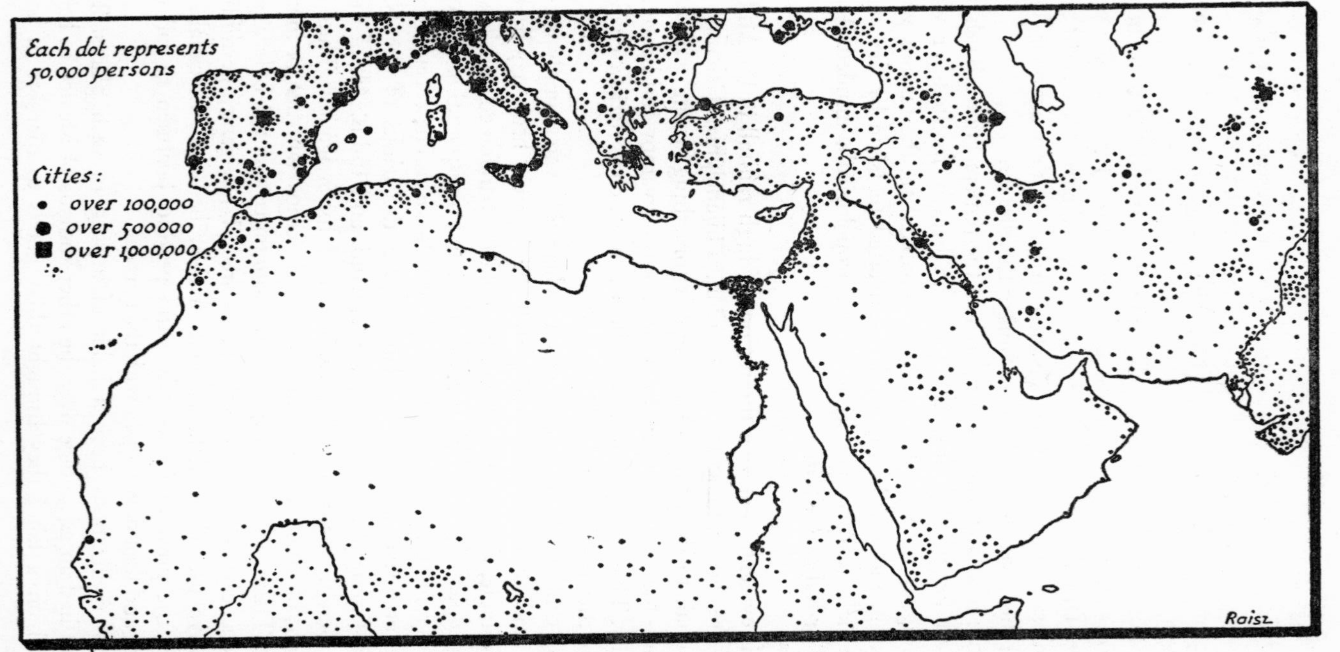

Map 2: *Population Density*

instead of lumping them in on their backs. It was no accident that theirs was the most vigorous civilization of Middle America at the time of discovery. The elaborate mounds of the Mississippi Valley are beginning to show American archaeologists that a high civilization had begun there too, with the aid of riverine navigation. In India, Siam, and China, rivers and canals, sampans, junks, and many other kinds of fresh-water craft have as much to do with the development of local civilization as the railroads in America.

Let not the historians and archaeologists skip lightly over this point and leave the impression that the Nile and Tigris-Euphrates systems became the seats of high ancient cultures by any kind of chance. It was a deliberate plot laid by the Supreme Geographer.

The Nile and the Tigris-Euphrates are undoubtedly the best known of these river valleys in terms of the civilizations they produced, and the most important in terms of results. But the lower Karun was the seat of a series of cultures related to those of the Tigris-Euphrates, as excavations at Susa and near Ahwaz have shown. Near its mouths in the Hammun-i-Sakari, the banks of the Helmand are lined with lofty mounds as big, to my unpracticed eye, as Ur of the Chaldees if not Nippur. These mounds await excavation. The banks of the Indus were also favored with an extensive and complicated Bronze Age civilization, as manifested by work done at Harappa and Mohenjo-Daro.

Eastern Pakistan, however, is out of bounds for this book. We end, then, with the eastern edge of the Iranian plateau, rather than face the vast complexity of what used to be India. Climatically speaking, however, Pakistan belongs with our territory, for its rivers drain partly from the mountains of Afghanistan, its rains are winter rains and not derived from the summer monsoons, and it is separated from the summer-rain country of India proper by the Thar Desert.

Returning to the Nile and Tigris-Euphrates, several important geographical differences meet the eye, and these have influenced history. The Nile is one stream, and the Tigris-Euphrates two. The *fellaḥīn* of Egypt can irrigate only a few miles to either side, for their valley is contained in cliffs and sandy deserts. The inhabitants of Mesopotamia could and did dig canals between the Tigris and Euphrates, thus rendering a much wider strip capable of cultivation and equally enlarging the territory covered by shipping. The Nile flows a long distance from its source before the cultivatable territory of Egypt begins. It is flanked by bleak and howling deserts, while its mouth is swampy and perennially silted. Egypt is a self-contained country, a geographical unit closely sealed off from the rest of the world. Migrations from the east strike the Delta and move on westward along the coast, leaving the main part of Egypt unaffected. Ships that sail the Nile cannot easily emerge into the Mediterranean, and besides, the types of hull, with shallow draft and low gunwales, which are suited for river traffic are not fit for Mediterranean storms; nor are the tall masts, stepped to scoop the upper air above the river, good for salt-water winds. From time immemorial the sea trade between Egypt and the outside has been in the hands of foreigners.

In Mesopotamia, however, we see a desert to the west and mountains to the east. Not as barren as that hemming in Egypt, the desert supports a thin population of herdsmen, who come to the river banks in summer and during rainless winters to pasture and water their flocks. The mountains also are inhabited by various hardy peoples, and they too have occasion to visit the river valley. Mesopotamia is not isolated like Egypt. Constant intercourse with nomads and mountaineers has repeatedly changed the genes of the population and permitted more cultural give-and-take. Mesopotamia is on the main road from India to the Mediterranean, and a crossroads of traffic. Egypt is, relatively speaking, a side pocket. That our own civilization is derived more from that of Mesopotamia, whence we get the three hundred and sixty-degree circle and the sixty-minute hour, is also no accident. Today the two greatest cities of the Middle East are Baghdad and Cairo, as strategically located on their rivers as New York, London, Shanghai, and Calcutta.

Climatologists hold vegetation in high esteem as a general index of climate, including all the aspects of rainfall, temperature, prevailing winds, and altitude. If one could have mingled among one's ancestors at the time when the modern postglacial climate already had come into being, but before these energetic forebears had succeeded in draining the swamps and denuding the hillsides, a botanist armed with notebook, camera, and a great deal of patience could have described the native flora of the Middle East with some nicety.

The fact is that except for China no part of the earth's surface seems to have been so denuded as the Middle East. We read of the orchard that was Morocco in Roman times, and see barren hillsides.

The Egyptians imported thousands and thousands of trunks of the cedars of Lebanon; and in every museum in the world which contains Egyptological specimens, pieces of that wood appear in the form of coffins or other types of furniture. Solomon used the cedar of Lebanon in building his temple. If you go to Lebanon today, you will see the cedar depicted on the flag of the republic and on the hats of its customs inspectors. But on Mount Lebanon itself, despite recent attempts at conservation and reforestation, not enough remains to furnish the timber for one Gloucester schooner.

One hundred years ago[2] lumberjacks from Baghdad used to go up to the Sulaimaniya hills in Kurdistan to fell timber. Floating it down the Tigris on the spring freshets, with men stationed every mile or so to prevent theft, they picked up the logs at Baghdad. Today it would be hard to find a suitable tree in the whole of Sulaimaniya Liwa. In Iran one is struck by the difference between the complete barrenness of the landscape, which is either under cultivation or within walking distance of a village, and that of the uninhabited deserts. In the inhabited land children go out overy morning with long-handled hoes and sacks to remove every spear of inflammable vegetation, including camel thorn, that the sheep and goats have left behind them; their work is thorough. In the desert, in places too distant from villages to warrant this attention, the traveler is impressed by the abundance of natural flora, in the form of sagebrush and dry stalks of aromatic annuals. Up on the eastern flank of the Elburz, near Sarrakhs, I once saw some juniper trees which had been lopped for firewood. "Aren't these protected by law?" I asked a soldier who was with me. "Yes," he replied, "but the government cannot afford to station one of us beside each tree."

The two big bottlenecks in the Middle East are water and wood. Utmost ingenuity is shown in the utilization of water. In the Riffian mountains the traveler climbing cat-footed along the sides of ravines finds his path serving also as the wall of an irrigation ditch. Here and there where the valley is narrow, the water crosses from one side to another in hollowed log aqueducts. Similar sights may be seen in all the mountains of the Middle East. When the water reaches the lowlands below, it already has been used many times. In the Yemen as many as three hundred terraces, one above another, can be counted on the side of the escarpment. In Egypt and in Syria the fellaḥin employ many devices, including wheels and buckets on

[2] Personal communication by Dr. George Cameron.

sweeps, to raise the water to the level of the fields. In the deserts Bedawin draw water from deep and ancient wells. In Iran, Afghanistan, and Oman, daring diggers burrow underground water tunnels from the springs at the feet of the mountains to artificial oases several miles out on the plain. Where the ground below is soft, they line the tunnels with baked clay culvert sections. Every fifty yards or so the traveler can see the earth-rimmed mouths of the vertical shafts through which the debris from the tunnel has been removed. These *qanats* go back at least to the time of Darius, and probably earlier.

Lumber is still to be obtained in commercial quantities in parts of North Africa, as in the Ktama forest in Spanish Morocco, the Sefru region of the Middle Atlas, and in the highlands of eastern Algeria, around Guelma. In Lebanon and Syria and in most of ʿIraq there is little left. The principal source of lumber in Iran is the northern slope of the Elburz, long exploited for boxwood and still heavily forested with oak and beech. These rare and distant forests are insufficient to supply the Middle East with the wood it needs. Most of the lumber used in the fine cabinetwork made in any *suq* or bazaar from Mogador to Kabul is imported, not so much from Europe and America as from the tropical forests of Africa, India, and Malaya.

It must be remembered that wood serves not only as building material but as fuel as well. Throughout the Middle East charcoal is the most prized fuel, for it gives a hot, smokeless flame, essential in houses designed for summer rather than winter habitation. It also is needed in metallurgy, pottery firing, and bread making. Most people use dung for fuel, for operations such as boiling soup or tea where a critical temperature of 1000° F. or more is not needed. Roasting meat, baking, smelting, and other technical operations requiring hotter fires are community or professional enterprises.

In Iran one of the most striking sights is the half-acre patch of dense poplar forest that grows up-ditch beside each village. These trees grow quickly, and their limbs cling close to the trunks; trees with four-inch stems grow no more than eighteen inches apart. No more efficient way of producing twenty-foot poles quickly and on a minimum space could be found. These poplar poles are the standard units of material for rafters, door jambs, window frames, and the like. The forest has moved from the mountain to the valley.

It is easy for us, newly aroused to an interest in conservation, to decry the deforestation of the Middle East. We have lived in a rich land for periods ranging from one to three hundred years, depending on the part of the country, and we have wasted probably no more than half our natural resources in forest and topsoil during that time. In a far poorer environment, over a period of five thousand years and more, the peoples of the Middle East have destroyed only ninety per cent of it. What if they had proceeded at our pace!

While destructive to timber, the Middle Easterners have been most appreciative of the edible botanical species with which their landscape was so richly endowed. Nowhere else in the world has man domesticated and improved so many cultivatable plants and trees. Most of the vegetable foods we eat originated in this area. Wheat, barley, and rye, of the small grains, and possibly millet. Broad beans, chick-peas, lentils, and vetches, of the legumes. Onions, leeks, garlic, of the lilies. Figs and the vine, and all the delicious varieties of muskmelon that cool and slake the thirsty traveler in the heat of summer. Pomegranates, a whole forest of which still grows wild in Mazandaran; olives and sesame for oil; apples, quinces, and pears, of the roses; a forest of wild pears covering the western slope of the Zagros near Sanandaj; peaches, plums, apricots, and almonds; walnuts, saffron. Dates in the desert oases and along the exotic rivers.

Incomplete as it is, this list will suffice to show that Middle Eastern man long ago learned to cultivate plants that yield carbohydrates, proteins, and oils, as well as sugars derived from simmering the dried fruits of his orchards, and from dates. No one knows exactly when and where agriculture began. There is evidence that people reaped grain-bearing grasses at Jericho in pre-pottery times, as early as 6000 B.C. This evidence includes the flint blades used as sickles, still bearing the polish of the silica from the stems of the grain, and the stone mills used to grind it into flour. There is also evidence of agriculture to the north, on the southern Caspian shore: flint sickles, grindstones, jade axes, and a crude, poorly baked pottery, as early as 5330 B.C.[3]

Perhaps agriculture began in more than one place, and the people practicing it in each expanded until they met and exchanged ideas and products. Much more work needs to be done, many more mounds and caves dug, methodically and to the bottom, before we can be certain. He who digs a mound or a cave must not be content

[3] E. K. Ralph, University of Pennsylvania, Radiocarbon Dates I, Science, Vol. 121, pp. 149–51, 1954.

with the careful recording of flint and stone and pottery, layer by layer. He must excavate animal bones with the same solicitude as human skeletons. The animal bones tell another part of the story, that of the origins of the domestication of our principal beasts of the farmyard and stable, the ox, the sheep, the goat, the pig, the horse, the ass, and even the dog.

We who eat roast beef on Sundays and pork with our beans seldom wonder whom to thank for these gifts, other than the ultimate and divine Source of all bounty. It was the ancient hunters and earliest farmers of the Middle East who first rounded up these animals and tamed them for their use. Try to imagine yourself on foot, armed with a bow and arrow, a length of cordage, and a stone ax, either alone or accompanied by a dozen of your fellows, setting out to catch a wild bull in the forest or a wild sheep on the mountain crags.

Once these animals had been caught and tamed most of them could be set to other uses than providing an easy source of meat and skins. The pig is the only exception. It consumes much food, is capable of rapid growth and excessive fattening, and bears a dozen young at a time; it is the prize food factory of the farmyard. But it cannot be led or put to useful work nor milked nor shorn. There is an old Arab story which tells of a sheep, a goat, and a pig living together in a pen. The sheep said, "Come, we are going to market with our master." The goat said, "Hurry, pig, we are going to market." Said the pig: "It is well for you to be happy and impatient. One of you is to be milked and the other shorn, but I am to be cut into pieces."

Except for the dog, the sheep and goat were probably the first mammals to be domesticated—even before the cultivation of cereals. The ox, which came later, was perhaps the earliest draft animal, followed by the horse. Both, plus the ass, became beasts of burden. Cows, goats, and sheep provided milk, the sheep wool as well. The ox needs well-watered country, being a native of forests and lush prairies; the horse requires grain. Goats can eat leaves in scrub forests, high on the hillsides; sheep need the grass of steppes and hill slopes. The pig, which joined the barnyard at about the same time as the ox, is economically useful only in a beech or oak forest, an extravagance elsewhere. Early Metal Age remains throughout the Middle East show an abundance of pig bones. As the people grew in numbers and the forests scarcer, pigs were replaced by more economical, all-purpose animals. Someone, somewhere, also domesticated the camel, apparently near the end of the second millennium B.C., in southwestern Asia.[4] It was not brought to Egypt until Assyrian times (about 671 B.C.), nor to North Africa until about 400 A.D. When it came to the Sahara it created a revolution, as we shall see.

From the beginning the Late Stone Age farmers of the Middle East, who soon became Metal Age farmers, understood the intimate relationship between agriculture and domestic animals. Oxen drew plows and smoothing boards and flint-studded harrows; oxen and horses trampled the grain on clay threshing floors. Cattle could pasture on the grain fields after the harvest, and their droppings—those not collected for fuel—would make the fields fertile.

Nowhere else in the world did such a close integration develop between animal husbandry and agriculture, except later, derivatively, in Europe. The Chinese rice farmer uses oxen, but his particular kind of cultivation requires much more human labor. He uses animals far less for transport, being much more dependent on inland shipping. The same is true in most of Negro Africa, where the environment, including the tsetse fly, divides the people into herdsmen or farmers, but rarely both. In aboriginal America only one economically useful animal was domesticated, the llama, and it was limited to a small area through its specialization in terms of altitude.

Many animals in the Middle East avoided domestication. The lion once roamed and roared from Tangier to the Khyber Pass. More than one hundred years ago, in 1846, Sir John Drummond-Hay shot one within sight of the Strait of Gibraltar,[5] and between 1840 and 1842 Sir Henry Layard hunted them with the Bakhtyari chiefs in the foothills of the Zagros.[6] A few lions are left on the northern edges of the Sahara, while others may survive here and there in Iran and Afghanistan, descendants of the proud beasts the Assyrian kings were wont to lead on leashes, according to their sculptors, and models for the national symbol of Iran, backed by the rising sun, and brandishing a sword.

Tigers still frighten charcoal burners in the Elburz forests, and black panthers provide good sport in the Middle Atlas. In the 1930's the Imām of al-Yemen kept two huge panthers in cages in his Ṣan'ā palace. Plenty of wild boar are left wherever there is oak

[4] This event is veiled in mystery. See Chap. 4, n. 10.

[5] B. Meakin, *The Land of the Moors* (London, 1901), p. 56.

[6] Sir A. H. Layard, *Early Adventures in Persia, Susiana, and Babylonia* (London, 1887), I, 438-446.

forest. Hyenas are plentiful on the edges of deserts, and wolves come down from the hills in Iran in winter to raid the sheep, while jackals slink into ditches everywhere.

The principal game animal, however, is the gazelle, hunted with greyhound (saluki) and hawk. Today the jeep threatens his extinction. Safe from the jeep are the audad or mouflon, the wild sheep of Asia, the ibex of the rocks in southern Arabia, and the hook-horned mountain goats of the Elburz. Quail, bustards, and pheasants provide sport in barren and lonely places. Along the marshes of the Shaṭṭ-al-ʿArab and the lower Helmand, and by the rice paddies of the Caspian shore, migrant ducks and geese draw hunters with nets and guns. The abundance of waterfowl must have been one of the primary inducements for men to settle the valleys of the Tigris-Euphrates and Nile in the earliest days when these streams were bordered by reeds and water-loving trees.

Another inducement must have been the fish to be caught in these waters. Today the only good fishing areas of the Middle East are, as elsewhere, off the mouths of large rivers. The brown water of the Nile, filled with vegetable matter to delight piscine palates, makes a great fishing ground between Egypt, Crete, and Lebanon. Another is the Persian Gulf, noted for its pearls, and another the southern Caspian waters and the small torrentlike streams draining the Elburz jungle. This is noted for its sturgeon and their caviar, formerly removed by the Russians through treaty rights.

Taken as a whole, the environment of the Middle Eastern countries was eminently suitable for the growth of high civilization in antiquity and the maintenance of that civilization in succeeding millenniums. The mild and variable climate, the presence of the world's most suitable plants and animals for cultivation and domestication, the exotic rivers with their steady supply of water and opportunities for inland water transport and need of control in irrigation, the scarcity of useful minerals and the consequent need of far travel and trade, this was a natural setting for exactly what happened. Shortages of fuel and water passed the initiative to richer lands more suited for the next stage of development after the preliminary techniques had been learned in the Middle East. Now, since new sources of fuel have been found in the Middle East, since dams built with modern machinery can not only help save water but also furnish power, and since these countries are strategically more important than ever, they are beginning to recapture the center of the stage.

3 THE PEOPLES, ANCIENT AND MARGINAL

THE PEOPLES OF THE MIDDLE EAST are many and varied. To list them country by country and language by language would make a book in itself. All of the peoples are related to each other in that all have their parts to play in the ethnic division of labor that makes up the first and most obvious dimension of our mosaic. Beyond this general relationship, the most convenient way to list them for treatment is to break them down into six main headings, on the basis of language. These are: (a) the ancient peoples whose languages are extinct (Sumerians, Egyptians, Elamites, etc.); (b) the Berbers; (c) the Dravidians; (d) the Semites; (e) the Indo-Europeans; and (f) the Turko-Mongols. This does not mean languages spoken exclusively, for few persons, particularly few adult males, in the Middle East speak only one language. It means the language traditionally spoken by each people, in the quiet of the home; the language the child learns first, with, or soon after, its mother's milk.

Ancient, Unique, and Extinct

Although many languages now spoken in the Middle East have been on the tongues of men for thousands of years, some have passed away. These include the speech of the most ancient ones of all of whom we have written record, the Sumerians. The Sumerians invented the cuneiform system of writing, on tablets of clay. This writing, starting as Chinese did with pictographs, passed into the rebus stage and developed several kinds of symbols, representing sounds and classes of phenomena. Luckily the medium on which it was written was relatively permanent. Although some tablets have crumbled, others remain whole; and scholars spend their lives reading these fascinating documents.

Most of the tablets are commercial accounts—so-and-so owes so-and-so a certain amount; I delivered three cows and a dozen measures of wheat to so-and-so; shipowner so-and-so enters into a contract with Captain so-and-so to sail his vessel to foreign parts, share and share alike in the profit, but if the ship is wrecked, it is the captain's responsibility. Some of them are concerned with the state of the holy treasury of a god, and others, like the Gilgamesh Epic, with the bold deeds of the heroes of a still older time.

The Sumerian language, worked out with much patience and skill by two generations of scholars, cannot be surely related to any other known form of speech. It was characteristically agglutinative, like Turkish, Finnish, Basque, and the languages of the Caucasus. It had a system of vowel harmony, in which the vowels of the different parts of a composite word were made to agree. The words themselves are unrelated to those of any other recorded language, probably because no other language of equal age, except Egyptian, is known. A few of its words survive today, as for example *abyss* and the name *Lilith*.

No one knows where the Sumerians came from. That they must have come from some other place is clear. The valley of the lower Tigris-Euphrates of their day, at around 4000 B.C., consisted entirely of alluvial soil, reaching the Persian Gulf a hundred miles farther to the northwest than at present. Not a piece of flint, not a scrap of stone, not an ounce of metal, awaited them there.

They came as farmers and boatmen, in a transitional stage between the Neolithic and the Bronze ages. They brought with them or soon obtained obsidian flakes for cutting skin, meat, and grain; jade and other hard-stone axes for woodcutting; bronze for weapons[1] and for a few tools; volcanic rock for grinding grain; luxury stones, such as steatite and crystal, for carving vessels; gold, turquoise, and other precious metals and stones for symbolic and ornamental use. They also brought wheat and barley and most of the other cultivated plants mentioned earlier, and the usual domestic animals, notably the ox, pig, sheep, goat, and, perhaps not at first but soon after, the horse.

In deciding whence they came, one scholar's guess is as good as another's. Some suggest that it was from the shores of the Persian Gulf by sea. What little digging has been done to date in the mounds of Baḥrain Island and of the Arabian coast has, however, turned up nothing very ancient. Others hazard a guess that it was

[1] This is based on the chemical analysis of specimens excavated at Ur by Sir Leonard Woolley. See H. J. Plenderleith, "Metals and Metal Technique," in C. L. Woolley, *Ur Excavations* (London and Philadelphia, 1934), II, 284–298, chap. 14. Dr. George Cameron questions this.

up along the Caspian and the Amu Darya, when the latter emptied into the Caspian, but here again not one scrap of concrete evidence, pro or con, is at hand. Virtually all we have to indicate the homeland of the ancient Sumerians is the hint that they came as sailors, with a complete vocabulary for hulls and sails, halyards and masts and yards.

The Sumerians invented, or at least perfected and spread, the early stages of two sequences of mechanical and chemical inventions that have shaken the world. The first was the principle of the rotating shaft. This sequence begins with fire making, the oldest human accomplishment not shared with other animals, the first way of producing nonmuscular energy by man. All over the world people make fire. Some make it with flint and iron pyrites, by stroking a spark into tinder. Others make it with a fireplow or firesaw, if they have the right kind of wood. Still others—and in the days before flint and steel and matches these were in the majority—make fire with a rotating wooden shaft in a wooden hearth. That the ancient Egyptians were among those who used the simple shaft and hearth is shown by their hieroglyphic sign (pronounced *d*ʿ), which when used with other symbols means *fire drill.*[2]

The simplest way to rotate a shaft is to turn it between the palms of the hands. But the hands have a tendency to slip down the shaft and thus necessitate a pause to begin again before the critical moment has been reached. It is better, therefore, to use some other device, such as a bow, a cord, or, even better, a pair of cords wound in opposite directions and hitched to a pump bar. From the pumped shaft to a pump drill is a simple step, and with the pump drill the Sumerians were able to carve intaglio designs on cylinder seals needed in their business and in their religious and political negotiations. The imprint of the seal, rolled out on clay, had the authority of a signature today but was more useful, for the average executive did not know how to write, leaving that detail to his professional scribes.

If you take a shaft and lower its socket two feet into a pit, fit it into a frame at the top, and attach to it a wooden disk, you have the makings of a potter's wheel. Hitch on the pumping device with a foot treadle and you can sit on the edge of the hole, turn the table

[2] Arthur Ungnad, *Zeitschrift für aegyptische Sprache* (1906), Bd. 43, pp. 161-162. See also its use in "The Tale of the Shipwrecked Sailor," *op. cit.*, p. 9, quoting the *Petersburg Papyrus 1115*, ll. 54-55.

with your feet, and shape lumps of clay with your hands as they whirl before you. The potter's wheel is a speed-up device, making it possible for one man to turn out many times as many vessels per day as he could by hand.

Now let us suppose that you, an ancient Sumerian, have a number of spare potter's wheels lying around your courtyard. The idea comes to you to fix two of the round wooden tables to one shaft, one to each end. You can roll this down the street. Or you can fix a stoneboat, summer sled, or box, which you already have, to the axle in the same way that you fix the shaft of the wheel to its upper bearing, and you have a cart. You have already seen teams of oxen yoked to plows. Attach the yoke to the end of the summer sled's pole, and all you need do now is load your cart and drive away. The invention of the wheeled vehicle required no new principles or new tools; all it needed was a little imagination in combining existing devices, with the use of existing tools. Whether or not the Sumerians or some of their unknown neighbors invented the wheeled vehicle in just this way, or not, we do not know. We do know that they had the necessary elements and that they made the vehicles.

In later times this sequence which the Sumerians had started was carried two steps farther along in applying the rotary shaft principle to milling. Sumerian women spent much time each day in needless drudgery, grinding grain on a metate-like hand mill of volcanic stone. These saddle querns occur in the earliest Neolithic cave level in the Caspian shore deposits and were by no means a Sumerian invention. As the Old Testament tells us, they were still used by the Israelites as late as the time of the Babylonian captivity. Tenth-century A.D. Arabs still used them in the region of Nippur; Tuareg slaves and Ethiopian women grind their flour with them today.

In Roman times, and perhaps earlier, the woman's grinding time was reduced by the invention of the rotary quern. Carve a nether stone in a circular form, fix a pin in the top, set on it a properly balanced upper stone with an asymetrical hole through which the grain can be poured from above, give it a handle, and turn. These devices are still used in the Hebrides and in the Middle East from one end to the other.

Along with this household improvement came a professional form, the larger mill operated by animal power. A shaft from the side of a huge upper stone is hitched to a blindfolded donkey, or to a pair of slaves, and the miller can grind enough for several families in an hour. There was, however, no need to use animals or slaves who required feeding. Extend the shaft downward as if it were a part of a potter's wheel, set paddles into it all around, and lead the water from an irrigation ditch through a pipe against the paddles. If the fall is great enough, the shaft will turn, and water will grind your grain. If you have no water, but a steady, prevailing wind, extend the shaft above the millstones and hitch on some wind vanes. Build a wall of brick to block out the wind on one side of the vanes, and let it blow through the other half. The wind will turn your mill and grind your grain. When these two devices were first invented is a mystery. Today they are widespread. They are simpler than the horizontal-shafted water wheel and windmill, familiar in Europe. A country carpenter can make them and keep them in repair with simple tools, for they can be made of wood and need no gears. We must remember that the more advanced applications of the principle of the rotating shaft, carried over in our civilization to the toolmaker's lathe, to the mammoth textile mill, to the automobile, to the piston-engined airplane, and to countless other devices, began with the Sumerians, to whom we are indebted for these things.

The other sequence has to do with the application of heat, once the shaft has produced its fire. Built outdoors without special flues or drafts, using wood as fuel, the ordinary fire will reach somewhere between 500° and 600° F. This is enough to cook meat and keep people warm. It is also enough to boil soups and stews in primitive clay pots, and to fire the pots themselves once they have been shaped. But the pots so fired are heavy, crumbly, and easily broken. If you examine the section of such a sherd you will see that while the surface may be hard and red, the inside is soft and black. This is a simple Neolithic-type pot, made by women in the back yard and fired in the same place.

The woman also must bake her family's bread. She can do this also over the back-yard fire, but this is wasteful of fuel, and since only the bottom of the bread receives the heat, she is limited to the *lawash* or unleavened cake, like the Mexican tortilla. Many people in the Middle East eat these cakes every day, and orthodox Jews eat them during the Passover in memory of a time when their ancestors had to revert to this system as an emergency kind of cooking. The people of the Middle East prefer, however, to eat loaves of raised bread when they can get them and if no religious restrictions intervene.

Raised bread involves what may be our oldest domestic plant, yeast. (Yeast probably was derived originally from beer brewing. All Neolithic-style peoples or primitive agriculturists in general enjoy some kind of brew, like the mealie beer of the African tribesmen, or the maize *chicha* of the South American Indians. Beer is probably as old as cultivated grain.) Once the dough has been raised it must be placed in an oven, an enclosed space which can be heated so that the temperature on all sides of the bread will be uniform. There can be no smoke in the oven or it will spoil the bread. Hence the preferred fuel is charcoal.

With charcoal and an enclosed oven, temperatures as high as 1000° to 1100° F. can be produced, if the draft is sufficient. The oven suitable for baking bread can be used as a kiln to fire pots. These pots can be thinner walled, for they will be of a uniform hardness throughout. The fine product of the potter's wheel requires this kind of kiln and a similar temperature. The same temperature will smelt copper and, once smelted, melt it again and again for casting. If tin is added to make bronze, the temperature can be a little lower, and a cleaner casting results.

No one knows the exact sequence of these events, nor who first did which, but the fact remains that fire, beer, bread, pots, and metal are all part of a single complex of biochemical and thermal discoveries that the Sumerians used and passed on to the rest of the world. With the sequence of the rotating shaft, these inventions form the base of metal-age Middle Eastern technology, and our own, along with agriculture, animal husbandry, and navigation, which they also possessed.

Such high skills require full-time specialists. In all societies woman's primary work is being a housewife and caring for her children. In most Neolithic societies the men are concerned with the care of animals, the heavier tasks of agriculture, hunting, fishing, toolmaking, and woodworking. Brewing, baking, pottery making, milling, and the like, along with weaving, are women's work. Hence, as each of these techniques rises to a certain threshold in its requirements of concentration and skill, it becomes the work of men. The brewer, the baker, the potter, the miller, the weaver, and the other craftsmen who have taken over women's work do not stand quite as high in the esteem of their fellows as those who continue the manly tasks of agriculture and animal husbandry; they live under a slight stigma. Landowners do not want to give them their daughters in marriage.

The tasks of irrigation, flood control, collection of food for the granaries, protection of traders, and defense of the land require still other specialists—kings and warriors, with their retinues. The maintenance of equilibrium by ritual, in which one passes the responsibility for crises into divine hands, requires still another group, the priests, who are closely connected with the kings, since each protects and bolsters the other. Both need scribes. The temples acquire landed property and the princes expand their estates.

Following this general pattern, on which they had no monopoly, the Sumerians developed a series of city-states, each with its capital and special god, and finally a united kingdom. The division of society into farmers, artisans, traders, priests, and royalty became firmly rooted, for it was the most efficient way for people living in such an environment to align themselves at the technological level in which they lived. Since that technological level has persisted in most respects until the present century, this kind of society still exists, in one guise or another, throughout the length and breadth of the Middle East.

Other peoples speaking ancient, extinct, and probably unique languages lived in the Middle East, but we have no evidence that they were as ancient, in the sense of being literate urban peoples, as the Sumerians. These include the Elamites, who lived on the lower Karun, to the east of Sumeria. They also used a cuneiform script, shared the general type of civilization just described, and also spoke an agglutinative language, with a lesser degree of vowel harmony. Their kings succeeded each other by matrilineal descent.[3]

Just as the Sumerians passed on the details of their civilization to their Semitic-speaking neighbors, so did the Elamites teach the Persians of the period of Cyrus, Darius, and Xerxes. Sumerian lived on as a ritual language, like Church Latin, long after it had died out as a household speech. In the same way Elamite was used by the Persians as the language of bookkeeping. As a local dialect in Khuzistan, some form of it may have survived until the end of the first millennium A.D.[4]

[3] George C. Cameron, *History of Early Iran* (Chicago, 1936), p. 227.

[4] George C. Cameron, *The Persepolis Treasury Tablets,* University of Chicago Oriental Institute Publications (Chicago, 1948), LXV, 18.

Thanks to the work of Dr. Ephraim A. Speiser,[5] among others, we also know about a number of other Middle Eastern Bronze Age peoples; some of these, the Lullu, Gutians, and Kassites, inhabited the slopes of the Zagros from Luristan to Lake Van; others, the Hurrians, lived in northern Syria and northern ʿIraq. Speiser believed that the languages of these peoples, similar to each other in structure, resembled the living languages of the Caucasus, such as Georgian, Circassian, Chechen, and Lesghian. That languages of this general category were once spoken much more widely than at present is certain. Much work, however, must still be done before this difficult and obscure linguistic problem can be unscrambled.

The Hamites

Of equal antiquity with the Sumerians were the ancient Egyptians. Their language, spared for us by their habit of carving hieroglyphs on stone and by the dry climate of Egypt which has preserved their hieratic and demotic papyri, belonged to the Hamitic family, which is purely African in historic distribution. Two other branches of the Hamitic stock are recognized: the Berber, spoken in North Africa, and Kushitic, in Ethiopia and in parts of Kenya and the Sudan. Ancient Egyptian still survives as Coptic, written in a modified Greek alphabet. This is the ritual language of the Coptic Christian Church of Egypt and Ethiopia.

Insofar as the archaeological evidence indicates, the ancestors of the ancient Egyptians who built the pyramids and carved their names on stone had lived in the Nile Valley for several centuries before they reached the Metal Age, with writing and architecture, kings and priests. It is hard to believe, however, that their culture is any more autochthonous than that of the Sumerians, since both cultivated the same plants and reared the same animals. Of these plants and animals only barley and the ass can possibly have had an African origin. Furthermore, the Egyptians lagged a little behind their Asiatic counterparts. Around 3500 B.C. the Sumerians started out in the full Bronze Age,[6] which lasted only a few centuries. Later they made their implements of copper, while their successors in Mesopotamia only resumed the use of bronze about 1400 B.C. The Egyptians began to mine and use copper commonly around 3000 B.C. and first

[5] Ephraim A. Speiser, *Mesopotamian Origins* (Philadelphia, 1930).
[6] See p. 28, n. 1.

obtained bronze by trade about 2200 B.C.[7] Although the peoples of Mesopotamia had long used carts and began driving horses about the beginning of the second millennium B.C., the Egyptians possessed neither horses nor wheeled vehicles until the Hyksos invasion, from Asia, about 1700 B.C.

Derived as the cultures of Egypt and Sumer may have been, and from where we do not know, they were both autochthonous in one most important sense, that urban civilization began with their efforts. The Egyptians and Sumerians spoke different languages and worshiped different gods, but in many other ways they were the same. They practiced the same system of agriculture with only one variation: the Egyptians' fields were flooded in the summer with the rise of the Nile, while the flooding in Mesopotamia came in the spring. Since neither depended on rain and both practiced irrigation, this made little difference. Both of them manufactured roughly the same kinds of goods. Both social systems were based on a division of labor between farmers, artisans, rulers, and priests. Both were concerned with the afterlife of their rulers and erected elaborate tombs, although the Sumerians built nothing comparable to the pyramids.

One notable difference may be seen in architecture. The Egyptians had an inexhaustible supply of excellent building stone, which they quarried near the banks of the Nile and floated on barges down to their building sites. This had its social aspect too, for the Egyptian rulers thus employed their farmers during the flood time, when horny hands otherwise would have been idle. The Sumerians, who had no stone within a reasonable distance, developed the use of bricks to a fine art. They made two kinds, the unfired, which is no more than adobe, and the fired. Because of the scarcity of fuel the latter were reserved for façades and public buildings. To make up for this shortage they invented the baked clay peg and thrust these cones into the adobe to form ornate patterns. More important, Mesopotamians invented the dome to compensate for the lack of wood, as the Eskimos did.

Ancient Egyptian civilization remained more or less uniform for two and a half millenniums. The Children of Israel came and went with no certain reference in the papyri. Cretans and other sea people traded along the ports of the Delta. The Hyksos invaded,

[7] The chemical analysis of ancient Egyptian metal objects is the basis for this statement also. A. Lucas, *Ancient Egyptian Materials and Industries* (2d ed.; London, 1934), pp. 146-229, chap. 7.

took over, and finally were expelled. The Persians under Cambyses, son of Cyrus, conquered Egypt in 525 B.C., and were followed by Alexander. Egypt was a prize colony of the Roman Empire, but Rome did little to change the Egyptians, who under their rule adopted Christianity of a non-Roman variety. It was not until the Arab invasion of 639 A.D. under ʿAmr ibn al-ʿĀṣ, that the turning point arrived. Many of the Egyptians retained their Christian faith and kept their ancient language for ritual purposes. These indigenous Christians, the Copts, are still there. Forming eight or nine per cent of the population, they are concentrated in Upper Egypt, where they are successful farmers. Many of them live in the city, where they hold a virtual monopoly on the bookkeeping trade, like the scribes among their ancestors. Their church has a hierarchy of moderate elaboration, with a metropolitan and two grades of priests, as well as monks and nuns. They have survived the Muslim invasion and adjusted themselves into the Middle Eastern mosaic as a special people.

No complexity such as the civilizations of the Sumerians and ancient Egyptians enjoyed can be attributed to the culture of the Berbers in North Africa. Excavations in the Caves of Hercules, outside Tangier, have shown that the local inhabitants, who were Berbers, lived in a Neolithic stage of culture at the time of the Roman arrival, and probably for some time afterward. These same caves and other sites give us some information about the ancestors of the Berbers and their predecessors.

Visitors to these photogenic grottoes, conveniently situated between a Spanish cantina and a first-class bathing beach, are often impressed by the similarity between the costumes worn by the local Moors and the Franciscan friars who stroll in that area. Both wear hooded robes with wide sleeves, skullcaps, and beards. The Franciscan garb is late Roman. So is the Moorish.

One day in 1947, as we finished digging, an expedition foreman brought in a Neolithic pot complete but for a hole in the bottom.

"What layer did this come from?" I asked.

Our foreman smiled. "No layer," he said. "The Spanish swineherd broke it yesterday, he had been cooking in it."

"Where did HE get it?" I asked.

"One of the women of our village made it."

Conservatism is the key to North Africa. The lower levels of the

High Cave yielded remains of a man in the Neanderthal stage.[8] His style of flint chipping, which was supplanted before the end of the Pleistocene in Europe by a blade culture, clung on in North Africa and in isolation attained perfection. Big, rugged, square-faced men with lantern jaws lived in Algeria as food gatherers until the dawn of the Neolithic. The Neolithic farmers, with their pigs, goats, and sheep, soft-cored pottery, barley, and wheat, reached Morocco from the East about the time of the first writing in Egypt and ʿIraq. Basically their culture is still there, overlaid with Punic, Roman, Arab, French, and Spanish accretions.

These Neolithic farmers brought in the Berber languages, now spoken by some sixty per cent of the people in Morocco, twenty-nine per cent in Algeria, not more than one per cent in Tunisia, and by the inhabitants of the Jabal Nafusa in Tripolitania and by those of the Siwa Oasis in the Libyan desert toward Egypt. Until the Spanish conquest of their territory in the fifteenth century, it was also spoken by the inhabitants of the Canary Islands, who were still in the Neolithic. Contemporary accounts of these warriors, who with stone and wooden weapons gave the invaders a hard time and held out for many years despite the superiority of the Spanish arms, yield our only eyewitness evidence[9] of Neolithic civilization of the Mediterranean-Middle Eastern type; as such it is of great value.

There are seven Canary Islands: Lanzarote, Fuertaventura, Gran Canaria, Teneriffe, Gomera, Hierro, and Palma. They are steep, precipitous, and lacking in harbors. The highest peak, in Teneriffe, reaches 12,152 feet. There is rain in winter, and it is dry in summer. Aside from grass, the principal vegetation is laurel and oak. Lacking means of intercommunication, the inhabitants of the seven islands developed many minor cultural differences, with the most elaborate social and political structure in the larger islands.

They made cutting tools of obsidian, basalt, and lava; no good material was available for polished stone axes, and the few that have been found must have been imported. From goat leg bones they fashioned a variety of other implements—awls, needles, and the like; from horn—ladles, spear tips, and fishhooks; from shell—more fishhooks and ornaments worn on the chest, like those of the American Indians. Despite the lack of good tools they carved bowls,

[8] M. S. Şenyürek, *Fossil Man in Tangier,* Peabody Museum Papers (Cambridge, Massachusetts, 1940), XVI, No. 3, 140.

[9] Unless there is some classical source on North Africa in pre-Roman times which I have missed.

spoons, lances, maces, shields, and coffins out of wood. They produced pottery in the Neolithic style, crude and underfired. For textiles they plaited much matting and basketry, but wove no cloth. Their clothing, in the form of hooded robes on at least one island, was of cured goatskin, finely stitched. They built their houses of stone, with pine rafters, earth roofs, and red-painted interior walls. The palace of the king of Teneriffe was lined with well-carved and

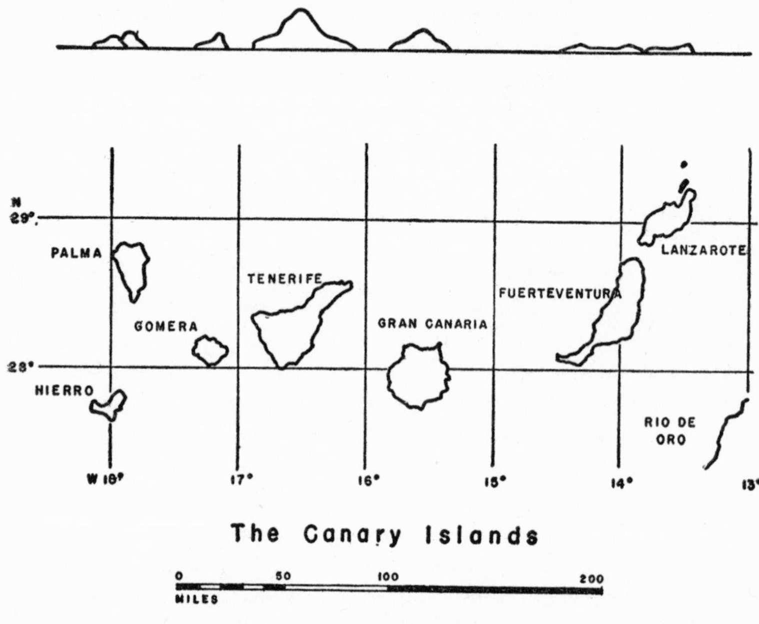

Map 3: *The Canary Islands*

jointed pine panels. They raised dogs, pigs, sheep, and goats, and grew wheat, barley, beans, and figs. They knew how to preserve meat and figs by drying, and milk by making cheese. They caught as much fish as they could by hook and line, torch and harpoon, seine nets, and by poisoning the still waters of inlets with euphorbia juice.

This outline of their material culture is little different from that of many living Middle Eastern peoples. Add metal, weaving, cattle, donkeys, a few more fruits and vegetables, tea or coffee, sugar and tobacco, and the chance to trade with towns and cities, and you have the technology of the average out-of-the-way Middle Eastern village of today.

On the basis of this Neolithic economy the Guanches, as they were called, were able to support a social, political, and religious institutional structure of some complexity, and with just as striking implications. Some islands were single kingdoms, others supported several sovereign states. The king was advised by a council of elders, who were nobles. Noblemen had to maintain a strict standard of conduct or they would be demoted. Specifically, a nobleman could not milk, slaughter, or skin an animal or do any other economically useful thing, any more than a Middle Eastern landlord or government official would do the same. The noblemen owned the flocks, the chief source of wealth of the islands, again putting them in the landlord class. The most important official beside the king was a high priest, who also acted as judge. Combining the judicial with the religious is straight Middle Eastern procedure, from the Sumerians and Egyptians down to Muslim law.

There seems to have been latitude in the succession to the throne. When the king died it went to his oldest surviving brother, and so on down the fraternal line; after the last brother it went to the first king's eldest son, and so on. This type of succession cannot be enforced; it is bound to make trouble and to be uncertain. Witness the recent difficulties in the Yemen, and the general scramble that takes place in Arab kingdoms, part of which is due to the large numbers of princes. Having *jus primae noctis* and choice of maidens while traveling, the Guanche kings also had many sons.

Beside the high priest the religious personnel included a sect of holy women who lived together in special houses and who wore white garments. Such a house served as sanctuary for any person fleeing vengeance. One of the women was abbess. These women served as oracles to those who came to consult them, and took part in religious processions and other rites. Some, if not all, of the islands contained particularly holy places, especially rocks, and to these shrines the people repaired in time of crisis, to circumambulate, to pray, to fast, and to sacrifice. Certain of these rites were mournful, and the suppliants wept and sang dirges and leaped about in extravagant fashion. A principal reason for ritual was rainmaking. In one such ceremony a man "esteemed as a saint" entered a cave to communicate with the god.

Aside from these public rites, individuals made pilgrimages to shrines on high places, where they swore oaths on the spirits of their ancestors and made sacrifices. The cult of the dead was as important to them as it was and still is in Egypt. Like the Egyptians, they embalmed the more important dead and sewed them in fine wrappings, which in this case were made of kidskins, specially selected. The mummies so produced were laid away in inaccessible caves in the sides of cliffs, complete with coffins. Much effort and their finest skills went into the care of the dead, and the undertakers formed a professional specialist caste. The gods themselves were not numerous; each kingdom would have its special deity, represented in some cases by a crude effigy and lodged in a stone temple. Hither suppliants came to offer sacrifices of milk and butter. In one island there were two images, of a man and a woman, each worshiped by its own sex.

The comparison between Guanche religion, as described by contemporary Spanish eyewitnesses, and the religious systems of Middle Eastern peoples from the beginning of writing to the present is very clear. One sees a greater participation of women than in Islam, but not greater than in some of the earlier historic faiths, and in some forms of Christianity. If the economy of the Neolithic as exemplified by the Guanches survives in the modern village, so the social, political, and ritual framework of modern Middle Eastern cultures goes back to the Neolithic. The city-states which arose at the beginning of the third millennium B.C. in the exotic river valleys to the east must have had a long Neolithic experience of the same kind of thing on a simpler scale. The shift from the Neolithic to the Bronze Age was an act of tightening, consolidating, elaborating, and perfecting, with the aid of better technology and increased trade, rather than an entirely new structure.

Returning to the living people of North Africa who speak Berber, we should look at Map 4. Most of the Berbers are concentrated in five groups: the Riffians, Beraber, Shluḥ, Kabyles, and Shawiya. These are all primarily mountain peoples, and most of them are farmers. The Beraber of the Middle Atlas was seminomadic. The others include the Ghomara, who have nearly lost their Berber speech; the Senhaja Srair (Bush Senhaja) of northern Morocco, who are forest people and specialists in leatherwork and woodwork; the Ṃzabites of Ghardaïa, who are both date farmers and merchants; the inhabitants of the island of Jerba, who are farmers, boatmen, and merchants; and the Siwans, who are date farmers. They also include what is left of the Tuareg.

These Berbers speak dialects which can be lumped into three

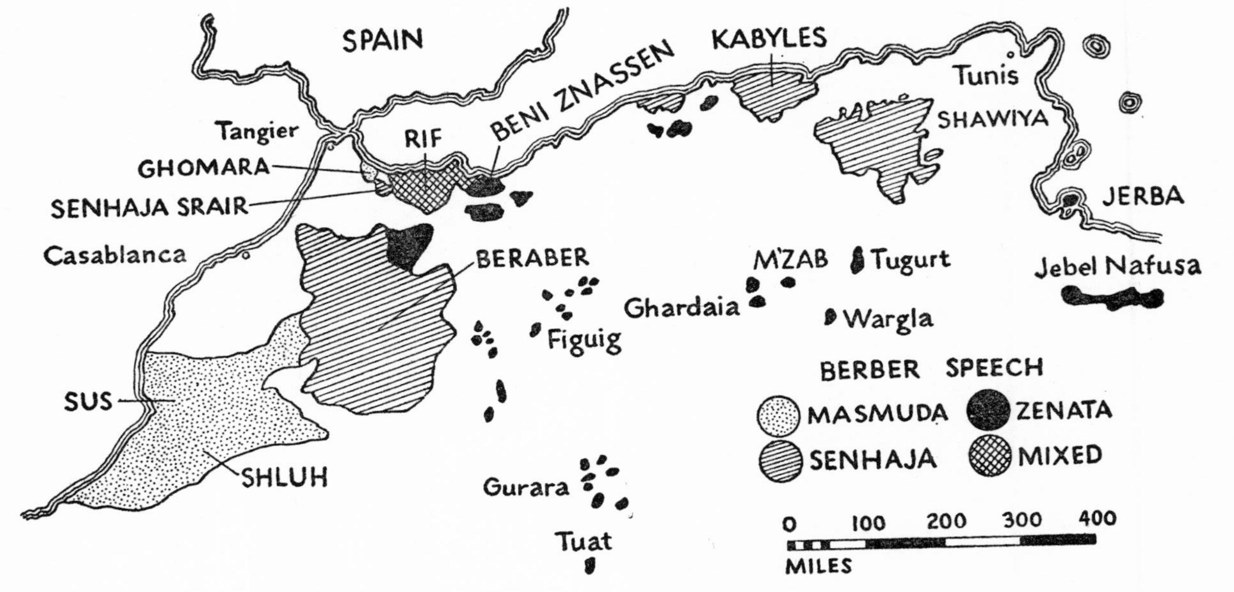

Map 4: *Berber Speech*

groups: Masmuda, Senhaja, and Zenata. Masmuda was the language of the majority of the agricultural peoples of Morocco before the Arab invasions. Today Shluḥ and Ghomara speak it, while Riffian is a mixed form. Senhaja was the speech of semisedentary shepherds and nomads; today it is spoken in the forests of northern Morocco, in the Middle Atlas, and among the Kabyles, Shawiya, and Tuareg. Zenatiya, formerly confined to the high plateaus of Algeria and the region of Ujda, was spread by the Almohads to many quarters, particularly to the oases of the Sahara, including Siwa.

Turning back to Map 4 we see that modern speakers of Berber languages are concentrated in the west and in the mountains and deserts; it is a typical refuge-area distribution. Since the establishment of Berber civilization, their country has been invaded many times, but principally in four waves. The first was from the east, and the intruders were Semitic-speaking Phoenicians. They built Carthage, settled the two wide valleys of Tunisia, and established trading posts along the coast at strategic places. Accompanied by Greeks and possibly by Jews, they gave the Neolithic Berbers a chance to trade, and particularly a source of metal.

The next wave came from the north, after the Romans had defeated Hannibal. Having destroyed Old Carthage they built a new one and colonized in depth. Some of the finest Roman architectural remains are to be seen in North Africa at Tebessa, Telepet, Constantine, Guelma, and elsewhere. Tunisia was culturally Roman territory, as was the Algerian coast. Many of the North Africans, both Puni-Romans and Berbers, had become Christian.

When wave three, that of the Arabs, struck, the blow again came from the east. They Arabized the previously Romanized population of Tunisia and moved westward along the natural highways to the Atlantic. Coming in several lots, the most important of which was the invasion of the Beni Hilāl in the middle of the eleventh century A.D., they gradually split the Berbers into local areas, took over the lowlands, and built cities. While eventually converting the Berbers to Islam, they failed in most instances to control them politically. In fact, two of the great Islamic dynasties of North Africa and Spain during the Middle Ages, the Almohad and the Almoravid, were of Berber origin.

Wave four, in true alternation, came again from the north; it began with the occupation of small islands and trading posts on the coasts by Spaniards and Portuguese. It rose with the conquest of

Algeria by France in the time of Napoleon and swelled with the creation of the French "protectorates" of Morocco and Tunisia, with the conquest of Tripolitania by the Italians, and with the Spanish acquisition of northern Morocco, Ifni, and Rio de Oro.

Wave five, again from the east, is in the making. Arab nationalism in North African countries is its first perceptible ripple.

These four waves, and the fifth which is beginning to roll, have affected the Berbers extraordinarily little. The Riffians are still farmers, still organized in tribes, although they no longer carry rifles. The Beraber of the Middle Atlas, those that are left, still herd their sheep in the mountains in the summer and retire to their *tighremts* in the winter. The Shluḥ continue to farm their terraced mountain slopes from their pueblo-like villages and weave red ovals on the seats of their robes against the evil eye. The Kabyles of Algeria wait on tables in Algiers and France; it is difficult to tell them from Europeans. When they have earned enough money they return to their villages and engage again in the local politics between *ṣofs,* the rival moities into which each village is divided.

The Shawiya of the Aures till their upland fields, and the Siwans fertilize their dates. Only the Tuareg (of whom more later) have drastically changed, and that is because their economy depended on their political independence, which all Berbers had—some until quite recently—lost. Yielding to the French and Spaniards is the first real change in their lengthy history since Jewish traders and craftsmen, moving inland from the Roman settlements, introduced the Neolithic mountaineers to the age of iron and formed their own special communities. These communities, Berber in speech, are still there.

Berbers practice every technique that any other people in North Africa know, except for some of the more recent European introductions, and these they learn quite quickly. Some are herdsmen; many are soldiers. Most are farmers. In the Sus there are Berber towns and one large city, Tarudant. Here all the skills of other oriental cities are practiced, including clerical work and government. Many automobile mechanics, bus drivers, and machinists in North Africa are Berbers. A fourteen-year-old Riffian boy was chief operator of ʿAbd el-Krīm's telephone system in 1926.

Many Berbers specialize. Susis in Morocco, Mzabites in Algeria, and Jerbans in Tunisia become keepers of small shops, similar to the neighborhood store in our country. Drawa become welldiggers. A debased class, *Imazilen,* centered in several places, serve as market criers, weighers, and musicians. Susis and men from Mogador become tumblers and acrobats and may be seen in the ring in the American circus and in vaudeville.

They have shown themselves to be intelligent, adaptable, brave, and dignified. The cultural conservatism so manifest in their camps and villages in no way hinders their capacity to adjust in the modern world. Europeans take a fancy to them because they seem more European than oriental in mental outlook. But let the Europeans remember: the Berbers are not of Europe, and they can adjust themselves to the fifth wave as readily as they have to the fourth, while retaining their essential rocklike quality of being and remaining Berbers no matter how much water splashes over them, from either direction.

The Dravidians

Although Pakistan is supposedly beyond the scope of this book, we cannot ignore the part played in the building of the mosaic by the civilization of the third great exotic river valley, that of the Indus. Less is known of the Indus Valley civilization than of those of ʿIraq and Egypt. Like the Sumerians and Egyptians, the Indus people had writing, but no Champollion has yet read it. As with the Sumerians, the Indus people seem to have started suddenly in the Bronze Age without a preceding local Neolithic. The word "seem," so often employed by scholars to cover all unforeseen contingencies, must here be taken seriously. No Neolithic has been found there yet, but a more extensive search is necessary before negative evidence can be taken as conclusive.

Some time in the latter half of the second millennium B.C. the Sanskrit-speaking ancestors of the modern Hindus and Pakistanis invaded Pakistan and India over the time-honored Khyber Pass, complete with Brahmins, warriors, and cattle. Whatever principal language or group of languages previously had been spoken in northwestern India and Pakistan disappeared under the Aryan impact. What this speech was like we may never know, but we have one kind of evidence on which to build a hypothesis. The principal languages of southern India, south and east of the present-day Aryan languages, are Dravidian. Dravidian is a linguistic stock, marked by long composite words and some rather difficult (to us) palatalized sounds. It is spoken not only in southern India by many

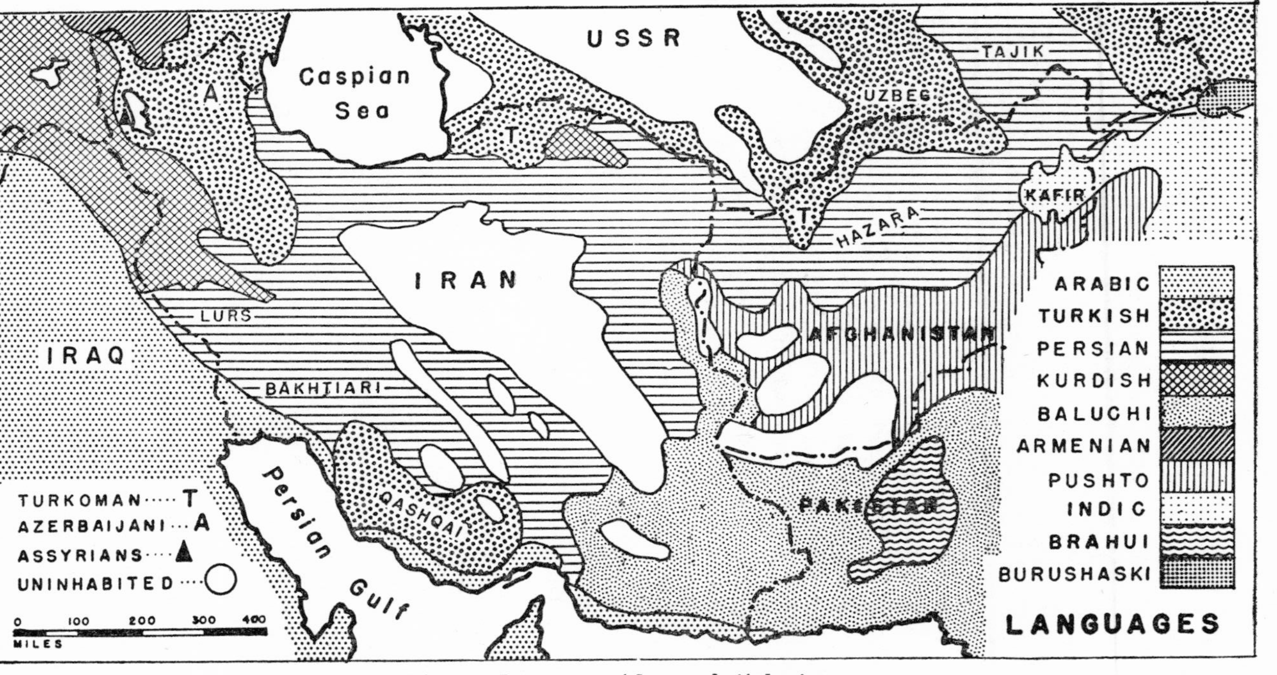

Map 5: *Languages of Iran and Afghanistan*

different kinds of people but also in the Middle East by one kind of people, the Brahui.

The country of the Brahui is the mountainous territory of southeastern Afghanistan and neighboring parts of Pakistan. Some of them also live in eastern Iran. The geographical location of these people to the west of the Indus Valley, and their linguistic kinship to the south Indians, suggests that the Dravidian languages were once spoken in the Indus Valley and that the Aryan drive both wiped out the earlier speech from the valley and split its periphery into the two logical geographical parts, both of which have survived.

The Brahui live as their environment dictates. Some are herdsmen, others are farmers. They are divided into two principal sections, inhabiting Jhalwan and Sarawan. Each of these districts supports a number of tribes, some of which are considered nobler than others, with corresponding restrictions on marriage. The noblest of all are the Aḥmadzai of Jhalwan, the family of the khans of Kalat. These people were the rulers of Baluchistan before the British intervention.

As one would expect so close to India, this corner of our mosaic is quite fine and complicated. The Brahui have many neighbors, including tribes of Baluchis, villages of Tajiks (Persians), Hindu merchants, and several castes of servants and entertainers, notably the Dombs, who go over into India. Being accustomed to authority the Brahui make excellent policemen and soldiers, and in Iran the *gendarmerie,* particularly in Khorasan, contains many.

I once went on a cave-hunting expedition with two Brahui gendarmes, a supersergeant (aspirant), and his gunbearer. The sergeant was six feet two and weighed well over two hundred pounds. He and his bearer sat in the back seat of the jeep talking their native tongue, which seemed full of th's. At one point he asked me to slow down, fired with his army rifle at a covey of grouse, and brought one down. He told me that he had three wives, a Kurd, a Persian, and one of his own people. He had spent his life hunting down smugglers and murderers. Later in the day he rode a horse up an almost perpendicular side of a mountain into a cave, to which the rest of us timorously climbed on foot. Men like him could have been responsible for any civilization, including that of the Indus Valley.

4 THE SEMITES

THE WORD SEMITE designates the peoples who have spoken in antiquity and still speak the Semitic languages and who are the most numerous of the inhabitants of the Middle East. Geographically, historically, and culturally they occupy a central position. Whatever color you may choose to assign to them is the most visible hue in the mosaic, the central base color to which the others stand in contrast. It is also the color of the fine cement which holds the pieces in place. If one were to select the most noticeable of the common elements in the civilization of the different Semitic-speaking peoples, they would include a disregard of time and space, a profound interest in the fine points of human relations, and a deep religiosity.

Our knowledge of early Semitic languages is limited to the beginnings of writing. We know that Semitic speakers lived in the valley of Mesopotamia, north of the Sumerians, during the Bronze Age, and probably also south of them, in the "Sealands" of Arabia, and that they took over the Sumerian cuneiform system of writing. The earliest Semitic language recorded is the Akkadian, from which were variously derived the later Babylonian and Assyrian.[1] The Babylonian civilization was the heir to that of the Sumerians; all of the technical processes which their cultural teachers had invented fell to the Babylonians, as well as the system of government, laws, and even the details of religious organization. Babylonian temples in turn became trust companies charged with landed estates, and Babylonian priests took over and further developed the mathematics and astronomy of their teachers.

The Assyrians, whose great period was the Early Iron Age, inhabited the rolling country and hills north of the alluvial plain, the same as the oil-well region of today near Kirkuk. Bordering the Armenian hills and the Zagros, they had access to supplies of metal,

[1] Arthur Ungnad, *Babylonisch-assyrische Grammatik* (Munich, 1925), p. 1. Dr. George Cameron states: "The later Assyrian is the lineal descendant of Akkadian while Babylonian is a development derived only in part from Akkadian but with weighty influences from the northwest in the time of the Amorites." Personal communication.

with which they made weapons and smote their enemies. Ancient history is full of accounts of the Assyrians killing thousands of one people and skinning others alive by the dozens, cutting off hands and impaling some bodies, while decapitating others by the hundreds. They invented the battering-ram and other *Panzerei* later perfected by the Romans; they were also the first experts at genocide and mass transfers to the Iron Age equivalent of Siberia. They ranged, robbed, and ravaged from the banks of the Nile to the snowy slopes of Demavend; from the deserts of Arabia to the forests of what is now Armenia and the shores of Lake Van. They have no direct linguistic or ethnic survivors, which is probably a mercy.[2]

The people who call themselves Assyrians today speak not Assyrian but a modern form of Syriac, a branch of Aramaic. Appearing about the eleventh century B.C., Aramaic became the language of the whole northwestern Semitic area, and the Aramaeans had their capital at Damascus, which is said to be the oldest continuously occupied city on the earth. During the time of Christ, Aramaic was also the common speech of northern and central Palestine west of the Jordan, as well as of ʿIraq. The Semitic peoples who adopted Christianity developed an extensive literature in this language and used the Syriac alphabet. The Nestorians particularly distinguished themselves as missionaries in Iran and Central Asia. They penetrated the Mongol capital in the lifetime of Jenghiz Khan and nearly succeeded in making Christianity the state religion of his empire. The present Mongol alphabet, and the Manchu as well, are nothing but a kind of Syriac script written vertically instead of horizontally.

At the time of the Arab invasion of ʿIraq the majority of the inhabitants of that country, while preserving the cultural pattern of earlier times, were Christian in religion, belonging to a number of different sects, of which the Nestorian was the principal one. Gradually most of these people learned Arabic and became Muslims.

[2] Dr. George Cameron objects vigorously to this whole paragraph, as follows: "Whoa! This was all Assyrian propaganda. If Olmstead ever performed a service it was in the introduction to his *History of Assyria* where he pointed out something of the following. The Assyrians realized that imperialism meant warfare and bloodshed. They saw no reason to minimize that fact. They tried to frighten people into salvation and subservience by boastful claims of gory victories. That was a propaganda machine of the first order. Why should we swallow it? Their administration was excellent, their search to recover the routes of trade across the Near East praiseworthy." Personal communication.

Some, however, assimilated the language but maintained their distinctive sects. The same thing happened in Syria and Lebanon. The Lebanese Christians, who are divided into Maronites (Uniates under the Church of Rome), Greek Orthodox, Jacobites, and Protestants, continue to use Syriac as a ritual language. In a few villages in Syria it is still spoken in daily life.

Decimated by the invasion of Hulagu in the thirteenth century, the Syriac speakers of ʿIraq moved up into the hills on the border of ʿIraq, Turkey, and Iran, and settled the fertile western shore of Lake Urmiya. They were the founders and principal inhabitants of Urmiya town, now called Rezaiyeh. During the ʿIraqi rebellion against the British in 1920-21, the British used these Nestorians as troops against the Muslims, and when the British left in 1932 the Muslims massacred the Nestorians, killing approximately six hundred, according to the most careful estimate. In Iran they have been the victims of massacre by their Azerbaijani Turkish neighbors on several occasions during the last century.

Although their indigenous church is tightly organized into a hierarchy (headed by a metropolitan called *Mar*), many Nestorians have become Catholics and Protestants as a result of the intense missionary effort directed toward them during the last century, particularly in Rezaiyeh where the Presbyterians and Catholics have had active centers. The Presbyterian mission in Rezaiyeh, with its schools and hospital, existed for exactly one century—from 1836 to 1936, when Riza Shah Pahlavi shut it down. As a result of the missionary work, most of the so-called Assyrians are literate, many of them are in government employ, and thousands have emigrated to America. Those who remain in ʿIraq specialize in being servants to Europeans, while in both ʿIraq and Iran they are truck drivers and automobile mechanics.

Turning back again to the beginning of the Iron Age we can postulate, but not prove, a migration of a Semitic-speaking special people, the Phoenicians, from the coast of the Persian Gulf to the Mediterranean shores of Lebanon and northern Palestine. Shipping in the Persian Gulf goes back to Sumerian and Babylonian times. According to the contemporary cuneiform records, the sailors lived on the shores of a country called Sealands, which apparently meant the coastal regions lying on the Arabian side of the Persian Gulf, the territory around the river mouths, and also Baḥrain Island. At one time it also may have been used to designate the Yamāma (part of the coast of Oman) and the Yemenite Tihāma. The last three place names are all based on Semitic roots of the word for sea.[3]

Many of the cargoes brought to Sumeria through the Persian Gulf originated in India or beyond. Indian Ocean navigation is a simple matter. The northeast monsoon can be used for sailing in both directions between the mouth of the Persian Gulf and various points on the west coast of India, as well as the east coast of Africa, with lateen sails. The route is a curved one, following the coasts. Although on this track such distant points as Madagascar and Indonesia can be joined, and were reached in antiquity, intermediate islands, including Reunion (ʿAbd el-Krīm's place of exile) and Mauritius (home of the dodo bird), remained undiscovered until modern times. It is probable that the early navigators of the Indian Ocean included both Indonesians and Indians. Exactly when Arab sailors began to ride the monsoon to India and Africa is unknown.

From the standpoint of navigation, the important point about the sea trade to the Persian Gulf, is that the cargoes were transshipped at several points, including Dilmun, believed to be the present Baḥrain Island, and another port called Malukhkha. All of these may have been within the gulf. Why, then, the transshipment? We do not know. One reason may have been the shallowness of the Persian Gulf above Baḥrain and the need for shallow draft vessels and highly specialized local pilots. Another may have been the simple desire to take over a share in the profits. Still another, the desire of the captains to get back out to sea while the monsoon still held, for once the boisterous southwest monsoon began they would be trapped in the gulf.

At any rate, around 1000 B.C. a number of events took place which must have been mutually related. These included the first recorded use of the domestic camel, the foundation of the South Arabian kingdoms, the development of the overland trade routes from southern Arabia through Ḥijāz to the Mediterranean, and the putative migration of the ancestors of the Phoenicians to the eastern shores of that sea. The relationship is logical and clear, although it cannot be proved. The camel is the key. Instead of having to unload their spices and other goods somewhere in the gulf for transshipment, the Indian Ocean sailors could by-pass that body of water and carry them on to some port or ports near or identical to the

[3] R. P. Dougherty, *The Sealand of Ancient Arabia,* Yale Oriental Series, *Researches* (New Haven, 1932), Vol. XIX.

modern Mukalla or Shihr. Here South Arabian caravan men would load them on camels and carry them through Ḥaḍramaut, Qataban, Saba, and Maʿīn, thence on to Mekka, Yathrib, and other oases of Ḥijāz to their destination. Thus it would be only logical for some of the sailors to move over to the Mediterranean and cut in on the rich maritime business formerly monopolized by the Minoans and now growing rapidly as the western Mediterranean was opened.[4]

The question arises as to whether the Phoenicians' variety of Semitic speech originated in the Sealands country or was derived from the local Canaanitic; the latter theory is now generally accepted. Despite this linguistic evidence, sailors could have come from the gulf to the Mediterranean, since languages can be learned and forgotten, and often are. In any case, having perfected their skills in these new waters and having ousted the Cretans as sea lords of the Mediterranean, the Phoenicians explored the rich western basin, settled Carthage, Cartagena, Cadiz, and other well-known places, and brought Portuguese and possibly Cornish tin back to the eastern centers of civilization. Homer has much to say about the Phoenicians, the principal navigators of the Aegean, who brought the barbarous Greeks of their time bronze armor and weapons, slaves, and fine cloths, and took away cattle and wine. By moving slaves by the tens of thousands the Phoenicians did much to spread and homogenize the various genes and local skills of the period.

Fine craftsmen themselves, they squeezed the paralyzing secretion from the juice sac of the deadly murex snail, and turned it into dye, the source of Tyrian purple. They built the Temple of Solomon of limestone with saws so that never the blow of a hammer could be heard, and cast complicated objects from bronze. Skilled as they were at trade, at manufacturing, and at the handling of ships at sea, the Phoenicians possessed still one other distinction: their excesses in religion, which brought down upon their heads the condemnation of the Old Testament prophets.

Long voyages at sea in the western Mediterranean and outer Atlantic; the uncertainty of the navigator's return after one month, two months, a year, several years; the extreme hazardousness of

[4] George Hourani, who read and criticized the earlier draft of this section, is opposed to the idea that the Phoenicians moved from the gulf to the Mediterranean as a people. My present attitude is that some of the gulf sailors came as individuals or as ships' companies and that from the intermixture of the immigrants and the local people the Phoenicians may have arisen.

commercial investments—so many acts of God confronted the Phoenician mariner that it is no wonder he committed himself to his deities in advance and even offered up his greatest prize, his first-born son, to the heated talons of the bronze idol, to insure success. These were rugged men, committed to an enterprise, and during the life span of their civilization, before Rome enveloped it, they did well.

Women left at home during lengthy voyages also developed quirks. The rites to the goddess Astarte at the sacred spring of Adonis were filled with abandon; neglected wives found the opportunity they needed, under a religious rationalization, and "soft" men mutilated themselves, forming groups of celibate devotees, the likes of which are still to be seen in some Middle Eastern lands, as well as elsewhere.

Although no one today calls himself a Phoenician, his heritage may be seen in several places. Arab sailors out of Kuwait and Muscat carry on his work in his traditional way. The Lebanese, Christians from the hills behind the very shore line the Phoenicians settled, sail to all lands to carry on trade. Christians and far voyagers likewise, the Maltese, tend the lighthouses in the Red Sea and speak a language part Semitic and part Italian, which some of them like to think contains Phoenician elements, although Philip Hitti, who may himself be a descendant of Phoenicians, calls it a corrupt North African Arabic.[5]

Speaking of linguistics, the Phoenicians distributed one important element in our modern civilization, the alphabet. Sometime between 1800 and 1500 B.C., their predecessors the Canaanites began a process which ended by taking the consonantal signs out of the Egyptian writing and forgetting the determinatives. From these consonantal signs which the Phoenicians spread to the west came the Hebrew, Aramaic, Sabaean, Arabic, Greek, and Etruscan alphabets, and from the Etruscan the Roman, which is now our own. From the Greek came the Coptic and the Cyrillic, which some of the Slavs enjoy. The loops of Armenian and Georgian came painfully from the same general source.

A series of points might be made about alphabets, determinatives, and consonants. The Egyptians had an alphabet at the start, combined with a syllabary, but at the end of each word they drew a picture of the object, action, or idea presented, to make sure that

[5] "Arabic Language," *Encyclopedia Americana* (1948), p. 124.

the reader understood. The reason why they did not drop these determinatives was the same reason why we do not adopt phonetic spelling: too many homophones. If we wrote *to, too,* and *two* all as TU, or *right* and *rite* as RAIT, *shoe* and *shoo* as SHU, etc., we might get into trouble also. French is much worse than English in this respect, with *mère, maire; foi, foie,* and *fois,* etc.

The Phoenicians were able to extract the alphabetic elements from Egyptian for one good reason: they had no serious homophone trouble. The Semitic languages have a great variety of consonants, which makes them so hard for the rest of us to learn. D, S, T, H, TH, and Z may all become palatalized. A smooth breathing, the *'alif,* is recognized; *hamza,* a glottal stop, and the indescribable *ʿain. Ghain,* somthing like the French *r* but farther back than an uvular trill, is also semantically employed. With twenty-eight consonants the Semites, including the Phoenicians, could ignore both vowels and homophones and introduce an alphabet which the later owners of both semantically significant vowels and homophones could use.

The most special people of all the special peoples of the Middle East are the Jews. They have been particularly important in history because they have served as the bridge between the world of the Middle East and the world of the West, from the time of the Roman Empire to that of the State of Israel. Except for the Persian Fire Worshipers, they are the only Middle Eastern people who have succeeded in keeping their ethnic identity, religion, and in a sense their language, intact for over three thousand years. They have been loved and hated, wooed, expelled, and in part assimilated, in country after country, millennium after millennium.

Probably no history of any people is better documented than that of the Jews, nor is there a single history in which the relation between changes in environment, technology, government, and religion can be so easily demonstrated. If we follow the narrative of the Old Testament they first appeared as nomadic herdsmen somewhere in the fertile crescent north and east of Palestine. As one of the tribal confederations descended from Abraham they fitted into the cultural pattern of semipastoral, tribal Semites, represented today by the Ruʿā'a. Spurred on no doubt by a series of dry years, they moved southward and westward looking for pasture. Their objective was the well-watered land of Canaan, but they missed it and ended up in Egypt, where some of them spent several generations as a tributary people. The Egyptians were probably accustomed to nomadic tribes being forced off the desert and seeking refuge.

Leaving Egypt in the belief that they were to be massacred, the Children of Israel again moved toward their goal, Canaan. Their leader, Moses, had a religious experience on the Mountain of Sinai. He persuaded his people to accept Yahweh, the mountain's particular god, as their God of Victory. Marching into Canaan under the divine protection of this god of a flaming mountain, they captured city after city and settled down as agriculturists. City life also implied technology and trade. Learning from the Canaanites they became craftsmen, jewelers, smiths, and traders. By the time of Solomon their clan and tribal organization had lost meaning; within a tribe some kin were poor, others rich. Judges ruled the cities in place of tribal shaikhs, and the prospects of international trade between the Indian Ocean and the Mediterranean spurred Solomon to promote national union. The center of government and of religion was established at Jerusalem, a recently captured city of the Jebusites which had no great symbolic meaning to any of the individual tribes, no matter how much it has acquired for so many people since.

Industrialization and trade produced social changes, some of which were uncomfortable. The rich grew richer and the poor grew poorer, and prophets arose to set things right in their own fashion. The prophets began as companies of shamans or dervishes or devotees; men who could put themselves into a state of trance by upsetting the work of the cerebellum and inner ear through gyrations, the repetition of formulas, and hyperventilation. This trick is as old as man. Once in their "state" the devotees could babble, and the crowd could extract meaning from the ravings according to taste. This was standard Semitic—and human—procedure. It is still done among the less sophisticated of the Semites in Arabia.

Like many other simple things it gave birth to something more complicated and more significant for the history of the world. From the groups of companions arose single prophets with their retinues. The prophets also claimed divine inspiration, but they furthermore were able to analyze the ills of the society they lived in and to prescribe the cure. Of forceful personality, they possessed secret sources of information and were a headache to the rulers of their day.

The principal achievement of the prophets was their realization and teaching that Yahweh was not merely the symbol of the success of the Children of Israel, not simply a private god in an Olympian

League of National Symbols. Yahweh was the symbol of all mankind, of justice and balance and equilibrium between social classes and professions and nations. Yahweh was on the side of anyone who sincerely worshiped him and followed his commandments, which in themselves insured peace and justice on earth. Yahweh so defined became a symbol which any human being of any race at any state of culture in any environment could sincerely and conscientiously worship, and in so worshiping could play his part in the evolution of man and the world in harmony with his fellow men and his surroundings. The Judaism of the prophets laid the groundwork for Christianity, for Islam, and for the civilization which we of the West try to defend against the godless and ungodly.

For a while and in places Judaism was evangelical. In North Africa, in Ethiopia, among the Khazars of the Crimea, Jewish missionaries accepted converts to what was otherwise a private faith. The great evangelism of Judaism, however, lay in the life and work of Jesus and in the efforts of His disciples. Historical forces in the Middle East and elsewhere propelled the Jews increasingly into the role of a special people. The Babylonian captivity of 587-537 B.C. took a few of the leading members of the southern kingdom of Judah to ʿIraq. Captured by the Assyrians, the tribes of Israel, the northern kingdom, disappeared, possibly through absorption into the surrounding population; no one knows what happened to them, and their disappearance has given rise to countless speculation ever since. Cyrus the Great, conqueror of Babylon, permitted the Jews to go home and rebuild their temple, but many stayed. Some penetrated the oases of Central Asia, either before or in the time of Alexander. Others went to Crimea with the Greeks. Jewish communities in North Africa and Ethiopia may, in some instances, date from before Roman times, even from before the Babylonian captivity, but this again is subject to argument. There were Jews in the Ḥijāz before Muḥammad and a large colony in the Yemen. In fact, at one time the kings of the Sabaeans, of whom more later, may have been Jewish.

The Roman expansion into western Europe brought along many Jews, among other Middle Easterners, to what now are France and Germany. Built to trade with the barbarians, the Roman cities on the west bank of the Rhine counted Jewish merchants among their personnel. The Arab conquest of North Africa found Jews *in situ* and brought re-enforcements. Similarly the Jewish population of

Spain and Portugal before 1492, when Ferdinand and Isabella ordered their expulsion along with the Muslims, was probably of complex origin. The German-speaking Jews from the Rhine moved historically eastward to join the Greek-speaking Jews from the Crimea in Galicia; the fusion of the two, with the predominance of the German speech produced the Yiddish-speaking Ashkenazim. Known as Sephardim, the Jews expelled from the Iberian Peninsula colonized North Africa (where Berber- and Arabic-speaking Jews had preceded them), the Netherlands, the British Isles, and various parts of the then Turkish Empire on the borders of the Mediterranean.

Until the formation of the State of Israel the world contained many kinds of Jews, with the Ashkenazim and Sephardim the most numerous and best known to the Western world. Descendants of Ashkenazim and Sephardim are citizens of nearly every Western country, and manifest every degree of absorption into the local populations, from complete to none. In the Orient local Jews (as distinguished from Jews newly arrived from the West) have retained their status as a special people, concentrating on finance, trade, education, and highly skilled handicrafts. In a few places, as in the Yemen and the Atlas Mountains, some have been farmers. In the West, while Jews tend to the professions, they have largely lost their special status, and had it not been for the events of World War II this change might have proceeded without interruption.

Hebrew, the language of the Israelites and hence of the Old Testament, was one of the so-called Western Semitic group, along with the Phoenician and Canaanite, to the latter of which it was quite close. For this relationship history furnishes a good reason: the Israelites conquered the Canaanites and absorbed them. Long reserved for scholarship and ritual, Hebrew has been revived as a living language. It is the official speech of the State of Israel, whose inhabitants, drawn from many speech areas, needed a lingua franca.

Another Semitic language, or rather group of languages, is that of southern Arabia. These were spoken in the ancient kingdoms of Maʿīn, Shabwa, Qataban, and Ḥaḍramaut, in the now desert country on the border between the Yemen, Saʿudi Arabia, and Aden Protectorate. The capitals of these four kingdoms were, respectively, Maʿīn, Ma'rib, Tamna, and Shabwa. Little is known about the peoples who lived there in pre-Islamic times. The country is virtually unexplored, the sites unexcavated, and the ancient literature, banned by the early Islamic purists, unavailable. From the Bible, the Qur'ān, and from al-Masʿudi's and al-Thaʿlabī's accounts, we know about Solomon's friend, Bilkis, the Queen of Sheba, who lived in Ma'rib. Book Eight of al-Hamdāni, on the Castles of al-Yemen, has been found and translated; Book Ten, which deals with the tribes, has also been recovered but awaits translation. Stone inscriptions[6] have yielded names of persons, gods, and places, and descriptions of a few events. Diodorus Siculus' secondhand account is at hand, along with Strabo's and the Periplus. And this is just about all.

These people practiced agriculture by virtue of irrigation. The irrigation depended on a series of dams, of which the largest and most famous was at Ma'rib. This dam broke twice, in 449 and 450 A.D., after which agriculture was no longer possible. Agriculture, however, served mainly to feed people whose main interests lay in transport and trade. The South Arabians carried goods from India and points east overland from their landing spots on the shore of the Indian Ocean, through the four kingdoms, up to Mekka, whence they went on to the Mediterranean. Solomon was interested in this trade at that end, and so were the Phoenicians. Among other objects carried were frankincense and myrrh, the product of the Qara Hills. These scented gums were needed for ritual, and ritual materials always bring a high price. They are still used throughout the Middle East, and beyond.

After the Arab conquest of the Yemen the local languages died out, but as is the habit of old forms of speech, they clung on in out-of-the-way places. Four dialects of this type[7] are spoken today among the cattle breeders of Qara and their neighbors, and on the island of Socotra, which itself is virtually unknown and a prime target for future anthropologists. The people who speak these languages are not good Muslims. They sacrifice to *jinn* and swear oaths over their ancestors' tombs. Relics of an earlier age, they des-

[6] Several thousand inscriptions have been copied. While many are simple tombstones or votive inscriptions, a considerable number are building inscriptions, including the one on the dam at Ma'rib, of 136 lines. Sir Hamilton Gibb. Personal communication.

[7] Bertram Thomas, "Four Strange Tongues from South Arabia, the Hadara Group," *Proceedings of the British Academy,* XXIII (London, 1937), 1–105. Thomas' work was of a preliminary nature. Dr. Charles Matthews of *Aramco* is making the definitive study.

perately need competent study before their old ways shall have been lost.

The greatest survival of South Arabian speech, however, is in Ethiopia and Eritrea. In the middle of the first millennium B.C. an invasion of the Ethiopian highlands by colonists from Ḥaḍramaut introduced Geez, a form of Ḥaḍramauti, which is still used as a ritual language and which has been supplanted by its linguistic descendants, Amharic, Tigré, and Tigrigna. The official language of Haile Selassie's empire, Amharic, thus perpetuates the speech of his alleged ancestress, the Queen of Sheba.

Arabic, meaning the language of the Qur'ān and its modern dialects, was historically the latest of the Semitic tongues to appear. By the seventh century A.D. it was apparently the speech of the people living between the Aramaic zone of Palestine, Syria, and ʿIraq, and the Sabaean zone of the Yemen and the Ḥaḍramaut. With Sabaean it is classed as South Semite. In the days before Muḥammad Arabic was undoubtedly spoken by fewer individuals than either of the other two. In several ways it merits attention.

In the first place, the Arabs who spoke Arabic were mostly sailors, caravan men, nomads, or city dwellers, making their living by transport, by trade, by crafts, and by catering to pilgrims. In all other linguistic provinces of the early Middle East, the backbone of the social system consisted of its villages with their farmers. The Arabs were specialists from the days before their expansion. Unlike farmers, nomads are accustomed to travel. So are merchants, particularly those engaged in seafaring and in the caravan trade. The Arabs were ready to move when their time came.

In the second place, Arabic was a special language. The Arabs spoke a number of related and mutually comprehensible dialects, but they also possessed a composite dialect reserved for poetry.[8] Different peoples in the world have selected different media for their most intimate and sacred artistic expression. The Germans go in for music, the French for a variety of arts including painting and cooking, while the Greeks are known to us for architecture, sculpture, and the drama. The Arabs had no special development of music, no painting, no *haute cuisine,* little architecture, no sculpture, and no drama. Their artistic equipment had to be portable. It was,

[8] C. Brockelmann, *History of the Islamic Peoples,* trans. by J. Carmichael and M. Perlmann (New York, 1947), p. 12. Philip Hitti, "Arabic Language," *op. cit.,* p. 123.

in fact, the vocal chords, sound box, and other speech organs of the poetic individual. Its product was speech, with and without song. The Yemenis say that even today one can find a whole tribe of fabulous Arabs in the Najrān, who speak to each other only in rhymed couplets. Hence to the Arabs language is much more than a means of communication. In its classical form it is the vehicle of the greater part of their aesthetic expression. How it fitted into the framework of the religion which the Arabs created and spread will be recounted later.

Today Arabic occupies a peculiar position. Learned men throughout Islamic countries can read and write the language of the Qur'ān, which crystallized this poetic form. Yet many of them cannot speak it. Once at a party in a provincial capital of Iran I was placed next to a professor of Arabic in the hopes that we might be able to converse together. His spoken Arabic, to my amazement, was even worse than mine; it was non-existent. He said to me in French: "I am a professor of Arabic; I read it, but I do not speak it." Of how many language professors in the Western world is this not true?

Beside the classical language exists another stereotyped literary form, the modern literary Arabic of the newspapers printed in Egypt, ʿIraq, Syria, and North Africa. Educated people in these countries can read it, but it is quite difficult for the Westerner who has learned to plow his way through the classical and to chatter in one or more kinds of colloquial. However, it is being successfully taught today in a number of American institutions at home and abroad.

The spoken language, which does not find its way into print or even into private correspondence, is divided into dozens of local dialects. Many of these are not mutually comprehensible. For example, when a Tangerine says *jero stitu* to mean "small dog," even a man from Fez, only some one hundred and thirty miles away, would not understand him. Algerian pilgrims have been known to greet fellow pilgrims at Jidda with *"Bonjour ʿalaiḳum"* with the imaginable results. North Africans say *muzien* for "good," while in ʿIraq *mu zen,* pronounced nearly the same way, means the opposite.

By drawing lines between areas in which the local forms of colloquial Arabic can be mutually understood, albeit with difficulty, and those in which the illiterate stranger draws a blank, one can divide the Arabic speech area into a number of over-all compartments.

These would correspond to Portuguese, Castilian, Catalan, and perhaps even Italian in the Romance world. The difference would be that while these four Romance languages are written as well as spoken, in the Arab world they are only spoken. If all learned conversations were held in the Latin of Horace and all newspapers printed in a modernized vulgate, the parallel would be better.

In North Africa a north-south line flanking the hills a few miles west of Tunis divides Moroccan-style speech from Egyptian-style. The Sinai peninsula bounds Egyptian Arabia on the east. Syria and Lebanon form another province; ʿIraq a fourth; and Arabia itself, including Jordan, a fifth. One is told that the Arabic of Jordan is particularly pleasing to the ear of those who like to hear the classical. Egyptians and Syrians consider their forms of Arabic sophisticated. The radio, gramophone, and movies are spreading these two styles widely, and television may soon add to the mechanical forces of homogenization.

That Arabic is not one language is shown by the need of interpreters between regional forms. In Ṣanʿāʾ I talked Moroccan to a Jew who translated what I said into Yemeni, and vice versa. In ʿIraq I have found that one of the best ways to relieve a long, dull winter's evening is for me to tell a story in Moroccan. One man usually understands more than the others and translates, while all howl with laughter. Despite this lack of mutual comprehension the language is basically one; the grammar is the same, and the vocabulary more or less a unit, except for the hundred or so most common words, which vary locally.

The early history of the Arabs, who spread this remarkable language, is exceedingly obscure.[9] Most of its details have yet to be revealed in the myriad archaeological sites of Saʿudi Arabia, still waiting to be excavated. Mound after mound, cromlechs, statues, inscribed stones, and caves invite the curiosity of the oil driller. That parts of this country, particularly along the shore of the Persian Gulf, once held a mighty civilization or series of civilizations is patent. Because of the lack of evidence one is entitled to a bit of speculation.

My theory is that the metal-age history of the Arabs before Islam can be broken down into three periods: before camel; with camel

[9] Georgio Levi della Vida, "Pre-Islamic Arabia," in N. A. Faris, *The Arab Heritage* (Princeton University Press, Princeton, 1944), pp. 25-57. See also Philip Hitti, *History of the Arabs,* Pt. I. (See also later editions, through the fourth.)

and with much trade along the western highlands; with camel and with little trade.

Period One, before Camel, may be represented by the rich sites along the Persian Gulf and on Baḥrain Island. Arabs derived food from oases, and great profit from the sea trade, feeding the civilizations of Mesopotamia seaborne goods from points east. Among others the ancestors of the Phoenicians may have figured prominently in this business.

Essentially it consisted of a combination of services by land and sea. Sealands navigators brought Indian Ocean cargoes to the mouths of the Tigris and Euphrates. There they were transferred again, and this time to riverboats, and poled or towed up these streams and their interlacing canals to near the head of navigation, where they were unloaded and carried to the bazaars of the ancient cities. Other goods came overland on pack animals from the Iranian plateau, following the Asadabad Pass-Bisitun-Khaniqin route (today an asphalted highway). More materials were brought from the Armenian hills by the Tigris Valley. A road around the curve of the Euphrates to Damascus led on across the Lebanese passes to the Mediterranean. Here again goods could be sent to sea and other items unloaded from ships which had coursed the western Mediterranean, the Black Sea, and even the Atlantic shores beyond the Pillars of Hercules.

During this period Arabs were able to have participated in the traffic at two sectors—sea trade in the Persian Gulf and possibly also the Indian Ocean, and pack animal transport along the banks of the Euphrates, from the region of Baghdad to that of Damascus.

Period Two, with Camel and Western Highland Trade, began probably no earlier than 1200 B.C., and possibly two centuries later. Our earliest contemporary historical notice of the camel is that in an inscription of Tiglath-Pilezer I, an Assyrian king, whose dates are 1115-1074 B.C.[10] The old Semitic word for camel[11] was *gammalu.* In writing this, however, they used the Sumerian cuneiform sign for sea, designating the new animal as *Beast of the Sealands.*

It would not be surprising were someone to discover that the

[10] Bruno Meissner, "In Assyrien wurde es (das Kamelle) von Tiglat-Pilezer I eingeführt und gezüchtet," *Babylonien und Assyrien* (Heidelberg, 1920), I, 220. For terminal date, see A. Poebel, "The Assyrian Kings' List," *Journal of the Near East Society,* II (1943), 87.

[11] Dougherty, *op. cit.,* p. 155.

Arabs, thus identified with this beast of burden by the Assyrians, had derived it from peoples farther east, as for example the Brahui or the ancestors or predecessors of the Baluchi. No evidence for this has yet appeared. In fact, "there is no evidence that the camel was ever known to the people of the Indus Valley,"[12] says Mackay, with reference to the Copper and Bronze Age civilization of Harrapa and Mohenjo Daro, which existed from around 3000 to 1400 B.C. This again caps the camel with a date beyond which we cannot proceed. When we move westward we find that the camel was introduced into Egypt by the Assyrians under their king, Esarhaddon, in 671 B.C.,[13] although the Persians, 150 years later, are generally given the credit. The Berbers of North Africa did not have the animal until the fourth century A.D.,[14] at which time it transformed the life of the local desert dwellers as it must have done a millennium and a half earlier in Arabia.

Wherever this unpleasant if indispensable animal came from, we may be sure that before his arrival the desert must have been a much quieter and less populous place than it is today. It must have harbored isolated communities of date growers and millet farmers in the infrequent oases, tribes of shepherds moving slowly along the fringes of cultivation, and bands of donkey people hurriedly crossing parts of it to hunt and to trade. The peoples of the date tree, the sheep, and the donkey are still there, but they serve largely to set a stage for the more exciting actions of the camel folk, with whose lives those of the others are in different ways entwined.

Trade, too, was fostered by the camel's arrival. The western route, which brought the spices of India and the incense of Ḥadramaut to the high-storied cities of the Yemen, passed through 'Asīr and the Ḥijāz. Mekka was one stop, Yathrib (later to be called al-Madīna or THE CITY) another. Higher up, the route forked, the west branch leading to the Mediterranean, the east to the Damascus-Ḥoms-Ḥama-Aleppo string of cities. During this period the influ-

[12] Ernest Mackay, *The Indus Civilization* (London, 1935), p. 44.

[13] A. J. Arkell, *The History of the Sudan up to 1821,* London, 1955, p. 128. Adolf Erman, *Life in Ancient Egypt* (London, 1894), p. 493. H. Ranke confirms this in his revision, *Aegypten und aegyptisches Leben in Altertum* (Tübingen, 1923), p. 586. I think we can ignore the efforts of E. A. W. Budge, *The Mummy* (Cambridge, 1925), p. 388, who supposes a knowledge of the camel in Egypt through some crude predynastic animal figurines found at Naqada.

[14] E. F. Gautier, *Sahara, the Great Desert,* trans. by Dorothy Ford Mayhew (New York, 1935), pp. 121–135, chap. 10. Gautier also says that the Persians brought the camel into Egypt in 525 B.C. (p. 124).

ence of south Arabia was dominant in the rest of the peninsula. The center had shifted from east to west.

Wherever water was permanent and abundant, as at Mekka and Yathrib, villages grew into cities whose inhabitants were competent to handle the caravans and the trade. The oases surrounding some of the cities may have been large enough to feed the local inhabitants and travelers. In some, at least part of the food had to be imported. Out on the desert ranged the Bedawin. They had kin in the cities and furnished the merchants with camels. Both camp and city were tribally organized. The intimate economic relationship between Bedawin and cityfolk must have already come into being, since without it there can be no Bedawin.

History is full of allusions to Arabs during the Graeco-Roman, or latter, part of this period. Tribe after tribe moved off the desert to the north, and became either oasis-centered traders or guardians of the marches for some sedentary power against their still unsubmitted kinsmen to the south, or both. During the third century B.C. the Nabateans occupied the land east of a line from the Dead Sea to the Gulf of ʿAqaba, now the Hashimite Kingdom of Jordan, and the cities of Petra, Bostra, Gerash, and Damascus. They took over the spice and incense trade from the Sabaeans, who had had trade representatives as far away as the Aegean isles, just as during the nineteenth century the import-export houses of Fez had agents in Manchester. Now the Nabateans become a special people, with representatives stationed as far west as Italy. As della Vida says:

> Nabatean civilization looks almost like the forerunner of what Islam achieved on a much larger scale, i.e., a merging of Arabian, Near Eastern, and Greek elements in a unitarian civilization. But the Nabateans not only lacked the tremendous religious enthusiasm of Islam; they also lacked the military impetus of the Arabian conquerors, and confronted the Roman Empire at the peak of its power.[15]

After the Nabateans came others, as for example the people of Palmyra,who have left behind them a neoclassical ruin as magnificent as Petra. They too spread all over the Roman world, as merchants and soldiers, a special people. When in the third century A.D. the Sassanian Empire arose in Persia, both Romans and Sassanians paid off Arabian chiefs to guard their borders, and Arab fought Arab

[15] Della Vida, *op. cit.*, p. 39.

in the pay of their masters. During the fourth century A.D. Ethiopians from Axum invaded southern Arabia, and even made an attempt to take Mekka, recorded in the Qur'ān. By this time the spice and incense trade had petered out; the dam burst at Ma'rib, and the Arabian Dark Age had begun.[16]

Della Vida's *Dark Age* is my *Period Three, with Camel and Little Trade.* It lasted from the third to seventh centuries A.D. What, we may ask, made it dark? Since Arabia has always been dependent on outside trade, events from without may be blamed. During this time the power of Rome declined, and the market for oriental goods shifted from Italy to Byzantium. The Byzantines had their own trade routes to the east, over the oases of Turkestan to the Caspian shore, through the Transcaucasian trough, and along the southern waters of the Black Sea.

With the dwindling of trade the cities grew weaker and probably less populous. Some of the erstwhile farmers of South Arabia turned to Bedawin life and moved north in search of pasture. Among these were the ancestors of the Beni Kalb and Ṭayyi' tribes of today. The oases with and without cities, needed by the nomads as trading centers and dry-weather havens for their camels, became so weak that the nomads forced them to pay tribute. Mekka was an exception. Thanks to its permanent spring, its holy and ancient pilgrim shrine, and the remnants of its caravan trade, the inhabitants of this city were able to maintain their independence. This is the background in which Muḥammad, whom more than three hundred million people today believe to have been God's Messenger, was born.

The work of his later years ushered in with almost incredible rapidity another period which in contrast might be called an *Age of Light.* The Arabs moved northward, to conquer 'Iraq, Iran, Egypt, North Africa, Spain, and eventually Sind. They spread their language where other forms of Semitic speech had formerly been spoken, but with non-Semitic speech populations they had less linguistic success. At any rate, this period initiated the situation which obtains today, in that millions of people speak Arabic in lands outside Arabia proper, and among these millions the economic situation is normal for the Middle East. In other words, most of the non-Arabian Arabic speakers are farmers, as they were before the Arabs came, however much or little Arab "blood" they may have absorbed.

[16] Here again I follow Della Vida. *Ibid.*, pp. 41 ff.

5 THE IRANIANS

WHILE FIRST PLACE IN THE MIDDLE EAST must go to the Semitic languages, second rank, in number of speakers, belongs to the Indo-European group. Semitic languages, however, are at home in this part of the world, while the Indo-European languages, spoken also by hundreds of millions of persons in Europe, the two Americas, India, Australia, New Zealand, and South Africa, originated outside it. While some of the world's greatest literature was first written in Semitic tongues, the majority of all written works in existence, including this volume, are in Indo-European languages. In the Middle East one Indo-European language, Persian, rivals Arabic as a literary medium.

Not counting outsiders such as missionaries, diplomats, archaeologists, and oil company executives, seven ethnically distinct groups of people speak their own distinctive Indo-European languages or groups of languages and dialects. These are the Persians (with the Kurds, Gilakis, and Baluchis), the Pathans, the Kafirs, the Armenians, the Greeks, the Gypsies, and the Sephardic Jews. Only the first four need mention beyond this paragraph. The Greeks today are largely confined to Egypt, where Hellenic colonies have existed continuously since classical times. The Gypsies, who move about through all the countries north of the peninsula and east of Suez as far as Turkey and beyond into Europe, speak various local forms of a composite language whose base is Indic. The Sephardic Jews speak Spanish.

No more in agreement than any other category of scholars, linguists have two ways of dividing Indo-European languages. The older way is to recognize a distinction between the western or *centum* and the eastern or *satem* branches, depending on whether they find a *k* or an *s* sound in certain key words. The satem branch concerns us here; it takes in Baltic, Slavic, Armenian, Iranian, and Indic (see Map 5). Iranian includes Persian, Kurdish, Gilaki, and Baluchi in one subgroup, and Pushtu in another. The only Indic that concerns us is the Dardic subdivision, spoken in Afghanistan by the Kafirs and some of their Muslim neighbors, called Parachis.[1]

[1] Georg Morgenstierne, *Indo-Iranian Frontier Languages,* Inst. für Sammenlignende Kulturforskning (Oslo, 1929), Serie B, Skrifter, XI, Vol. I.

The second and more modern linguistic approach is to classify the languages by their degree of structural resemblance to the supposed mother tongue, on the theory that instead of splitting they left the fold one by one. On this basis the most conservative of the Middle-Eastern Indo-European languages would be the extinct Hittite of Anatolia, placed in the centum group; the next most con-

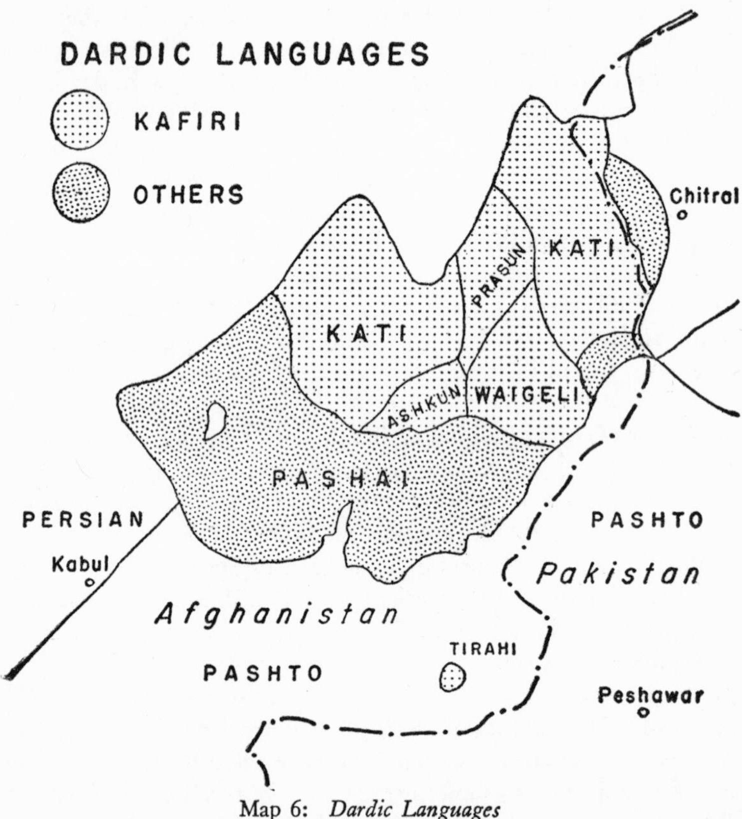

Map 6: *Dardic Languages*

servative would be Armenian, labeled satem. Greek, centum, would come third. Both Hittite and Armenian may mirror a time before the centum-satem split, if such a division ever occurred. Both further reflect the influence of local non-Indo-European languages related to those now spoken in the Caucasus.[2]

[2] I am indebted to Professor Henry Hoenigswald of the University of Pennsylvania for help in elucidating this problem, and particularly for the loan of his unpublished paper, on the position of Armenian.

A century ago linguists were less cautious than today. Under the leadership of Max Müller, they not only shaped the hypothetical mother tongue from which historic Indo-European languages have been derived, but also deduced the common cultural details and located the parent people who spoke this tongue, in space. They postulated an early metal age civilization, with the same agricultural species and domestic animals in use as in the Middle East. On the basis of geographic features, common names for trees, and the like, the philologists placed the seat of this culture in the Hindu Kush mountains, a region conveniently remote enough to prevent checking for many years to come.

Indo-European-speaking peoples of antiquity, from the Kelts to the Hindus, did have certain things in common, including an emphasis on the ox rather than the sheep; clothing with built-in legs and sleeves, rather than the sheetlike garments of the early Middle Eastern and Mediterranean peoples; a three-class social structure, which can be rendered alliteratively as consisting of earls, churls, and thralls, plus a priesthood; a high regard for the horse as a means of locomotion in war; a contempt for fish as human food; cremation with or without human sacrifice; and a family of gods symbolizing the segments of the universe and sources of disturbance to men, whether coming from outside, such as war, thunder, and stormy weather, or from inside, such as sickness and love. Only one god reflects a trade—the smith.

While much of this coincides with a Middle Eastern pattern, particularly if we try to reconstruct the heroic age before the rise of urban civilization, some of it does not. The ox, the trousers, and cremation carry us to a wetter and colder country.[3] We cannot go far wrong if we locate the earliest speakers of Indo-European languages, before they split or began to "peel off," somewhere on the plains between the Pripet Marshes and the Altai Mountains and south to the Caucasus, Elburz, and Hindu Kush. This civilization may or may not have been as old as that of the Middle East. As far as we know now, the two developed side by side, each borrowing from the other, while the Middle Eastern culture advanced more rapidly, passing into the urban stage with guilds of specialists and writing.

For some reason not as yet understood, the several Indo-European-

[3] Wetter because of the need for firewood, colder because the ground is frozen in winter, preventing burial.

speaking peoples have peeled off in a cultural and political sense, too. The Illyrians had their day of expansion. So did the Greeks, the Romans, the Kelts, the Germanic people, and now the Slavs are doing the crowding. What happened in the West also took place in the East, for we know that the ancestors of the Persians, the Afghans, and the Hindus moved down into eastern Iran and western Afghanistan during the middle and second half of the second millennium B.C. There the stream splits; the Iranians moved westward and the future Indians eastward. Indo-European speakers also invaded and settled Anatolia, probably from more than one direction. In the Middle Eastern area, the spread of the Persian Empire can serve as counterpart to that of Rome.

No Bronze Age survivors of this early Indo-European push remain to match the Guanches of the Canary Islands. As far as we know, in the whole world the Bronze Age is dead. However, if the reader will overlook a few iron tools and an arsenal of matchlocks, we can supply a brief account of an extremely conservative, culturally archaic, idolatrous Indo-European-speaking Middle Eastern people, the Kafirs of the Hindu Kush,[4] who were forcibly converted to Islam in 1896 by the Afghani Amīr ʿAbd ur-Raḥmān Khan, after the government of India had recognized his rights to that territory.

The country of the Kafirs consists of a number of high, precipitous valleys in the Hindu Kush, draining the waters of the snow fields into the Kabul River. Near the top are lush alpine meadows, flanked by dense forests of pine. Lower down the slopes olive, pomegranate, and other Mediterranean fruit trees grow wild. Walnut trees cast shade. So steep are the valleys that only foot trails approach them, and these are easily defended, which is why the Kafirs were able to hold out for so long. Although rain is lacking most of the year, perennial torrents furnish abundant irrigation water, thanks to which the Kafirs are able to till narrow terraces by plowing with small oxen. Their chief crop is hay, needed for winter fodder, and their chief business herding cattle, goats, and a few sheep. With livestock, hides, wool, and butter as capital, they trade over the Pakistan border for cotton goods, jewelry, and other manufactured products. They

[4] An expedition from the Danish National Museum has just returned from a three-year study of these people. My account, based on old documents and particularly on Robertson, soon may be not only outdated but proved wrong in detail.

also sell some produce in the neighborhood of Kabul. Peddlers from India, non-Muslims, were allowed in their territory.

The inhabitants of each valley live in a number of large and crowded villages. In order to spare agricultural land and to insure defense, they build their houses on rocks, and the ground plan of the village depends on the terrain. Some of these villages contain as many as five hundred houses, made of wood, usually three stories high and built when possible around a courtyard. The lower floor serves as winter stable, manure pile, and latrine; the second as storehouse, and the top as living quarters. An open hearth in the middle of the floor provides much smoke, some of which escapes through a hole in the roof; in comparison with a Muslim household a lack of cleanliness is apparent. Furthermore the room is equipped with wooden beds, tables, and stools, for the Kafirs both sit and sleep off the ground, like Europeans. Inside the house one sees many containers, some of carved wood, others of goatskin. Notable among these are skins of wine of several colors, and jars of intoxicating grape jelly. The Kafir family, when it sits at table, clothed in goatskins and black wool, starts its meal with a grace and washes down its bread and cheese, and now and then a dish of rare meat, with wine. What seems odd and even scandalous to Muslims gives the Christian observer from Europe or America a sense of nostalgia.

The traveler entering the outskirts of the village will notice a number of small wooden buildings, some distance from the community itself. These are what might be labeled female contamination houses. Women seclude themselves there during their menstrual periods and retire there to give birth to children. Among the Kafirs, as among many primitive peoples, female sexual phenomena are considered unclean. This may be interpreted as follows: both menses and childbirth create disturbances in the lives of the woman and her husband, and disturbances can best be allayed by a reduction of interaction and by seclusion. After a child has been born a period of high interaction, with joyful celebration involving kinfolk and neighbors, prepares the community for the presence of a new citizen.

Once the village itself has been reached the traveler may discover that his path winds between the booths of craftsmen; some are carving wood, others stitching boots, and still others are banging hammer on glowing iron. The music of stringed instruments may greet his ear from behind closed doors. He has entered the section of slaves. Supposedly the descendants of aborigines, plus captives from other tribes and from the lowlands, the slaves furnish the industrial power of the Kafirs; they do all the skilled labor. They provide their masters with clothing, tools, and household furnishings and utensils. Other slaves not so easily distinguished act as servants in the freemen's houses. All of them are quartered in this outlying ward and are forbidden to approach the holy places, which the traveler sees when he reaches the center of the village.

Here an open space awaits him. At first glance it looks like a tennis court or other gaming field. Actually it is an outdoor dance floor. Near it is a large wooden building with an altar in the middle; this is the winter dance hall. In this same nucleus of the village there are several small buildings, with open doors. One is a temple to the war god Gish, and his crudely carved wooden idol, with white stone eyes, can be seen inside. Another is a shrine to several gods at once; their images can be seen peering through windows. A number of other wooden images, driven into the ground like stakes, represent powerful ancestors. Really great men have been known to immortalize themselves in this fashion before death, but usually it takes a year afterward, and even then a period of purgatory while the idol weathers in a less holy area, before deification has been accomplished.

The basic unit of Kafir society is an extended family consisting of anywhere up to fifty or sixty persons, living in a house or group of houses and ruled by the oldest group of brothers. This family is an economic unit, particularly in the ownership and care of sheep, goats, and cattle. If it is a large family it is an important one, for in numbers lie strength. If it is small its members may hire themselves out to a larger one, particularly as herdsmen. Three kinds of work are considered men's work, and all are dangerous: fighting tribal enemies, guarding flocks, and going on trading expeditions. Of these three the second takes most of the men's time and effort. The pastures are up the steep slopes of the alpine valleys. During the summer most of the men will be there watching their property. Cultivation is women's work, probably because it comes at the same time as herding. The hay that the women grow will feed the animals during the winter while they are stabled.

The political system is a function of isolation. Restricted to foot travel, which can be blocked by cutting a few shaky wood and rope bridges, the valleys themselves in some cases form two or three self-contained units. Sometimes the upper reaches of two neighboring valleys are more nearly united than two parts of the same valley. A tribe, therefore, consists of the inhabitants of a number of villages in reasonable touch with each other. This fragmentation is reflected in the fact that the Kafirs speak four separate languages, Kati, Waigeli, Ashkun, and Prasun,[5] which more or less coincide with tribal units. Of these tribes the Prasun are considered aboriginal. They are said to differ physically from the others, with darker skins and broader faces, and to be poor fighters. The indigenous slaves among the other tribes are said to be of the Prasun type, but the Prasun themselves hold slaves. One suspects that there is more to be learned here.

The government of a tribe has two departments, for foreign and for domestic affairs. Since war is nearly constant and since it is also much more critical than internal adjustments, the foreign office is the more powerful. A rich man, or a man of strong personality who can raise sufficient contributions among his kin and followers, gives a series of big feasts, over a period of two years. These feasts involve much ceremony, like the potlatches of the northwest coast Indians or the social-climbing feasts of the Solomon Islanders.[6] At the end of this period he is given the official rank of *jast,* or elder, and joins the council of his peers. This council handles the foreign relations of the tribe. Usually two or three of them are more powerful than the others and wield control. At their head is the chief of the tribe, the *mir,* who obtains his position after a series of even more generous feasts. The freemen of the tribe, while content to leave most foreign affairs in the hands of the chief and his elders, come together in tribal meeting over matters of the greatest gravity, such as war or peace, and enter long debates on the floor. Oratory flourishes, and orators are esteemed. When they decide on war, they declare it honorably by sending their enemy a package of bullets or arrowheads, and await a reply.

The department of the interior is managed by a magistrate elected annually and by twelve assistants. These men handle quarrels

[5] Georg Morgenstierne, *Report on a Linguistic Mission to Afghanistan,* Inst. für Sammenlignende Kulturforskning (Oslo, 1926), Serie C-1-2, Vol. I.

[6] F. Boas, *The Social Organization and the Secret Societies of the Kwakiutl Indians,* Report of the Smithsonian Institute (Washington, D.C., 1895). Douglas Oliver, *Human Relations and Language in a Papuan-speaking Tribe of Southern Bougainville, Solomon Islands,* Peabody Museum Papers (Cambridge, Massachusetts, 1949), XXX, No. 2, 13-38.

over irrigation water and keep the ditches in repair; they see that crops are sown and harvested at the proper time. They also manage the weekly dances which provide the villagers with their principal outlet for community action and recreation. They impose fines on offending citizens, and if the offense is serious, they exile the culprit and burn down his house, with the help of the whole population. The chief magistrate also entertains guests of the tribe, at public expense.

A third set of officials cares for the emotional needs of the Kafirs. In each village one used to find three kinds of clergy: one or more hereditary sacrificing priests, the counterpart of the Brahmins of India, the Magi of the Medes and Persians, and the Godes of the Anglo-Saxons and Norsemen; a "well-born chanter of praise,"[7] apparently some kind of Druidlike bard; and a combination clown and oracle, whose dual function was to break the tension when emotions approached the threshold of control, and to go into a state of ecstasy in which he communed with spirits and transmitted their wishes to the people.

The chief god was Imra, the Creator, a distant deity. Moni, his go-between, interceded with him for suppliants. The most popular god was Gish, the personification of war, who symbolized the fragile independence of the Kafirs and their hatred of Muslims. Every village had at least one shrine to Gish, while the other gods often had to double up in single edifices. Imra received cows in sacrifices, Gish got bulls and billygoats, while other gods were satisfied with mutton, particularly the god of wealth, which is chiefly in sheep.

At the ceremonies the priest killed the animal after sprinkling it and gifts of inanimate foods with water.[8] Once the animal was killed, the priest collected the blood, mixed it with flour, wine, and butter, symbolizing the principal foodstuffs of the Kafirs, and smeared this concoction on the already encrusted shrine. The meat and bread and wine were now dedicated, and the feast began. One can imagine pious Muslims from the flatlands viewing this ceremony with the same horror with which Cortes beheld the sacrifices of Montezuma

[7] Sir G. S. Robertson, "Kafiristan," *Encyclopaedia Britannica* (13th ed.; 1926), XV, 630-634.

[8] The heathen Finns also sprinkled water on a victim to make it shiver as a sign of acceptance from the god. If it failed to react they would bring in a second animal.

on the altar of the Temple of the Sun in Mexico. The archery and the matchlocks of the Kafirs could not hold out against the conquering wrath of ʿAbd ur-Raḥmān, aided by imported ordnance, any more than the Aztecs with their obsidian-bladed swords could long resist the pikes and muskets of the mounted Spaniards. The Kafirs are still there, but their Bronze Age religion has become history.

The Iranian languages form two large divisions, Persian and Pushtu. The Persians, the most numerous of the Indo-European-speaking nationalities in the Middle East, possess an ancient culture of which they have reason to be proud. Their contributions to painting, architecture, poetry, the theory of government, and the art of civilized living are too well known to need description here. In Afghanistan, Persian has long been the language of the court, as of the bazaar; it was not long ago that in Baghdad it was the language of polite social conversation. In Kipling's India, British officers like H. St. John Philby[9] knit their brows learning Persian which, before English supplanted it, was the official language.

Although back in the Bronze Age the ancestors of the Persians and our own forebears in Europe may have shared a Kafirlike way of life, the Persians in Iran have been a civilized people for at least three millenniums. It was Cyrus, a Persian, who freed the Israelites from their captivity by another Semitic-speaking people, and it is a successor, Muḥammad Riza Pahlevi, who through drastic reforms and military preparation, is today trying to prevent the more ominous captivity of the whole free world.

Persian society is made up of two categories of people, villagers and citydwellers. In the parts of the Iranian plateau not occupied by peoples of Turkish speech, one sees a village wherever there is enough water bubbling forth naturally or led from the mountains in tunnels. These villages ring the deserts and flank the mountains. Humble and unassuming, their occupants are splendid farmers, and often skilled at simple crafts. Some live in Soviet territory, where they are called Tajiks; other Tajiks inhabit parts of Afghanistan. Down in Baluchistan the occupants of similar villages are called Dehwars or Dehkans.[10] Wherever they live or whatever others call

[9] *Arabian Days* (London, 1948), pp. 32 ff.

[10] Lieutenant Henry Pottinger, *Travels in Beloochistan and Sinde* (London, 1816), pp. 79-81.

them, these villagers are a single people, Persians. How numerous they are is not known, since in existing censuses they are not distinguished from other ethnic elements.

The rest of the Persians are townsmen or citydwellers. In the urban centers a rough distinction may be made between the working classes and the aristocrats. The working people are recruited from the villages and according to their specialty from various parts of the country. The aristocrat too has an intimate tie with the villages since he is usually a landlord, and it is the villagers who furnish his income. The wise landlord visits his property from time to time and builds up friendly relations with his tenants, caring for their simple needs. The foolish landlord leaves all this in the hands of a *ḳatḳhodā,* or resident agent, and is interested only in the amount of income. Villages have been known to change masters over a deal of cards, like banknotes or stock certificates. Wise and foolish alike, these landowners make up the educated classes, from which civil servants, army officers, clergy, professors, and some of the big merchants are drawn. It is they who constitute the majority in Parliament, where some of them, struggling to preserve their incomes, resist reform.

The early history of the Persians is known to us from four kinds of sources: archaeology, folklore, foreign literary accounts, and contemporary Persian documents. Thousands of mounds dot the Iranian landscape. The few that have been excavated show that in late Neolithic or early Metal Age times, villagers began tilling fields, grazing flocks, and building houses, and that this has been kept up ever since. The villagers originally must have come from some more fruitful place, for it is evident that the barren, wind-swept plateau, with its sparsity of water and intense winter cold, could have been settled only by farmers who had learned their agriculture elsewhere.[11] To the north, off the plateau, the winters are milder and the rainfall more abundant. At present the evidence points shakily to a northern origin for the early villagers of the Iranian plateau. What they spoke, no one knows. Today they speak Persian.

Philologists and historians have reconstructed an invasion of satem-speaking peoples from Turkestan into the Iranian plateau. The principal route may have led across the Oxus into Afghanistan; the date is set at about 2000 B.C., well after the establishment of our

[11] Wheat grows as well in Pennsylvania as in the Dakotas. We think of it as a grasslands crop because in the forestlands water-loving food plants are more profitable.

villages. The eastern wing of this invasion went to India, where it arrived about 1500-1400 B.C., introducing Sanskrit, reducing the ancient Indus Valley civilization, and setting up the caste system which has endured to this day. The western wing moved across the Iranian plateau, dodging the deserts, to settle the more fertile regions. Some must have gone to the Helmand country of Seistan and into Khorasan, others across the narrow band of tillage south of the Elburz to the plains of Azerbaijan, and the Lake Urmiya country.

> Advance groups penetrated the Zagros Mountains shortly after 2000 B.C., introducing Indo-European god names and numerals to the indigenous population. About a thousand years later the newcomers were re-enforced, perhaps from across the Caucasus, by other bands of Indo-Europeans, some of whom settled in a new land which they called Parsua.[12]

For a while the older speech won out, as English did over Norman French in England; as late as the seventh century B.C. some of the Zagros peoples may have still been speaking locally older languages. By the time of Xenophon (401 B.C.), however, after a putative Indo-European re-enforcement, the Carduchoi, or Kurds, apparently were speaking Indo-European as they are today. Yet the social structure of the Kurds, with the custom of marriage between the children of brothers, and their glottal singing, remind one of non-Indo-European practices. Mountains are refuge areas; mountain populations are usually complex in origin.

Herodotus divided the western plateau people into Medes and Persians. The Medes lived in the country from Tehran to Hamadan. They were organized into six tribes, each of which inhabited a number of villages. In 728 B.C. a wise judge, Deioces, was elected king.[13] He built Ecbatana, the modern Hamadan, within whose bounds aerial photography has revealed the outlines of the former Median capital, still unexcavated. One tribe of the Medes was that of the Magi, who specialized in ritual, like the Levites in Israel.

In 815 B.C. the Persians moved southeastward from Parsua (the Urmiya region) to the present province of Fars, which their descendants consider the home of Persian civilization. It includes today the city of Isfahan, long the capital of the Persian Empire and a

[12] These two sentences were written by Dr. George Cameron for this passage. See his *Persepolis Treasury Tablets,* Vol. LXV, 17 ff., especially p. 18, n. 116.

[13] Herodotus, *Historia,* Bk. I, ll. 95-101, trans. by George Rawlinson (London, Everyman's Library, 1910), pp. 51-54.

jewel of architecture, and the equally beautiful Shiraz. It was the Medes who first set up a kingdom, but the Persians under Cyrus II (the Great) took over from them in 559 B.C. and expanded it into an empire. Cyrus, Darius, and Xerxes were great conquerors and great builders. Unlike the Assyrians they left conquered peoples in peace, gave them a measure of self-government, and granted them religious freedom. They even restored the idols and sacred vessels taken from the conquered peoples by the Assyrians.

Darius and Xerxes built huge palaces and treasuries at Susa, on the lowlands of Elam, and at Persepolis, in Fars. The tablets found in the Persepolis treasury by a Chicago expedition[14] reveal much of interest about these building activities. The tablets were written between 492 and 460 B.C. when the Persian Empire was at its height. We know from the Behistun inscription that Old Persian was a written language at that time. All but one of the tablets, however, are in the Elamitic language. Darius and Xerxes imported Elamite scribes from the lowlands to do their accounting, just as today some of the scribes there are Assyrians and Armenians.

Many of the tablets are payroll bookkeeping. They show that at least twenty-four skilled trades were represented, including woodworkers, specialists in columned halls, inscription carvers, "up-carriers," relief carvers in wood, relief carvers in stone, goldworkers, gold-inlay workers specializing in reliefs, coppersmiths, sculptors, makers of iron doors, and specialists in services, such as beer tenders, wine makers, and *haoma* priests (of whom more presently); foremen, accountants, and food providers such as farmers and shepherds.

These specialists came from distant places. In Susa "Babylonians molded bricks; Assyrians brought cedar timber to Babylon whence Carians and Ionians conveyed it to Susa; Ionians and Sardians wrought the stone; Medes and Egyptians wrought the gold and adorned the walls; Sardians and Egyptians applied the inlays."[15] In Persepolis Egyptians served as woodworkers, while others of their country carved the inscriptions in stone. Carians did the gold work, while Syrians, Egyptians, and Ionians were the up-carriers. If their job had been simple hod carrying, there would have been no need to import specialists. Whatever up-carrying was it must have required skill. Could it have meant hoisting and rigging ridgepoles, beams, and rafters?

[14] Cameron, *The Persepolis Treasury Tablets,* Vol. LXV.

[15] *Ibid.,* p. 11.

The evidence of these treasury tablets shows that in the time of Darius, Iran already had acquired a complex division of labor on ethnic lines. The Persians themselves, concentrated in the territory of Fars, constituted or included an elite, a nobility. Fars was their home and hence free of taxation. There the noble Persians were trained from infancy in handling arms and in meting out justice to equals and inferiors, as Xenophon has shown so clearly in his *Cyropedaea*.

The Achaemenian Empire of Cyrus and Darius (650-329 B.C.) was the earliest true empire in the world, in that it constituted a government of many different peoples under a single ruler. While kingdoms had existed during the Bronze Age, in Egypt, Sumeria, Babylonia, China, and elsewhere the technological facilities for rapid transport and communication needed by an imperial government had not yet been invented. In China this came about three hundred years later with iron, the standardization of the gauge of cart tracks in the different provinces, and the development of inland waterways.[16] In Iran also, iron tools meant a speed-up of processing, while the introduction of the camel made long-distance hauling of heavy burdens practical, and the practice of riding astride, introduced from the northern plains, permitted the development of both cavalry and post-horse routes by which messages could be carried quickly by special riders to the head of the government from all corners of the empire. In Iran as in China the introduction of coined money greatly facilitated trade.

Aside from its historical importance, the political structure of the Achaemenian Empire deserves our attention because it served as the prototype of others. Not only did the Arabs copy some aspects of it in the generation following the death of the Prophet and in fact staff their caliphate with Persian clerks and officials, but it served as a much closer model for the Ottoman Empire, which controlled most of the Middle Eastern peoples from the thirteenth to the nineteenth and even twentieth centuries.

The Persian emperors held themselves so aloof from their subjects that it was possible for many of the latter to believe that the imperial head wore a light-giving halo.

> This king, an absolute autocrat, ruled from afar; the subject populations kept their special organization, their religion, even

[16] For this I am indebted to my colleague Dr. Schuyler van R. Cammann of the University of Pennsylvania.

> their chiefs; the Phoenicians continued to be governed by kings; the Egyptians had their nome chiefs; the Jews tranquilly carried out the establishment of their theocratic state; as long as these vassal provinces recognized the power of the king and paid taxes, the populations lived in peace and quiet. However all the subjects without exception, up to the highest dignitaries, including ministers and generals, were considered to be the slaves (*bandaka*) of the king . . . [17]

The Persian Empire, which stretched from Cyrenaica to India, and from Ethiopia to the oases of Russian Turkestan, was divided into satrapies or provinces. Including Parsis (Fars) which was the seat of government, these had reached the number of thirty-one by the death of Darius in 486 B.C. Each was controlled by three officers, a satrap or governor, a secretary whose duty was to watch over the satrap and report any irregularities to the court, and a general. In fortified towns there was a commander of the citadel under the general. These three officers were separately appointed by the crown and reported to it independently via the post-horse couriers. In addition, a corps of special inspectors, called the "Eyes and Ears of the King," traveled about the whole empire, protected by a special guard of troops. At their recommendation the emperor would remove a governor, or even have him killed, without trial.

The satrap's chief duties were keeping the peace and collecting taxes. With the help of the military he saw to it that the roads were kept free of highwaymen and that farmers could grow their crops and graze their animals without fear of raids. In some provinces the satraps also laid out, forested, stocked, and protected royal hunting preserves, called Paradises (whence our word). The crown assessed each province a fixed sum of money, plus certain special products in kind. For this purpose the satrapy was divided into tax areas, some of which coincided with nationalities. Asia Minor, in four sections, had an annual assessment of 1,760 silver talents, Egypt with Cyrenaica 700, and so on, to an annual total of more than 16,000 talents, equivalent to about twenty million dollars, gold. It is no wonder that the royal treasury needed a considerable clerical staff and an efficient guard.

India's share was not paid in silver, but in gold dust equivalent to 4,625 talents, plus a pack of hunting dogs for the palace. The

[17] Clement Huart, *La Perse antique,* Vol. XXV, *L'Evolution de l'humanité* (Paris, 1925), p. 88. My translation.

Egyptians had to provide 120,000 measures of wheat to the Persian army garrisoned there, Babylonia furnished 500 eunuchs, Media 100,000 sheep, 4,000 mules, and 3,000 horses of the special Nisean breed raised around Hamadan, Armenia gave 30,000 colts, and Arabia (the Yemen) 100 quintals of myrrh and frankincense. Every three years the Ethiopians yielded treasures in gold, ebony, and ivory, as well as five children, while every five years Colchis (Georgia) had to send 100 boys and 100 girls. The demand for eunuchs, Ethiopians, and handsome Caucasians anticipated the Ottoman practice as clearly as the concept that every man is the emperor's slave.

These taxes were fixed. The satrap could take what he liked and keep what was left over, providing that he did not create enough disturbance to cause his two rivals to inform on him or to draw a visit from the Eyes and Ears of the King. From time to time the latter sent other agents into the provinces to estimate the tax load anew; if he found that it was too great, including a reasonable surplus for the satrap, he would reduce the figure, and vice versa.

The king himself was supreme judge of his peoples, but he delegated most cases to judges whom he himself appointed. Persian justice was famed in the ancient world, and with reason. Cambyses once caught a judge taking bribes; he had him executed and flayed and his skin cut into strips. With these strips he covered the seat of justice on which the victim's son was then forced to sit. Artaxerxes I flayed a judge alive for the same cause, and with the same postmortem treatment. According to the law of the Medes and the Persians, no man could be put to death for a single crime, nor could any slave be brutalized by his master for a first offense. High treason drew beheading and the amputation of the right arm; rebels had their ears and noses removed, were publicly exhibited, then taken to the scene of revolt and executed.

To protect the emperor and to execute his orders, there was a royal guard composed of Persians and Medes, with perhaps some Susians from the hot lowlands. They were organized in three corps. Two thousand cavalry and two thousand infantry, all noblemen, carried lances with a gold or silver apple at the butt. Each man was also armed with a six-foot pike and a bow and arrows. The third corps consisted of ten thousand men called The Immortals, organized in ten battalions, of which the first carried lances with golden pomegranates at the butts.

These three corps formed the backbone of the army. Other troops garrisoned the forts in the provinces, and the local satraps and their generals raised militia to help put down small revolts. If these got out of hand the king himself would come in the midst of his guard. In wars of conquest he would take along the militia from all provinces, clad, armed, and sometimes mounted, all in the fashions of their own countries. While the guard would fight with unflinching discipline, this motley host, which by sheer weight conquered most of the less regimented countries, would break in the face of a well-organized and determined foe, such as the Macedonian phalanxes of Alexander, who brought about the fall of the First Persian Empire.

For five and a half centuries the Persians remained under what began as foreign rule. Although Alexander's empire soon collapsed, a horde of Scyth-like horsemen from the northern plains invaded Iran, adopted Persian customs, and moved on to the lowlands of ʿIraq, where they buried their dead in blue-glazed coffins resembling bathtubs (much to the dismay of archaeologists who wish to get through this "modern" deposit as quickly as possible for the sake of the older material beneath). These horsemen were the so-called Parthians, illiterate and rough. In 226 A.D. the Persian Empire was re-established and lasted until the arrival of the Muslim Arabs in 636 A.D. This four-hundred-year period, known as that of the Sassanian Empire, is of interest here because these, and not the Achaemenians, were the Persians whom the Muslims met and by whom they were influenced.

During Sassanian times the Persian population was divided into four classes: priests, warriors, clerks, and farmers. The first class also included the judiciary, for as with the Arabs justice was sacred. The warriors were the noblemen of supposedly pure Persian descent, comparable to the youths of Fars who had formed Cyrus' bodyguard. They possessed landed estates, rode horses, and were comparable to the landowning aristocracy of today. The scribes and clerks also included physicians and astrologers, while the lowest grade was shared by skilled craftsmen and merchants along with the peasants. In each village a *dehgan,* acting as chief and landowner's agent, was responsible for rent in kind, just like the katkhodā of today (see Chapter X). Seven privileged families held large estates, in return for which the chief of each supposedly exercised a special function. One set the crown on the king's head, another was a generalissimo, a third commander of cavalry, a fourth head steward, a fifth overseer of civil affairs, a sixth arbitration judge, and the seventh a combination tax collector and chief of treasury. Since the abilities needed for all these jobs obviously are not hereditary, these were honorary titles and except for the first, which needed little more than a steady hand, they were capable of delegation. Nonhereditary officers with real power were the prime minister, high priest (hereditary in a tribal sense only), guardian of the sacred fire (same situation), chief secretary, and commander of armed forces. The tribe of the Magi nominated the high priest from among their number, and the king had the choice of confirmation. Like the Grand Mufti whom we will encounter later, the high priest decided all questions of dogma and procedure in ritual matters.

Just as the state underwent a gradual transformation, religion evolved and changed in Iran. In Achaemenian times the Persians had three cults or faiths: for the king, for the people, and for the Median tribe of Magi, who were the hereditary priesthood. The king worshiped a creator-god Ahura-Mazda, who gave the sovereign his power and helped him conquer rebels and enemies. This god, although invisible, was symbolized by a flame burning on an open-air altar, with the sun shining overhead. Mithra, an ancient god who served as intermediary between the upper world of light and the lower world of darkness, came to be honored by the kings as the dispenser of royal glory.

The people worshiped the four elements: light, water, earth, and air. To these they sacrificed animals in ritually purified places, in the presence of one of the Magi, who chanted a sacred hymn. During the ceremony the sacrificer cut up the animal and boiled the meat, after which he could remove it for consumption. In my search for caves in eastern Iran I have come across two places where this kind of sacrifice, without benefit of Magi, is still done.

The Magi officiated at ceremonies for kings and commoners and had their own cult as well. One of its features was the habit of drinking a mixture of milk and the crushed juice of a plant called *haoma,* which was probably the milkweed *Asclepias acida,* which had a narcotic effect. While under the influence of this drug the priests could participate in the spiritual world. They prayed to this plant as the giver of health, longevity, strength, wealth, and physical and moral victory. The practice of this cult has been confirmed archaeologically through the discovery of the greenstone mortars and stone pestles with which the plant was crushed.[18]

[18] Cameron, *The Persepolis Treasury Tablets,* LXV, 5.

Out of the cult of the Magi grew the Zoroastrian religion. While Zoroaster himself may have lived in Achaemenian times, there is no contemporary evidence of his cult. By Sassanian times it had become the state religion of Iran, like Shīʿism today. It is noteworthy that its efflorescence followed the Parthian period, that the Parthians were plainsmen from the north where a dualism between the forces of light and darkness, good and evil, was earlier attributed to the Scythians and was the dominant element in the pre-Islamic religion of the Turks and Mongols.

In Zoroaster's teachings Ormuzd is the good principle, Ahriman the evil. Each has an army of spirits to do his will, and Ormuzd's army is commanded by Ahura-Mazda, here a general. Each force has six counselors, charged with the welfare or the reverse of the following departments: domestic animals, fire, metals, the earth, water, and vegetation. Ahura-Mazda is the creator of life, Ahriman that of death. Ahriman's home is in the lower shades, which is in the north, beyond the Elburz, and its entrance is in a mountain. He has at his command a stable of particularly unwholesome monsters who dwell in the forests of Mazandaran and the malarial swamps of Gilan.

The soul is immortal, and after death it wanders for a bit, finally coming to rest at the foot of a bridge. Here it faces three judges who weigh it in the scales. Its good deeds during life are placed on one pan, its bad deeds on the other. If the beam tips to the good side, the bridge widens before it and the soul crosses safely to a land of eternal light. If the reverse, the bridge shrinks and the soul falls off into the shadows. A few whose good and bad deeds exactly balance each other are consigned to a purgatory. The last of twelve cycles of earthly time will be completed three thousand years after the appearance of Zoroaster. In 2340 A.D., according to West's reckoning, a messiah will arrive and a flood of molten metal will cover the earth, purifying it.Then Ormuzd and Ahriman will fight their last battle, Ormuzd will win, and the last judgment will come.

Although some Muslims consider Zoroastrians to be People of the Book like Christians and Jews and hence inviolate if they pay a tax, others have persecuted them. Between seven and ten thousand remain in Iran, apart from the colonies in India (Parsis) and those in Baku. Most of them live in Yezd and Kerman, where they worship in fire temples today; the priests wear gauze mouth masks like surgeons' to prevent contamination of the holy flame. Some have moved to

Tehran, where they serve as gardeners. They have developed a system of disposing of the dead which fails to offend the elements. It is to place the body in one of the famous "Towers of Silence," of which there are but five in all Iran. Here vultures eat the flesh, and the bones are later lodged in ossuaries. The Parsis, coreligionaries who have been in India over a thousand years, are merchants and traders, some of whom own and manage large international firms and bear British titles of knighthood, and one of whom, a few years ago, taught mathematics at Harvard.

Three other languages are closely related to Persian: Kurdish, Gilaki, and Baluchi. Each is spoken by a particular people. The Kurds, who live in valleys of the Zagros Mountains north of Kermanshah, within the political boundaries of 'Iraq, Turkey, and Iran, have had sufficient time to develop a speech of their own, and even a number of dialects. The Gilakis are the forest people who live on the southwestern shore of the Caspian, with colonies in the provinces of Mazandaran and Gurgan. The traveler usually is surprised to see their wooden houses, built on piles and topped with steep, thatched roofs. The men themselves walk about with formidable billhooks over their shoulders, carve dugout canoes out of huge logs, and haul their goods on summer sleds with teams of oxen. In their native setting they look like an archaeologists's reconstruction of a western European scene during the Iron Age. Their speech has not been adequately studied, and their distinctive material culture may soon be lost, since this is the most industrialized part of Iran. The Baluchis, who live in parts of Pakistan, Afghanistan, and Iran, are camel nomads. (Their way of life will be described in Chapter XI.) Their language is a deviant form of Persian, in some ways similar to Kurdish.

Pushtu, or Pashto, forms the eastern division of the Iranian languages, spoken in Afghanistan east of a line from Kabul to Kandahar, and in the Northwestern Frontier Province of Pakistan, by some five million people whom Kipling made known to the English-speaking world. These are the Pathans, whom Captain C. C. Davies called "the most expert guerilla fighters in the world."[19] This may or may not be true, and certainly the Riffian *meḥallas* of 'Abd el-Krīm could have issued them a challenge. For several generations they gave the British army a testing ground for its officer material,

[19] C. Collin Davies, *The Problem of the Northwest Frontier, 1890-1908* (Cambridge, England, 1932), p. 179.

and now the Pakistanis are being favored with the same expensive privilege.

These warriors live in contiguous tribes from the high mountains of Kafiristan on the north to the Baluchi country in the south, occupying a ridge of barren hills. Here and there in narrow valleys one sees a thin line of green, indicating cultivation, and the roofs of village houses. The Pathans, like the Persians, are expert irrigators, with open ditches and qanats, but because of the deforestation and soil erosion of their country, the rain is torrential, the run-off rapid, and ninety per cent of the water lost to cultivation. In their miniature farms they grow two crops, harvesting in the spring and fall. The spring crop consists of wheat, barley, tobacco, melons, and legumes; in fall they gather in maize, sugar cane, cotton, and, in a few favored spots, rice. Where they have enough water they also grow the usual fruit and nut trees including apricots, walnuts, and almonds. Their chief livelihood comes from herding sheep and goats. The land is too poor for cattle, although they breed a few horses and more asses, needed for transport.

This country is palpably too poor to support its population. Several ways have been found to alleviate the situation. Some of the tribes drive their sheep to high pastures in the summer; this is particularly true of the Durranis, a favored group from whom the reigning house of Afghanistan is derived. Some of them descend through the Khyber Pass in November to pasture their flocks on the lowlands, while some of their men seek agricultural work among the settled population, and others trade. In April they come home, and that is the time of danger for the unprotected plainsmen, for the Pathans have left no hostages below. Raiding and brigandage bring in food and cash; caravan "protection" does the same. The British government used to pay subsidies in return for peace and quiet; meanwhile raiding and blood feuding reduce the male population and the number of mouths to be fed.

The Pathans follow a code which dictates hospitality to all guests, sanctuary and protection to all who flee vengeance, and the strict execution of the law of an eye for an eye and a tooth for a tooth. Each village has its *mulla* or religious leader, who trains boys to follow him. When a mulla learns to heal, by acquiring a little medical knowledge and the power of suggestion, he may attract a ring of disciples and thus gain power. As this power grows it ceases to be purely religious, but takes on a political aspect, and holy men like the famous Mirza 'Alī Khān, the Faqīr of Ipi, once a figure in the daily press, stir up whole tribes and lead warlike expeditions into the lowlands. In the old days many of the Pathans found a way out of the population problem by enlisting in the British Indian army. In these days they would make a splendid corps in the army of the United Nations.

The most nearly international people of the Middle East, aside from the Jews, are the Armenians. Christians longer than any other whole nation, according to their own careful histories, they, like the Poles, have been victims of geography.

Located north of the Mesopotamian cultural center, their country always has been in the conflict zone between the nuclei of great powers; Persia and Byzantium, Turkey and Russia. While this position has given them only alternate periods of political freedom, at the same time it has exposed them to many cultural influences of which they have been quick to take advantage. Like the Pathans, they breed more people than the land will support, but unlike the Pathans their outlet is the book and the saddler's knife rather than the dagger. For centuries skilled human beings have been their chief export. Today they can be found among the citizens of every civilized country. Dr. Varaztad Kazanjian of Boston is the father of plastic surgery; Heinz Guderian was one of Hitler's brightest generals, while Calouste Gulbenkian was said to be the world's richest man. In the Middle East their importance far outweighs their numbers, for they serve as merchants, financiers, teachers, doctors, dentists, skilled metalworkers, bankers, truck drivers, and, of course, rug dealers. Outside of Turkey and Soviet Armenia they are probably most numerous in Iran, where they have an entire city of their own, New Julfa, on the outskirts of Isfahan. In Egypt they have purchased land and buildings on which to establish an Armenian cultural center. Wherever they live in numbers, in Boston or Tehran, they continue to speak their own language and to publish their own newspapers. Loath to lose their nationality, their assimilation has been a headache to more than one oriental monarch, and the question of what will become of the Armenians is still far from settled.

6 THE PROPHET AND THE LAW

WE NOW HAVE BEFORE US, in all too little detail, a picture of the lands with which we are concerned and of the peoples who inhabited them up to the beginning of the seventh century of our era. Two centuries later the descendants of all these people already had learned to participate in an international civilization. In that period which lasted with a few interruptions, almost until the nineteenth century, a scholar like Ibn Baṭṭūṭa could travel unarmed from Tangier to Amoy and from the steppes of southern Russia to Zanzibar and to Timbuktu, resting his head night after night in publicly endowed hostels, in palaces, and in the monasteries of rival dervish orders competing for the honor of showing him hospitality.

It can be truthfully said that this was an economic unit, this vast Middle East and its neighboring regions. It was not economics, however, that held it together. Trade was essential, but trade is curiously sensitive to interruptions. What held it together was the mutual confidence of human beings. Throughout history only one force has been found which will furnish this kind of confidence among peoples far removed from each other, and that force is religion.

Before the time of Muḥammad the Middle East had possessed many religions. Some were local, confined to special places, like the worship of Enlil and Marduk in Nippur and Nineveh. Others were the property of special peoples, like that of Yahweh, the God of the Children of Israel, in the early history of that nation. Others were universal, like Zoroastrianism; the Buddhism which affected so much of Afghanistan; ethical later-Judaism; and Christianity.

Whatever the moral and ethical values of each of the other faiths and whatever the historical reason involved, none of them fully succeeded in uniting this vast area before the rise of Islam. This golden age was made possible by the common belief of the majority of the people (or at least of the ruling class in each country) in the divine inspiration of Muḥammad's message, and by the common practice of the ethical standards in human relations which had arisen in conjunction with the development of his religion. Christians and Jews, whose own religions set equal standards, were free to maintain their existence as special peoples within the confines of the Islamic realm, except in a few places such as the holy cities of the Ḥijāz.

Historians and theologians have spent much time and effort scouring musty documents to find earlier prototypes for many of Muḥammad's sayings and for the ritual and legal devices that he and his followers specified. Islam is a religion of the same general category as Judaism and Christianity, derived in part from a common Semitic cultural background and in part from those two older faiths by the process which anthropologists call "stimulus diffusion." Some of the Islamic ritual, such as the position of the hands clasped in prayer, may go back to the practices of the Sumerians. Like other religious systems, Islam had to grow up out of something; while interesting historically, the careful tracing of the origin of each trait has no bearing on the validity of a system of beliefs. Islam is valid because Muḥammad believed himself to be God's vehicle of communication to mankind and because enough people were so persuaded that they could bring themselves to behave autonomously as members of a world community, following a single code of ethics.

What is that code? What are the beliefs on which it is based and the rituals by which it is implemented? Before we can attempt to answer these questions it will be well to learn something of the setting in which the Prophet appeared, and the broader features of his life on earth. Out of a host of detail, we learn that Muḥammad ibn ʿAbdullah ibn ʿAbd ul-Muṭṭalib was born in Mekka in or about 570 A.D. It will be remembered that this was a period of economic depression and political uncertainty in Arabia and to varying degrees throughout the Middle East. It will also be remembered that the overland camel caravan trade which passed from the Indian Ocean to the Yemen through Ḥijāz to Syria and the Mediterranean had fallen off, that the South Arabian kingdoms were in a state of decline, and that in the Ḥijāz itself Bedawin shaikhs had reduced most of the commercial cities to a tributary state. Mekka itself was the principal exception, with its abundant and constant supply of water and its possession of the holy places, to which pilgrims brought a steady and life-saving revenue. The Mekkans were rich traders.

Remember further that few of the Arabs of Muḥammad's day were farmers. Many were pastoral nomads, but these were not the primary targets of Muḥammad's evangelical effort. Still more, probably, were businessmen: traders, shopkeepers, caravan men, and sailors. Although primarily concerned with the techniques of transport and travel, the caravan men and sailors also were traders on the side. It was these businessmen to whom Muḥammad chiefly addressed his message.

To these men, trading and travel were the breath of life. As traders and travelers over stony deserts and treacherous seas, they were accustomed to hardships; danger was a part of their routine. Ships and caravans, as we shall see presently, require top-level leadership and highly coordinated, intelligent obedience on the part of free and equal men who have selected their own leader. Such men are accustomed to subordinate their individual wills and personal interests to the orders of such a leader in situations where combined and coordinated action is necessary for the success of a mission, or even for survival. Such men, furthermore, have no patience with arbitrary commands or incompetence and can be trusted soon to replace bad leadership with good. Accustomed to interaction within the framework of small, personal, and forceful organizations, they have no feeling for elaborate hierarchies nor skill at creating them.

In discussing the Phoenicians it was stated that those ancient merchants and seamen had an unusually powerful need for ritual because of their long absences from home, the dangers inherent in their way of life, and the uncertainty of their business enterprises. The same is true of the Arabs of Muḥammad's time. They were accustomed to satisfy this need by the practices of their ancient cults, localized in the three principal idols[1] of the Kaʿba. By the beginning of the seventh century A.D., however, the conceptual crudity of the beliefs on which these cults were based must have impressed a number of the Arabs, what with the diffusion of sophisticated ideas from the Hellenistic centers of learning to the north and of more abstract theological notions from their peripheral contact with Judaism and Christianity, as well as from other sources. The situation was, roughly, that the Arabs were in a state of disequilibrium resulting from the world depression of their time, the political situation outside was ripe for a change, they felt a great need of ritual, and some of them may have been losing faith in their old symbols. The stage could not have been better set for a prophet. And a prophet was born.

Any child psychologist would, I think, agree that what happened to Muḥammad during his infancy and early childhood could not

[1] Lāt, ʿUzzā, and Manāt, all females. T. P. Hughes, *Dictionary of Islam* (London, 1885), p. 371.

have prepared him better for the role of prophecy if it had been so planned. His grandfather, ʿAbd ul-Muṭṭalib, was one of the most important men in Mekka. Not only did he belong to the prominent Hashimite family of the noble tribe of Quraish, but he was also the official custodian of the Kaʿba, that religious center at which the citizens of Mekka worshiped and from which they derived much of their income.

ʿAbd ul-Muṭṭalib's son ʿAbdullah, unfortunately, had no chance to rise to equal prominence. He died young, leaving his wife Āmina pregnant, to be delivered in due time of the future prophet. When the boy was born his grandfather made much of him and gave him the name by which he is still known, which means The Praised One. The baby was then given to a slave girl to be suckled, but after a few days he was taken from her and sent out to a Bedawin encampment to live in fosterage with a second nurse, Ḥalīma, a woman of good family among the Bani Saʿd. It was there that Muḥammad learned to talk, and the purity of his speech was afterward attributed to this circumstance.

After two years of this he suffered a traumatic experience, the details of which are not too clear. Two men supposedly approached the infant and threw him to the ground. One of his foster brothers then ran back to the tent screaming that the strangers had ripped open Muḥammad's belly. The child, however, was on his feet when rescued, and apparently unharmed. Whatever actually occurred, it was clear that the child needed a change. Ḥalīma took Muḥammad back to his mother.

When Muḥammad was six, Āmina went to al-Madina, carrying her son with her. On the way back she fell ill and died. The child was then put in the charge of his grandfather, who died when Muḥammad was eight. At this point he was given over to the care of his uncle Abu Ṭālib, who lived until after Muḥammad's marriage at the age of twenty-five.

During his adolescence Muḥammad served as a shepherd, which gave him much time for contemplation. When he was seventeen he went to Syria with his uncle and also had some combat experience in a local religious war. During the year which preceded his marriage he traveled to Damascus and Aleppo with a caravan as commercial representative for the wealthy widow whom he shortly wed—Khadīja, who was then forty, had been married twice before and had borne her former husbands two sons and a daughter. His life before twenty-six, therefore, had given him much insecurity, a succession of deaths at critical moments of those dearest to him, a shocking experience in infancy, much isolation, a lowering of financial and prestige status during adolescence, a tempering of body and spirit in camp and caravan and battle, a glimpse of the outer world, a familiarity with the local cult and the quarrels which arose over it, and the final attainment of security through marriage to a woman old enough and wise enough to fill the added role of mother.

From 570 to 595 A.D., his first twenty-five years of life, Muḥammad passed through what we may call the first cycle of his career, marked by insecurity, trial in adversity, and final success. Cycle two fell between ages twenty-five and forty, from 595 to 610 A.D. This was marked by a tranquil existence in Mekka as a respected member of the community. He achieved the surname al-Amīn, or The Just, from his capacity for judgment. (It was he who settled the quarrel between rival clans as to who should lift the Black Stone[2] into its new position in the rebuilding of the Kaʿba by placing it on a blanket and having the competitors each raise a corner.) During this period Khadīja bore him two sons who died in childhood[3] and four daughters: Fāṭima, Zainab, Umm Kulthūm, and Ruqaiya. In place of his sons he adopted two others: ʿAlī the son of his uncle and guardian Abu Ṭālib, when the boy was six and Muḥammad himself thirty-five, and Zaid, a Syrian Arab slave boy who belonged to Muḥammad and who refused to be ransomed by his kinsmen. Freedom and adoption were the rewards of this loyalty.

The reader unacquainted with Muḥammad's earlier life might imagine that the story would end here, that our subject would have spent his middle age and declining years in comfort and tranquillity. About the age of forty, however, he began to feel a growing dissatisfaction, and he entered a third cycle of twelve years during which the trials and ordeals of his early life were in a sense repeated. Feeling increasingly dissatisfied with the local religious situation he retired for periods of meditation in a cave, known as Ḥirā, outside the city. This was not an eccentric action, since the Quraish had long used the cave for that purpose.

[2] The holiest object in the Kaʿba; presumably a meteorite. It is set in a corner of the Kaʿba edifice.

[3] In 631 A.D. a slave girl, Mary the Copt, bore him a third son, Ibrahīm, who died at the age of two. None of the Prophet's other nine wives presented him with offspring.

At first Muḥammad's revelations took the form of dreams, until finally revelation came to him while fully conscious, in the form of the angel Gabriel. Muḥammad seems to have resisted his new role for some time and to have been particularly anxious not to fall into the category of *ḳāhins,* soothsayers said to owe their ecstasy to possession by jinn. It became increasingly clear to him, however, that God had selected him as the vehicle of revelation, and after several years of resistance he accepted this mission. His first converts were his wife Khadīja and his two adopted sons, ʿAlī and Zaid. The fourth was a loyal friend Abu Bakr, the fifth his first cousin ʿUthmān, also a grandson of ʿAbd ul-Muṭṭalib. The first two men of local importance to join him were Ḥamza and ʿUmar, both famous warriors.

Muḥammad moved his flock into a house directly facing the Kaʿba, which greatly incensed the other Quraish, to whose religious system this was an unwelcome affront. For a while they broke off relations with the Muslims, as Muḥammad's group of about fifty converts now called themselves. Khadīja died in 619 A.D., aged sixty-five, and Muḥammad, desolate, sought various means of distraction. One was a further marriage with a widow, Sauda, and a betrothal to ʿĀ'isha, the seven-year-old daughter of his friend Abu Bakr. Another was a search for a more fertile field of activity. He tried aṭ-Ṭā'if, where he went on a mission of conversion, without success. Then he decided upon Yathrib, the rich oasis to the north which later became al-Madīna (The City). Meanwhile ʿAlī had married Faṭima, and Ruqaiya (after one divorce) ʿUthmān. Ruqaiya died, and Umm Kulthūm (also after an unsuccessful earlier marriage) became ʿUthmān's next wife. Zainab married one Abu l-ʿĀs, whom she led into the fold.

After having gradually exfiltrated most of his followers, Muḥammad left Mekka quietly on June 20, 622 A.D., to join them in al-Madīna. This departure is known as *al-Hijra.* The word is commonly translated as "flight," a term justified perhaps in that it was done secretly. However, a better translation is "emigration,"[4] since it was a well-planned and orderly retreat. It marked the turning point between periods three and four in Muḥammad's career, between his second period of trial and his second time of success and victory, now calibrated on a much larger scale. So deeply did its significance impress Muḥammad and his followers that they made the year in which it occurred the first of their new calendar.

[4] Thanks to Dr. E. E. Calverley.

This calendar begins on April 19, 622 A.D., on the first day of the lunar month preceding the Hijra. The Muslim calendar, with dates in A.H. (*Anno Hegirae*), is lunar and eleven days short of a full solar year. The Arabs had possessed a system of intercalation to make the adjustment between the two systems before Muḥammad's time, but he chose to omit this rather complicated correction. We do not know exactly why but can only point out that in the Ḥijāz there is no regular rain anyhow, and hence no alternation of precipitation seasons. Summer and winter alike are hot. Caravan men habitually travel by night to avoid the heat of the day, and their favorite time for journeys is in the full of the moon. The moon is a friend, the sun a foe. In early South Arabian lore the moon was a man and the sun a lascivious woman who made periodic demands on him which sapped his glow. The lunar system was adequate for everyday business in its time and place.

Muḥammad and his followers made the lunar year the yardstick for the succession of Muslim festivals which thus fall at different times of year in other lands where seasonal change is profound. To have a given ritual period come first in summer, and then gradually work its way around to winter, provides a sharp distinction between these rites, which unite the Muslim community, and the local chthonic festivals which follow the cycle of vegetation, and the solar round. This facilitated the act of conversion later on. Farmers in Egypt, North Africa, Syria, 'Iraq, Iran, and elsewhere could keep up their ancient rites which tided them over the critical turns of the year without disturbance, and adopt the Muslim cycle in addition. The former set provided for local satisfaction, and the latter linked them with the Muslim community as a whole.

Once Muḥammad had settled in al-Madīna his personality again seemed to change. His powers of leadership and his appetite for human relations grew. He led his armies personally into battle against the forces sent by the Quraish from Mekka and against hostile tribes of both Jewish and pagan persuasions. Converts flocked to the great mosque which he built during the year 1 of his new calendar. He married wife after wife until his total of eleven was reached. None of these women bore him offspring which survived infancy, and none seemed to fill the place of Khadīja.

During the year 8 (630 A.D.) he made the pilgrimage to Mekka under a truce, with two thousand followers. There he converted two men who were to become great: Khālid and 'Amr. (The latter a few years afterward carried out the conquest of Egypt and the first Muslim invasion of North Africa.) Marching northward to what is now Hashimite Jordan, Muḥammad suffered a defeat by a combined army of Arabs and Romans and lost both Zaid and a brother of ʿAlī. A month later ʿAmr led another force in that territory and compelled the tribes of the Syrian frontier to submit. Still in 630 A.D. Muḥammad marched on Mekka, took it without a battle and destroyed the three hundred and sixty idols in the Kaʿba, including a wooden pigeon which he personally dismembered. But he left the Black Stone intact. ʿUmar took for him the oath of all the people of Mekka who had assembled for that purpose.

In eight years the Prophet had received control of al-Madīna and won that of Mekka and the tribal lands north to Syria. In the ninth year delegations from the various tribes of the rest of Arabia visited him to submit to his rule and to acknowledge his prophetic status. This was a period of consolidation, during which Muḥammad built up the machinery of government, sent out his lieutenants to conquer more territory, and appointed tax collectors to gather the quarter tithe from all who had submitted. Still in the ninth year he caused ʿAlī to announce in Mekka that no more idolators would be permitted to make the pilgrimage, which from then on was reserved for Muslims. He further ruled that idolators must either be slain or converted and made to pay the regular alms tax (*zaḳā,* of which see later), while the People of the Book, meaning Christians and Jews and perhaps also Magians, were to be spared, allowed to continue their own worship, and made to pay a special tax designed for subject people. In the tenth year he made a final pilgrimage, to set an example of procedure for all time, and in the eleventh year, on June 8, 632, he died. According to the Sunnis his dying head rested on ʿĀ'isha's bosom, while the Shīʿa say on that of ʿAlī.

Muḥammad died at sixty-two, old for a prophet. He died a successful man, which is again out of pattern. One of the secrets of his success was that he was a man's man—a herdsman, a trader, and a warrior. He knew how to exercise the exact kind of leadership that the Arabs of his day understood. Another secret was that his doctrine was clear and easily understood. Although the Qur'ān bristles with obscure illusions that mean little or nothing to the modern reader, they referred specifically to contemporaneous events of which everyone concerned was well aware. A third secret is that he did not ask his followers to change their way of life too drastically; he asked them to change from a tribal or blood allegiance to a religious allegiance. He understood the cultural pattern to which they were conditioned, and he required those changes which would bring about unity, and no more. A fourth is that he came from an upper social level from the start; a fifth that his prophetic mission began when he was in his late forties, at an age to command respect in an age-graded society.

If ever a religion were built to fit a cultural situation, Islam was it. Its principal differences from Christianity (and here I expose myself to criticism from both sides) are: that it was suited to a particular environment and culture, while Christianity is applicable to all time and space, and that by so limiting itself Islam became correspondingly more practical in the immediate situation, and surer of success within its smaller field. Conceptually a less ambitious and more certain venture, it produced its golden age earlier than that of Christianity, which, though older, required a wider canvas, greater resources, and a more elaborate technology for its fruition.

During the last ten years of Muḥammad's lifetime the Arabian peninsula became a Muslim island. During the next eleven his successors conquered Egypt, Syria, ʿIraq, and Iran. In less than a quarter of a century, therefore, all of the Middle Eastern lands covered in this book, except North Africa, had become Muslim territory, and North Africa was to follow fifty years later, along with most of Spain and Portugal. The critical quarter century between 622 and 643 witnessed the spread of Islam from a community of traders and camelmen to a wider and more varied as well as much more numerous community of farmers, townsmen, and urban sophisticates. This rapid expansion taxed the ingenuity of Muḥammad's successors in providing the proper machinery of government for so many different kinds of people. This period, then, is just as important from the standpoint of the crystallization of Islamic ritual and procedure as the lifetime of Muḥammad is for their conception.

Backed by hoary tradition, it is standard practice among Arabs to choose the successor to a deceased leader from among his sons, or at least from among the male kin of the noble family to which he belonged. Any attempt to designate an heir before the death of his predecessor meets with disapproval, and the tribe, council of shaikhs, or whatever body is concerned reserves the right of election. Hence a scramble usually ensues, and after a little disorder the most competent man usually comes out on top.

When Muḥammad died Abu Bakr, the father of his favorite wife ʿĀ'isha, was in the pulpit of the great mosque at al-Madīna. Muḥammad had designated him as his substitute several days before, to act as *imām* during his illness. Muḥammad had no surviving sons, although his grandsons al-Ḥasan and al-Ḥusain, the offspring of ʿAlī and Fāṭima, were then seven and six years old,[5] too young to be considered. It was clear that the new imām, as the leader of Islam was called, must be from the tribe of Quraish. Abu Bakr qualified in this respect, and he was in fact acting as imām at the moment of the Prophet's death, by Muḥammad's own order. So the company of the faithful elected Abu Bakr head of the religious state which his son-in-law had created.

Imām properly means "prayer leader." In a wider sense it was also given to the head of state. A second title still used for the same office is *Amīr ul-Mu'minīn* or "Commander of the Faithful." Rightly or wrongly, the Imām of the Yemen so calls himself today. A third title is *Khalīfa,* with its European rendition, Caliph. This is the term most commonly understood by non-Muslims. It means literally "he who is left behind" and hence "successor."

Abu Bakr, who was an old man when he took office, died after two years. He is remembered chiefly for having collected the Qur'ān into one official volume. ʿUmar, a man of energetic, outgoing personality, followed him, and it was under his leadership that the Muslims conquered Egypt, Syria, and Persia which at that time included Afghanistan. ʿUmar rode into Jerusalem on a camel, and probably built there the mosque bearing his name. He was murdered in 644, after ten years in office, and was succeeded by ʿUthmān, Muḥammad's fifth convert and first cousin, who also had been the husband of two of the Prophet's daughters. ʿUthmān reigned for twelve years; in 655 A.D. when he died, Islam was now thirty-five years old. The first three caliphs had been members of the Prophet's own age group at Mekka. It was now time for a change.

Following the general principle of keeping the office within the Quraish and as close to the prophet's own kin as possible, the Muslim community was faced with one logical candidate. He was the Prophet's *ibn ul-ʿamm* (son of the paternal uncle), a relationship which the Arabs hold nearly as close as that of brother. He was also Muḥammad's adopted son, the husband of his favorite daughter, and the father of his two grandsons, al-Ḥasan and al-Ḥusain. Short

[5] Or eight and seven.

of a son, it would be hard to find anyone closer to the Prophet than ʿAlī. He had shown himself a brave man on several occasions, but he was not noted for his decision. Now that the older generation was gone, he and many others considered it his turn.

Owing to the northward shift of the center of population in the new Muslim world, and particularly in view of the difficulties of travel, al-Madīna made an awkward capital. Two other cities were much more conveniently situated, al-Kūfa in ʿIraq and Damascus in Syria, separated by the long arm of the Nafud Desert. ʿAlī, duly elected, set himself up in al-Kūfa. A rival, Muʿāwiya, who had become governor of Damascus, revolted. He was the son of one of the Prophet's early opponents, who later became an ally and thus a member of the Companions.[6] On January 24, 661, A.D., a Khārijite seeking, among other things, to avenge the death of some kinsmen of a lady friend,[7] slashed ʿAlī's forehead with a poisoned sword, penetrating the brain and thus bringing to an end the first or "rightly directed" caliphate. Members of the same sect also succeeded in wounding Muʿāwiya, during the same year.

Al-Ḥasan succeeded his father briefly, but Muʿāwiya forced him to abdicate. He lived on for eight more years in al-Medina, during which time he married and divorced some eighty wives. Al-Ḥusain tried to start a rebellion at al-Kūfa nearly twenty years later (in 680 A.D.), after the death of Muʿāwiya, and was stopped and fought to death by the army of al-Kūfa itself. The drama of al-Ḥusain's demise, suitably heightened, has furnished a plot for thousands of passion plays acted out ever since. Muʿāwiya founded the Umayyad dynasty at Damascus, which ruled until 749 A.D. and seated fourteen caliphs, chiefly by direct hereditary succession. In 750 the seat of power again shifted to ʿIraq, with the formation of the ʿAbbasid dynasty at al-Kūfa, and the building of Baghdad. Hārūn ar-Rashīd, the hero of the Thousand and One Nights, was the fifth of this line, reigning from 786 to 809 A.D. The ʿAbbasid caliphs numbered thirty-seven and

[6] *Aṣḥāb.* There is no agreement as to the exact meaning of this term. Everyone who embraced Islam, saw the Prophet, and accompanied him on some expedition, certainly belonged. There is said to have been 144,000 Companions at his death, arranged in thirteen classes, with Khadīja, ʿAlī, Abu Bakr, etc., at the top, and those who, as children, had seen him, at the bottom. Hughes, *op. cit.*, p. 24.

[7] This detail is from Hitti, *History of the Arabs,* p. 182. The rest of this passage is a close paraphrase of a personal communication from Gibb.

ended only with the capture of Baghdad by Hulagu, a grandson of Jenghiz Khan, in 1258.

The ʿAbbasid caliphs had been in the direct, orthodox Sunni line. With the destruction of Baghdad the uncle of the last Khalīfa retired to Egypt where he maintained the office as a spiritual power. Some forty years later, in 1299 A.D., the Turkish sultan Othman I, founded the Ottoman dynasty which bore his name. Salim I, the eleventh sultan in this line, made Istanbul the official seat of Muslim spiritual power after his conquest of Egypt in 1517, and his descendants gradually came to be regarded as caliphs, with himself reckoned as first. (Needless to say, others contested this.) At any rate they lasted until the overthrow of the thirty-seventh sultan and twenty-seventh caliph of their line, ʿAbd ul-Ḥamid, in 1909.

Even before the rise of the Turks, rival caliphates had arisen, fostered by the great distances within the various parts of the Muslim world. The Fāṭimids, who were not Sunnis at all but derived from the Ismāʿīli Shīʿa (see later), ruled parts of North Africa and all of Egypt from 910 to 1171 A.D., numbering fourteen caliphs. In Spain the caliphate of Cordova, which later moved to Granada and which was an offshoot of the Umayyad line of Damascus, lasted from 755 A.D. to 1032. The later dynasties of Spain, which did not claim the caliphate, lasted until 1492, the year Ferdinand and Isabella expelled the last of the Muslims from the Iberian Peninsula.

It was a far cry from the company of faithful, assembled in the great Mosque of al-Madīna, electing Abu Bakr to the office of imām by acclamation, to the shaded patios of Granada, and the pomp of the Sublime Porte. The rules by which these later caliphs made their decisions were set down within the first two centuries of the Muslim calendar, in a manner which we shall attempt to explain, along with the skeleton of the religious organization which they created.

The basis for Muslim dogma, ritual procedure, and religious law rests in the words and action of the Prophet. His successors found two sources: the Qur'ān and the *Ḥadīth*. The Qur'ān is the sum total of the statements which Muḥammad made while in a state of inspiration. These statements are considered to be not his words, but those of God. His followers wrote them down on scraps of parchment, sheep's shoulder blades, and other informal materials, in an alphabet which was then less perfect than it later became, because of the lack of diacritical points to distinguish the consonants. This caused little trouble, however, since his devotees memorized his statements as soon as they were uttered.

When the *sūras* (chapters or verses) of the Qur'ān were assembled, the question of their proper order arose. This was arbitrarily solved. One verse, the *Fātiḥa* or "opening" obviously should come first. The rest were arranged in order of length, from longest to shortest, except at the very end where the extremely short and very euphonic verses, revealed in Mekka early in the Prophet's career, were arranged in a more logical sequence. The Qur'ān contains one hundred and fourteen chapters in all. The one which is listed as Number 112 may, as some but not all Muslims believe, have been the first revealed. It reads:

> Say, the fact is, Allah is one, Allah the Eternal. He did not beget and he was not begotten and there was no one meet (or sufficient) for him.[8]

The great virtue of the Qur'ān is its beauty of language. Its proper recitation is moving, whether or not one understands the Arabic. It is obviously not suited for translation, and Muslims recite it in the original tongue, no matter how little of it they understand. The sequence of sounds has a ritual meaning wholly apart from their literal semantic significance. Many Muslims have committed it to memory. It can be read through, aloud, in a single night, and often is in critical moments, such as the watch over the dead. The Qur'ān thus furnished Islam with two tools: a set of rules to be culled from its context and an all-purpose litany.

The second source is the Ḥadīth, or Tradition (literally, a saying). No sooner had the Prophet died than the learned scribes of Islam began a scramble to collect and write down all of his noninspirational sayings, no matter how brief and fragmentary, and an account of all his actions. This went on for several generations after the death of the last person who, as a small child, had caught a glimpse of the Prophet and thus ranked as a Companion, thirteenth grade. The favorite scene of this reportorial activity was al-Madīna, where most of the Companions and their descendants remained, happy to be debriefed. The compilers worked out a critical code to test the reliability of each item. Three grades were given the per-

[8] Translation supplied by Dr. E. E. Calverley.

sons handing down each tradition; pious and reliable, medium, and weak or untrustworthy. Some traditions were complete, that is, the chain of narrators was continuous, while others which showed gaps in the chain were incomplete. Traditions which had been handed down by many different chains are considered beyond dispute; only five such are admitted. A tradition with three chains is also considered reliable, and so on down the line to traditions which are known to have been fabricated.

A typical ḥadīth goes as follows:

> Abu Kuraib said to us that Ibrahīm ibn Yūsuf ibn Abi Isḥāq said to us from his father from Abu Isḥāq from Tulātā ibn Musārif, that he said, I have heard, from ʿAbd ur-Raḥmān ibn Ausaja, that he said, I have heard from Barā ibn ʿĀzib that he said, I have heard that the Prophet said, Whoever shall give in charity a milch cow, or silver, or a leathern bottle of water, it shall be equal to the freeing of a slave.[9]

Two names are prominent in the field of ḥadīth-collecting, those of al-Bukhāri and Muslim. As a result of their efforts and those of others, the body of Muslim *Sunna,* or custom, their code of traditional behavior, was established. Each tribe in Arabia had had its own sunna, or unwritten law. Muḥammad's followers, through the Qur'ān and the Ḥadīth, set up a new sunna, which resembled English common law in that it was based on case histories and precedent. The validity of each article in the sunna was established by Muḥammad's statement favoring it, his statement forbidding it, or his example in reference to it. Even when speaking on his own and not as God's vehicle, Muḥammad is believed to have possessed *ḥikma,* or wisdom, which in itself serves as a basis for authority.

Brought up in the Arab tradition of small, personal organizations, Muḥammad distrusted hierarchies and wanted none in his religion. In fact, he conceived of the office of imām as that of a lay prayer leader and preacher elected by his fellows for the occasion, since all faithful were equally religious, equally close to the deity. Specialists in religion, however, were bound to arise. By the second century of Islam a body of learned doctors called *ʿulamā* had come into existence in each urban center, and it was to them that questions of dogma were referred. They were, in effect, a supreme court to advise

[9] Hughes, *op. cit.,* p. 640.

the administrators of the law. It was they who therefore compiled the Muslim legal system, called *sharīʿa,* out of the Qur'ān and Ḥadīth through the sunna.

Sharīʿa means "highway." There was more than one school of learned doctors, and hence more than one highway was built. The difference between sunna and sharīʿa, then, is that the sunna is a single body of recorded customs common to all Sunnis, or orthodox Muslims, and the sharīʿa is one of several alternative codes of law based on the sunna.

The ʿulamā were localized naturally in the several capitals such as Baghdad, Damascus, and Cairo, and while scholars often moved from one center of learning to another, these places were far enough apart and the local needs of the conquered and converted populations different enough, to warrant the growth of different systems. Out of many schools which arose during the second and third centuries of Islam, only four produced legal codes which are still in effect, the *Ḥanafi, Māliḳi, Shāfiʿi,* and *Ḥanbali.* These four codes are official in different countries. The Ḥanafi in Lower Egypt, India, and most of the orthodox area of western Asia outside of Arabia; the Māliki in North Africa, the Muslim portions of the western Sudan, and Upper Egypt; the Shāfiʿi in the Ḥaḍramaut and Indonesia; and the Ḥanbali in Saʿudi Arabia. Except for the Ḥanbalis, each admits the equality of the others, and all of the other three are allowed to co-exist in a single community.

The ʿulamā of each school arrived at their decisions by a careful perusal of the Qur'ān and Ḥadīth, and by the use of the principle of *qiyās* (analogy) in the case of some new substance or situation with which Muḥammad was not acquainted, such as tobacco, coffee, and distilled liquors. One of the points of disagreement between schools, for example, is the legality of the use of the closable water tap, which is called *ḥanafīya* in Arabic because the Ḥanafis permit it.

The Ḥanafi school was founded by Abu Ḥanīfa, in Baghdad, to provide a code for the ʿAbbasid caliphs. His is the oldest and most liberal. He was born in al-Kūfa in 700 A.D. and died in 767. The ʿulamā of al-Madīna disapproved of his liberality and under Abu ʿAbdullah Mālik ibn Anas (716-795 A.D.), a native of al-Madīna and judge in Mekka, set up their own, or Malikite, system, depending rigidly on the Ḥadīth and claiming superiority through the claim that Abu ʿAbdullah knew the last surviving Companion, Sahl ibn Sa'd, who must then have been over one hundred years old.

Mālik taught ash-Shāfi'i (772-826 A.D.), who was born in Palestine of Quraish parentage and who worked out his own system from a combination of the Ḥanafi and Māliki codes, with a freer use of qiyās (analogy) than either. His contemporary, Aḥmad ibn Ḥanbal (780-855), who was born and died in Baghdad, was by far the most strict and severe of all. Popular in 'Iraq and Syria with certain elements up to the time of the Turkish conquest, his school petered out, to be revived in central Arabia during the eighteenth century as the code of the reforming and puritanical Wahhābis, whose present leader is now in control of much of the peninsula. It is they who will not permit other rites in their territories and who enforce the rules against silk, gold, perfume, tobacco, and the like. It is they who wear Arab costumes in New York while other Muslims move about unnoticed in Western clothing.

At this point one may legitimately ask how it happens that several codes of law may coexist in a single community. The answer is that this has always been the case throughout the Middle East. Jews, for example, were judged by their own chief rabbi in Ṣan'ā, and only when a question arose between a Jew and a Muslim did the the case come before the Imām's court. Until recently, in Morocco, Americans were tried by their own consuls, in accordance with our old treaties of extra-territoriality which have only just been abandoned. The three systems of sharī'a which are considered interchangeable differ from each other chiefly in the details of performing ritual and not in any provisions likely to cause difficulty in a mixed community. Only the Ḥanbali is so different that its coexistence might cause trouble, but even here the others have expressed their willingness to admit equality.

Before Muḥammad's time the administration of justice in Arabia was handled on a simple and informal level. Tribal shaikhs rendered judgments on matters involving disputes between their constituents, while religious leaders, established in various shrines, did the same for purely ritual affairs. Two litigants might choose a third party, either a man of probity in whom they both had confidence or a stranger passing by chance or, as in the case of Muḥammad at the time when he decided on the procedure for replacement of the Black Stone, the first person to enter the courtyard or room. Such a judge was called a *qāḍī*.

Under the mushoom ritual state of Islam, all sorts of litigation arose with the commotion of expansion, and permanent specialists in justice were needed to administer the sharīʿa. These were the qāḍīs, who were appointed regionally by the sultans, ḳhalīfas, governors, etc. to sit in judgment in terms of the various codes locally in fashion. ʿUmar created a supreme court, called the *Diwān al-Maẓālim,* to sit in the entourage of the caliph. Another kind of court, also called maẓālim, was held in certain places to redress minor secular wrongs, and some of these had qāḍīs.

All of this was fairly disorganized and individualistic, in accordance with Arab tradition. The Turks, however, lovers of order and organizers of hierarchies, introduced further complexities. They created the office of *mufti.* A mufti is a professional jurist who makes a collection of *fatwas,* or decisions, just as a professor in a law school compiles a book of case histories. These fatwas are useful as an addition to the less inclusive specific items in the sharīʿa of the four rites, which alone are often inadequate as a basis for decision. Parallel to the administrative hierarchy of sultan, pashas, beys, and so on down, the Turks set up a legal hierarchy topped by the Shaikh ul-Islam, otherwise known as the Grand Mufti of Istanbul. Under him were the qāḍīs, and under them in rank the ordinary muftis, who might be called into court for consultation for a fee. In each portion of the Islamic world which the Turks ruled as a special province, a deputy grand mufti was established, and with the dissolution of Turkish power these became autonomous. The Shaikh ul-Islam or Grand Mufti system has persisted in Egypt, and until the rise of Israel the same was true in Palestine, with the well-known Ḥajj Amīn al-Ḥusaini.

Among the Arabs as among the ancient Children of Israel and other Semitic-speaking peoples, no clear distinction was made between religious and civil law. What was offensive to the community was offensive to God, their symbol of the mutual relationships of its members. Only what we call torts, or offenses to the individual rather than to the community, fell into a secular category, and these usually were nothing more than quarrels over physical property, such as when A's cow ate B's millet or when a man broke a twig from another's tree. In the tightly intimate familial communities in which Semitic-speaking peoples lived, few offenses which affected an individual failed to disturb the group as a whole.

Among the peoples whom the Arabs conquered, converted, or both, disputes over such matters had arisen long before Islam, and ways of settling them had been perfected. These people tended to draw the line between interpersonal disturbances which they were already equipped to resolve and disturbances involving the new religion which they had adopted, and hence outside their previous experience. This was particularly true of peoples who did not speak Semitic languages in the first place and who failed to take over Arabic except as a ritual medium. Each preserved its old code, written or oral: the *'Ādat* of the Turks, the *Qanūn* or *Izref* of the Berbers, and the *'Urf* of the Persians. Each accordingly followed a dual system of legal administration, the old and the new, the civil and the religious.

During the last century the contact with the West and the rise of new problems have led to further legal developments. In most cases the capitulations came first; the foreigner, if a citizen of a sufficiently powerful nation, was tried in a mixed court or in the consulate of his own country. With the rise of nationalism and Westernization and the introduction of parliaments and frock coats, most of the nations with which we are concerned adopted civil codes, based on one or another of the standard European models. Only the kingdoms of the peninsula have yet to do this. The Prophet's law is still enough in the land for which it was designed.

7 THE FIVE PILLARS OF ISLAM

So MUCH for the codification and administration of the sharīʿa, as established by Muḥammad and his followers during the first two centuries of Islam. What of its content? Briefly, it is a list of things that people might consider doing, with a judgment as to the ritual legality of each action. While in our legal system the emphasis is on what one may *not* do, the sharīʿa divides human activities into five categories: (1) those which are obligatory on all believers, (2) those desirable and recommended but not obligatory, (3) optional actions to which the tenets of the faith are indifferent, (4) objectionable actions which are to be discouraged but are not forbidden, and (5) those forbidden.

In legal as contrasted with purely ritual practice, the emphasis is on two extremes, the *ḥalāl,* clean or permitted, and the *ḥarām,* unclean or forbidden.[1] Such decisions, made on the basis of the Prophet's word and example, cover nearly every category of human behavior which a person could undertake, in the cultural situation in which the Prophet lived. At the top of the list of actions of the first category, in the *must* class, are the famous Five Pillars of Islam: *shahāda, salā, zakā, ṣaum,* and *ḥajj,* meaning Profession of Faith, Prayer, Almsgiving, Fasting, and Pilgrimage.

The first of these, the Profession of Faith, literally *bearing witness* or *testifying,* is simply the repetition of the formula, *"La ilaha-illa-llah, wa Muḥammad rasūlu-llah."* "There is no god at all but Allah, and Muḥammad is the messenger of Allah."[2] It forms part of every prayer. Merely to repeat the first part of it, in a critical situation, makes one a believer. Before the Spaniards took the beach of Ajdir in the Rif in 1924, Christian prisoners held on the rock of Alhucemas offshore, an old and famous Spanish penal island, would escape now and then, and swim ashore. The refugee would find

[1] The injunctions and taboos against all things which the Prophet Muḥammad labeled as ḥarām or unclean, such as pork and wine, will be discussed in some detail in Chap. 18.

[2] I originally rendered *Allah* as *The God,* but Dr. Calverley states: "Allah is a proper name, perhaps originally The God, but not to Muḥammad and the Muslims."

Riffians awaiting him on the beach, their rifles cocked. Staggering to his feet in the surf, the Christian, already instructed by his fellows who had learned this from Riffian traders allowed on the island, would raise the forefinger of his right hand and recite: *La ilah illa-llah,* and be allowed ashore unmolested. Often he would be given a complete set of clothing, a house, a wife, and a job. (I have measured some of these *renegados,* who were in a cold sweat for fear my calipers would reveal their origin to the Spanish authorities.)

The second pillar, Prayer, varies considerably among the schools. Within all, however, it is required five times a day, at dawn, noon, midafternoon, sunset, and dusk. Every word must be in Arabic, and it must be done in a state of ritual purity. This means washing the hands up to the elbows, the feet, and the ankles. Sand may be used instead of water if necessary. Purity is destroyed by sleep or by contact with impure substances such as corpses, urine, excrement, seminal fluid, wine, pork, and dogs. One must wash the parts affected thoroughly after acts of elimination or copulation, which is why Muslims use spouted jars that look like watering pots, instead of toilet paper. Even if one has washed carefully after each contamination, it is best to be sure and purify oneself in any case before prayer.

In cities and smaller settlements which possess mosques, the faithful is reminded of the hours of prayer by the call of the muezzin.[3] In small mosques it is the imām himself who vocalizes, but in large city congregations a special man is appointed. If the mosque has a minaret or tower, he climbs it so that his voice will carry over a wider distance. If not, he stands beside the door. The words of his call vary with the sect. In the Ḥanafi manner, he cries: *Allah Akbār* (God is most great) four times; *Ashhadu anna la ilaha illa-llah* (I testify that there is no God at all but Allah) twice; *Ashhadu anna Muḥammad rasūlu-llah* (I testify that Muḥammad is the Messenger of God) twice; *Ḥayya 'ala 'ṣ-Ṣalā* (Come to Prayer) twice; and *Ḥayya 'ala 'l-Falāḥ* (Come to Prosperity) twice.

Some of you may have heard this call, early in the morning, wafted softly over the cool, still air from dozens of mosques. Surely you will agree that there are few experiences more pleasant or stimulating, when one has just awakened after weeks of travel. Less agree-

[3] This familiar word is the Turkish-Persian form for the Arabac *mu'adhdhin,* the man who calls the *adhān.*

able is the mechanized muezzin whose canned call is blasted out of loud-speakers wired to the railing of the minaret gallery. In some of the more frequented capitals of Muslim nations, this dubious tribute to the mechanical age has unfortunately been installed.

The worshiper has a choice of praying privately, in the open air or in a house, or praying in a group, with an imām, either out of doors or in a mosque. The mosque contains facilities for purification, a niche indicating the direction of Mekka, which all must face, and a pulpit from which the imām delivers his Friday sermon. The prayer consists of a number of cycles of acts; two at dawn, three at sunset, and four each at noon, midafternoon, and sunset. Each cycle consists of standing, bowing, prostrating, and sitting. Its details again vary with the sect, and indeed between the three equivalent sects these are their principal points of difference.

Let us study, for example, a two-prostration prayer. The worshiper stands with his hands to his sides, saying: "I propose to offer God a worship of two cycles, with a sincere heart, facing the *qibla*." He then places his thumbs to his earlobes and opens his hands to either side of his face, saying: "God is most great." Third, he places his right hand over his left and holds both below navel height (in the position familiar in Sumerian statuary). He recites a long prayer, including the *Fātiḥa*[4] and at least two other short sūras or one long one. Fourth: knees straight, he bows at the waist, hands on knees, head down, and says: "God is most Great." Fifth: while holding the same position he says: "I extol the holiness of my Lord, the Great," twice. Sixth: body erect, hands to sides, head slightly bowed, the imām says: "God hears him who praises him," to which the company responds gently, "O Lord, thou art praised." If the worshiper is alone he says both. Seventh: the worshiper drops to his knees, his arms stretched forward from the elbow, and says: "God is great!" Eighth: now he places first his nose and then his forehead on the ground. (If there is a little dust, so much the better, so that when he is through people can see he has been praying.) Thrice he repeats: "I extol the holiness of my Lord, the most high." Ninth: he sits up on his heels, hands on thighs, and says, "God is Great!" Tenth:

[4] "In the name of God the Compassionate, the Merciful, Praise be unto God, the Lord of Creatures, the Compassionate, the Merciful; Possessor of the Day of Judgment; Behold, thee do we worship, and to thee do we cry for help; Lead us on the right path; the path of those to whom there is given grace, not (the path) of those against whom there is anger, nor those who have gone astray." Hughes, *Dictionary of Islam,* pp. 465-469.

Seven Attitudes of Prayer

falling again on his face, as in number eight, he first says "God is Great!" and then recites three times, as before, "I extol the holiness of the Lord, the most high."

If this is the end of the first cycle, he rises and says, "God is Great!" in a standing position. If it is the end of the second, or the end of the whole prayer, he does this sitting, and at the end of each two cycles three extra sitting or kneeling positions and recitations are added. At the end of the entire prayer comes the supplication, in which the worshiper, while kneeling, holds his hands together in front of him, palms inward, and fingers up, as he recites special prayers selected for the occasion. Although this is contrary to the rules, the supplication sometimes is rendered in a language other than Arabic, and thus constitutes the most personal part of the ritual.

This is the Ḥanafi manner. The others differ in details, but the total amount of energy expended and the number of words recited are more or less the same. Praying in company is one of the best-known methods of building up satisfactory relationships between the members of a group, in Islam as in other religions. The prayer partly described above also furnishes splendid exercise, particularly beneficial to middle-aged shopkeepers who walk but short distances each day and tend to overeat. Going to the mosque together provides one of their principal opportunities for interaction with their fellows.

The modern traveler who has visited Islamic lands, with the exception of Saʿudi Arabia, may say: "Why, I have never seen anyone pray!" He must remember that most praying is done in private, that few Muslims other than Wahhābis and professional religious men of other sects find time to perform all five prayers each day, and that even those who omit their daily prayers often go to the noonday service in the mosque on Fridays. This is for men only, and forty or more must attend; the imām lectures from the pulpit and in his discourse must mention the name of the head of the state. After this he descends and prays with the others.

The traveler may now remark: "I have been in Muslim cities on Fridays, and business was going on as usual." This is partly true. Muḥammad did not designate Friday as a day of rest. It is a day part of which is devoted to a special religious service, as partly described above. Before and after the service merchants are free to open their shops, as many do. However, no special markets are held on that day, and government offices are usually closed. Only where the Muslims have taken over the idea of the week end from the British and Americans does one find a close-down from Thursday afternoon to Saturday morning. Archaeologists, accustomed to the routine of working only six days a week, welcome a seventh day to catch up on their sorting and paper work. Hence most of them who excavate in the Middle East lay off their men on Fridays. This never fails to puzzle new workmen, who inevitably ask: "Aren't we going to be paid for Friday? We are ready to work then, like any other day." Something that the workmen appreciate more is giving them time off on Thursday afternoon, so that they can go to the steam bath (*ḥammām*) and purify themselves for the services which, in many communities, take place that evening.

Pillar number three, zakā or Almsgiving, is another kind of purification. The theory is that by giving away part of one's property one purifies the rest. It is the age-old first-fruits concept and the principle of maintaining group equilibrium by sharing. As old as man, this principle is one of the traits of human behavior that distinguishes him from his primate relatives. The zakā is a tax on negotiable property possessed more than a year and free from debt. Payment is not required on personal possessions in daily use nor on the tools of one's trade. Thus dwelling houses, clothing, personal armor and weapons, house slaves, cattle which provide food, the scholar's books, and the craftman's tools are all exempt.

Nine classes of property are taxable: camels which are out grazing, but only when the owner possesses five or more; oxen, including water buffaloes, also grazing, when numbering thirty or more; sheep and goats of the same category, numbering forty or more; horses not used for transportation or war or farming, but herded together, stallions and mares, as a capital reserve, and also horses and mules kept for sale; a minimum of two hundred *dirhams* of silver; a minimum of twenty *mithqāls* of gold; merchandise, which shall be found on appraisal to be worth a minimum of 200 dirhams; mines and buried treasure (when discovered) which are not located on one's immediate residential property (precious stones are exempt); agricultural produce—everything grown, except articles made of inedible substances, wood, cane or bamboo, and grass.

This is an income tax designed to take from the rich and spare the poor, as can be seen by the fact that the donkey, the poor man's beast of burden and by far the most numerous species, is tax-exempt. The distinction between working property and negotiable capital is similar to our own. The inclusion of buried treasure as a source equal to mines means simply that mines are scarce in the Middle East, while buried treasure is common. Metal age civilization was nearly four thousand years old there when Muḥammad was born, and archaeological sites were innumerable, as recent aerial photographs of Arabia have shown. Tomb robbing is nearly as old as tombs.

The reckoning of the tax was just as complicated then as it is now. Each of the nine categories had its own scale. The tax on 5 to 9 camels was 1 goat or sheep; on 10 to 14, 2 goats; on 20 to 24, 3 goats; on 25 to 35, 1 female yearling camel; on 36 to 45, a two-year-old female camel; on 46 to 60, a three-year-old female camel; on 61 to 75, a four-year-old female camel; on 75 to 90, 2 female two-year-olds; on 91 to 120, 2 female three-year-olds; and beyond 120 the same general progression may be continued.[5] For horses, the rate is one *dīnār* a head or 5 per cent of the total value. For gold, silver, and merchandise it is 2½ per cent. This rate is to be paid on the total, not on the amount in excess of the free allowance. The rate for mines and buried treasure is 20 per cent, which seems liberal since in most modern states buried treasure is 100 per cent state property. On crops, 10 per cent, the regular tithe, is exacted, except for those grown on land irrigated by buckets or other machinery, by the labor of men or of animals.

At this point we may well pause to congratulate Muḥammad on his mathematical ability, which reflects his long years of business experience. Add to this the fact that he was illiterate and had to carry all these figures in his head, and it is even more marvelous. (I remember an occasion some quarter century ago when I was proposing to change some American money into *pesetas* through a double exchange via the medium of *francs.* The money was to be given to two illiterate Riffian traders whom I was meeting in a friend's house in Fez. I laboriously worked out the transaction on paper, but before I was half through they told me the answer. I checked it, to their visible scorn, and found that they were correct. They had done it in their heads.)

The amounts of property, in cash and kind, so accurately specified,

[5] Space and the putative patience of the reader prevent inclusion of all the details concerning the tax on cattle, sheep, and goats. Those interested should consult Hughes, *op. cit.,* pp. 699-700. It is surprising to me that sheep and goats were considered of equal value, which is not the case today in most Muslim countries.

were considered not as taxes but as voluntary contributions. Hence the capitalist was frèe to distribute it himself as alms. If he did not choose to do this, or if he had distributed only a part of it, he could come to the collector, appointed by the religious head of the community, and make a declaration on oath, which the officials were obliged to accept. A third alternative was to await the collector's visit.

Two points must here be made. Muḥammad, who was no man's dupe, expected a high level of honesty among his followers. For several reasons he was justified. This zakā was a religious obligation and few believers make light with articles of faith. The amount earned and owed was sworn to under oath, and to Arabs an oath is an extremely serious matter. Furthermore the community in the Middle East is a compact organization in which everyone knows everyone else's business.

The second point is that the almsgiver could hand out his charity in person. This gave him the satisfaction of seeing where it went and of gaining personal credit for having given it, as well as the thanks of the recipients. I recall a long line of ragged persons, old, maimed, blind, and diseased, standing along a certain white wall in Marrakesh early one Friday morning, many years ago. A gate opened. Out stepped a tall, corpulent man, covered with many layers of gossamer white robes. By his side stood a tame gazelle on a leash. A slave held a bowl full of coins, which the master handed out one at a time to each supplicant. One by one they bowed to kiss his hand, murmuring *"Baraḳa Laufig,"* the local corruption of *baraḳat Ullahi fiḳ* (May the blessing of God be upon you). The wealthy man was paying part of his zakā. You may call this exhibitionism, but I do not. How many rich men in our society take the time and trouble to see the recipients of their charities (duly noted in the daily press) face to face?

To whom were these alms to be distributed? On this point as on all others, Muḥammad was quite specific. He named seven categories of persons, as follows: *fuqarā* (plural of *faqīr* or *faḳīr*), persons who owned property, but less than the amount required for payment of the zakā, in any category; *masāḳīn* (plural of *misḳīn,* whence the derived words in French and Spanish), persons without property; the collectors and distributors of the zakā, who had to be paid for their work; new converts; insolvent debtors; and wayfaring strangers. He also specified two purposes for which the zakā could be spent: the redemption of captives and the advancement of Allah's religion.[6]

The direct care of the poor and the option of giving alms personally instead of through the collector of the zakā of course fostered begging, which was no innovation. In the world of Islam the beggar assumes a religious quality. Many are members of religious orders, and there is no doubt the feeling, whether or not expressed, that a person who will humble him or herself to the point of begging deserves some compensation. Add to this the lack of facilities for the crippled and blind, and the opportunity of doing some visible good to one's fellow man, and the practice is easily explained.

In 1949 I was traveling by bus from Tehran to Hamadan. At a certain ford the driver stopped. A blind woman, nursing a baby, arose from a brush shelter beside the road and approached the bus. The driver passed the hat, everyone put in a coin or a bill, and he handed the collection to the poor woman, who replied with an invocation to God to bless her benefactors. The blessing was returned by the occupants of the bus, and the driver drove on. (If, in visiting an oriental city, you find yourself pestered with beggars and remark, "There ought to be an institution to take care of these people," remember that there is an institution, and an old one, the zakā. Give, in moderation as the Muslims do, and take it off your income tax.)

The zakā is not the only tax imposed in Muslim states. There is a special tax on Christians and Jews, which was abusively levied on Berber converts to Islam in the early days of the conquest of North Africa. There are also customs, gate taxes, market taxes, and other sources of revenue most of which appeared after Muḥammad's death. But the zakā differs from those in that it was not originally designed to support the state,[7] being rather a means of leveling out the income of the various elements in the community so that no one would go hungry, of financing the conversion of the heathen and of facilitating travel between the various parts of the Islamic world.

The fourth pillar is ṣaum or Fasting, which means keeping Ramaḍān. Ramaḍān is a month, the one during which it is written that God

[6] *Qur'ān* 9:60.

[7] In Sa'udi Arabia the king's agents collect the zakā during the summer when the nomads are immobilized. In return for this he offers them protection. He does not take the tax from visiting tribes from other states unless they summer there. Colonel H. R. P. Dickson, *The Arab of the Desert* (London, 1949), p. 440.

sent the Qur'ān to the lowest heaven where Gabriel received it and whence he revealed it, bit by bit, to Muḥammad. It made its descent on the Night of Decree, which may have been on the twenty-first, twenty-third, twenty-fifth, twenty-seventh, or twenty-ninth of Ramaḍān; no one is sure. The twenty-seventh, however, is given the best chances, and on that night, whichever it is, all eight doors to Paradise are opened simultaneously and in a row. The believer who is watching and who has been keeping the fast may then see the sky open and glimpse God. Such a lucky man dies immediately and enters Paradise at once. It is difficult to estimate how many people believe this today, but it is certain that the death rate is high during Ramaḍān, particularly when it falls in summer.

Originally Ramaḍān came in the hot season. With the removal of the intercalary month, Muḥammad caused it to rotate, so that it now inches its way around the year. In the latitude of Mekka, 21° North, the seasonal variation in the length of the day, as in temperature, is not profound. In the latitude of Tabriz, or Bukhara, these variations take on importance. Summer fasting and winter fasting are two quite different things. Geography imposes a definite limit upon the performance of the fourth pillar of Islam.

The fast begins before dawn of the day after the first appearance of the new moon of Ramaḍān. Muḥammad provided a system whereby men of known integrity could be counted on to record their having seen the moon, and thus start the ceremony in each camp or community. It was not long, however, before the viewing of the moon became the duty of the ʿulamā in each principal city, and their word was to hold for the countryside around it. Today each Muslim nation has its own corps of moon viewers who telegraph or telephone the news to the corners of the kingdom. This news is greeted with the booming of cannon and the roll of drums. Sometimes, on the first night, the venerable watchers of the skies find the crescent satellite obscured by clouds and must try again the next night. Hence the exact day on which the fast is to begin is not known in advance, and this suspense adds to the excitement of the season.

In 1942 Ramaḍān began in September. In Tangier the Spanish army officers, who had seized the city and its surrounding international zone illegally, decided to impress the local Muslim population with their beneficence as Protectors of Islam, a role which both Kaiser Wilhelm and Mussolini had also assumed. Accordingly they rolled, by dark of night, a number of French 75's to strategic points about the city. When the moon appeared, they fired. The Christian inhabitants of Tangier, chronically nervous and expecting invasion, had spasms. The Muslims walked out in the streets and began beating drums. "The natives have risen," said many a European, reaching for his illegal gun. At dawn the fast began, but by midday the news had filtered through the town. The ʿulamā of Fez had failed to see the moon. The inhabitants of Tangier, deceived by the conniving Christians, had begun to fast too soon.

Certain categories of persons are exempt from fasting. These include children under the age of puberty, the sick and infirm, pregnant women, and travelers. The travelers should make it up later. He who breaks the fast is supposed to support a poor man for a whole year. Fasting is begun at that moment when it is first possible, in the waxing light of day, to distinguish a black thread from a white thread, and, in ordinary usage, continues until the rim of the sun is below the horizon. Fasting means abstaining from food and drink, from smoking, from sexual intercourse, and from shedding blood. Seclusion and contemplation are recommended for the daytime, as well as frequent visits to mosques. Reading the Qur'ān is also recommended. In towns and cities the faithful usually know when to begin and when to stop, for cannons are fired or drums beaten at the critical moments.

Needless to say, those who can afford to do so sit up late at night feasting. At the moment when the evening cannon is about to boom, it is customary for the faster to sit with a bowl of rich soup, called the "soup of Ramaḍān" in his hand, and water nearby. Although the night prayer during Ramaḍān is supposed to include twenty prostrations, there is still time for a good meal, followed later by an early breakfast. The faster then goes to sleep, to awaken, if he is lucky, around noon. This is the rich man's routine. The poor man must work all day without food or drink, and many a laborer collapses under this ordeal, especially in the summer. If he is a smoker of tobacco, hashish, or opium, his plight is the worse.

Tempers run short during Ramaḍān. It is an angry season, and a good one to avoid if possible. Men are not supposed to fight, and if A draws B's blood in a scuffle, B has broken his fast. It is the poorest time of all for archaeological work, engineering projects, or other enterprises that require the supervision of labor. The wise supervisor of excavation or public works determines when Ramaḍān is coming each year, and builds his schedule around it, for most Muslims of the laboring class keep the fast. In North Africa everyone does, for fasting is a symbol of resistance (like wearing *jellabas*), a protest against European rule. In autonomous Muslim countries where large Christian and Jewish minorities also live, fasting serves to emphasize the solidarity of the majority group. In the same way, the Jews have their Passover ceremonies, and the Christians Lent, which serve the same purpose.

The end of Ramaḍān is celebrated by a ceremony known as ʿĪd ul-Fiṭr, ʿAid eṣ-Ṣaghir, or Bairam, depending on the locality. Usually this lasts for three days, and it is as much a work holiday as Christmas is in America. Everyone must have a new set of clothing. Men go to the mosque, women to the cemetery. Everyone visits relatives and distributes alms. Dancing (with the sexes segregated), feasting, and the beating of drums are the order of the day. For weeks in advance, if you walk by the potter's drying yard, you will see him setting out the clay tubes for new drums.

The fifth pillar is ḥajj, the Pilgrimage to Mekka. This takes place in a special month, Dhu 'l-Ḥijja, the twelfth of the lunar calendar. This pilgrimage existed long before Muḥammad's day and was one of the chief sources of income to the Quraish. The procedure also had been worked out in the dim past; Muḥammad made a few changes, to eliminate the role of the idols which he destroyed, but otherwise he left it much the same. ʿAbd ul-ʿAziz Āl Saʿūd, the late king of Saʿudi Arabia, repeated in a sense Muḥammad's experience. When he took al-Hijāz in 1924 he destroyed a number of tombs which he considered idolatrous, and closely policed the pilgrimage to make sure that no corruptions should be practiced. At first he attempted to halt it altogether, but soon realized that its income was essential.

Anthropologically speaking the pilgrimage is one of a whole galaxy of phenomena which seem to satisfy the human need for a periodic, large-scale interaction between widely scattered peoples in terms of a continuity with the mytho-historical past. Australian aborigines, stone-age hunters, gather once a year to holy places in which their ancestors are believed to have first appeared on earth or to have performed miraculous deeds. Here they act out the details of these myths and make use of the opportunity for social intercourse with persons from distant parts whom they otherwise rarely see. In Plymouth, Massachusetts, tourists convene each summer from all the states of the union to look at the granite boulder on which the first female passenger to leave the *Mayflower* supposedly set foot. These visitors buy banners and stickers which announce to the world at large that they have visited the sacred premises. In Lexington, Massachusetts, on April 19 each year a committee of citizens, dressed in buff and blue, acts out Paul Revere's ride and the Battle of Lexington. If the Congregational Church had chosen to make the visit to the stone at Plymouth and the acting out of the Battle of Lexington parts of its ritual, then we could validly compare these ceremonies to the pilgrimage.

The analogy is less complete in another sense; no one today knows the original rationale for the pilgrimage, probably as old as Stonehenge, nor what events it was meant to celebrate. When Muḥammad appropriated it, he converted it to his own use and gave it a new mythology. Such a ritual provides its own justification in the function it serves. In the present instance this function is clear. Men and women from the length and breadth of the world of Islam come together to a free and holy place. They dress alike and act alike, subordinating their own wills and personalities to a greater power. They undergo a long and arduous routine together, which gives them a common experience and an opportunity to get acquainted. They attain the symbols of initiation which enhance their prestige.

On the way out, as on the way in, they pass through a number of other countries and have a chance to see what is happening in them and to tell others what goes on in their homes. Muḥammad specifically said that it is lawful to trade while on pilgrimage, and this along with numerous charitable devices makes it unnecessary to amass capital before departure. On his journey a pilgrim may find a better spot in which to settle and practice his craft, profession, or trade, or he may meet someone from a distant land whom it would be good to have at home. This pilgrimage, therefore, is one of the principal media for interaction in the world of Islam, one of the chief vehicles by which it was unified. For Muḥammad to have rejected it on the grounds that it was the property of an older faith would have been as logical as to have rejected prayer for the same reason. In these days of turmoil when many Muslims are the subjects of Christian or antireligious states, the pilgrimage gives the subject a chance to meet free men and to compare notes. For this reason some governments have forbidden it or salted it with puppet pilgrims of their own choosing who deceive no one.

Every Muslim is supposed to make the pilgrimage at least once. In Muḥammad's lifetime this was simple, for his congregation did not yet extend from Morocco to Mindanao. It was possible to send a substitute, and women could go with their husbands or with kin such as fathers and brothers to whom they were ineligible in marriage.

The pilgrims set out well in advance, in order to arrive at one of the six rest houses, situated five or six miles outside the city on the six roads which lead into it, on the sixth day of Dhu 'l-Ḥijja. At the rest house the pilgrim bathes, makes two prostrations, and exchanges his clothing for the *iḥrām*, which consists of two pieces of cotton cloth, without seams, about the size of ordinary towels. Females, however, are not required to wear this revealing costume. Their uniform consists of five pieces: trousers, overdress and frock of green, a black robe, and a veil.[8] The male pilgrim may wear sandals, but not shoes. He may not shave, pare his nails, oil his head, or even scratch his skin until the pilgrimage has been completed.

He now walks to the city in the company of his fellows, singing a special pilgrim song. Once in Mekka he goes to the great mosque, performs his ablutions, and kisses the Black Stone which is still in the same position to which it was raised by Muḥammad's direction. He then circumambulates the Ka'ba seven times counterclockwise, three of these running and four at a slow walk, and on each circuit he touches the so-called Yemeni corner and kisses the Black Stone. Next he goes to a spot known as the Place of Abraham, where he recites: "Take ye the place of Abraham for a place of prayer." Two more prostrations, and he returns to the Ka'ba to kiss the Black Stone once more. Then out the gate to Mount Ṣafā, a hill on the outskirts of the city, he goes, reciting: "Verily aṣ-Ṣafā and al-Marwa are signs of God." Having climbed the hill he recites this thrice more, after which he runs from the top of aṣ-Ṣafā to the top of al-Marwa seven times, repeating his prayers each time he reaches the summit of each hill. The pilgrim then returns to Mekka and circumambulates the Ka'ba once again.

After this day of strenuous exercise he rests, for on the seventh of Dhu 'l Ḥijja he need only listen to a speech in the Great Mosque

[8] *Ibid.*, p. 158.

about the pilgrimage. On the eighth day he walks with his companions to a village called Mina, where they all pray and sleep. On the morning of the ninth, they pray at Mina and then proceed to Mount ʿArafāt, where they pray some more and hear another sermon. Then they go to a place called al-Muzdafila, halfway between ʿArafāt and Mina, arriving in time for the sunset prayer, and there they sleep.

On the tenth day the pilgrimage reaches its climax. This is the day of sacrifice, called variously Yaum-an-Naḥr, al-Aẓḥa, and ʿAid-el-Kabīr. The pilgrim rises early, prays, and then goes to Mina where three ancient pillars mark some archaeological site. Each has a name, the first being *shaiṭān ul-ḳabīr* (the big devil). The pilgrim picks up twenty-one stones, which he finds conveniently lying on the ground at his feet, and throws seven at each pillar, from a distance of fifteen feet or more, with his right hand. In 1300 years and over, several millions of pilgrims have thrown these pebbles, or their replacements, several tens or even hundreds of millions of times at the same three pillars, and no one knows how many times this was done before Muḥammad's day. The pillars are still standing. This is indeed a miracle.

Still at Mina the pilgrim now acquires an animal, preferably a sheep. He cuts the throat of this animal ritually, while exclaiming, "God is most Great!" He gets a shave, has his nails pared, and removes his iḥrām. Now he can put on his regular clothing and resume the character of an individual. After a three-day rest at Mekka and a few other duties, including a final circumambulation, he is free to go home, wearing a green turban, and from now on people will address him as al-Ḥajj (or al-Ḥajji), the Pilgrim, and this will add greatly to his prestige.

Needless to say the logistics of the pilgrimage is big business. Wholly aside from the caravans, which will be discussed later, the modern pilgrim ships and planes, the details of admitting some hundreds of thousands of human beings from some dozens of countries into the Ḥijāz each year, caring for their health, feeding and lodging them, providing them with the iḥrām, taking care of their civilian clothing in the meantime (the Saʿudi government fumigates it), selling them souvenirs, keeping them from extravagant acts in moments of pious frenzy, and sending them home again, is full-time work for a large number of people. Jidda is full of Javanese, Moroccans, Pakistanis, Persians, etc., who interpret for their countrymen and provide for their needs. The British, Dutch, and French have long maintained large legation staffs there, as doubtless now do the Pakistanis and Indonesians. Ibn Sa'ūd charged five golden sovereigns for the privilege of making the pilgrimage—some of this he no doubt spent in looking after them and caring for the holy places. Now it is free. Each pilgrim must have his ticket home before he is admitted. Once in a while some devotee, overcome with pious indigestion, desecrates the Black Stone by vomiting on it, and he, it is said, is instantly decapitated. Two such instances have involved a Persian and a Yemeni and have brought about correspondence with these governments.

Meanwhile at home, throughout Islam, the tenth of Dhu 'l-Ḥijja is celebrated by all believers, whether or not past or potential pilgrims. Every family must have its sheep,[9] just as we need turkeys for the proper celebration of Thanksgiving. The head of each family kills at least one, which is supposed to provide meat for seven persons. Of the meat of each beast, one third goes to the immediate family, a third to its kin, and the last third to the poor who cannot afford one. Providing the proper number of sheep is a problem everywhere, but it must be particularly difficult in Mekka where pasturage is thin and the animals must be brought from a distance. This is the central feast of Islam, comparable to and derived from the feast of the atonement, Abraham's substitute sacrifice, for the remission of sins. Hence the animal must be mature and without blemish.

The traveler in Muslim lands who happens to be in a town or city during the two or three days preceding the tenth of Dhu 'l Ḥijja will notice the profusion of sheep in the streets. The Great Feast is observed just as wholeheartedly today as it was in the Prophet's own lifetime. One may say of the Five Pillars of Islam as a whole that they were expertly chosen, for they have stood the test of time. Muslims still profess their faith, still pray, still give alms, still fast, and still go on pilgrimage. Automobiles, airplanes, and even the radio, far from impeding these acts of devotion, have served to foster them.

[9] A goat, cow, or camel can be substituted.

8 STRENGTH IN DIVERSITY

EXCEPT FOR BRIEF REFERENCES to the heterodoxy of the now extinct Fāṭimids and to the Kharijites, we have proceeded so far as if all Muslims belonged to the same religious community. The Christian Church is made up of several great religious divisions, while the Buddhist community is split into the adherents of the Greater and Lesser Vehicle. That Islam should be similarly divided is to be expected.

So far, then, only the four schools of the sharīʿa—the Ḥanafi, Māliki, Shāfiʿi, and Ḥanbali—have been offered in the way of diversity. Their followers form the largest of three main theological divisions and call themselves Sunni, or Followers of the Sunna. The two remaining theological branches are the *Khawārij* and the *Shīʿa.*

The first to branch off, and by far the less numerous, are those of the Khawārij, or Kharijites, which means "Seceders." In general their dogma agrees closely with that of the stricter Sunni rites, but they differ on two points: the succession to the caliphate and the obligation of a Muslim to do good in order to keep others from doing evil. The Kharijite movement began in 657 A.D., when twelve thousand soldiers deserted the Caliph ʿAlī at the Battle of Siffīn. The question had arisen as to his right to continue as caliph. A group of soldiers stated their belief that the caliph need not be of the Quraish, nor must there always be a caliph at all; that if there was to be a caliph, God himself should make the decision and reveal this to the faithful in some way.

This decision ruptured their relations with ʿAlī. They left him and formed an independent community in northern Arabia. In 658 A.D. most of them were killed and the remnants dispersed. Their position on the second point of dogma made them particularly expendable, since they maintained that one *must* do good in order to prevent others from doing evil, even if at the cost of one's own life. Members of other sects are permitted to look the other way, if occasion warrants.

Today the few Khawārij remaining live in Oman, in Zanzibar, and in two isolated places in North Africa: the city of Ghardaïa in the Mzab and the Isle of Jerba. In the two latter places the communities consist of Zenatan-speaking Berbers, who are specialists in shopkeeping in Algerian and Tunisian cities, and whose heterodoxy doubtless serves to help them preserve their special-people role.

The major branch of non-Sunnis is that of the Shīʿa, or "Partisans." While the Khawārij rejected ʿAlī, the Shīʿa endorsed him. Shīʿism began as a political movement. ʿAlī established his capital in ʿIraq at al-Kūfa, and the Arabs and rapidly Arabized townsmen of the region were eager to make this country the center of the new Islamic world. Because of the hostility of Muʿāwiya and of the Khawārij, however, their leader and one of his sons were killed, and Damascus became the capital.

Hence the Arabs of al-Kūfa worked out a system of dogma which produced a rival theology, if not theocracy. They rejected the first three caliphs entirely and claimed that the succession passed directly from Muḥammad to ʿAlī. ʿAlī's place was taken by a succession of imāms, who had the power of interpreting religious dogma. The caliph, on the other hand, was an executive, while the limited interpretation permitted by the Sunnis was in the hands of the doctors of the four schools, and the Shaikh ul-Islam. Muḥammad was said to have possessed secret knowledge, which he passed on to ʿAlī, and which then went to the other imāms in turn. Gradually the imāms came to be regarded as infallible, the vehicles of divine light transmitted since the time of Adam, and in some sects the actual incarnation of the deity.

Although the Shīʿa soon split into many fragments, only three sects have survived, the Imāmi, Zaidi, and Ismāʿīli. The first, which has been the state religion of Iran since 1499, is the most numerous and also the most liberal. It began in ʿIraq where most of the Arabs living south of Baghdad are Imāmi Shīʿa. In Iran nearly all Muslims belong, the principal exceptions being the northern Kurds and the Turkomans, who are Sunnis, like most of the Afghans.

The Imāmis recognize twelve imāms: (1) ʿAlī, (2) al-Ḥasan, (3) al-Ḥusain, (4) ʿAlī Zain ul-ʿAbidīn, (5) Muḥammad al-Bāqir, (6) Jaʿfar aṣ-Ṣādiq, (7) Mūsa al-Kāẓim, (8) ʿAli ar-Riza (Riḍa), (9) Muḥammad at-Taqi, (10) ʿAlī an-Naqi, (11) Al-Ḥasan al-ʿAskari, and (12) Muḥammad al-Mahdi. The fourth was a son of al-Ḥusain, and from there on son succeeded father down the line. Al-Mahdi, who is said to have disappeared down a well at Samarra, also is said to be still alive and prepared to return at the right moment.

The Zaidis branched off at the fifth imām, rejecting Muḥammad al-Bāqir and taking his brother Zaid instead. Their line has continued to the present day. They are the Muslims of the plateau of the Yemen, whose capital is at Ṣanʿā. The Imām Yaḥya, who was murdered in 1948, was of this dynasty, as is his son Imām Aḥmad who has succeeded him. The Zaidis attribute no supernatural powers to their imāms and in general seem to fall closest to the Sunnis in their general practices.

The Ismāʿīlis split off over the succession to Jaʿfar aṣ-Ṣādiq, the sixth imām. His eldest son, who should have inherited, was Ismāʿīl. One day Jaʿfar found Ismāʿīl drunk and disinherited him, setting up his second son Mūsa in his stead. Ismāʿīl had his following, and they founded a sect of their own. His son Muḥammad, the eighth imām of their line, was also the last one visible to men. Since then a whole line of "concealed" imāms is believed to have succeeded him. Today they live mostly in India and in some villages of Syria and of Khorasan. The much publicized Agha Khan died in 1957. He has been succeeded by his Harvard-trained grandson, His Highness Kerīm. Although most of his subjects live in Pakistan, some of them occupy a number of villages in the Qaʿinat of Khorasan, and a few remain in the mountains of Syria, particularly at Salamīya, just west of a point halfway between the cities of Ḥimṣ and Ḥamā (Homs and Hama).

These harmless Syrian hill farmers are the last remnants of a once sinister offshoot of the Ismāʿīli body,[1] the Assassins, who under their famed leader Ḥasan ibn aṣ-Ṣabāḥ, the Old Man of the Mountain, became a special people expert in the activity which their name now implies. (Originally it meant hashish [hemp] eaters.) Their main stronghold was in Iran, but after it was destroyed by the Mongols in 1256[2] only the Syrian remnant remained. In 1326, some seventy years later, Ibn Baṭṭūṭa described the Syrian branch as a going concern:

[1] According to Gibb, via the Fāṭimids. Ibn Baṭṭūṭa, *Travels in Asia and Africa, 1325-1354,* trans. by H. A. R. Gibb (New York, 1929), p. 349, n. 49. Also H. A. R. Gibb, *Mohammedanism* (London, 1949), pp. 124-125; also Henri Lammens, *Islam, Beliefs and Institutions,* trans. by T. Denison Ross (New York, 1929), p. 158. How and when the Syrian branch was reunited with the Ismāʿīli parent body I do not know.

[2] Brockelmann, *History of the Islamic Peoples,* p. 250.

> Thence I visited the fortress of Baghras . . . and many other castles and fortresses, several of which belong to a sect called Ismāʿīlites or Fidāwis, and may be entered by none but members of the sect. They are the arrows of the sultan; by means of them he strikes those of his enemies who escape into ʿIraq and other lands. They receive fixed salaries, and when the sultan desires to send one of them to assassinate one of his enemies, he pays him his blood-money. If after carrying out his allotted task he escapes with his life, the money is his, but if he is killed it goes to his sons. They carry poisoned daggers, with which they strike their victim, but sometimes their plans miscarry and they themselves are killed.[3]

He fails to mention the earthly paradise which the founder of the sect had set up in his Iranian fastness, complete with gardens and fountains and beautiful girls, as a resting place between jobs for his envoys; and the famous hashish with which they are said to have steeled their nerves is also missing. More important to the anthropologist is the fact that they were able to establish a graded hierarchy, in five steps. At the bottom were the common people, ordinary Muslims. Next up the ladder were novices, and above them the men who did the actual murdering (after a glimpse of paradise and under the influence of the drug). The two top grades included the executives, who must have viewed life with a colder realism. We presume that only the fifth grade exists in numbers today.

A special group of Imāmis also live in that area. The Matāwila,[4] who live in the cities of Ṣūr and Ṣaidā (Tyre and Sidon) and in the Baalbek Valley (Coelo-Syria), number one hundred and fifty thousand and are said to be so fanatical that some of them carry packets of Persian soil on their persons and smash the pottery out of which either Sunnis or Christians have eaten.

One must not, however, judge the Shīʿa as a whole in terms of these odd survivors. The main branch, that of the Imāmis, number at least twenty-five million, in Iran and ʿIraq and the Arabian coastlands alone. In their opinion it is they rather than the Sunnis who are the orthodox of Islam, and the least fanatical. In practice, they reject Muḥammad's injunction against the graphic representation of the human face and figure, as of other forms of animal life. One

[3] Ibn Baṭṭūṭa, *op. cit.*, pp. 61-62.

[4] Hitti, *History of the Arabs*, p. 249 n.

can buy lithographed portraits of both ʿAlī and the Imām ar-Riza at the latter's shrine in Mashhad. One must remember that painting was and is a fine art in Persia, something which it would have been hard to give up.

The Shīʿa manner of praying differs somewhat from each of the four Sunni forms, and they also have their own ideas about the rules of inheriting property. Unlike the Sunnis they include the Zoroastrians with the Jews and Christians among the People of the Book, who are allowed to practice their own religions without disturbance. It is a general belief, fostered by the quatrains of ʿOmar Khayyam, that the Persian Shīʿa are more liberal about wine than the Sunnis, but actually drinking has come and gone in different regions at various times, without much regard to sect. Wine making and selling are privileges of Jews and Christians. The Shīʿa stress different dates on the ritual calendar from the Sunnis. Aside from the Great Feast their principal ceremony culminates on the tenth of Muḥarram, the anniversary of al-Ḥusain's tragic death at Kerbala, in 680 A.D., the sixty-first year of the Ḥijrā.

On this day and the several preceding it, Christians are well advised to keep off the streets in many Shīʿa cities, and particularly not to try to take photographs. Crowds of men parade through the main thoroughfares shouting, "Ya Ḥasān! Ya Ḥusain!" in rhythm, weeping, and lacerating themselves with swords, sticks, and chains. On the tenth day itself some work themselves into a frenzy of grief and slice their heads with axes or swords. In many cases the barber has already made a few incisions, calculated to produce the maximum blood for the least injury, and the ax or sword, turned broadside, merely opens them and starts them bleeding again. In others, however, there is less deception, and some men actually injure themselves severely, if not fatally.

During this period also it is the fashion to produce passion plays in alfresco theaters erected in different parts of the city, at the expense of the wealthier inhabitants. Some of those produced in Tehran during the nineteenth century were extremely realistic. In the fateful battlefield scene, certain intrepid volunteers had themselves buried to the neck to represent decapitated heads, while others by concealing their heads became the corresponding torsos. At these plays, pathos is the main theme, and it is fashionable to weep. Weeping also is part of the regular Thursday night religious service among rural Shīʿa, who beat their breasts tearfully at the mention of ʿAlī's name and of those of his murdered offspring. It is interesting to note that Shīʿa celebrations commemorate the deaths rather than the births of their heroes.

While Shīʿa make the pilgrimage to Mekka, they are not limited to this journey alone. They have other shrines nearly as holy: the tomb of ʿAlī's head at Najaf, that of al-Ḥusain at Kerbala, and that of the eighth imām, ar-Riza at Mashhad. Thousands of ʿIraqi Shīʿa visit Mashhad every year, crossing Iran to do so, and the Persians come to ʿIraq for Kerbala and Najaf, riding sometimes in busses draped with black and sometimes in private vehicles. Often they sell carpets and even their pushtins, or reversed sheepskin coats, on the way to obtain funds for their return home. The Mashhad pilgrimage is especially perilous for the impecunious pilgrim who travels on foot, for he must cross the Dasht-i-Lut Desert if he comes from the south, or the northern reaches of the Dasht-i-Kavir from the west. A common sight on both roads is a group of pilgrims, or a family, holding up empty jars and begging water. Some of these sometimes fail to reach their destinations.

The pilgrimage at Mashhad requires no special costume. In fact, many perform it today in Western clothing. It also involves no strenuous physical exercise and can be done in a few hours. The pilgrim, on the completion of his holy rounds, is entitled to call himself Mashhadi, a designation somewhat less impressive than Ḥajji but still valuable in Shīʿa circles. The name Ḥajji itself is subject to qualification because some Shīʿa, born during the month of Dhu 'l Ḥijja, are so named, just as those born during the month of fasting may be called Ramaḍān.

As in the case of their minor branch, the Assassins, the Shīʿa, like the Turks, have a capacity for hierarchical organization foreign to the Arabs of the peninsula, and this applies also to the Imāmi majority. Their mullahs are graded, with *mujtahids* at the top. A mujtahid is equal to a member of the ʿulamā among the Sunnis. In Kerbala and Najaf are located companies of mujtahids, who pass upon questions of doctrine. For this purpose they use their own books, compilations of the traditions parallel to those of the four Sunni schools, but they differ from the Sunni doctors in their comparatively greater freedom to exercise personal judgment, for they are said to partake of the inner light of their imāms. In Iran, where Shīʿism is official, the shah appoints a head mujtahid in each major city. This officer serves as the top religious authority, comparable to the Grand Mufti or Shaikh-ul-Islam of the Ottoman creation.

In considering this matter of schisms and sects, then, it may be said that Islam is a world religion, comparable to Christianity and Buddhism. No religion encompassing millions of persons in dozens of countries, exposed to local variations of environment and historical circumstance, can hope to maintain a rigid structure. In its very variety lies one of the sources of its strength.

Another source is the great amount of attention paid to the maintenance of equilibrium within each community and the preservation of good relations between communities, by means of support for the poor and needy and provision for the comfort and well-being of travelers. We have already seen how the zakā, as specified in great detail by Muḥammad, takes part of this load. An equal share of the burden is borne by endowments known as *waqf* from Egypt eastward, and in North Africa as *ḥabūs*. All Muslim sects have them, while in Lebanon and Syria, Christians do also.

A waqf or ḥabūs is a charitable foundation. A wealthy merchant or landlord will insert a provision into his will that a certain share of his property is to be given to a certain waqf. If he chooses, he may found one. Some wealthy waqfs are associated with the tombs of saints or other religious edifices and provide for their care, as in the case of the magnificent tomb of Imām ar-Riza in Mashhad. Others are set up like trust funds so that part of their income will be distributed to certain persons, often the descendants of the founders, particularly in the case of families descended from the Prophet. Still others are designated for special duties, like the waqf for putting baby storks back in their nests in Turkey,[5] or that for feeding pigeons in Fez—the point being that the pigeons defecate on the corners of the university buildings, and the students collect the droppings and sell them to the tanners, this waqf constituting a form of student aid. Ibn Baṭṭūṭa tells of a waqf in Damascus conducted expressly for the purpose of buying Chinese porcelain dishes to replace those broken by servants or slaves, to save the latter from punishment by their masters.[6]

In the same city he lists five other and more important classes of waqfs, maintained for the following purposes: to pay the expenses of the pilgrimage to substitutes for persons unable to go; to supply wedding outfits to girls whose families were unable to pay for them;

[5] Private communication from Myron B. Smith.

[6] Ibn Baṭṭūṭa, *op. cit.*, pp. 69-70.

to ransom prisoners and free them; to care for travelers by giving them food, clothing, and the expenses of conveyance to their countries; and to improve and pave the streets. The variety of these few examples indicates the wide range of purposes to which these foundations are dedicated.

The property from which a waqf derives its income may be agricultural lands or rent-yielding urban real estate such as a tannery or row of shops. It may not be capital in the sense of money invested in stocks or bonds which pay interest, since this falls under the heading of usury, forbidden in Islam (although permitted to Christians and Jews). The waqf system gives employment to thousands of persons, for a poor man who owns no property may work for a waqf, which may in fact own part or all of his village. In at least some countries the waqf gives him a larger share of the produce than if he were privately employed. The shopkeeper or artisan is likewise better off than if he rented private space in the city, for he is sure that no landlord will sell his work place and force him to move. Waqf property cannot be sold, although under certain special circumstances and after much negotiation, some classes of it may be exchanged.

A waqf is administered by an officer called a *nāẓir,* who presides over a board of overseers or trustees and who is responsible to the government. In the case of large waqfs this may become a full-time job and require a staff. Each mosque is in a sense waqf property, since the man who finances the building of a mosque loses control over it once it is prayed in, it then becoming the responsibility of its officers. Like those in the larger cities, small country mosques own property, employ landless workers, and offer hospitality to travelers. The number of these foundations in the Muslim world is legion, and their benefits to the social structure profound.

The waqf is not, however, the only kind of institution in the Islamic community which helps maintain equilibrium within the social structure. Essentially it serves to iron out the differences between high and low, rich and poor, familiar and strange, bringing the extremes closer to the mean. A complex society, however, characterized by an extreme division of labor, needs a further kind of strengthening. People in such a society fall naturally into horizontal categories based on wealth, degree of education and sophistication, and general standard of living; and these categories, particularly those near the middle. require structure, within which the mutual interactions of their members may be channeled and ordered.

Muḥammad and his immediate successors failed to provide for this need because they did not live in that kind of society, but found it only after the lands to the north, east, and west had been conquered. The Arab social system in which they had been born and reared consisted of an aggregation of closely integrated kinship units. In a city such as Mekka it was the tribes that ruled, and the relations between tribes were not always smooth. A man's loyalty was to his kin, and within the kinship unit the head of the extended family ruled. All members were more or less equal, and differences in wealth were made up by mutual aid.

In a city like Cairo, Damascus, or Baghdad, and in the rural areas around such centers, people lived in wards or villages, and those who still retained tribal affiliations soon lost them or filed them on the shelf of honored but infrequently used tradition (like the clan affiliations of Americans of Scottish origin). Something else was needed. This something else was a galaxy of associations.

An association is an institution which persons of equal status and similar interests join to provide a supplement or compensation for the interaction within their families, businesses, and formal religious communities, which in sum total may not be wholly satisfactory. The associations which a man may join must have as the framework of interaction some central activity in which all can participate. The nature of that activity reflects the basic interest of the particular society. Among the Plains Indians, whose main preoccupation was war, societies of warriors arose. In early Islam the society was slanted toward religion, and hence the associations took a religious form. This was particularly facilitated by the Christians and Buddhists who already had developed monastic orders, convents, and the like, while the institution of a holy man and his circle of devotees was as old and as basic as the early prophets of the Old Testament.

If we look back over the program of Islamic procedure as developed by the Prophet and his immediate successors, we see that two things are emphasized: a lengthy and time-consuming ritual which serves to break down tribal differences and to consolidate the Islamic community as a whole, in its widest sense, and a close attention to the letter of the law, involving much legal hairsplitting. The latter was carried on at a highly intellectual level by the learned doctors, who had little time for the immediate needs of their constituents. Outside Arabia itself Islamic society was highly segmented and each segment needed its own set of symbols, its own organization, and its own procedure, to supplement the over-all structure. It needed a weft as well as a warp, and the religious brotherhoods arose to fill this need.

They were the result of a movement which began in al-Kūfa in the eighth century A.D., through the agency of a group of penitents, after the Early Christian pattern, called *ṣūfis*. Ṣūfi means woolly. The Ṣūfis wore wool shirts, to mortify the flesh. They met together in groups to recite aloud from the Qur'ān. The rationale for these recitations was to induce in the devotee a state known as *ḥāl* (literally, "condition"), in which he would be able to perceive God and interact with, and even unite himself to, the deity. The derivation of this practice is clear; people all over the world do it, in every level of cultural complexity. We have our own ḥāl in Appalachian coal-mining communities where members of obscure religious communities handle snakes, stamping up and down, open mouthed, with eyes raised and glazed in ecstasy.

It is one of the easiest and cheapest ways known of satisfying certain physiological and psychological needs, of relaxing the nervous system and relieving emotional anxieties, while merging oneself with a group of persons of equal status and in a similar condition. It is much more satisfactory and much less expensive for the common man, living in a crowded community, than alcohol or adultery. Being religious in nature, it tends to be socially acceptable, especially since it creates no neighborhood disturbance.

Few physiologists and psychologists have studied the details of this interesting practice, which closely resembles, and may even have been derived from, the breathing exercises of the Yogi.[7] One excellent description, however, made by Dr. W. S. Haas on the modern Raḥmaniya dervishes of Algeria, will serve as illustration. The essential medium of recitation in this and other orders is the name of God in some ritual context. Every order has one; it is called the *dhikr,* usually pronounced *zikr,* of that order. Each group of brethren consists of two classes, the professionals and the laymen. The

[7] According to William S. Haas, who has made the only detailed study of this subject I have been able to find. Haas, "The Zikr of the Raḥmaniya Order, a Psycho-physiological Analysis," *The Moslem World,* XXXIII, No. 1 (January, 1943), 16-28. China is another possible point of origin, as suggested by my colleague Dr. S. van R. Cammann. It is not known at what exact period the formal breathing exercises entered these rituals.

professionals include the leader and his helpers, who do not enter into the state—they attain their spiritual satisfaction in other ways.

The routine is divided into three parts, an introduction or warming-up period, the zikr proper in four double sequences, and the breaking up of the spell.

Part One starts off as follows: the lay brethren sit cross-legged in a circle, with the imām or leader outside the ring. After they have been quiet for a few minutes he begins to recite the first half of the shahāda, or Profession of Faith; "La ilaha illa 'llah," over and over again, rhythmically. This does not last long. He shifts to a number of suras or passages from the Qur'ān and finishes with a special prayer, private to the order. From time to time individual brothers in the circle may join in and repeat his words, as the spirit moves them. This first period lasts about a quarter of an hour. The brethren are now in a mood for the next step.

The members of the circle rise, and others who arrived late and have been waiting outside enter. The shaikh steps into the center, the brethren join hands, and the shaikh orders them to begin. For eight minutes they now go through what may be called Routine A. They pronounce in unison, "*Al*-lah, *Al*-lah, *Al*-lah," again and again, exhaling on the first syllable and inhaling on the second. This soon becomes *ha*-ha, *ha*-ha, then *a*-a, and eventually a pair of rattling noises (probably unvoiced aspirates). With the exhalation on the first syllable the brother bends his knees, with the inhalation on the second, he straightens up again.

The shaikh, who is not participating in all of this, watches each brother carefully. Now he will approach one of the brothers and gaze fixedly into his eyes. Again, he will leave the center and stand near another of his company, facing in the same direction and going through a few strokes of the routine, as if to guide the brother back from some deviation. With these two kinds of personal attention the shaikh apparently manages to keep everyone more or less at the same level of consciousness.

Suddenly he gives a command, and they all pass into Routine B. This is the opposite of A, and easier. The brothers inhale shortly on the first syllable and exhale at greater length on the second. They now keep their legs still, transferring the motion to their chests. On the inhale they throw out the chest, and on the exhale pull it back. While Routine A moves at sixty paired strokes a minute, B's rate is only forty-five. Each lasts eight minutes. During

Routine B. the shaikh watches his company attentively as before; in the session which Dr. Haas witnessed he drew one brother out of the circle and made him change places with a fellow devotee.

As Dr. Haas explains, these two routines differ in rhythm as well as in degree of strenuousness. During Part A members outside the circle, presumably mostly the shaikh's professional assistants, clap their hands to set the beat, for it is not a natural routine. The shaikh shifts to B when he sees that the brothers are beginning to lose consciousness. The easier routine of B levels them off. He wants them to enter a trance but not to pass out.

A sequence of A and B constitutes a turn. The first two turns are alike and as above. In the third, the shaikh leaves his relatively passive role and moves about, approaching individual brothers in turn. Suddenly one of them will step forward out of the circle, moving independently in a state of ecstasy and crying ALLAH "in an imploring tone of rapture where pain and bliss are melting into one."[8] Both shaikh and brother utter inarticulate sounds apart from the zikr, and when the excitement has reached its climax and all the brothers seems to have been affected, the shaikh cries out, throws up his right arm, and wiggles his index and middle fingers rapidly for half a minute. He moves his arms backward and forward, presumably in a different rhythm from what has gone before, and now he leads them into Routine B.

The fourth turns starts out like the third, except that when the climax arrives and the company is shifted to B, they all fall on their knees and do the chest exercise by moving the body backward and forward. At the end they all throw themselves forward, touch their foreheads on the floor, and remain that way, forming a star-shaped ring around the shaikh, who remains on his knees, with his body upright.

They are now in the "state." The shaikh leaves them this way for several minutes, and then he repeats in a low monotone, "Allahu AKBAR!" stressing the last syllable. He moves his head to that of each brother, repeating it individually. Gradually they begin to relax. They stretch their limbs, shift about, and rise to their feet. One of the staff wipes the face and kisses the head of each man. *Exeunt omnes*. It has taken about an hour and a half, and they have merged with the deity.

So much for the details. It is easy to see how participation in this

[8] *Ibid.*, p. 23.

kind of ritual will leave a believer in a calm and satisfied state. It is also obvious why the learned and dignified ʿulamā would look down their aristocratic noses at it. As Gibb points out, while this kind of mysticism may not have appealed overmuch to the Arabs themselves, it was welcomed by the newly converted outlanders whom the Arabs liked to treat as inferiors, notably the Turks, Iranians, and Berbers, each of whom may already have had some more or less similar practice.

Dr. Haas' description applies to only one order. Each has its own routine, by which the same end, however, is achieved. The more vulgar and spectacular orders, like that of the ʿAissāwa in Morocco, may help along the achievement of the state by the use of drugs, notably hashish, and they may go in for extravagant public exhibitions, in which they wave long heads of hair in circles, and bend over from a standing posture to pick up offal from the ground with their teeth. The Ḥamadsha even steal a leaf from the Shīʿa's book (or vice versa) by head chopping and self-flagellation. These orders are horizontally stratified to fill the needs of the various social levels in the community, and the coarser ways of getting into a state are, as one would expect, confined to those orders which serve the needs of the lowest strata. One may be sure that the higher orders like the Tijaniyin, for example, to which wealthy business and professional men belong, go in for no such exhibitions. It would be interesting, of course, to discover what they actually do.

As the requirements of the zikr have made clear, each order consists of two classes, professional and lay. Each has a central headquarters, often containing the tomb of its founder. Most of them also have chapter houses located in different cities and often in many countries. This real estate is the property of the order, somewhat in the manner of a waqf, although in some cases the head of the order may have the power to dispose of it personally. The usual means of support is by voluntary contributions from the lay members, although there also may be endowments.

Each order started originally at the initiative of some learned shaikh[9] who studied with others, at some center of learning, often in a university. He established his own *ṭarīqa,* or way, which is an individual interpretation of the religious philosophy of Islam. Gathering about him a group of devotees, he set up his own estab-

[9] The word shaikh or shaykh simply means "leader." He may be the leader of a tribe or of a religious community.

lishment known as a *ribāṭ,* which is usually translated as "retreat" or monastery. The common North African word *murabiṭ,* usually rendered in the French form *marabout,* means a member of such a community.

Scholars have spent much time and effort tracing the lineage of the different orders, most of which are interconnected. They find that the earliest to take shape in the modern sense was that of the Qādiriyin, founded by Sīdi ʿAbd al-Qādir al-Jilāni, a native of the province of Gilan on the Caspian shore of Iran, the wettest spot in the whole Middle East. The mother ribāṭ is in Baghdad, with chapters all the way from Morocco to India, and with thousands of chapters of the orders derived from it.

Of the Ṣūfi retreats in Cairo, Ibn Baṭṭūṭa says, in 1326:

> . . . the nobles vie with each other in building them. Each is set apart for a separate school of darwishes, mostly Persians, who are men of good education and adept in the mystical doctrines. Each has a superior and a doorkeeper and their affairs are admirably organized. They have many special customs, one of which has to do with their food. The steward of the house comes in the morning to the darwishes, each of whom indicates what food he desires, and when they assemble for meals, each person is given his bread and soup in a separate dish, none sharing with another. They eat twice a day. They are each given winter clothes and summer clothes, and a monthly allowance of from twenty to thirty *dirhams.*[10] Every Thursday night they receive sugar cakes, soap to wash their clothes, the price of a bath, and oil for their lamps. These men are celibate; the married men have separate convents.[11]

These orders served as one of the most important vehicles by which individuals were motivated to move about from country to country, and most of the retreats also served as hostels for travelers, in competition with the mosques and some of the waqfs. Their contribution to the homogeneity and internationalism of Muslim culture in the past was thus great. Despite the development of modern nationalism and the rise of a Western-educated class in Muslim lands, their work is far from finished. The Derqāwi order in Morocco, with its mother ribāṭ in Tangier, was a closely coordinated organization,

[10] A silver coin of about 14 carats. Hughes, *Dictionary of Islam,* p. 85.
[11] Ibn Baṭṭūṭa, *op. cit.,* p. 51.

with branches all over North Africa, until the spring of 1950 when its shaikh, Sīdī Aḥmad ben Ṣādiq, was arrested for fomenting a revolt in Spanish Morocco and thrown into jail at Mazagan. This story is not yet finished.

Another even more powerful brotherhood is that of the Sanūsi of Cyrenaica,[12] a well-watered plateau with a narrow coastal strip and desert behind. Before the Italian occupation—one of the most inhuman ever perpetrated by a modern Christian nation—this country was occupied by about one hundred and fifty thousand Bedawin, whose relations with the outside world were handled by a mere twenty-five thousand Arab townsmen, three to four thousand Jews, and a handful of Europeans. The Bedawin were organized into autonomous tribes which shared the seasonal pasture, with occasional disputes. Their social organization and over-all political situation was little different from that of the Bedawin in the days of Muḥammad, except that they were nominally Muslims. Some of the regular Ṣūfi brotherhoods had their chapters there, but only in the towns, since the particular tensions which they allay do not exist among Bedawin.

About 1787 A.D., a holy man named Sayyid Muḥammad ibn ʿAlī as-Sanūsi was born near Mustaganim in western Algeria. He studied at Fez, under the Tijāñi order, and then went to Mekka, gathering disciples on the road. He remained in the holy city for six years and then went home, but finding the French in occupation, he returned to the Ḥijāz where he stayed eight years more. During this period he attached himself to the head of the Moroccan Qadiriya branch[13] and when the latter was exiled for unorthodoxy to the Yemen, the Sanūsi also went along. His master having died in exile in 1837, the Sanūsi returned to Mekka, where he founded his own order. He did this only after having tried many Ṣūfi doctrines and other orders personally; he evolved a highly dignified, conservative, and orthodox system slanted toward the Bedawin, who were notably uninterested in religious practices.

In 1841 the Turkish authorities, with the sanction of the religious leaders of Mekka, expelled him, and he went to Cyrenaica where he set up his Mother Lodge in 1843 near Cyrene. He managed to return

[12] Incomparably well described by E. E. Evans-Pritchard, *The Sanūsi of Cyrenaica* (Oxford, 1949). The author is professor of anthropology at Oxford.

[13] The parent order founded by Mūlay (or Sīdī) ʿAbd el Qādir al Jīlānī.

to Mekka for seven more years, and in 1856 he moved his headquarters to the previously uninhabited oasis of Jaghabub, where he established not only a ribāṭ but also a university second only to al-Azhar of Cairo. He died and was buried at Jaghabub in 1859. Jaghabub was the crossroads of the northwest caravans to the Sudan and those going east and west between North Africa and Egypt, over the inland route. It thus became a great center for travelers, whom the Sanūsi and his followers entertained.

He had two classes of members: the *ikhwān* or brothers, who were literate and recited the zikr, and the *muntasibīn,* who were illiterate and belonged because their tribal shaikhs were members. Although they were not required to follow any religious ritual which failed to interest them, the shaikhs were interested because the order provided them with certain advantages. They were able to stop at the Sanūsi chapter houses all along the caravan routes, which by the acquisition of waqf property were in a position to offer hospitality. Furthermore the Sanūsi leaders had assumed the role of previously unorganized holy men, of arbitrating disputes between tribes and keeping the peace.

The order was organized as follows: at the head was the *shaikh aṭ-ṭarīqa,* who was advised by the *khawaṣṣ,* an inner circle of other descendants of the founder plus two or three unrelated but learned ikhwān. On the next level were the shaikhs of regional lodges, who had the power to ordain the ikhwān, who in turn were allowed to recruit the lay members.

As the Arab traders and political leaders spread into Fezzan, Kufra, and the central Sudan, Sanūsi missionaries went with them and set up their lodges. These served as social centers for travelers and local converts. When the French took over this part of Africa they killed the lodge masters, while the Italians did the same in Cyrenaica. At this point the Grand Sanūsi became militant, and the previously peaceful dervish order turned into an army.

This is not a book of modern history. The activities of the Sanūsis in Cyrenaica and Egypt can be read in books devoted to that discipline. It is worthy of note, however, that on November 25, 1950, the present head of the order became ruler of all three parts of the former Italian colony. It is a far cry from the small circle of men in wool shirts calling ecstatically on the name of God.

It is an equally far cry from the Sanūsi to the itinerant Rifaʿi dervishes whom one could still see, a few years ago, biting the heads off puff-adders in the public square of Marrakesh, the member of the same order who used to lick hot irons in the Ringling Brothers-Barnum and Bailey Circus side show, and the few remaining straggling mendicants in Iran, who hold up an ancient battle-ax and a begging bowl made from an African nutshell and belong to no regular organization. This show-business fringe of dervishdom is on the way out. A hundred years ago in all Muslim lands, and much later in some, it was still a power. Dervishes in Iran would camp before the door of a rich man, and make his life so miserable that he would have to buy them off. In parts of southern Iran and Baluchistan it is possible that some of the so-called dervishes are really members of debased ethnic groups, comparable to Gypsies, who have taken over the less intellectual aspects of the mendicant Ṣūfi way of life as a means of subsistence.

Despite their great heterogeneity, and their capacity to merge into other types of institutions, the Ṣūfi organizations share one common function. They served, and still serve, as mechanisms for the organization and stabilization of comparable segments of populations living under regular governments and standard Muslim political systems. They add to the number and variety of pieces in our mosaic. However esoteric or unorthodox their beliefs and practices, these still fall within the conceptual framework of Islam.

Still another set of organizations accomplished similar results, setting up hierarchies with different degrees of participation and giving the believer that mystical sense of union with his deity with which the whole Ṣūfi cycle started. These are the heretical cults, based on fragments of Muslim, Christian, and other doctrines, which grew up and still exist on the borderlands between the Muslim and Byzantine culture areas, of the period between 622 and 1453 A.D., the Hijra and the Fall of Constantinople. These borderlands follow the mountains of Lebanon and Syria northward and eastward to Kurdistan. The mountains are high enough and steep enough to discourage pursuit by the outraged orthodox, and far enough from the two cultural centers to have permitted a number of groups of heretics to develop and crystallize their schisms.

We are concerned now not with the various branches of Christianity, however archaic and aberrant, nor with the comparable Muslim sects such as those of the Assassins and Matawali, but with the religious systems of other little groups of peoples sandwiched in mountain valleys and on the flanks of steep tablelands. These systems are reckoned as separate religions. They are four in number: those of the Druzes, the Nuṣairis, the Yezidis, and the ʿAlī Ilāhis.

The Druzes are about one hundred and twenty-four thousand strong. Many of them still live on Mount Lebanon, their earlier home. In 1860 the French, who have always been their enemies, drove out many of them, and the majority now inhabit the Hauran plateau, now called Jabal Druz. Many have emigrated, and colonies are to be found in Flint, Michigan; Danbury, Connecticut; and elsewhere in America. At home they are farmers, stock breeders, and landlords employing many Christian villagers. Ten great families rule them, each with its amīr and his palace. Often quarreling and even fighting in peacetime, in war these families unite, and they are noted fighters.

They grade themselves into three classes. At the top there are the very few who know all the mysteries of their secret religion. Next comes a larger group of initiated people, who study the mysteries and from whom the upper class is recruited. These wear special garments and observe certain taboos such as refraining from tobacco, coffee, and alcohol. The remaining eighty-five per cent are laymen who know none of the secrets and obey orders in matter of ritual.

The Druzes practice *taqīya,* or concealment.[14] This means that they may pretend to belong to some other religion when this subterfuge is necessary for their safety. While they will not talk about their religion, a certain amount is known.

Like so many other deviations, it began with Ismāʿīli Shīʿism through the Fāṭimids. The sixth Fāṭimid caliph of Cairo, al-Ḥakīm (966-1020 A.D.), was an unattractive and eccentric young man. He ordered the citizens to work by night and sleep by day, and he forced the Christians to wear heavy wooden crosses in the streets, while Jews were made to drag along oversized replicas of the bronze calf mentioned in *Exodus* and in Sura 2 of the Qur'ān (entitled The Cow). He invited the debutantes of Cairo to a party and then walled them up inside a mosque and left them there to starve. No one seemed to mind much when he rode out on the desert one day on a white ass and disappeared without a trace.

His career caused much speculation among those who had not known him, including one Ismāʿīl ad-Durāzi, a Persian, who used

[14] "This *taqīya* is common to the Shīʿa generally and is not unknown to other religions, including early Christian circles." Personal communication by Dr. Calverley.

the disappearance of the youthful monster and his predicted reappearance as the basis of the schism which took the Persian's name. Later a second Persian, called Hamza, and surnamed al-Hādi, or The Guide, wrote a number of sacred books which are said to form the basis of the Druze religion. These books are available to scholars. They emphasize the unity of God and claim that He has been reincarnated in human form some seventy times. They also profess a belief in the transmigration of souls. Despite the disclosure of the contents of al-Hādi's books, all the Druze secrets have not been revealed; the essential rituals are said to be transmitted only by word and by example.

Between Alexandretta and Latakiya, in the mountains of northern Syria which form an extension of Mount Lebanon, live an equal number of equally deviant sectaries, the Nuṣairis. They are farmers and herdsmen, living in isolation. When they come into the city, they too practice deception, when necessary. They too have their own sacred book and divide themselves into three stages of initiation. They believe in a trinity in which ʿAlī is God; Muḥammad, whom ʿAlī created, is the Name; and a certain Salman al-Farisi, the Door. They are divided into four subsects, three of which variously identify these individuals with the sun and moon and the lion, while the fourth sect worships the air, considering God invisible.

The Druzes and Nuṣairis speak Arabic. The other two sects, Yezidi and ʿAlī Ilāhi, are Kurdish. The Yezidis are a group of farmers who occupy Jabal Sinjar in the very northeastern part of Syria, while others live in villages in ʿIraqi territory, and even in Soviet Armenia. They are divided into laity and clergy. As with other Kurds the laymen include both nobles and commoners, a somewhat fluid stratification (which will be explained later). The clergy are in six classes, at the top of which are the shaikhs, all descended from their founder, Shaikh ʿAd, and over this body is the chief shaikh. These priests wear white garments. Next is a second grade of priests called *pirs* (Persian for "old man," and hence "holy man"), who wear black. Third are the faqirs, who are mendicant brothers, often shaikhs and pirs who have renounced the world. The fourth class is that of the *ḳavals,* who rank on the same level as the faqirs. These are the executive officers of the shaikhs who collect taxes and gifts from the villages and serve as circuit judges. When the matters under dispute are beyond their powers of decision they refer them to the shaikhs and report the answer. Fifth down the line, and fourth in rank, are the *ankhans,* the ordinary clergy, and sixth the "Servants of Shaikh ʿAd's Hearth," who act as curates and temple janitors.

Wholly apart from this religious hierarchy, the Yezidis, like other Kurds, are organized into tribes and governed in the usual manner. Their religious structure, while more elaborate, parallels the Muslim organization among the other Kurds. The old Ottoman government treated the Yezidis with the same tolerance and laissez-faire shown to other autonomous and self-contained minorities which would be difficult to subdue and hardly worth the effort. Generally these various heretics and schismatics have developed hierarchies of some elaboration for a good reason. They are ethnically homogeneous closed corporations, living apart. The hierarchies serve as a substitute for the mosaic system in force elsewhere, or vice versa.

With the Yezidis, the office of shaikh is hereditary, but goes only to the sons who bother to become instructed. Apparently there is much to be learned, including a veneration for the hearth of Shaikh ʿAd which is their holy of holies; a Zoroastrian-style dualism between the forces of Good and Evil, God and Satan; a reverence for the four elements of earth, water, air, and fire; and a ceremonial greeting of the sun at daybreak. Satan, apparently, heads the pantheon, followed by seven standard Semitic archangels; Christ, risen to heaven, who will someday return; and a host of other deities, some of whom seem to be departmental.

The Yezidi dogma includes an absolute belief in God and in his infinite love, the worship of his prophets and servants, filial piety, neighborly love, and mutual aid, alms to the poor, and the equality of all men before God. It forbids pork and blue clothing and restricts relations with Muslims. The Yezidis believe in the immortality of the soul, the efficacy of graveyard sacrifices to their ancestors, and the ability of the latter to intercede with God on their behalf. One can detect not only ancient Iranian elements in this complex of beliefs, along with elements taken from Christianity and Islam, but also the shadow of a survival of practices reminiscent of the paganism of the native peoples of the Caucasus, outside our present field.

Last, possibly least, and certainly least known of these separate religious groups are the so-called ʿAlī-Allahis (ʿAlī Ilāhis) or Ahl al-Ḥaqq, meaning in order, ʿAlī is God, and People of the Truth. Their name for themselves, however, is said to be Ahl-i-Allah, or

God's People.[15] According to two contemporary Presbyterian missionaries who have carried on evangelical work among them, they are confined to a few villages in the mountains north of Kermanshah, and are Kurds. According to both Mrs. Bishop and Wilson, whose observations were made sixty years earlier, they include Lurs as well, and Wilson claimed that they were several hundred thousand strong and divided into seven sects.

Since they too practice taqīya, it is not easy to learn much about them. Like the Zoroastrians, they deem light sacred; they also identify it with ʿAlī. They believe in transmigration, with ultimate absorption into the person of the Infinite One. In some of their villages they have two shrines, one for each sex. The village leader is considered holy, healing by touch; his office is hereditary. During religious services they invoke ʿAlī, pray responsively, kiss bread, eat, and then the men sway, whirl, and work themselves into a state of ecstasy. Although not technically Ṣūfi brethren, they have a zikr, which consists of repeating *Yā hū!* (O he!)

In southern Kurdistan they venerate an ancestor associated in some way with King David, to whose shrine, situated in a gorge, they pay visits. Here they offer up sacrifices of animals. They also are said to eat pork. Mrs. Bishop was told that they were once Jewish, and some of the missionaries working in this area today feel that they retain a number of definitely Christian elements in their belief and ritual. The reverence for light, however, is undoubtedly old Persian. A number of them have been converted to Christianity and are members of the Presbyterian community of Kermanshah.

During this discussion of the various marginal, obscure, and even secret religious systems, the reader may have formed the opinion that paganism survives in solution only in these out-of-the-way places. Nothing could be less true. All over the Islamic world, as in many Christian lands, ancient and homely practices form part of the ritual life of illiterate people—on the desert, in the mountains, in the villages, and in the city streets. Saints cure sick children by spitting in their mouths, and childless women spend the night in rustic tombs to attain the power of conception. Blue beads shelter the

[15] Mrs. Isabella (Bird) Bishop, *Journeys in Persia and Kurdistan* (London, 1891), p. 85. S. G. Wilson, *Persian Life and Customs* (New York, 1895), pp. 234-242.

child and the horse from the evil eye, and the mark of Fāṭima's hand on a door protects the house inside. Like Ṣūfism, these practices and devices are part of the equipment needed to maintain equilibrium in a stratified society. They serve their purpose. Many books have been written about them. Many Muslim clerics have preached against them. They still exist and even arise anew, like Our Lady of Fatima across the Strait in what once was a Muslim land.

9 MORE PEOPLES, THE TURKS AND MONGOLS

THE FAITH OF ISLAM already had been formulated and carried to Morocco and India before the last of the great peoples of the Middle East, the Turks, had stepped onto the local stage. They came from the wide grasslands to the north, like the ancestors of the Persians, Afghans, and Hindus in earlier times. To understand the culture of the Turks, and their contributions to Middle Eastern civilization, we must return (see Chapter 5) to a consideration of what went on across those open plains during the Bronze Age. In those days Turks had not been heard of, but their teachers were already in evidence.

These teachers, the Indo-European-speaking peoples, followed a way of life from which some of the simpler elements in our own culture are also derived and which we can reconstruct from several sources. Homer's immortal epic, one of the earliest sources, depicts a three-class society dependent on cattle herding and agriculture, with the smith-carpenter the only technician and a class of priests deriving their income from the care of open-air altars to a galaxy of gods. Kingdoms were small and communication difficult, for aside from the seaways, transport depended on bumpy springless chariots drawn by oxen or mules and, for royal visits and war, by horses. Warriors in Homer's epic used to drive up to the enemy at a gallop, leap out, fight, and leap back in again for the getaway.

Sometime between about 1000 B.C. and the time of Herodotus (born 484 B.C.) the Indo-European-speaking peoples of the northern plains learned to ride astride and to shoot from the saddle with short, sinew-backed bows. This accomplishment, which produced an empire father south, was as revolutionary and as devastating as the invention of the tank in World War I. By its means a resolute commander could organize a mobile force of archers on horseback, sweep across the plains, build up a huge ephemeral empire, and cross the mountain rim into the literate lands of the Middle East. There the warriors could obtain gold, fine garments, and other luxuries that rough plainsmen love, including the luxury of power.

In the spring these plainsmen would drive their herds out onto the open steppes, shifting camp frequently as the grass was exhausted. In the fall they would lead them back to winter quarters, in the fold of the foothills where water from the mountains made haying possible and where grain could be had from dependent villagers. Some, instead, went to the banks of streams, where irrigation water supported other villages and produced the same result. Two social units were produced by these annual shifts: the winter camp of ten to a hundred tents and the summer camp of two or three related households, with servants and slaves. Servants and slaves were needed to do the herding, for freemen were warriors. Their job was to raid and to keep others from doing the same. Raiding brought slaves, and some slaves were women. The Scythians kept portable harems of women in covered wagons, shielded by side curtains from public gaze.

The chief of the winter camp was an absolute lord, for a strong hand is needed to direct migrations and organize raids, as well as to punish those who raid out of turn. He in turn would owe homage to a greater lord, and the greater lord to a king. The king had an army of noble youths, and when the king died he was buried under a huge mound in a special country. In the grave with him was much gold, fashioned into ornaments by the Crimean Greeks, and a number of women and animals slain to accompany him to the other world. Around his mound sat a ring of noble guardsmen, rigid in death on the backs of rigid horses, held up by spears which pinned together man and mount.

Darius the Great led an expedition into the grasslands to rid his northern frontier of this menace. The Scythians appeared in the distance to lure the invaders on, then faded over the horizon, burning fodder and polluting wells as they went. Finally, when the two forces came face to face, Darius sent the king of the Scythians earth and water which meant that they should surrender. The Scythians sent back a bird, a mouse, a frog, and five arrows. While the Persians did not immediately succeed in interpreting these symbols, one Gobryas finally read them as follows:

> Unless, Persians, ye can turn into birds and fly up into the sky, or become mice and burrow into the ground, or make yourself frogs and take refuge in the fens, ye will never escape from this land but will die pierced by our arrows.[1]

[1] Herodotus, *Historia,* I, Bk. IV, 338, § 132.

Since the Persians were unable to fulfill these requirements, the Scythians won. Darius, like Napoleon over two millenniums later, had overextended his supply line and could not feed his troops or animals off the blackened land.

The Scythians invaded Asia Minor, Syria, Iran, and 'Iraq. So later did their kinsmen the Parthians, as related earlier.[2] Scythian-like peoples also extended their domain eastward, over the Altai into Chinese Turkestan and to the borders of the settled provinces of Great China, where their presence is recorded not only in writing but also in images of clay and porcelain. Here the bearded, Nordic-looking plainsmen encountered old populations of Mongoloid peoples, who soon learned the way of the saddle and the short, powerful bow. The grasslands of Mongolia became a breeding ground, just as the lands fringed by the Black and Caspian seas had earlier done, and new nations of mounted archers arose.

The first of these to achieve fame were the Huns. They bothered the Chinese, who defeated them. Turning westward in flight, they rode across the Eurasiatic plain as far as France, only to meet defeat at the Battle of Châlons in 451 A.D. These Huns were racially Mongoloid. We know this from contemporary accounts and from their skulls dug up in Scyth-like royal graves in Hungary. Their followers, however, were drawn from every land between China and France and represented a racial medley. The language of the Huns was an early form of Turkish.

Turkish is a branch of the Ural-Altaic family of languages, which contains a primary split between Uralic, meaning several kinds of Finnish, Magyar, and a number of Siberian languages, and Altaic, meaning Turkish, Mongol, Tungus, and Samoyedic. The Uralic languages are spoken by peoples who, when first known, were racially European, and the Altaic by peoples who were, at their first historic appearance, Mongoloid, although some of them, like the Ottoman Turks, are today racially members of the white group.

During the seventh century A.D. Turkish tribes began infiltrating the grasslands and desert borders east of the Caspian, and by the tenth century they were firmly in possession of the grasslands of the present Turkoman country. At this time, under the influence of the Muslims in the great cities of Turkestan, the Turkish tribes were converted to Sunni Islam, a faith which they have since maintained. As Muslims, some of these tribes, collectively known as Ghuzz, in-

[2] See Chap. 5, p. 80.

vaded Asia Minor, where they set up a kingdom, the Saljuq sultanate of Rum. Few of the subjects of this kingdom were Ghuzz, for the land already had been fully inhabited by Christians, including Greeks, Armenians, and Syrians, and by Kurds. The process of assimilation which has since made Anatolia Turkish in speech as well as in government must have begun at that time.

In the thirteenth century Jenghiz Khan's Mongols took over Khwarizm, as the land of oases and cities in the present Russian Turkestan was then called, moved westward to Sarrakhs and Nishapur in present-day Iran, over to the present-day Azerbaijan, and into Armenia and Georgia, which they conquered. From here, with the help of Armenians and Georgian cavalry, in 1258 A.D., they conquered Baghdad and brought the ʿAbbasid caliphate to an end. Like those of Cyrus and Darius in earlier times, the Mongol forces consisted of a bodyguard of nobles from the ruler's own people and varied units drawn from the peoples they had conquered. Among these foreign legions were many Turks; in fact the Turks far outnumbered the Mongols.

After the fall of Baghdad the Mongols set up Tabriz as their administrative capital for the Middle East. This city grew to be the greatest East-West trade center of its time, replacing Baghdad, and it was the gate of entry for Chinese goods and Chinese cultural influences. Its language was Azerbaijani Turkish, which like the ʿOsmanli tongue became filled with Arabic and Persian words. Turkish speech became the common tongue of villagers from the Caucasus to below Hamadan. That some of these farmers were actually Turks is possible, since the Mongols and their Turkish followers pursued a scorched earth policy, massacring people by the thousands; after eight centuries men still bristle in ʿIraq and Iran at the mention of the name of Hulagu, the destroyer of Baghdad, the son of Tuli and grandson of Jenghiz Khan.

The Mongol dynasty in Iran and ʿIraq lasted until 1499 A.D. Although today it is but an ugly memory, it produced some lasting results. A few hundreds of thousands of racially recognizable Mongols still live in villages in eastern Iran and western Afghanistan. Known in the former as Berberis and in the latter as Hazara, they are now a peaceful people, Shīʿa Muslims and speakers of Persian, acting as professional servants in the cities and towns.

A far greater result was the establishment of the Ottoman sultanate as a result of the fall of the Saljuq kingdom of Rum at Mongol hands; a tribe of Anatolian Turks, under their leader 'Osman, began their steady rise to power which in a few centuries brought them the Caliphate of Islam and temporal dominion over the Arab world. A less tangible result was the increase of trade and exchange of personnel between China and the Middle East, with the establishment of actual Chinese craftsmen at Tabriz. What this did for the ceramics and textile industries, and for the development of architecture and pictorial art, has been covered too well elsewhere to need repetition here.

The principal contribution of the Turks and Mongols to Islamic Middle Eastern civilization lay in the field of government, but to understand this we must fit it into their over-all cultural picture, which may be introduced by a few excerpts from contemporary accounts. When first seen, the Turks and Mongols affected their viewers with fear and revulsion. An early Armenian writer[3] says that the first Mongols:

> . . . were terrible to look at and indescribable, with large heads like a buffalo's, narrow eyes like a fledgling's, a snub nose like a cat's, projecting snout like a dog's, narrow loins like an ant's, short legs like a hog's, and by nature with no beards at all. With a lion's strength they have voices more shrill than an eagle. They appear where least expected.

(What the Mongols thought of the physical appearance of the Armenians is not recorded.)

This excursion into physical anthropology explains one of the secrets of the success of the Turks and Mongols. The Mongoloid physique was something new to Persians, Arabs, and Armenians, whom it struck with horror. Unable to explain these visitors on the Old Testament basis of the sons of Ham, Shem, and Japheth, they were inclined to consider them both less and more than human.

Before they became Muslims the Turanians also failed to wash, and Ibn Faḍlān, describing the Ghuzz of the tenth century,[4] states that Muslims traveling among them were forced to perform their

[3] Robert P. Blake and Richard N. Frye, "*History of the Nation of the Archers,* by Grigor of Akanc," *Harvard Journal of Asiatic Studies,* XII, Nos. 3, 4 (1949), 269-399 [1-131]. This quotation is found in chap. 3, p. 295 [p. 27].

[4] R. P. Blake and R. N. Frye, "Notes on the *Risala* of Ibn-Faḍlan," *Byzantine Metabyzantina,* I, Pt. 2 (1949), 7-37.

postcopulatory ablutions in secret, lest the Turks think they were bewitching them with water. The diarist admired their aversion to pederasty and adultery, and their punishment of adulterers by tearing them apart (tying them between the limbs of two trees bent toward each other). The immodesty of their unveiled women shocked him deeply, although it did not impair his accuracy as a reporter, as the following passage will illustrate.

> One day we stopped off with one of them and were seated there. The man's wife was present. As we conversed, the woman uncovered her pudenda and scratched it, and we saw her. Then we veiled our faces and said, "I beg God's pardon." Her husband laughed and said to the interpreter, "Tell them we uncover it in your presence so that you may see it and be abashed, but it is not to be attained. This, however, is better than when you cover it up and yet it is reachable."[5]

Three centuries later most of the Turks had become Muslims of whom in general even Ibn Faḍlān might have approved, but the Mongols perpetrated further insults of a much more serious character. Grigor of Akanc who described the rape of Baghdad by the Mongols states in one passage that "Hulagu Khan was very good, loving Christians, the church, and priests."[6] In another he tells how Hulagu had the caliph of Baghdad thrown in jail without food or water for three days. At the end of this rigorous fast the caliph was brought before him. The caliph angrily demanded food and drink, at which Hulagu had a plate of gold set before him, declaring that if the caliph had sent him the gold earlier, he would not now have to eat it.[7]

After throwing the caliph to the Mongol soldiers to be killed, Hulagu conceived still another humiliation. Grigor reports:

> He [Hulagu] loved the Christians so much that he took pigs for the one yearly tribute from the Armenians—100,000 shoats, and he sent two thousand pigs to every Arab city, and ordered Arab swineherds appointed to wash them every Saturday with a piece of soap, and in addition to give them fodder every morn-

[5] *Ibid.*, p. 14 [MS p. 21].
[6] Blake and Frye, *"History of the Nation of the Archers,"* p. 341 [73].
[7] *Ibid.*, pp. 333-334 [65-67].

> ing, and at evening to give the pigs almonds and dates to eat. Every Arab man, were he great or small, who did not eat the flesh of swine was decapitated. So he honored the Arabs.[8]

Another point that Grigor makes repeatedly is that actually the Armenian and Georgian cavalry won Baghdad for the Mongols. If true, this could have fostered little sweetness and light between the Muslims and their Christian neighbors to the north, whose very participation in this episode must have seemed unpleasant enough. Even more harmful than either the sack of Baghdad or this Viking-like piece of pleasantry was the Mongols' destruction of the network of ancient canals between the Tigris and Euphrates rivers, turning farm lands into desert. From this ʿIraq has never fully recovered.

From these excerpts two things are clear: the Turks and Mongols differed profoundly from the Muslims in the basic symbols of daily life, and they were much more strictly organized. Individualists almost to the point of anarchy, the Arabs had, by the thirteenth century, produced no hierarchies or complex institutions. The clerical offices of the ʿAbbasids were staffed by Persians and Aramaic-speaking Christians, guards recruited from the Turks settled in northern ʿIraq and Anatolia. The destruction of Baghdad placed the already divergent realms of Syria, Egypt, North Africa, and Spain even farther out on their respective limbs. The time for a new empire could not have been riper, and the ʿOsmanli Turks—Sunni Muslims who had learned to wash and to say their prayers, and whose faces, through wholesale mixture with more familiar-looking peoples, no longer chilled the hearts of the faithful—were on hand and ready to take over.

They were ready because they retained the basic system of organization which their ancestors had brought from the grasslands and which the same remote ancestors had learned from the Eastern brethren of the Scythians. As with other peoples, their smallest unit of society was the family, but their families were large and varied. A rich herdsman might have any number of wives, many of whom had been taken in war. When he died his eldest son inherited the harem, except for his own mother. There was no question of succession nor any of inheritance. Everything went by primogeniture, so that fortunes and positions of authority were kept intact, as with the British and most other European aristocracies, and unlike the Arab system

[8] *Ibid.*, p. 343 [75].

where sons share alike and two daughters equal one son and where uccession is by election and a scramble for power.

Next to the family comes the *ulu,* a group based on those who winter together. As the population grows these ulus divide and subdivide, and each obtains a chief. As with sons in a family the ulus are graded by seniority, and in a tribe the chief of the oldest ulu is he *beg.* These chiefs belong to noble families, and their daughters are noble ladies who ride and hunt with the men and who have been known to manage the affairs of their husbands in widowhood. The nobles exact a tribute from common men, while nobles and commoners alike own slaves. Among the commoners some are craftsmen, and the principal and most honored craft is ironworking, combined with carpentry, the only craft recorded for the earliest known Indo-Europeans.

Although the word of the tribal chief is absolute and his punishments ingenious and awe inspiring, he does not rule in an arbitrary fashion. When important events arise he calls a council of freemen, at which each has the right to speak. Only after long debate and a thorough airing of all issues does he make his decision. Once it has been made, however, he expects all to follow him to the death.

Even more important events may bring a council of tribes into being, for the system is flexible; just as ulus can grow out of ulus, so supertribes can grow from tribes, and from supertribes, empires. From a meeting of begs may issue rivalries and combats, and the pooling of loyalties under a khan. This khan holds together his far-flung empire through the same general device as the ancient Persians, with its system of inspections and counterchecks, facilitated by rapid communication through the maintenance of post-horse stations with professional riders. Such an empire can collapse as quickly as it has arisen, if the crisis which brought it into being has passed and if the command falls into weak hands. The tribes, however, will remain, for the crisis which holds them together is perennial, seasonal, and economic—the need for order in the search for grass.

When the Turks and Mongols conquered they were as ruthless at first impact as our early sources reported. After they had devastated and depopulated a region, however, the Turks, at least, caused some of the towns and villages to be rebuilt, and settled them with new or surviving inhabitants, giving them to deserving veterans in fief. In return for half the produce, the descendants of these veterans were bound to military service on call and in some cases to bring along a fixed number of men. Thus a new aristocracy, one of landowners, arose in the Turko-Mongol wake. It was new in personnel. In some of the lands which the Turks conquered it was also an innovation. In Persian-held lands, however, it was as old as the Persian aristocracy which had been established on the same lines.

Although the Turks became devout Sunnis, their devotion did not prevent their retention of parts of their old oral legal system, which was indeed necessary to maintain their division into classes, and their political concepts. First to go, of course, were the outer symbols of their old religion. This bore a striking resemblance to Zoroastrianism in that it recognized two opposing spiritual forces, one of goodness and light and warmth, and the other of evil and darkness and cold, the summer and winter seasons of the northern plains. The Lord of Light lived in the east, whence the sun rose and the Turks had come; the Lord of Darkness in the west. Each had his company of winged spirits, which helped men or brought them sickness. Other symbols were images of felt, carried around in carts or hung over the men's and women's sides of the yurt, and over the kumiss butt next to the door.

The practitioners of religion were shamans, expert at showmanship—sleight of hand, ventriloquism, and dramatic dancing. By their chanting and gyrations they worked themselves into a state of ecstasy, during which they communicated with the Spirit of Light if they were white shamans, or the Lord of Darkness if they were black ones. In the spring priests of the white fraternity sacrificed horses to the Lord of the East, in the fall black shamans did the same to the Lord of the West. After the conversion of the Turks, this shamanism was rerouted into several channels, particularly into the Ṣūfi brotherhoods, which at the time were probably stronger and more popular in Anatolia than anywhere else. Here arose the whirling dervishes and the monastic Bektāshi order, while the sleight-of-hand and ventriloquism element survived in companies of performers who wandered from village to village attracting crowds in the open spaces outside the gates. The old Turkish habit of erecting high Scythian-style mounds over the tombs of their chiefs was abandoned, along with multiple horse sacrifices, although some Turkomans today bury their dead in the sides of ancient tumuli (hindering excavation) and kill an occasional horse.

One must not forget that the rise of the Turks took place during

1. A Descendant of the Prophet, a Khunik Sayyid

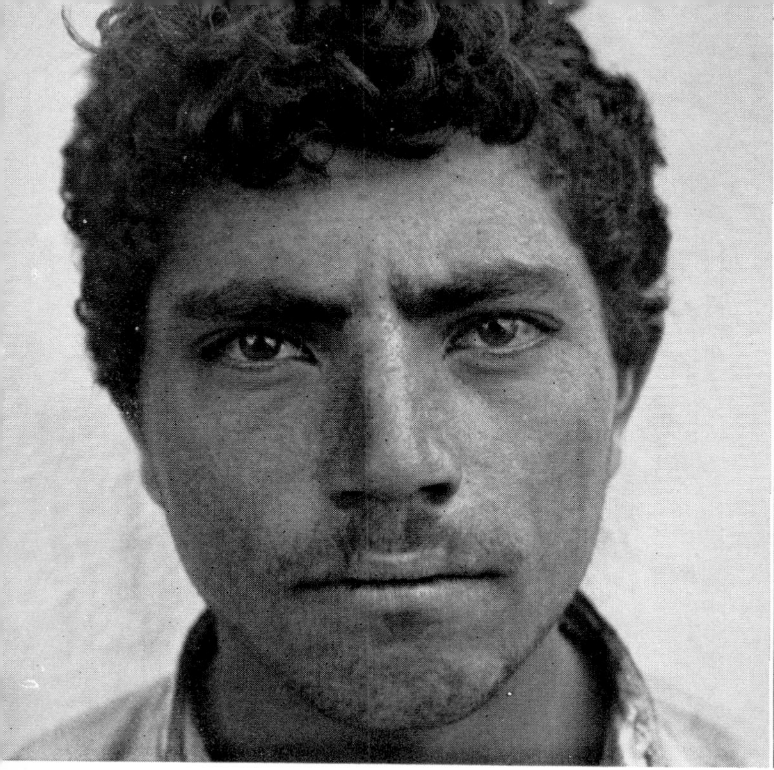

2. Non-Mediterranean Types:

A young Kurdish warrior

A Ṣā'id of Zabol

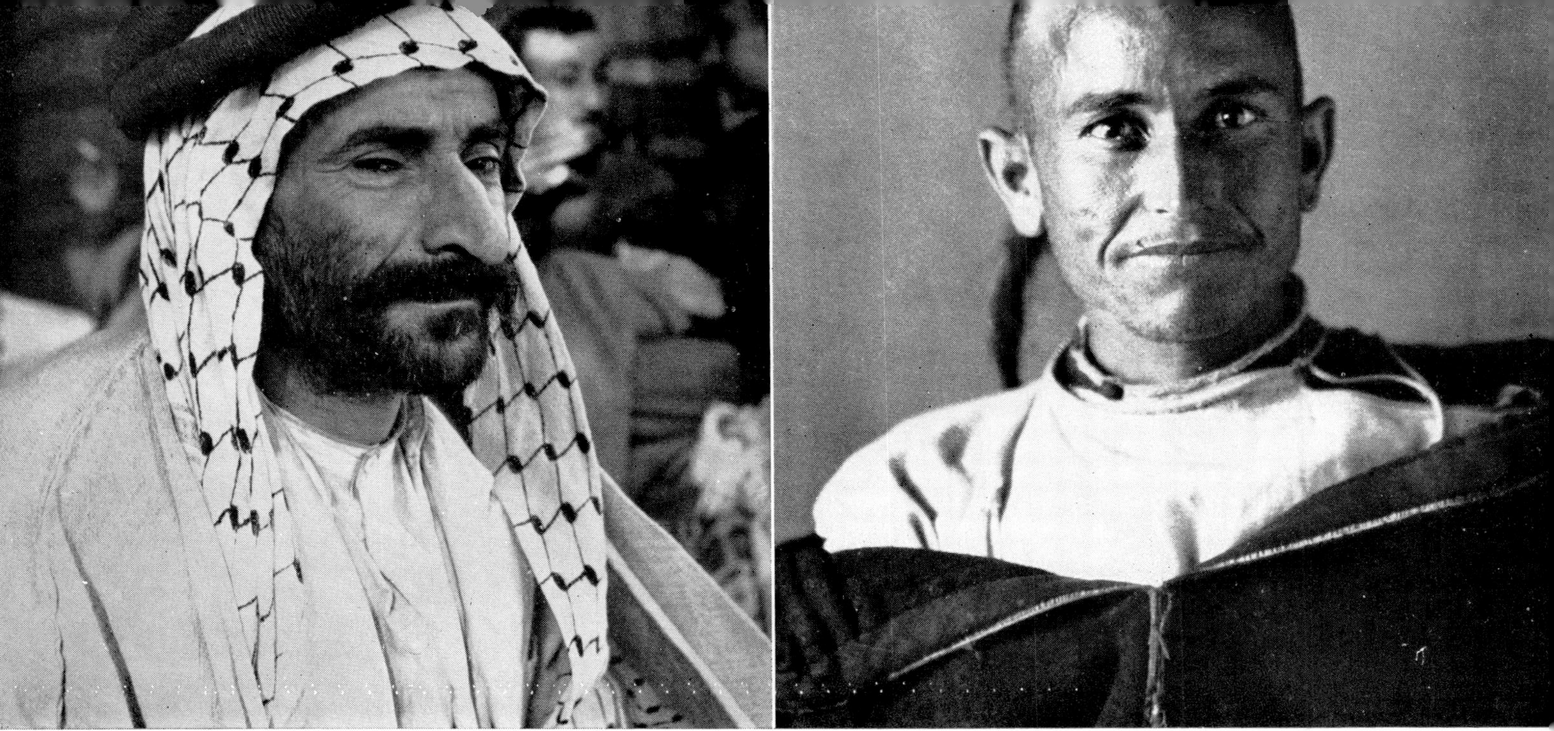

3. Mediterranean Types:

A Badāwi

A Riffian

4. Of Pride and Humility:

A Shikkak Kurd in tribal headdress

Three old cronies, Jewish Quarter, Ṣanʿā

5. Of Heathendom:
three Kafirs of the Hindu Kush and their ancestral statues *(Courtesy of the Danish National Museum, Copenhagen, and Dr. Halfdan Siiger)*

6. Mongoloids and Negroids:

A Yamut Turkoman

A Ḥarratīn youth from the Draʿa

7. The Environment:

The Arabian desert (*Courtesy of the Arabian American Oil Company*)

A summer pasture, Moroccan Middle Atlas

8. The Free Village of Khunik, Khorasan, Iran

9. a. The Mediterranean Landscape, Lebanon
(Courtesy of Ivan Dmitri for American Export Lines)

b. Oasis Irrigation
(Courtesy of the Arabian American Oil Company)

10. Housing:
Khorasan: domed houses with ventilators

Arabia: a Badāwi tent
(Courtesy of the Arabian American Oil Company)

Gurgan Plain, Yamut: a Turkoman yurt

11. Technology:

(top) The potter's wheel, Safi, Morocco

(bottom) Weaving woolen cloth, Tangier *(Courtesy of W. D. Schorger)*

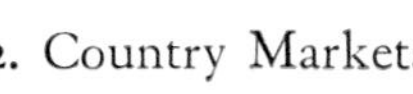

12. Country Markets:

Secret information: Rif

Butcher inflating goat before skinning: Shluh

13. Social Classes, Fez:

Two *tājirs* and an Idrīsite *sharīf*

A retail merchant, potter's *sūq*

14. a. Shammar Warriors atop Nippur Mound, Watching Their Flocks
(Courtesy of the University Museum)

b. The Camel, Baalbek, Lebanon
(Courtesy of W. D. Schorger)

15. The Ship and the Caravan:

Caulking a *būm*, Hodeida

Inside a caravanserai, ʿIraq *(Courtesy of the University Museum)*

16. The Feast of the ʿAissāwa, at Meknes, 1926:
the fantasia—powderplay (last public performance)

the height of the Crusades and that beyond the din of battle many opportunities were offered for cultural exchange. The Turks, the Persians, and the Kurds all had a rigid class system in which armed horsemen formed an elite, and although less formally organized, the Arabs had a similar tradition. The concept of chivalry was no stranger to the Muslims; the celebrated exchanges of mutual courtesy between Richard the Lionhearted and the Kurdish chieftain Saladin (Ṣalāḥ ad-Dīn, or The Welfare of the Faith) serve to illustrate the fact that the obligations and delicacies of knighthood were known to both sides. Parallel origins and mutual growth may well explain this similarity.

Among the Anatolian Turks chivalry took on an additional aspect, the development of associations within the cities, of men who called themselves *Ahl al-Futuwwa,* or People of Virtue.[9] The members of these brotherhoods (they called themselves brothers) were not nobles but young unmarried artisans and merchants, who pooled their resources and lived together. During the day the members worked at different trades, and at night each brought his pay to the chief. Their hospice was elaborately furnished. If guests were at hand, the brothers entertained them lavishly. Sometimes rival groups in the same city went to great lengths to win guests away from each other. Ibn Baṭṭūṭa received and described their hospitality; he states that in "towns that are not the residence of a sultan one of the Young Brothers acts as governor, exercising the same authority and appearing in public with the retinue as a king."[10]

These youth-movement members believed in "manliness, they abstain from injury, give without stint, and make no complaint."[11] They wore special insignia consisting of fancy trousers, and the investiture of a novice with these trousers was a solemn rite. The brotherhoods were neither guilds nor Ṣūfi chapters but resembled more the rifle companies of at least one modern Muslim city (as will be explained in Chapter 14) and also the *zurkhané* (gymnasium) of the Persians. Whatever their origin, relationship, or fate, they served a purpose in the social fabric of the Muslim cities of the early Turkish Empire and were tied into the whole complex of chivalry which the Crusaders shared with their Muslim adversaries. Historically

[9] H. A. R. Gibb and Harold Bowen, *Islamic Society and the West: Islamic Society in the Eighteenth Century* (London, 1950), I, Pt. I, 59, 286.

[10] Ibn Baṭṭūṭa, *Travels in Asia and Africa, 1325-1354,* p. 131.

[11] *Ibid.,* pp. 125-127.

they served as a springboard for other kinds of institutions which helped hold Muslim society together, in which role they represent a Turkish contribution to the over-all institutional picture (unless scholars find the contrary). Whatever else one may say about the early Turks, no one can deny that they injected a breath of fresh air into a system which had reached its prime and stood slightly uncertain about the future, as well as giving it a link with the greener lands of Europe and the Far East.

10 DIFFERENCES, INHERITED AND ACQUIRED

IN OUR AMERICAN VERSION of the modern Western culture, we are under great pressure to look, act, and think alike. No matter where our grandparents came from, or what race we belong to, we dress alike, comb our hair in the same general fashion, and in our conversations avoid specific references to each other in terms of race, religion, or ethnic origin. Many newspapers, for example, have definite rules about identifying the race or religion of a person apprehended for a crime, either by picture or by word. Our cultural system functions most smoothly on this basis. (This tendency has been carried so far that it is difficult to have a purely scientific, objective book on race published or reviewed, while there are many books decrying race as a "myth.")

In the old Middle Eastern culture the opposite situation prevailed. There the ideal was to emphasize not the uniformity of the citizens of a country as a whole but a uniformity within each special segment, and the greatest possible contrast between segments. The members of each ethnic unit feel the need to identify themselves by some configuration of symbols. If by virtue of their history they possess some racial peculiarity, this they will enhance by special haircuts and the like; in any case they will wear distinctive garments and behave in a distinctive fashion. Walking through the bazaar you have no trouble identifying everyone you meet, once you have learned the sets of symbols. These people want to be identified. If you know who they are, you will know what to expect of them and how to deal with them, and human relations will operate smoothly in a crowded space.

Obviously the mosaic system is best suited for a civilization in which trades require a maximum of skill, taught from father to son, and a minimum of organizational complexity. Our unitary system is necessary in a civilization in which the greatest skill goes into the making of the machinery for production and into the handling of human beings in a large and complex economic institution. It is the designer, the toolmaker, and the executive who must have consummate skill, not the individual workman. Individual workmen are drawn from many ethnic groups, religious communities, and racial populations. To keep them working together peacefully and harmoniously is our ideal. The Middle Eastern ideal is to have a streetful of small, independent shops, and in each shop a group of three or four highly skilled men, all kin, all brought up in a single tradition, and all doing the same thing at once. In the political field the exaggeration of differences symbolizes and reinforces a kind of internationalism which modern nationalism cannot tolerate.

This discourse has two purposes. The first is to demonstrate why the Middle Eastern peoples emphasize visual differences between groups, just as they persist in speaking their private languages and worshiping God in their various ways. The second is to point out that attitudes toward racial and cultural differences and degrees of uniformity are themselves culturally conditioned; that our own rather violent swing in the direction of uniformity is a requirement of our particular cultural pattern, and hence possesses a relative rather than absolute value. Each attitude is "right," in its own setting. A third attitude, the objective scientific study of race and of culture, however unpopular, is "right" in any setting, for only through the truth can freedom and justice to all men be ultimately achieved.

The physical differences which Middle Easterners choose to emphasize are partly inherited and partly acquired. Geneticists know that we inherit not specific features but capacities for performance and development, and that these capacities trigger and limit each other, in a regular order through the life of the individual. The extent to which individual capacities are attained depends on nutrition, exercise, and other culturally determined forces. In our country where nutrition and exercise are more or less equal, and where medical care is for all, certain traits level out. The son of an undersized Sicilian couple may be as tall as his neighbor, whose lanky parents came from Ireland. The flat-headed Albanian's son has as rounded an occiput as the son of the bun-headed Englishman. In the Middle East differences in nutrition continue to produce differences in stature, and cradling practices differences in head form.

Overlooking momentarily these culturally acquired exaggerations of nature, we discover first that Middle Easterners do vary in race. Our area, from Morocco to Afghanistan, is the homeland and cradle of the Mediterranean race. Mediterraneans are found also in Spain, Portugal, most of Italy, Greece, and the Mediterranean islands, and in all these places, as in the Middle East, they form the major genetic element in the local populations. In a dark-skinned and finer-boned form they are also found as the major population element in Pakistan and northern India.

The Sumerians were Mediterraneans skeletally. So were the ancient Egyptians, the Babylonians, the Children of Israel, and the Arabs of the early Islamic period whose skeletons I had the privilege of measuring at Nippur. A Mediterranean is a white man of variable stature—as whites go, usually short to medium; his bones are light, but strongly marked for muscle attachments if these muscles have been well developed through use. His legs are relatively long compared to his trunk, and his hands and feet rather small. His chest is relatively flat, his neck of medium length, his head of medium size, long-oval in shape with parallel sides; his face is small and delicate, with only slight bony ridges over the eyes. The upper part of his face is large in proportion to the lower part, so that when he is old his nose looks large for his jaw. Of all human beings the Mediterranean has the most human, the most highly evolved, masticatory apparatus. His teeth are small, and so are the muscles that operate his jaw. His face is narrow, and his nose consequently is often prominent when compared to the lower-bridged and flatter noses of wider or longer-jawed races in Europe and other parts of Africa and Asia. The Mediterranean man is a relatively hairy fellow. His head is covered with a heavy growth of straight, wavy, or ringleted hair, usually fine in texture; rarely does the true Mediterranean go bald. His eyebrows are full, often meeting over the nose. His beard develops throughout adult life. While it is not the heaviest beard of all mankind, it is often a close runner-up. His body hair also increases throughout life and individually varies greatly in quantity.

As a rule his skin is some shade of white, from pink or peaches-and-cream to a light brown. Skin color should always be taken on some unexposed part of the body. Among Middle Easterners this is simple, because they cover as much of the body as is consistent with their work. The exposed skin color may be a dark brown, while the skin of the underarm is ten shades lighter. (The sun shines brightly in the Middle East.) While fair-skinned people are to be seen, they live chiefly in shaded bazaars and government offices, whence they rarely emerge into the dazzling light of day.

The Mediterranean's hair is usually black or dark brown, while his whiskers may reveal a few strands of red or even blond. Blond hair may be seen, but it is the exception. Its presence does not require some invasion of Goths or Scyths or the miscegenation of Crusaders. One of the characteristics of the Mediterranean race is a minority tendency toward blondism. This is seen much more frequently in the eyes, since blond hair, which appears in infants, usually darkens as the hair coarsens with age.

Among Mediterraneans every shade of eye color appears. Coal black is exceptional, a dark or medium brown most common. Nearly a fourth of any sample, however, will have blue, gray, or green eyes, usually mixed with brown in the iris pattern. Eyes do not darken with age; hence the greater prevalence of light eyes rather than blond hair among the adult. Like pink skin, blue eyes and blond hair appear most often among people whose work or social status keeps them indoors. Descendants of the Prophet, courtiers, and wealthy merchants are more often blond than farmers or camel drivers. In my opinion this does not mean that blonds are in any way superior to brunets, in the Middle East or elsewhere. It rather indicates that in a hot, brightly illuminated environment blonds are at a disadvantage when out of doors. Those who can manage it gravitate toward work in shaded quarters; furthermore the natural selection that may operate against them in the field and desert would fail to limit their increase in the shade. Middle Eastern urban civilization may thus have produced artificially an environment comparable to the Baltic fog, from which the Nordic emerged.

Who, then, are these Mediterraneans? Nearly all the Arabs, practically all the oriental Jews, most of the inhabitants of Egypt whatever their religion, most of the Berbers, most of the Persians proper, many of the Kurds, most of the Baluchis, a large number of the Afghans, and many of the Turks of Anatolia and Azerbaijan. Nearly eighty per cent of the individuals living in the Middle East and participating in its civilization (excluding Europeans) are Mediterraneans of one variety or another; of the other twenty per cent at least half probably show an increment of Mediterranean genes. The Mediterranean race, then, is indigenous to, and the principal element in, the Middle East, and the greatest concentration of a highly evolved Mediterranean type falls among two of the most ancient Semitic-speaking peoples, notably the Arabs and the Jews. (Although it may please neither party, this is the truth.)

The Mediterraneans occupy the center of the stage; their areas of greatest concentration are precisely those where civilization is the oldest. This is to be expected, since it was they who produced it and it, in a sense, that produced them. In the more remote and inaccessible parts of the Middle East, however, in high mountain valleys, on the far side of the desert, and in impenetrable swamps, other kinds of white men are still to be found as elements in local populations. In some if not all cases, they are survivors of earlier preagricultural peoples. Their continued existence is a function of geography.

In 1922 the Western world was first made abundantly aware of the westernmost of these survivors through the extreme bravery and warlike ability of the Riffian tribesmen of Morocco against first Spain and then France, under the leadership of Sīdī Muḥammad ben ʿAbd el-Krīm al-Khattābi, now a resident of Cairo. Between 1924 and 1928 the author had the good fortune to visit Morocco four times for the express purpose of studying the racial characteristics of ʿAbd el-Krīm's warriors, a task which was successful enough to permit a working evaluation of their racial position.

Like all other Berbers, the Riffians include standard Mediterraneans in their tribal populations. Among these Mediterraneans the incidence of elements of blond hair and blue eyes is a bit higher than the usual twenty-five per cent. I attribute the slight excess to several factors: isolation in a cloudy and cool mountain habitat and mixture with an older strain. Concentrated in the more isolated tribes in the central Rif, the older strain is characterized by individuals of stocky build, with large heads, broad faces, low orbits, large teeth, and broad noses. While variable in pigmentation, these individuals, who look like Irishmen, run to red hair, green eyes, and freckles. They cannot be explained by any historical invasion of North Africa, real or fancied; the bones of their preagricultural ancestors have been excavated from North African soil in sufficient quantity to confirm the local antiquity of the genes which produce them. A broad head, a wide face, a snub nose, freckles, and other individual traits derived from this racial combination may be seen in other Riffians and in other Berber populations. Green eyes, for example, are common among the Middle Atlas Beraber (as anyone who was with the Goums in the last war may remember). Fair hair has been recorded from the Kabyles in Algeria, but actual statistical work shows them to be almost entirely Mediterranean with only a slight excess of blondism.

Our next stop on the way east is the mountains of Lebanon and

Syria. The Lebanese and the Druzes have a different appearance from the Arabs whose language they speak. Many, but not all, Lebanese and Druzes are stocky, long-trunked, short-legged, barrel-chested people, with short necks, broad heads, and broad faces. Their hands and feet are large and particularly wide, at the opposite human pole from the tapering extremities of the Bedawin. They run to dark brown hair and light brown eyes, and are often very hairy, with the tendency of hairy men to go bald at an early age. They look more like Bavarians and Abruzzi Italians than like Arabs. They are not Mediterraneans at all but Alpines. The populations of which this extreme type is part are genetically composed of Alpine and Mediterranean elements, in varying proportions. One can, of course, find individuals of straight Mediterranean type in these populations, but the majority show some combination of traits derived from both extremes. Thousands of these people have migrated to America and have been studied both here and in their homelands. They have produced a number of distinguished anthropologists as well as historians.[1]

The next step eastward takes us to the northern Zagros Mountains and their northern extension in the Armenian highlands. The most numerous and characteristic population of the Zagros is that of the Kurds, who are racially as well as culturally the eastern counterpart of the Riffians. Like the Riffians they inhabit high valleys and mix little with outsiders. Like the Riffians they are Mediterraneans in the majority, but of a heavier bone structure than most of the plainsmen and citydwellers. A few more than to be expected are blond, and the deep jaw and larger teeth characteristic of some northern Europeans is also found here. Now and then, however, an individual appears who may be compared to the broad-faced Riffian; he is not tall, but quite broad and robust. His neck is short and thick, his head large but not round; his face is broad, his jaw heavy, and his upper lip long. This man does not differ in pigmentation from the rest, nor is he particularly hairy. He again represents the survival of an ancient population preserved in his mountains by an act of geography. His heaviness of bone and particularly of jaw has undoubtedly influenced the physique of his more typically Medi-

[1] I refer in particular to Dr. Afif Tannous, whose services have been of incalculable benefit to the United States government, to Professor Philip Hitti of Princeton University, and to Professor N. A. Faris of the American University of Beirut.

terranean cousins. In a series of thirty-four Shikak Kurds whom I measured in 1949, all but two had green eyes of a single homogeneous hue. Of the two one had blue eyes, the other dark brown. The brown-eyed Kurd was an outsider, the local mulla. Nothing could illustrate better the inbreeding of this population.

Two other populations in this region also show the presence of a broad-headed, heavily built strain—the "Assyrians" and the Armenians. Darker in skin color as befits their more southerly origin, and dark in hair and eye color as a rule, the Assyrians run to broad faces and snub noses, a combination of Mediterranean with some other, presumably Alpine, strain.

Racially the Armenians are extremely complex and regionally variable. One may see individual Armenians who are blond and look like Nordics; others are perceptibly Mongoloid. The majority, however, are brunet white varying between an Alpine prototype and at least two strains of Mediterranean—a small, fine-boned variety like the Arabs and a heavy-boned, darker-skinned type like the Afghans. The Armenian is characteristically quite hairy, while another Armenian specialty is the high frequency of a large, prominent nose. Some of the Armenian truck drivers whom one sees on the Tabriz run are huge men, and on the whole Armenians are larger and heavier than most of the other peoples among whom they live. (Like the Lebanese and Assyrians, they are most easily measured in America.)

Still moving eastward we come to a fourth refuge area, the swamps at the mouth of the Helmand River, where the so-called "hunters" (*Ṣayyād*)[2] catch fish and fowl alike in their nets, in season. Although many of these hunters are palpably mixed, and others are ordinary Mediterraneans, they include a strain of older vintage, which appears startlingly in rare individuals. These individuals look like nothing in the world more than the "Murrayian" type of Australian aborigine and the hairy Ainu of northern Japan. Broad, thickset, muscular, and hairy, wide faced, and heavy browed, they stand before one calmly, like an apparition from the past. My driver (an Iranian citizen of mixed Armenian and Assyrian ancestry) said to me in Zabol when we first saw these men, "Professor, these are the men you have been digging up in caves." He was not far wrong.

Many of the Persians of Khorasan, and many Afghans and

[2] This word must not be confused with *sayyid,* one of the terms for a descendant of the Prophet.

Pathans across the border, are too big, too bony, and too broad faced to qualify as standard Mediterraneans, although in pigment and in hair form they rate perfectly. In my opinion they represent either an old mixture between the type of hunters and a Mediterranean, or else an evolutionary stage in the progression from hunter to Mediterranean, or both.

This ancient strain is also prominent in the Brahui. Another marginal white group remains to be studied, that of the Kafirs, but they have never been properly measured. They seem to run to an excess of blondism, and probably of archaic features, but this determination rests for the future. In southern Arabia, particularly in the Ḥaḍramaut and Dhufar, a strongly spiral-haired, dark-skinned strain survives which like the hunters of the Helmand reflects population elements in southern India and beyond, and which, in being undifferentiated for heat or cold, may be classed as archaic white. This too needs much more study.

So much for the non-Mediterranean white elements in the Middle East. They are striking in appearance, they are localized in geographical refuge areas, and they characterize sharply a number of special peoples who have moved from their refuges into the cities and towns to take over special occupations. They are more commonly to be found overseas than the majority—Mediterranean peoples—among and between whom they live.

The world of Islam takes in large portions of Africa outside the bounds of the Middle East as we have chosen to describe it, and much of Asia and its fringing islands. Many Negroes and many Mongoloids outside our area are Muslims. This can be studied most clearly by anyone fortunate enough to live in Jidda, the great pilgrim port (very probably as an employee of the State Department or the oil company). A physical anthropologist resident in Jidda could obtain fabulous series from many distant and inaccessible lands. Ideally, of course, this would be the task of a Muslim anthropologist, of which there already are a certain number.

Within the narrow confines of the area covered in this book, however, both black men and Mongoloids live. They are exotic to the region, they are in the minority, and their presence may in all cases be historically explained. Negroes have been introduced into the Middle East by three routes: from the western Sudan to North Africa over the Sahara, down the Nile into Egypt, and across the

Indian Ocean and/or Red Sea by ship. Most of them were so introduced since the spread of Islam to the Sudan and East Africa by Arab traders. Most if not all of them came as slaves. They have filled several needs, of which the following are most notable.

In the oases of the Sahara, in the fetid Tihāma (the coastal plain of the Yemen), and in the sweltering valley of Ḥaḍramaut, African blacks took over agricultural tasks for which white Arabs and Berbers were physically unsuited under conditions of extreme heat and humidity. In the capital cities of Morocco companies of Negro soldiers served as the faithful bodyguards of despotic sultans who could trust no other human beings. In the Sahara, hired Negro guards protected caravans from nomadic raiders. Negro women with their desirable "cool" skins accompanied their Tuareg masters on raiding expeditions and became the first bedfellows of the pubescent sons of Moroccan aristocrats. In Arabia, trusted Negro slaves accompanied their masters everywhere, advised their sons, and fought furiously for their patrons, who fed and clothed them as well as their own children. On the date ships out of Basra and Kuwait, Negroes served as cooks. In harems from Marrakesh to Istanbul and Samarqand, ebony-skinned eunuchs made themselves responsible for the chastity of their masters' wives and concubines, and the Turkish sultans gave some of these black eunuchs high government posts, including governorships. From Morocco to 'Iraq freed slaves and their mixed descendants specialize in a number of occupations, of which blacksmithing is the most common.

It is a common belief in America that the Muslims, and particularly the Arabs, draw much less of a color line than that present in our own country. This belief is not founded on fact. Arabs admire and trust their slaves and often set them free. Muslims of Negro ancestry are as free as anyone else to earn a living, and their lives and property are protected by law to the same extent as anyone else's, but not all kinds of employment are open to Negroes in all Muslim lands. And when it comes to intermarriage, the Arab is indistinguishable from the Southern colonel. No one takes greater pride in his ancestry than an Arab, who (at least in 'Iraq) can obtain a legal judgment against a person falsely accusing him of Negro ancestry.

Slavery has been officially abolished for varying lengths of time in all countries of the Middle East excepting the autonomous Arab states of the peninsula. In some other countries there has been a time lag between abolition and emancipation. In Morocco all a slave need do is declare himself before a government tribunal, and he will be set free. But as recently as World War II there were still some old slaves who did not wish or dare to do this, and an underground slave traffic of small dimensions was still going on. In peninsular Arabia even without emancipation slavery is on the wane; the supply has been notably cut down by the British fleet.

Just as the Negro slave traffic awaited the spread of Muslim missionaries and the traders to Black Africa, so the entry of Mongoloids into the Middle East failed to take place before the rise of the Turks in the tenth century, and the reign of Jenghiz Khan. The earliest Turkish movements penetrated our area. They brought in the Turkomans, who established themselves on the Gurgan plain and who formed a number of isolated enclaves in northern 'Iraq, in the Kirkuk region, and in Syria. In Anatolia itself the Turks became the dominant element in the population, but it was not for several centuries that they rose to the status of most numerous people, through conversion and absorption.

The old Ottoman Empire was built around the mosaic theory, and communities of Greeks, Armenians, Kurds, and other nationalities dotted Anatolia alongside the Turkish areas. Only with the fall of the Ottoman Empire and the modernization of Turkey after World War I did this picture change. Nationalism meant uniformity, and an ethnically Turkish Turkey. Hundreds of thousands of Greeks were exchanged, those Armenians who were not killed left the country by the hundreds of thousands, and the Kurds were made equally unhappy. From the racial standpoint this made little difference. Only partially Mongoloid when they arrived, the Turks had intermarried so extensively with the descendants of their predecessors, with Balkan Christians, and with Caucasians that it is difficult to find an Anatolian Turk today who appears completely Mongoloid. The Turks are Mediterranean plus Alpine, like their neighbors to either side.

Among the Turkomans, however, the old Mongoloid strain is still evident. Despite generations of mixture, the families who consider themselves noble take pride in being the more Mongoloid, which can be seen particularly in the breadth of the face, the prominence of the cheekbones, and in the form of the external eye. A high incidence of blondism also indicates a strong Nordic strain. The Turkish-speakers of Azerbaijan (the seat of the Mongol power in

Iran) fall between the Ottoman Turks to the west and the Turkomans to the east. Most of them look Mediterranean, but are often wider headed and larger jawed. A partially Mongoloid type of eyefold is also common. The same is true of the Qashqai in the southern Zagros.

More pronounced Mongoloid types appear farther east. In the outskirts of Gurgan one will see today a village of virtually pure Mongoloids, Kirghiz who fled the Soviet Union some twenty-five years ago. They are locally employed as carters, and in this short time have become a special people. Other Kirghiz have sought refuge in Afghanistan. The Berberis, Persian-speaking Shī'a villagers who live between Herat and Mashhad, are pure Mongols, said to be leftovers from the days of Jenghiz Khan. They, too, have taken on special jobs, as domestic servants and cooks. Intermediate in Mongoloid intensity between the Turkomans and Kirghiz are the Uzbegs, properly Turkestan people, some of whom inhabit the southern bank of the Amu Darya in Afghanistan, and who form the chief element in the population of the region of Balkh.

The rare traveler to southern Arabia's Ḥaḍramaut Valley quite unexpectedly finds the towns to contain a large number of rather small and fine-boned Mongoloids, in addition to the regular Arab and African types. These are the children of Ḥaḍramauti traders and their Javanese or Malay wives, brought back from the East Indies.

Today Middle Eastern peoples are much more localized than they were several centuries ago, when caravans carried the trade from China to Iran, and from Morocco to Egypt, and from Iran to Syria and Egypt in turn. Persians went to Spain (where among other things, as some believe, they gave the Spaniards the word *Ustéd*), and Andalusians went to India. Unhindered by passport regulations or quotas, a free movement of peoples distributed the genes of Middle Easterners with their technical skills. Even the Christian minorities entered the genetics of the Muslim majority through the harem gates, and those of wealthy Jews did the same through conversion. Much of the uniformity of the Mediterranean race may be due to this re-enforcement of a basic and original similarity.

As if race were not enough, members of the various minorities enhance their peculiarities through artifice. These include some actual alterations of the human physique, intentional or otherwise. If you will look at the back of the head of an old-country Lebanese,—

and its usual baldness will be of help—you will see that it is flat, in a vertical plane. This flatness also appears to bring the vault to a peak, and to tilt the axis of the ears so that they converge toward the lobes. When your victim turns in profile you will see that the distance from earhole to the back of the head is quite short, while that from the earhole to the nose is normal. The nose may often appear to owe some of its projection to the pressure from behind.

This type of head form is produced by cradling the very young. The mother or her helpers swaddle the infant and tie it in a cradle in such a fashion that the shoulders are held down, and while the head is free to move within these limitations, it naturally rests on the back instead of the side. The pillow is hard. The mother can carry this cradle on her back while walking, leaving her hands free to spin wool as she goes. She can set the cradle down on the side of a field, or even hang it from a branch, and her baby is safe while she works. She thus solves the baby-sitter problem by giving her child a flat head. Flat heads of this kind are considered beautiful, and women also mold the baby's skull with their fingers, pressing the forehead and pinching up the nose.

The result is the so-called Armenoid or Dinaric type of head and face, which anthropologists for decades considered the special property of a separate race. Lebanese, Syrians, Druzes, Armenians, Assyrians, some Kurds, Gilakis, Turkomans, Kirghiz, and probably others all do this, and thus exaggerate the physical differences between themselves and the other peoples of the Middle East.

Less permanent but equally conspicuous is the treatment of the hair and beard. Whether Sunni or Shīʿa, the conventional, old-fashioned Muslim who belongs to no special minority or brotherhood has his head shaved at regular intervals and his beard trimmed with the razor. Unless he is an old man, he wears his beard short. There are many variations, however, symbolizing many different situations and conditions. The Badāwi of the Arabian desert, particularly when a young man, wears his hair long and braids it into four "love" locks. Long, unbraided hair is worn by countrymen in the Yemen. The mountain Berbers wear single pigtails, some on the right, some on the left, and others in the middle, and the side chosen indicates basic differences between traditional Berber ancestral stocks. The old-fashioned Persian hairdo is a page-boy bob with the crown shaved and full locks over the ears. The orthodox Jewish coiffure is a head shaven behind, with hair of medium length left over the forehead, and a long curl hanging at the temple in front of each ear.

Full, rather than clipped, beards are *de rigueur* with professional holy men of all persuasions. The members of the Derqāwi sect in North Africa shave the upper lip and let the chin beard grow rampant, and the same is done in the Ḥaḍramaut. (My friend Frederick Wulsin swears that while he was digging at Tureng Tepe in 1932 he saw one of the Turkoman chiefs wearing a beard which started out bifurcated, but below the chin the two strands were braided together, with the combined tail tucked into his shirt.)

Long, unclipped mustaches of the handlebar type are a specialty of the members of the Ṣūfi sect of Gunabad, in Khorasan. They were also popular among the Turks and Armenians but now linger on only in the most marginal reaches of the former Turkish culture area, in Albania and Montenegro. Many of the present-day Armenians and Assyrians of the Middle East affect a miniature mustache under the nostrils only, which they call "Swiss."

One may add to these barbering details the practice of dyeing the hair, and further distinctions are achieved. Among Arabs a hennaed beard indicates a descendant of the Prophet, or at least an extremely holy man. In Iran men henna their head hair out of vanity when it begins to turn white. Women dye blond hair black, and white hair red; they also paint their hands and feet with henna in different designs which indicate marital status or relation to a particular crisis in life. Prostitutes sometimes playfully paint patterns in henna on their clients' hands, to keep them from going home before it wears off.

Berber and Arab women are often tattooed in various distinctive tribal patterns, on the arms, hands, face, neck, body, and legs. Among some of the Middle Atlas Berber tribes of Morocco, the men have a cross tattooed on the end of the nose. Eyebrow plucking is prevalent, as is the use of *k̜oḥl* (antimony) about the eyes—both as a medicament and to give one the large-eyed appearance only recently fashionable in Europe and America. In southern Arabia malachite is employed by women as a green eye-shadow, and everywhere women use some kind of rouge.

Clothing is also distinctive. The headgear employed is ritually important to the Muslim, who like the Jew must be decently covered in any formal situation. The most respectable and conservative head covering is the turban. Ideally it should be large enough, when unwound and spread, to cover its owner's body as a shroud. Under the turban one may wear some type of brimless cap, which may be of felt or of cloth, plain or ornate. If the wearer is a pious man the cap should not contain precious metals or silk. Both the size and the method of winding the turban have special meanings, some quite subtle and denoting conservatism, gaiety, and other personality traits, as well as status, in a general way. Green turbans are reserved for those who have completed the pilgrimage to Mekka and for descendants of the Prophet through his daughters Umm Qulthūm, Ruqaiya, and Zainab, while a blue turban denotes a descendant of the Prophet through ʿAlī and Fāṭima.[3] Riffians wear yellow turbans of a special kind made in Lyons, France, while the Afghan, the Pathan, and the Baluchi wear a large white turban, with a long tail hanging to the shoulder.

The old-fashioned oriental Jew wears a small black felt cap on the back of his head, over the area shaved. On the Sabbath he may change it for a red one. Back in the days before they adopted European clothing, Christians in what used to be the Turkish Empire (including Lebanon, Syria, and Armenia) usually wore some kind of felt cap held on by a headcloth. The Armenian and Lebanese caps were truncated cones of red, eminently suited to their shape of head. The Assyrians' caps were, in some instances at least, white. Zoroastrians in Yezd and Kerman used to wear a loosely wound yellow turban; they were forbidden to tighten it like those of the Muslim Persians.

When I was in the Yemen in 1933, we Christians were obliged to wear black karakul lambskin kalpaks, of general Central-Asiatic style.

A broad-based version of this, surmounting the broad Turki head like a wheel, is still worn by the Gurgan Turkomans. Smaller kalpaks of various colors are the principal headgear of the Afghans. The Ottoman Turks formerly wore the famous fez, which is said to have been of Byzantine origin. They introduced it to Egypt and North Africa, and the city of Fez took over its manufacture. While banned in Turkey today it is official in Egypt; in Northwest Africa the fez is a variant headgear worn mostly in the cities. Some wealthy and conservative Moors use it as a skullcap over which to wrap a white turban, leaving the tip of the fez visible. Conical fezzes with

[3] Local usage produces much variation in the use of these two colors. Whatever I say will be wrong somewhere.

blue tassels are worn in Morocco by the *makhzānis,* the Sherifian government's official police, while in the old days Persian policemen also wore them. Copts wear browns caps. Before Riza Shah Pahlevi, Persians wore high, brimless, sugar-loaf felt hats of brown or black; the Lurs had especially large ones. In many rural parts of Iran these hats have come back into use. The Kurds, who never gave up their ethnic headgear, differ from tribe to tribe, the most distinctive being the Shikak, whose huge mushroom-shaped headpiece of white felt is held on by a black or navy blue band.

Both Mustafa Kemal of Turkey and Riza Shah Pahlevi of Iran emphasized headgear as the principal symbol of reaction on the one hand and of progress on the other, and ordered their peoples to wear the horrendous brimmed hat of the Christians throughout their realms. No Arab potentate, however, has followed suit. The traditional headgear of the desert is the *kufīya* and *ʿiqāl* (pronounced *ʿaghāl*), the headcloth and band, a garment which is intensely practical in duststorms, and one of which Arabs are intensely proud.

The rest of the costume is often equally symbolic. The garb of the Jew is black, of the Zoroastrian yellow, of the Copt brown, and of the Sussi blue. The city Arab wears white, except for the slave dealer whose outer garment may be fearfully red. If the Arab wears trousers, they are not evident; he usually wears drawers. The Kurd, the Turkoman, and the Christian all wear some kind of pants, usually the baggy kind so much more comfortable than ours.

Add to these basic ethnic differences the rosary and staff of the religious devotee, the cross of the Christian cleric, and variations in material based on wealth and position, and the knowledgeable observer can tell all he needs to know about his man at a glance. He knows his language, his religion, his profession, and his degree of wealth. Before he comes within speaking distance, he knows exactly how to behave toward this individual, and what behavior to expect. This exaggeration of symbolic devices greatly facilitates business and social intercourse in a segmented society. It saves people from embarrassing questions, from "breaks," from anger, and from violence. It is an essential part of the mechanism which makes the mosaic function. Those rulers, like the king of Egypt, the regent of ʿIraq, and the present shah of Iran, who are leaving the question of the adoption of Western clothing to the discretion of the individual, have made a wise choice. In the larger cities of their kingdoms, Western garb is predominant. In the rural districts and the mountains the retention of the old costumes is a function of isolation.

In parts of North Africa where Europeans still hold political control, it is not the wealthy and sophisticated who wear European clothing, but the poor who can afford nothing else. The wealthy and sophisticated Arabs and Berbers cling to their fezzes and jellabas, although they may wear fine European underwear, shirts, and jackets underneath. To them the fez and jellaba symbolize their unity in the desire for freedom as Muslim peoples. By wearing them they carry on the age-old tradition of the Middle East, by which the costume designates the group, with all its traditions and ideals, to which belongs the man.

But what about the man himself, inside his ethnic clothing, and under his variously clipped and shaven beard? What about the brain within the skull, flattened by cradling or rounded as nature intended it, and what about the mind of the mature man, which this tangle of gray and white cells houses? What kind of a personality does this individual, guided by his variously trained mind, his general health, and a number of glands, express in his everyday behavior? Do Riffians behave differently from city Arabs? Are the actions of Jews in the Millaḥ different still? Is it true that you can predict what an Armenian will do in a given situation?

In the Middle East, the man in the street firmly believes that each ethnic group is characterized by a standard pattern of behavior. I need not outline these hypothetical patterns here, for they should be patent enough from what is said in other chapters. What is needed is an objective evaluation of the subject of culture-personality as it applies to the peoples of the Middle East. It must be objective because this is explosive stuff. Much of the success or failure of the Westernization of Middle Eastern countries depends on a gradual shift in the mutual relations of the ethnic elements of the mosaic within each sovereign state. We who are watching this process from a distance must have the picture clear.

Anthropologists, as might be expected, differ widely on this subject. Their difference takes two forms. In the first place, some find profound differences in standard types of personality between ethnic groups in various parts of the world, while others deny that cultures have special personalities. Among those who accept the existence of these differences, a further division takes place between the environmentalists and the hereditarians. The left wing of the former would ascribe culture-personality to habits of suckling and cradling infants and of toilet training. Members of this wing seem to think little of what happens to the child once he begins to eat solid food and to squat in the cornfield with his peers. The right wing of the latter link personality to somatotype, which is another way of saying body-build. They believe somatotypes to be hereditary. Since types of body-build differ among populations, the standard personalities of populations could be said to differ accordingly.

I believe that ethnic groups *do* possess standard types of personality, at least in the Middle East. I know that were I to speak rudely to a Turk he would probably grow visibly angry and might even strike me, while a Persian in the same situation could be expected to grow coldly polite. Within reasonable ranges and allowing for probable errors, it is possible to predict what persons of different ethnic groups would do under given situations in which outsiders were involved, and I would not be surprised to learn that both heredity and environment were responsible, each force, in certain respects, limiting the other.

It would be hard to believe that the mountain tribesman does not owe part of his ferocity to the fact that he has been constantly reminded, through childhood and adolescence, of the slight to his family's honor through the death of Uncle ʿAlī in a feud twenty years ago, nor can one easily eliminate the factors of nutrition, exercise, and the presence or absence of mountain air which, combined with genes, make some people physically more vigorous than others. Speech, fire, and the capacity for a belief in supernatural powers distinguish man from the lower animals. What a man hears, eats, does, and is persuaded to believe, from the time he learns to talk to the time when he assumes the duties of manhood, cannot fail to influence his adult personality.

So far most of the studies on personality and culture have been conducted on relatively homogenous peoples, living in a state of mutual isolation. In the Middle East the situation is reversed. Here we find dozens of ethnic groups living in daily contact with each other. Each group preserves its ethnic personality, while daily intergroup contacts seem to place a premium on accentuating these differences, as part of the ethnic division of labor, which is the key to the whole social system. In other words, in his daily contacts with members of other ethnic groups, it behooves the individual to behave as expected. Whether the ethnic personality pattern to which a man has been trained suits his natural capacities and tendencies or not, he must conform. He must exhibit this stereotyped personality to the outside world.

His personality within his ethnic group is another matter. In our own society, a drygoods clerk is supposed to smile politely to all customers, however vexing they may be, but there is nothing to prevent him from becoming the Grand High Mogul of his lodge when he is off duty, ordering his fellow members to approach him, on his throne, crawling on their knees. Similarly the Jew who effaces himself all day behind a pile of merchandise in the bazaar may assume a role of respect and importance in the evening inside the Millaḥ, after he has washed and put on clean and comfortable clothing. The villager who bows deeply before his landlord in the morning may, a few hours later, act with considerable hauteur toward a poorer farmer who wishes to borrow his ox.

Within each group of people living together as an ethnic unit in the Middle East, it is safe to say that all of the normal types of human personality are found. These include leaders and followers, wise men and simpletons, garrulous gaffers and silent, nose-rubbing thinkers. Anyone who wishes to test this need only live in such a community long enough and gracefully enough for its members to forget that a stranger is among them, and then to observe, clinically, what goes on. Such a person cannot fail to agree that two kinds of personality are at play; that which your man presents to the outside world and that which is known to his kin.

As barriers between ethnic groups break down, and as differences in opportunities for education, nutrition, health, and occupation are ironed out, the former type of personality is bound to shrink as the latter grows in importance. As a person's kin come to include his nation and then his world, so must the true or inherited personality of the individual increasingly assert itself. That is an ideal for which all who love freedom are groping. From this standpoint we must recognize that the old-fashioned Middle Easterner was always free in his hours off duty. A totalitarian in a homogenized society is never free. How to achieve cultural unity without the loss of individual personality is a problem.

II THE VILLAGE

SO FAR THIS BOOK has been written around one principal thesis, which may be summarized as follows. The Middle East, a relatively arid section of the earth's surface, is less richly endowed by nature than the wetter lands which lie to either side. Its principal if not its only advantage[1] is its strategic position between Europe, Black Africa, the Central Asiatic realm, India, and China. Since the beginning of history its inhabitants have served as middle men, and being at the crossroads were leaders in the arts of civilization for millenniums.

Probably their greatest accomplishment has been their success at working out a rather complicated way of living, which consists basically of treating the various segments of the landscape as parts of a coordinated whole, rather than as separate economic realms. To do this they have developed an elaborate division of labor on several discrete levels. The first is the ethnic level, which we have already considered. A second is a division into three mutually dependent kinds of communities, the village, the nomadic camp, and the city, which distinctively offer each other, in the same order, vegetable foodstuffs, animals suited for transport, and processed goods, including tools. Both village and camp supply the city with meat, milk products, skins, and wool. Not only is each of these three types of community dependent on the others for the maintenance of its way of life, but each is equally specialized. Of the three, however, the village is the most conservative, most permanent, and least variable in population, because it is least subject to the whims of kings, trade, and weather, and because it can feed itself almost indefinitely if cut off from its trade outlets and sources of supply.

Both the city people and the nomads need vegetable foodstuffs, which they consume chiefly in the form of grain. Although the cities include (among other specialists) enough farmers to till the soil immediately outside the walls, as well as rich men who raise fruits in their gardens, these efforts do not produce one tenth of the food eaten.

[1] Other than oil, the development of which falls beyond the scope of this book.

The villagers concentrate on the cultivation of cereals. Cereals need water. If there is sufficient rain in the winter, wheat and barley can be grown by dry farming, while millet and maize will grow without irrigation in the few favored places which receive summer rain. In most villages, if they are grown at all, millet and maize are planted in the fields or terraces near the bottom of the slopes, where they can be irrigated. They are highly prized, not because Middle Easterners like their taste but because of their yield and the value of their stalks and leaves as cattle fodder. Rice, of the only kind grown in the Middle East, always needs irrigation, and it is the greatest prize of all, since not only do people like it but it yields ten times as much as wheat or barley.

The location of the village, then, depends on water. There must be enough rainfall to grow winter cereals, usually wheat or barley, but in a few mountain regions rye. There must be sufficient permanent water for drinking, watering the animals, cooking, an occasional bath, and if possible operating a grist mill. The runoff of this permanent water should be sufficient to irrigate a few precious plots of terraced land, in which to grow some protein-rich legumes and enough onions to flavor the food, with perhaps some millet, maize, or even rice. If the soil is just right, most of this land may be used for a valuable cash crop, such as saffron, madder[2], opium, or tobacco.

Provision also must be made to feed the animals, for this is a mixed economy in which animal by-products, particularly milk and wool, are important. Sheep and goats can be grazed outside the tilled area while the crops are growing, and after the harvest, on the stubble of the grains grown by dry farming. In the winter they may need straw. The asses used for transport also need straw as well as grain and what little grass grows beside the stream. The milch cows and the oxen, needed for plowing, are even more expensive to feed, for they are heavy-boned, water-loving creatures and must have grass, millet, or maize stalks, and even grain at times. In return, however, they furnish not only milk and traction but also dung for fuel. Horses and camels are seldom seen in villages, except when ridden by outsiders or unless the village is the seat of a local chieftain.

The balance between cultivation and stock raising is a fine one, and the villagers calculate it down to the last goat. When the animals

[2] The reader can find a detailed account of the elaborate technique of madder cultivation in Pottinger, *Travels in Beloochistan and Sinde,* pp. 324-325.

are too numerous for the tillage, enough are sold or slaughtered at appropriate intervals to restore the balance, and when too few they are saved.

In parts of the Middle East where enough forest cover remains within reasonable distance of the source of water, provision need not be made for growing timber. On the Iranian plateau, however, where whatever trees may once have grown there have long since been felled, the villagers reserve part of their land lying along the stream for the growth of poplars. These weed trees grow extremely close together, forming almost a wall of trunks, which the carpenter uses in house building and furnishing and in the manufacture of plows, rakes, and other implements.

Where there is more water still, the villagers cultivate fruit and nut trees, the species depending on the climate. Dried figs, apricots, almonds, walnuts, with raisins, supply quick energy in the early spring when cereal stocks are low and the milk animals dry. Dried fruits also can be boiled down into syrups, an excellent substitute for sugar. Oranges, pomegranates, and other ripe fruits bring cash on the urban market, if they can be carried there fresh. So do eggs, everywhere the special property of women.

If there is a sufficiently large perennial supply of water, villages can be built where there is little or no rainfall, and all the crops can be grown under irrigation. This is the situation in the exotic river valleys and oases. In these places, however, the farmers must work continually to keep the water on their fields and the desert off them.

If the narrow valley of the Nile were not tilled to the last inch year after year, swamps with impenetrable reedy jungles would return. In ʿIraq, few of the interriverine canals smashed by Hulagu's horde have been repaired, and even these are continually silting. The mighty Nippur, with its tremendous ruins, stands in a patch of fine sand, blowing over sterile furrows, and a wolf sleeps in the old expedition house atop the ziggurat. The previously unpeopled oasis of Jaghabub needed much work by the Sanūsi's faithful before it could be made to feed even a portion of its new inhabitants. When the Marib dam broke, a whole countryside, perhaps a fourth of the arable land in the Yemen, reverted to desert.

Despite the work involved, the exotic valleys contain the largest populations in the Middle East, and their villages rub elbows. In large oases as well, village succeeds village—a good example being the Tafilelt oasis in southeastern Morocco, one of whose towns was the famous caravan port, Sijilmāsa. It is in the regions where permanent water comes from nearby mountains in quantities insufficient to provide much irrigation, and where rainfall permits the dry farming of cereals, that villages are more widely spaced. This permits elbow room between communities and a patch of country suitable for goat grazing and the collection of dry weeds and faggots.

Even these villagers who depend partly on the rain must work hard to control their permanent water supply and to get the maximum use from it. They lead most of this water out of its natural channels into ditches contouring the slopes, from which it can filter down from terrace to terrace; the dry beds fill only with flash floods. In narrow valleys the traveler will see a system of tree trunks adzed into troughs, carrying the water across gullies, and even over the stream bed itself.

In the wide, shadeless basins of Iran, Oman, and Turkestan the water would soon evaporate if left to flow in the open. Hence their qanats. These underground water tunnels need much work to keep them free of silt. Crawling about in tunnels fifty feet underground, with the only exits a series of narrow, unfaced wells, takes courage as well as skill; many men have been crushed or smothered in them. The qanats extend the area of cultivation away from the mountain slopes onto the borders of the deserts, making use of water which otherwise would be wasted. Like the oases and settlements of exotic river banks, these villages are liable to destruction if the source of water is neglected.

Water determines the location of villages, but subject to the temperature. If the summer heat is too great, the water goes underground; if the winter cold is too severe, however, the village may be uninhabitable. Persians, Turks, and Berbers can endure an occasional winter temperature of 15° below zero, provided there is not too much snow. If, in addition to low temperatures, they are regularly faced with snow three or four feet deep, for months at a time, they cannot tolerate this because it will kill their animals. Hence the lush upland meadows of the Atlas, Zagros, and Hindu Kush become summer pastures, abandoned by nomads in winter.

Water will also determine the minimum size of a village. The supply must be more than enough for a single biological family of a man, his wife, and unmarried children, because such a family cannot perform all the tasks needed in the peasant economy at the proper times. Although one man can handle a plow alone, he can seldom afford the two oxen needed to haul it, and thus usually doubles up with a neighbor. Although the combined hands of the family can reap the amount of grain needed to feed them, it will take them a long time, and it will take the father of the family even longer to thresh it, thus cutting in on his time needed to care for the crops under irrigation. One boy will have to spend all his time with the sheep and goats during this season, for these animals must be driven well beyond the range of cultivation until the crops are in. In a village of twenty or thirty families, that one boy can look after the combined flock, leaving twenty or thirty other boys, at the very least, to help their fathers.

The father of the single family may not be skilled at woodworking or the construction of rough stone or adobe walls. No midwife is available to deliver his children, and his wife may die in childbirth. He himself may be stricken, with no one to take his place or care for his widow and babies. A one-family community is impractical. Middle Easterners, even in villages, live by sharing tasks and by specialization. A village must include several families, a carpenter, a midwife, and someone who can lead the prayers.

A dozen households is about as small as a village can be and still function and perpetuate itself. While some of its inhabitants are part- or full-time specialists, others pool their strength to work together at bees, such as house raising, to get large and heavy jobs done quickly in a brief, slack season. Even if the father of the family were the best carpenter-mason in the countryside, he would still never find time to build his house and outbuildings alone.

Having discovered the minimum, what is the maximum size for a village? If there is enough water, villages may succeed each other along its course or shore. If the water is a mountain stream flowing between steep, narrow banks, and the tillage consists of two rows of two or three terraces each spaced at intervals, the houses of the village may be separated and extend for a mile or more, but this situation is unusual. As a rule the village houses are built wall to wall, huddled on a relatively sterile piece of ground near its water and surrounded by its fields, with shade trees, walnut, fig, or poplar, planted near enough to form a pleasant lounging place, and threshing floors also in the foreground.

The men of the village must leave their houses in the morning and go out to their fields, returning in the late afternoon for the principal meal of the day. The farther the outermost fields the longer the walk each way. Since much of the work requires oxen or donkeys, progress is held down to their speed, which seldom is more than two miles an hour. Four hours a day commuting time is about all that is economically profitable, which means that the periphery of the cultivated fields should not be more than four miles from the village. Add to that a mile or two for pasture, and the villages should not be more than ten miles apart, providing that all the land between is potentially cultivable.

Usually they are closer, for walking distance is not the only consideration. Fields two hours away are difficult to protect from animals and thieves. Furthermore, in times of political unrest it may be essential to have the manpower of the village within calling distance. More important still, the village is an extremely intimate community of individuals, each of whom knows all the others, and whose mutual relations are subject to a close and fine adjustment based on mutual help and informal give and take. In most countries the leadership of the village is in the hands of one or more old men who have seen all of the others grow up and who know how to handle each individual on the basis of his observed traits of personality and character. Were the village to grow beyond a certain compass this informal type of government, which requires no full-time political specialists, and takes no one away from his agricultural duties, could not succeed. Fifty or sixty households is about the maximum limit.

Beyond that, the alternative to a full-time political specialist or group of specialists is a constant succession of quarrels, contests for leadership, and side-taking. In fact, when a village grows too large for its human safety factor, it splits, and one faction will remove itself. If there is vacant land elsewhere, a new village will rise. If not, the dissidents may move to a city and be absorbed in its already fragmented population.

Another mechanism to keep the population within the limits of its framework of equilibrium is permanent or temporary emigration. If the villagers specialize in some work they earn their livings by these specialties throughout the countryside. If they later come home to retire, the capital that they bring may make it possible for younger men to set out on their travels well equipped, and also provide the village with some of the luxuries of the city.

When a village is located along a much traveled trade route, and its position is favorable for overnight or noonday rests, some of the villagers may set up roadside stands to sell travelers melons, bread, and tea; in fact hostels may be built, and this is bound to affect the size and status of the community. If water is abundant and the land is good, one village may become a trading center for its neighbors, develop a row of shops, and cease to be a village. Its organization will become more complicated and its one specialty, that of farming, will be replaced by many.

Towns which arise in this way are much fatter prizes to the lawless than ordinary villages. The village has grain and livestock, which the ungodly can consume if they can find it, and a few poor souls to sell as slaves. But it has no boxes of gold, no horses, no bolts of fine silks and woolens, no firearms, and no barrels or skins of gunpowder. Towns therefore need garrisons, and garrisons eat food and cost money. In many ways a community is better off if it remains a village. If both well situated for trading and supplied with sufficient water, the village can grow into a town or city under one of two conditions. Either it is geographically so placed that the soldiers of the central government can reach and protect it at any time of year, under normal political conditions, or else it is so remote that they cannot reach it at all and the whole district will become an autonomous area, with the new town or city as its capital. The second circumstance requires the decay of the central government, the rise of a gifted leader, or occupation by a powerful invading people. The vagaries of history have thus changed the status of numerous communities from village to city, and back again. Many villages are built on elaborate ruins.

Going to town with his produce is one way for the farmer to trade, and in certain relatively arid regions the only way. Elsewhere two other methods are possible. In the exotic river valleys villages are often less than a mile apart, and river boats carry heavy loads of produce, as well as passengers. Permanent markets may be established along the river banks, and the farmer can sell his produce and buy most of the goods he wants at any time, without going far from home. Ibn Baṭṭūṭa, on his first visit to Egypt, said in amazement that he saw an uninterrupted chain of bazaars from Alexandria to Cairo, and that it reached as far upstream as Aswan.[3]

In the larger oases the same system obtains. Villages are just as close together, or even closer, and the camel replaces the boat as a fast

[3] Gibb and Bowen, *Islamic Society and the West,* I, Pt. I, 50.

carrier of large loads. The entire oasis is a market. In Oman, where whole populations of cities and villages alike move out to the date orchards in the picking season, merchants move out as well and set up their shops.

The second method is a staggered series of weekly markets. This is found in regions where villages are situated fairly close together, not in a line as along exotic rivers and the underground channels of oases, but radially, in open country and in adjacent mountain valleys, where the chief source of agricultural water is the rainfall. Instead of going to a town, the farmer carries his goods to a weekly market located between villages. Here he trades with merchants from a large city. One such market is held within walking distance of every village every day of the week except Friday, and the largest ones are held on Thursdays. The market is run by professional criers, weighers, and butchers, who keep order and prevent cheating and quarrels and who make the rounds of six markets every week.

These markets have several advantages. As with the town the farmer can trade six days a week if he likes, but can go and return the same day, while a visit to a town might mean remaining overnight. He can be sure to see his friends from other villages any day he likes, while his wife may count on a few hours of gossip with the other women selling eggs. With the town, it is not easy to predict when other villagers will come in. Instead of trading with a town or small city, where the variety of goods is limited and the quality variable, since the goods are manufactured locally, he deals through intermediaries with a big city. The professional trader soon learns what his regular clients like and sees that they are supplied. This kind of market is not only advantageous but necessary in regions where lawlessness prevails and no towns have arisen. Politics is not the only limiting factor, however; the rainfall must be sufficient to permit the villages whose inhabitants use these markets to be situated close enough to each other for this purpose. On the other hand, if the villages are too close, as in oases or along the banks of the Nile, separate weekly markets are unnecessary. In some of the more densely settled rural parts of the Middle East conditions are right for the existence of the weekly markets, as for example in North Africa and on the Caspian shore of Iran.

That the germ of this system is latent thoughout the Middle East is clear. In every city the shopper will learn that it is only on special days of the week that he can buy certain products, produced not in the bazaar itself but in the surrounding villages. Straw mats appear early in the morning on Mondays. Tuesday is the day for bidding on mules, while camels are sold on Thursdays, and so on. People in both the villages and the city know this schedule, and both bring in their goods accordingly. Where certain villages specialize in certain products, it may pay them to spend several days on the road.

Up to a certain point we may say that villages are alike from one end of our territory to the other, but beyond that point we cannot go. Two related factors produce differences. They are: who owns the land and whether the village is located in government territory or in free tribal country. If it is in tribal country, it makes a further difference whether the villagers themselves belong to the system of tribes or merely serve tribal masters. These are questions which properly belong in Chapters 15 and 16, but certain aspects of them should be considered here. From now on, examples are in order.

Ten miles south of Qaʿin, in Khorasan, and not far from the Afghan border, there is a village known as Khunik Pai Godar. This community consists of some fifty houses built wall-to-wall and roofed with some three to four hundred domes (as shown illustration 8). It is built on the flank of a hill, not far from a pass in the mountains. A few miles to the east is the watershed between the central Iranian basin, draining into the Dasht-i-Lut Desert, and the Helmand basin. Usually these mountains draw enough rain from the westerlies to support life among two hundred-odd human beings and their animals, but in some years rain does not fall. Then the people pull their belts the tighter, and some of them must go to the cities to find work. The year 1949 was the seventh in succession in which it had failed to rain. The people were in desperate straits, but they were still cheerful. Most of them are Sayyid, descended from the holy Prophet himself, and they own their own land. Rain will come, and life will go on as before.

These fifty houses contain forty families. The houses are chiefly single-storied dwellings, except where the slope of the hill makes a lower room possible. Built of sun-dried brick and cleverly domed to save wood, they have floors of natural cement and clean white walls hung with cloths and other ornaments, including a charm made from the seeds of the wild rue. Some of the rooms have fireplaces, although there is little fuel to burn in them. Under the village itself one can see the doors of two artificial caves, large enough to hold the sheep and goats of all the families during the winter, and above the caves, to the east, two stone-walled sheepfolds to provide shelter while the women do their milking.

On the western slope, in the shade of a majestic walnut tree, stands a row of threshing floors. This is the village gathering place, where strangers pause, and where poor travelers ask for alms. Over to the east, a small stream flows out of a qanat hole, from up the mountain. This, together with a spring, provides the village water supply. Anyone may help himself to water for drinking and cooking, and even for washing, but irrigating water must be measured off by the old water-clock method, in what amounts to six-minute units of flow. Most of these units are allocated to the fields around. Some, however, go to the bath, a long, low building just over the edge of the stream.

The beautifully kept terraces which surround the village are farmed by the men of Khunik, who have nothing to learn from anyone about methods of agriculture. On some of the terraces they grow enough grain to feed their families and a few vegetables; on the rest they grow saffron. Saffron is a crocus, a perennial plant which grows from a bulb. It requires just the right conditions of soil, sun, and moisture and will grow in few places in the world. The saffron itself consists of the pistils and stamens of the flower, and to pick these requires nimble fingers cheaply hired. One quarter of a million flowers makes a pound of saffron, which sells at retail in New York for forty-eight dollars. In Khunik it brings the equivalent of fifteen dollars. This is the cash crop of these villagers. While they live in a marginal country for agriculture, they have found the right crop to bring them the maximum income.

Their fields provide them with vegetable food, and their flocks with milk and what meat they eat. The flocks also provide wool, which the men spin when they have nothing else to do. Their women weave some of it into a brownish tweed and the men full this cloth and take it to Qaʿin, where a tailor makes it into winter clothing for them. In some of the other villages cotton is raised; the Khunik people buy it raw, and their women spin it, using the hand-operated spinning wheel. Then they weave the cotton and dye it with indigo, which also must be purchased. The blue cotton cloth makes the everyday clothing of both sexes. Other home techniques are grinding grain and pressing seeds for oil. Having neither water power nor strong prevailing winds, they grind most of their grain on hand querns, but one man in recent years built a donkey power mill run with a belt made of old automobile tires.

So far we have mentioned skills shared more or less by all the villagers. Two men, however, are full-time specialists. One is the village carpenter. He buys both tools and lumber in Qaʿin. He can build doors and door frames and make plows and rakes; most of the needs of the villagers in the woodworking line are within his skill and means. The second man is the bath-keeper. He leads the water into the bath and heats it (his children glean the hills for fuel), and shaves his customers, the other villagers. The bath is village property, and he is paid a few rials a month by each bather.

Four other people are part-time specialists: two sisters who are midwives and who would be full time if births were frequent enough, a second carpenter, and a butcher, who also would be full time if animals were slaughtered often enough. This is all. An interesting fact which ties these people together is that both the full-time specialists are outsiders, and so are the midwives and the butcher. Only the one part-time carpenter is a local. Only three other residents are outsiders, two poor men who work on other people's land for a share and a deaf mute who came into the village one day many years ago, seeking alms, and has never left. The villagers feed and clothe him out of charity. He watched us every day for nearly a month while we were digging near the village, and never begged.

Although there is a small mosque in Khunik, the villagers prefer to hold their Thursday evening religious services in any one of several houses with larger rooms. There is no resident mulla. If they cannot borrow one from a neighboring village, one of the older men acts as imām. There also is no formal government in Khunik, but everyone tacitly recognizes Ḥajji ʿAbbās, a handsome old man who owns more property than most of the others, as the leader. When they want to sing and dance in the evening, they ask his permission. It was he who brought us melons while we were digging, and arranged for the rooms in which we lived.

Every February the district tax collector comes, and the villagers give him one fifteenth of their crop, in grain, saffron, opium, or money. While opium is grown, they do not smoke it. One tenth of the crop they give as zakā to the imām of the mosque at Qaʿin; this goes to the shrine at Qum. A fifth goes into the waqf of their family in Qaʿin. The remaining three fifths, more or less, they keep. With this they buy their raw cotton, felt caps, hardware, jars, indigo, shoes, lamps, kerosene, charcoal, tea, sugar, spices, rugs, painted pottery, decorated wooden chests, and the turbans which mark them as Sayyid. Most of these items they can find at Qaʿin, but for some, such as women's shoes, they must go to Birjand, while the search for painted chests and green turbans may take them to Mashhad. Only three green turbans were actually worn in 1949. One of the wearers was Ḥajji ʿAbbās. The remaining men make shift with blue ones, dyed by their own women.

Much more can be said about Khunik.[4] It is a model village. Its inhabitants are virtuous, industrious, gentle, and happy. They participate little if any in the affairs of government outside their own domain, and the government interferes very little with them. Theoretically, if a crime were committed, the Ḥajji ʿAbbās would inform the katkhodā of the next village, and news of it would get to Qaʿin, where there are policemen. Happily no one commits crimes in Khunik, and hence this arrangement is entirely theoretical. Aside from private business, villagers go to Qaʿin only to register births and deaths.

Persian villages more or less like Khunik are to be found not only in Iran but also in Afghanistan, Pakistani Baluchistan, and parts of the U.S.S.R. In Khunik the people pay taxes to the government. In regions where nomadic tribesmen are in control, the villagers pay tribute instead to the chiefs, in return for which the latter attempt, like the government, to keep them free from raiders. The tribute is undoubtedly greater than the tax. Even in government territory, however, few villages are as well off as Khunik, since most of them belong to landlords. Attempts have been made in Iran to remedy this situation. Historically, some of the lands were given in fief to noble warriors or government officials as a reward for public service. Since the fields belonged to the landlord, (called in Persian *arbob*) the farmers whom he found or brought there worked for him. Some arbobs have begun as shrewd and industrious farmers and worked their way up by buying out their neighbors, but this is rare.

In a landlord-owned village near Tehran, fictitiously known as ʿAliabad,[5] one hundred and ten human beings lead lives char-

[4] Eventually one of my students, Paul Schumacher, who is making an intensive study of this village, will say it.

[5] L. J. Hayden, "Living Standards in Rural Iran," *The Middle East Journal,* III, No. 2 (1949), 140-150.

acterized by hard work, little food, and great monotony. Although the houses are kept as clean as in Khunik, there is no white plaster on the walls, and few windows are glazed. The men group together in teams of four, with two yokes of oxen (one ox per man involved), and such a team forms a unit in preparing land for tillage. One team can handle forty acres and there are six teams in ʿAliabad. Each man gets his portion of the income from ten acres, which yield between eighteen to twenty bushels per acre. The one hundred and eighty to two hundred bushels so produced are supposed to be divided into five parts: one for the owner of the land, one for the water, one for the seed, one for the owner of the oxen, and one for the farmer who has done the work.

The landlord owns the land, and also the water, and usually he is called upon to supply the seed as well, which gives him three fifths of the crop. The oxen are owned by only a few men in the village; if he owns ten oxen an ox owner (called *gavband*), can earn as much as five men. In which case he need no longer work. Most of the farmers, who own no ox, receive only a fifth of what they produce, which will not exceed forty bushels. This is barely enough to support life for the farmer and his family, aside from buying clothing; his wife can glean about five bushels more after the harvest. All together this gives them enough grain for about four hundred days.

In such a village the arbob is rarely in residence. Usually he lives in a large city, preferably the capital, where he may have some government post or practice law or medicine. A village may have several arbobs, each owning shares, and it may change hands rather frequently, to settle debts, even those incurred in gambling. Some landlords come to the village in the summer or early fall, and a few visit frequently, providing medical care and other conveniences, but such men are rare. In any case the landlord needs an agent or intermediary, a man of strong enough character to exist between two fires and to withstand the villagers' wrath against their fate. This is the katkhodā; he may grow rich, but his days will not be happy ones. (Every katkhodā I have seen has worn a permanent look of harassment.)

Often the houses too belong to the landlord, and then there is a constant struggle to get them repaired; the tools too may be loaned, in which case the tenant leaves them in the field to rust or breaks them carelessly. Such men whom I have hired as excavators have started off breaking my tools in the same way and finding excuses to avoid work. Many were so poor that they had to be paid each night, and some even wanted to be paid in the middle of the day as well. These attitudes, however, seldom last long. With steady wages and a few benefits such as sanitary working conditions and free pills, they soon learn to work with interest and skill. They are splendid human material and well worth the effort being made to improve their condition. Lately we have heard much about these villagers in Iran. Similar villagers live on similar shoestrings in other countries. In Iran the government is trying to do something about it, which is why we hear of them.

West of the Zagros, east of the Mediterranean, and north of the Arabian peninsula lie the lands in which Arabic-speaking peasants, who form nearly seventy per cent of the total population,[6] till some twenty-two per cent of the land, the rest of which is mostly mountain and desert. Like their ten million counterparts in Iran, these seven-and-a-half million farmers live almost exclusively in villages and follow more or less the same agricultural rounds. There are certain differences in crops because of geography; for example, the principal vegetable fat along the Mediterranean coast of Palestine, Lebanon, and Syria is olive oil. Olives will grow in only a few favored spots farther east, and there sesame and other seeds furnish the needed oil. ʿIraq produces dates in quantity, while the Mediterranean littoral is citrus country, and even bananas grow near the shore in Lebanon. Today, with rapid transportation and despite customs barriers, these fruits are exchanged. One can buy Lebanese bananas in Baghdad and Baṣra dates in Beirut (if one has the money).

The differences of crop make little difference in the structure of the village, since the problems of cultivation are the same. The forces which dictate the size of the village are constant, and the relation of village to town and city is such that the number of specialists in the village is always at a minimum. Whether Muslim or Christian, the village is divided into a number of extended families, comprising three generations and dwarfing in importance the biological family of father, mother, and children. Such an extended family may include ten to thirty people who live in the same compound, who own or rent their land collectively, and who cultivate it together, sharing

[6] Computed as of the period before the intensive migration to Israel. See Elizabeth Monroe, ed., *The Middle East,* Royal Institute of International Affairs (London and New York, 1950), p. 475.

alike in the portion of the produce which they receive.[7] At the death of the grandfather, whose presence holds this group together, it will split into its component elements, and the cycle will begin again. Since this has been a continuous process and since kinship is remembered and prized, the village itself consists of a number of larger groups each of which claims descent from some ancestor who either founded the village or entered it soon after its foundation.

The extended family lives together. If everyone cannot fit into the same house, other dwellings are built with common walls. As the kin grow, these groups of dwellings expand, and the village acquires wards. In the middle of the village is an open space, serving as general gathering place, and behind the open space the religious edifice, either mosque or church, which serves as the spatial nucleus of the community. If the villagers are divided in religion, there will be two squares, and two religious nuclei; the village will, in Tannous' term, be bipolar. In recent decades another focus has grown up in certain villages, particularly Christian communities in the Lebanon: the post office. Here the kin of emigrants to America and other foreign ports gather when the mail is in, to receive news of relatives abroad, and remittances.[8] (The former may contain instructions for the marriage of a man in Detroit with a girl whom he has never seen, and the latter will make this union financially possible.)

It is partly because of their practice of receiving money from abroad, and partly because of other circumstances, including female education, that the Christian villagers of Lebanon and Syria own a greater proportion of the land they till than do their Muslim neighbors. Land ownership in the Near East is a complicated business. A man may own a fruit tree growing on someone else's field or merely a share in the fruit tree. One reason for this is the Arab laws of inheritance, which divide landed property, or the right to work other people's landed property, between the children, with boys sharing equally and two girls equaling one boy. This causes complex fragmentation. A certain amount of it is useful, since through its agency each farmer will obtain the use of the different

[7] This discussion is based on several articles by Dr. Afif Tannous, notably: "The Arab Village Community in the Middle East," *Smithsonian Report for 1943,* Pub. 3760 (Washington, D.C., 1944), pp. 523-544; and "Land Tenure in the Middle East," *Foreign Agriculture,* Office of Agricultural Relations, VII, No. 8 (Washington, D.C., August, 1943), 170-177.

[8] Afif I. Tannous, "Emigration, a Force of Social Change in an Arab Village," *Rural Sociology,* VII (1942), 62-74.

kinds of land, irrigated and dry-farmed, bottom and hill slope, vineyard and orchard. Too much, however, slows down working hours at the expense of walking between plots, starting and stopping too many times, and separate cultivation of contiguous segments of terraces. After a certain threshold of wasted time and energy has been reached, steps must be taken. What these steps are to be depends on the kind of land involved, designated on the basis of ownership.

Tannous distinguishes between four kinds of land on this basis. The simplest, known as *mulk* land, is private property, held in fee simple. Aside from paying taxes in kind, the owner may do with it as he likes. Some of it was privately owned before the Arab conquest, and has never been alienated, while some of it was granted outright to tribal chiefs or soldiers at the time of the conquest or later. Some of it may have been given to powerful chiefs in return for their protection. Mulk land can be either worked by its owner or rented.

More of the acreage of cultivable land is in a second category, that of *mīri* (Amīr's Land), or state property, which is leased either temporarily or in perpetuity, under four qualifying conditions: (1) if it remains unworked for three consecutive years or (2) if no heirs claim it, it reverts to the state; (3) the owner cannot bequeath it to designated persons, since its inheritance can only take place automatically in accordance with Muslim law; and (4) the owner cannot leave or give it to a religious foundation.

This fourth condition brings up the third class of land, that which belongs to a waqf, either Muslim or Christian. As far as villagers are concerned, waqf property may consist of buildings, fields, orchards, individual trees, or public fountains; it is fixed property of any conceivable category. While mīri land may not be given to a waqf, its produce can be so dedicated. This second kind of waqf property is called false waqf, as distinguished from true waqf, which is owned outright by the foundation and is inalienable. All waqfs, it will be remembered, do not belong to mosques or churches. Some are dedicated to specific charities, while others provide a secure income to the descendants of the donor and thus serve as trust fund. The waqf which maintains a public drinking place, however, is of benefit to everyone.

The fourth kind of land is called *mashā,* or "shared." As its name implies, it is owned by the village in common. Each farmer or family has the right to a certain number of shares. Every so often at from one to five-year intervals, the village elders redistribute these lands, and this cancels fragmentation due to recent death and inheritance. The uncultivated grazing lands on the edge of the village not only belong to all its citizens but are not even allotted; the common flocks are driven out to it and allowed to graze wherever the animals can find enough herbage. Similarly roads, paths, and threshing floors are common property. Such land which is shared by all without allotment is called *matrūḳa* (leftover).

Allotment in rotation, then, solves the problem of fragmentation on the mashā land, while there is no problem at all with the land which provides the meat, wool, skins, and milk. Since the villagers (in the Lebanon at least) eat as much milk products as grain, pound for pound, this is an important consideration. With the other classes of land other mechanisms obtain. Land which belongs to a waqf has only one owner, the foundation. Hence it cannot be divided. Since mīri land reverts to the state when unworked or when there are no heirs, a certain amount of consolidation occurs in this fashion. With mulk land, even if several persons own a piece of land, they may be willing to rent it to a single farmer. It is only in the case of mulk land worked by its owners that the problem becomes critical, and here the only solution is a process of buying and selling to produce consolidation. (In the Lebanon much of the correspondence with kinfolk in the Americas which Tannous analyzed concerned deals of this nature.)

One hears much about land reforms in the Middle East. It should be clear that reforms are needed not only in the amount of land owned by the individual farmer but in the manner of ownership. All of these complications, however, have their function in a pre-industrial society. Absentee ownership maintains a needed literate, sophisticated upper class in the cities, while the waqfs, the mashā arrangement, the common pasture, and the rules which permit the poor to glean the fields and gather windfalls from the orchards, keep most of the villagers from falling below a critical subsistence level.

Along the fringes of the Arabian desert, in ʿIraq, Syria, and Jordan, some of the villages are organized in a strictly feudal fashion, with a shaikh holding absolute power over his fellow villagers, who are normally all kinsmen. However the land may be owned, it is the shaikh who allocates jobs, and if some outside agency is conducting work in the neighborhood (as for example an archaeological expedition), he rules on who shall be employed and who shall not. He furthermore takes a cut of all wages as his hereditary privilege. This shaikh holds court in an audience chamber, which may be a tent, or in southern ʿIraq, one of those picturesque Quonset-like reed *diwāns.* Here he sits patiently day after day, serving coffee to all comers, producing feasts of roast meat on occasion, and listening to the grievances of his constituents. He in turn pays homage to a higher shaikh, and so on up the tribal hierarchy.

In ʿIraq and Syria the historical explanation is given that these are nomads who had but recently settled down and taken over agriculture and hence have preserved a tribal organization. However, one finds the same thing all over North Africa, where the tribes in question have been farming for centuries. The functional explanation, as contrasted with the historical, is that farmers become or remain organized in this way if and when the central government of the country is unable to supply troops to protect them against raids by nomads. Farmers who are so organized can, if they have the courage, hope to hold off their attackers and thus avoid plunder and tribute.

Because tribal organization is the rule in North Africa, further discussion of village structure in that part of the Middle East should be postponed until after we have considered the subject of tribes in general in the next chapters. Similarly, consideration of the agricultural parts of the Arabian peninsula must also wait. A few words may be said about village life in Egypt, however, where the population is dense and long settled and where many of the usages go back to pre-Islamic times.

In the first place, Egyptian villages were larger than most others. This was because there was no frost and the soil yielded two to three crops a year, and because the principal food crops were rice and durra, which feed many more mouths per square mile than wheat or barley. In some areas rice yielded thirty times as much grain per unit of land as wheat.[9] Thus the Egyptian village was more comparable to those of India and China than to most other Middle Eastern agricultural communities. The banks of the Nile did not provide much grazing, however, and the population of sheep and goats was much less per capita than in most other parts of the Middle East. The situation was more favorable for cattle and water buffaloes, useful for milk and traction. The lack of sheep meant a shortage of wool; in compensation, the climate is mild, and clothing could be

[9] E. R. Leach, *Social and Economic Organization of the Rowanduz Kurds,* London School of Economics and Political Science Monographs on Social Anthropology, No. 3 (London, 1940).

made of cotton and flax, grown locally. Cotton also provided an edible fat, cotton-seed oil.

Being larger than most others, the Egyptian village could and did support more specialists. Usually there were one or two shopkeepers, a potter or two, one or two carpenters, a barber, and perhaps a smith. A dozen or so men spent their time patrolling the river dikes and guarding granaries. An imām ran the mosque and religious school. At least three other officials intervened between the fellaḥīn and the landowners or owners. The latter were always to be reckoned with; the villages belonged to capitalists, known as *multazims,* meaning tax collectors. Such was their original function under the Ottoman Empire, but from tax collecting for the government to ownership required but two easy steps historically. In ancient Egypt the fellaḥ was bound to the soil. Although the sharīʿa freed him, old customs persisted, and under the Ottomans a multazim could bring back a runaway cultivator. A Copt called *ṣarraf* (literally, money-changer) served in the village as the multazim's treasurer, a *shaikh al-balad* as headman, and a *shahīd* or village lawyer watched over the interests of the fellaḥīn.

Not all villages were owned by single multazims. In case the property was divided, each owner was represented by a separate shaikh, one of whom was the head shaikh responsible for order in the community. His task was made a bit easier than it might otherwise have been through the mechanism of certain rules. One was that dates were not taxed; the fellaḥīn could keep all they produced. Another was the division of the village land into two classes, *al-waṣīya* or seignoral land, which was one tenth of the whole, and the fellaḥ's land, comprising the other nine tenths. The former was for the support of the multazim, who was supposed to hand over the taxes from the rest to the government. Law prevented the multazim from selling the former class of land alone. The whole village was divided into twenty-four agricultural units, each of which contained nine tenths of fellaḥ's land and one tenth of al-waṣīya; the multazim could sell as many of these units as he liked, but he could not break them up.[10]

[10] This material on Egyptian villages is derived from Gibb and Bowen, *op. cit.*, I, Pt. I, 261-263. Gibb states: "The description of the Egyptian village in Bowen's and my book relates to the eighteenth century. All these usages were swept away by Mehmed ʿAlī, who substituted a state monopoly of the land, and under his successors the regime of individual and almost unrestricted private property was gradually established." Private communication.

The foregoing generalizations and series of sketches by no means cover the subject of the village in Middle Eastern society. This is but a crude beginning. Much more work must be done in every Middle Eastern country before we can stand on firm factual ground. It will be noted that only the barest mention has been made of village organization outside the realm of governmental control; to deal with it now would be to jump subjects in our table of contents.

One final point can be made, however, and this concerns another level of division of labor. It is the division between villages which possess special geographical advantages and those which do not. In Morocco, for example, the village of Mediuna, located just south of Cape Spartel on the Atlantic coast, has sufficient land to feed its inhabitants, but not enough to supply a surplus which could be traded for finished goods and small luxuries. Ways to supplement this paucity are found. Most of the men work intermittently in the millstone quarries of the Caves of Hercules, a half hour's walk away. Here they find a gritty conglomerate ideal for milling. The *m'allimīn* (masters) who hew out these stones carry them by mule to the market in Tangier, whence they are traded all over Morocco.[11]

Another example is the famous tribe of Taghzuth, in the Senhaja Srair country just north of Fez, where the inhabitants of several chilly forest villages make a living tanning skins and producing leather bags famous all over Morocco. Other examples could be listed by the dozens. The effect of this kind of a division of labor is, of course, to increase the rural population by giving the inhabitants of infertile regions a way to buy food to supplement their own meager crops. If the region is still less fertile, however, it can support human beings only if they move about from place to place and season to season, as we shall see in the next chapter.

[11] William D. Schorger submitted a study of this village as his doctor's thesis at Harvard University in 1952.

12 THE CAMP IN THE DESERT

We have seen how important geography is in determining the location of villages, their spacing, and the ways in which their inhabitants are able to trade with urban centers. This exercise can be carried further; we can divide the entire Middle East into three principal geographical components on the basis of the suitability of each for occupation. These are the lands suitable for sedentary village and urban life, the lands unfit for human occupation on any basis, and those in between, where human life can be supported if the inhabitants are equipped to move around, either seasonally or at the whim of the rain, or both.

The in-between lands again fall into three categories: the habitable portions of deserts, of mountain pastures, and of steppes. In each case the transition from village land to pasture is gradual, and consequently transitional economic systems are also encountered in each. The animals available to the nomads of these three kinds of terrain are the same: the camel, the horse, the ass, the ox, the water buffalo, the sheep, and the goat. These are the same animals available to the villagers, and except for the camel and water buffalo, they go back far into Middle Eastern antiquity.

The nomadic peoples of each of the three kinds of terrain have found different combinations of these seven animal species to be best suited to their purposes. Their experience has been based on the interplay of a number of considerations, aside from the value of the animal as a source of wool or hair, milk, and meat. These are its feeding requirements, its resistance to thirst, its resistance to cold, its traveling speed, its tractability, and the amount of load it can carry. The camel is thus the animal par excellence of the open desert, and the horse of the steppe. The sheep, favorite of the villagers, is also suitable for slow nomads on the edges of cultivation in both desert and steppe, and for mountain pastoralists who make but two shifts a year, between the chill upland meadows and the warmer plain.

The deserts of the Middle East belong to two separate categories. The Sahara and the Arabian deserts are of the Plateau and Dune type, while the deserts of the Iranian plateau are of the Mountain and

Bolson variety. In the former the landscape consists of plateaus of varying height, with some mountains and many deeply eroded, dry valleys. Part of the desert is covered by huge stones and other parts with sand, but most of it is merely rubble. During the winter months rain falls on the desert in varying amounts and with great seasonal variability. The higher plateaus and mountains usually receive more rain than the lowlands, all else equal, but in the parts of the deserts between the westerly and monsoon storm tracks, the rainfall is negligible, regardless of altitude. The Libyan desert and the Rubʿ al-Khāli are the two driest places. Elsewhere thunderstorms scatter moisture erratically, and the dry wadis run with flash floods. In the wadi bottoms the underground water table is often high enough to be reached by the roots of date palms, and wells furnish water for camels as well as for some patches of irrigation. At one time or another, large sections of the Sahara and Arabian deserts support the animals of nomads.

The Mountain and Bolson type of desert is far less hospitable. The Iranian plateau, including most of Iran and Afghanistan, consists of a rim of mountains enclosing a series of basins, and in the hollow center of each basin is a desert, the Dasht-i-Kavir, Dasht-i-Lut, and Dasht-i-Margo. These basins get no rain whatever. Water from the westerlies descends on the crests of the surrounding mountains. That which falls on the outer slopes runs off in short streams to the oceans and seas, but the share of the inner slopes drains into the desert basins, where it becomes saline and alkaline and unfit for drinking, even by camels. Hence land suitable for nomads is scarce and limited to southwestern portions of the outer rim of the plateau (except for the Indus gap, this country joins onto the Thar Desert of Pakistan, which is of the Plateau and Dune category), where the rainfall is too scant for agriculture, and to the country around the Helmand mouth.

In the three separate parts of the Middle East which will support them, we find three different aggregations of camel nomads: the Baluchi and some of the Brahui in Baluchistan; the Bedawin in Arabia; and the Berber-speaking Tuareg, along with other Bedawin from Arabia, in the Saraha.[1] As might be expected, all of these

[1] The Sahara also contains Beja and their subgroups, the Bisharin and Hadendoa, Kushitic-speaking "Fuzzy-Wuzzies," who live between the Upper Nile, south of Aswan, and the Red Sea. Being Sudanese and Ethiopian in cultural affiliation, they fall outside the range of this work.

possess a number of traits in common, and these traits distinguish them sharply from most villagers.

The village has an optimum size, which remains constant from season to season and from year to year. The camp of nomads, however, has not one but several optimum sizes which vary greatly by seasons and may even vary in the same season of different years. Both the villager and the nomad lead hard, healthy, out-of-door lives, but the activities of the villager are repetitive and cyclical while those of the nomad are erratic. The villager knows what is going to happen each season, each day, and each hour; his calendar has been prearranged for hundreds of years. The nomad does not, and consequently he must be more alert.

Unless he is a mountain tribesman and his home has natural defenses, the villager does not like to fight. Even if he lives on flat, open country he will defend his home bitterly if the need arises, but he finds it easier to pay tax or tribute than to suffer the loss of his crops and livestock, for he is extremely vulnerable. On the other hand, vagaries of weather throw nomads into fierce competition with each other and survival depends on warfare. The nomad is a warrior, with all the pride and aristocratic bearing that this profession denotes.

The village has a simple organization. Areas of conflict have long since been defined by custom, and leadership is loose and informal. The camp has a more complex system because it includes several categories of people, and leadership must be firm and decisive because life depends upon it. The warriors, particularly those of leading families, develop a pride of race and a concern for the purity of their breeding, a matter of relative indifference in the village.

The amount of ethnographic information available on the nomads of these three areas varies greatly. We have more on the Bedawin than on any other people in the Middle East, and four excellent monographs on the Tuareg, but on the Baluchis and nomadic Brahuis many reports but little of an anthropological nature. These people may have been the first to develop a camel culture in the desert. What we know about them refers chiefly to a period a hundred years ago and more, when the British, who were worried about them, sent out a number of army officers to investigate.

Brahuis and Baluchis may be considered equivalent peoples, in that each maintained political independence until within the last century, and each consists of a number of tribes, graded into more and less noble categories on the basis of birth order within their traditional genealogies. In each the leading or most aristocratic tribe refuses to give its daughters in marriage to outsiders. The tribes are divided in *ḳaums,* or camps, each with its local chief, who may or may not have a fixed headquarters in some fortified place furnished with permanent water.

Each kaum has its regular territory and its seasonal camping places where its members pasture their animals. They live in black tents, said to be covered in some cases with felt,[2] although the ones I have seen were made of woven goathair, like those of Bedawin. No one would think of making a black tent for use in a northern latitude, because black is supposed to absorb the heat. But the nomads of the Middle East all use black tents. Why? The answer is that they move about much by night and like to sleep or sit under cover by day. They pitch their tents in such a way that it gets the maximum of ventilation needed. Whatever else is wrong with the desert, it usually has a breeze. Being loosely woven, the goathair cloth allows air to pass through, and becomes tight and rainproof when wet. The air in the tent moves, and hence absorbed heat is no problem. Light, however, is a problem, particularly ultraviolet rays. The thick, black material of the tent keeps out all light, and the nomad, his wives, and children can rest in the shade, which is actually cooler than outside, and much cooler than the interior of a translucent, breeze-choking tent made for the camping trade.

Those Baluchis who are still nomadic (in the Indus Valley and India many have settled down as landlords, landlords' agents, and mercenary soldiers) make two principal moves a year, to the higher country of the interior in summer and to the lower coastal regions in winter. In the late autumn they butcher a number of animals and preserve the meat by sun-drying and smoking over fires of green wood. They also convert milk into cheese and ghee, which like the meat will keep through the lean season. Their women convert surplus wool into rugs, blankets, and felt carpets for sale.

Each of the Baluchi tribes was headed by an amīr who, while holding executive authority in time of war, served as the moderator of a tribal council, in which all freemen were entitled to speak. The camps into which the tribe was divided for purposes of pasture each had its *sirdar,* or leader, who decided when and where to shift, and

[2] Pottinger, *Travels in Beloochistan and Sinde,* p. 61.

on the conduct of *chapaos,* or raids. The sirdar had his guest tent in which he entertained travelers, at common expense.

Aside from stockbreeding the Baluchis protected the villages of Persian-speaking farmers for which they were responsible and raided those for which they were not. They conducted merchants through their individual territories as guides and guards, for a fee, and under their protection caravans had little trouble. Their raiding grounds reached west to Yezd, east to the Indus, and north to the Helmand. Their favorite weapons are the rifle and the sword; a hundred years ago their amīrs would send emissaries as far as Istanbul to buy sword blades and matchlock barrels, although good ones were made locally. The warrior wore a shield of rhinoceros hide between his shoulder-blades, and he might even carry a bow and a quiver of blunt arrows, for hunting birds. Between raids the warriors exercised with martial games, and by hunting. One sport was for the horseman, at full gallop, to pierce a stake lightly driven into the ground with the tip of his lance, and carry it away. They also coursed salukis after gazelles, and a good saluki would sell for three camels or even more. Hawking was another of their pastimes.

The warriors of a camp would spend much time planning a chapao down to the last detail. Under the command of their chief they would set out on camels, leading baggage camels, and mares for the final dash, and leaving their stallions to avoid whinnying. They took rations of dates, cheese and bread, and water in leather bags. Riding to the neighborhood of the victim village, they would halt in a thicket or lonely canyon to rest the camels, and as soon as the inhabitants were believed to be asleep, they would dash in, burning, destroying, and carrying off whatever they could find. They would keep this up, moving from village to village, riding eighty or ninety miles a day, until the baggage camels were loaded, ten or twelve to a man, and then they would return home via a different route.

This was dangerous work. Some were killed, others caught and mutilated, while still others died of fatigue. Some of their camels might be lost, others might die of overexertion. Sometimes the victims would be alerted and waiting for them, but now and then they struck it rich, and each man would get several thousands of rupees and a number of slaves.

These slaves were of both sexes. Once captured, they would be blindfolded and tied on the camels, so that they could not tell where they were taken. The raiders shaved off the women's hair and the men's beards and rubbed the scalp and beard skin with a quicklime preparation to kill the follicles, and thus to discourage the slaves from wishing to go home. Many of these slaves were sold to the north and east, while a few were kept around the camp as workers. The Baluchis themselves were thus able to concentrate on their martial exercises and hunting.

Among the Baluchis we now see a dual division of labor, in the first place between the tribesmen and their subject villagers, which provided vegetable foodstuffs in return for protection, and in the second between the warriors in the camp and their slaves, who did the routine work. A third is between the warriors and the trading caravans, which they protected for a fee, and a fourth between the Baluchis and various kinds of specialists whom they considered beneath them socially and hence not to be harmed. These were the Hindu traders, who brought the products of the cities, and the Loris or Dōms, a gypsy-like people who served in the camps as blacksmiths, tinkers, musicians, and serving maids. Having a safe-conduct and the entree to the women's quarters in the camps, the female Dōms acted as go-betweens in the initial prospecting for marital partners for the sons of their masters.

A fifth arrangement was with the holy men who formed settlements of their own and traveled about with the camps, always ready to be called on to officiate at a funeral or to write an amulet for a sufferer. Many of these claimed the rank of sayyid, or descendant of the Prophet through ʿAlī and Fāṭima. When a particularly holy one died, his clients would build a tomb over him, and he thus became a pīr. As time went on, his reputation would increase. If his tomb were beside a spring, then he was believed to have brought that spring forth from the rock with a stroke of his lance. Litigants would travel to his tomb to swear oaths over his grave, and so great was their fear of his retributive power if an oath should be false, that each party would be satisfied with the other's truthfulness.

This is a complex social system, and nothing could illustrate better the ethnic mosaic of the Middle East. Being situated between large centers of population which in themselves are varied, the Baluchis had many sources from which to draw. The Bedawin, however, have achieved an equal complexity from a smaller ethnic pool. This in itself demonstrates that the complexity is a matter not of chance but of necessity.

Bedawin occupy most of the Arabian peninsula, except for the

Rub ʿal-Khāli and its northward finger of the Nafūd, the agricultural lands of the Yemen, ʿAsīr, Ḥaḍramaut, and Oman, the cities of Ḥijāz, and the palm orchards and shipping centers of Kuwait and al-Ḥasa. The Bedawin discussed here are those living north and west of the Empty Quarter. Those between Ḥaḍramaut and the sea, and in the Qara hills, are a different people with their own culture. The northern Arabian desert lands occupied by the Bedawin with whom we are concerned stretch across the pipeline where Jordan and ʿIraq join wings, into Syrian territory. Damascus and Baghdad and the semicircle of cities between them all stand on the edge of Bedawin territory, and owe part of their prosperity to trade with these nomads.

In the world of the Bedawin permanent water may be obtained on the banks of rivers, particularly the Euphrates, and from wells. Some of these wells are in the open desert, while others support oases. During the rainy season, from October to March, local showers may create pools which will remain for a week or two, and in the wadi bottoms it is often possible to reach water for several months after these rains by digging shallow pits. During the summer, from the first of June until the end of September, everyone who lives in the desert is obliged to camp near permanent water, for in this season camels must be watered every day because of the lack of moisture in the tinder-dry perennials which form their fodder and because of the heat. After the rains fall, succulent annuals grow rapidly, and the desert air is filled with the sweet perfume of their flowers. Camels need water only once in five days in the fall, and at much rarer intervals in the full flowering of the springtime. Then the Bedawin can move their camps farther and farther from the wells, since only they need daily water, and expeditions of a few men can be sent several days' journey to fetch it.

The storms which bring the rain do not distribute it evenly. Watching a thundercloud and the flashes of distant lightning, the Bedawin will send scouts to locate the rainfall, and then race to reach it. If the only livestock in the camp are camels and horses, he will attain his goal. If encumbered with sheep, however, he might fail, although he could afford to keep sheep if he were content to stay on the edges of the desert or in a few favored places where the rain is sure. Like the Persian villager in Baluchi territory, the shepherd is a fat but sitting duck.

These environmental considerations provide one of the axes on which the Arab of the desert bases his complex classification of his fellows, whom he divides into two broad categories, sedentaries and nomads. By sedentaries he means both the full-time agriculturalists and traders who live in the oases and along the rivers, and the transhumants. The transhumants are people who own or rent tillage and houses, plant cereal crops with the first rain, and then drive their sheep a little way into the desert for the winter. In April or May they come home for the harvest and pasture their sheep on the stubble.

The nomads he further divides three ways, into the *Badw* or *Aʿrāb,* the *ʿArab ud-Dār,* and the *Shawaiya.* The *Badāwi* or *Aʿrābi* (singular of the words given above), is a camelman. Since sheep would hinder his mobility, he does without them. He spends the summer months camped about his wells or near the bank of a stream, and the rest of the year out on the desert. These people are the true Bedawīn (a word used only by non-Arabs) about whom many books have been written. The *ʿArabi ud-Dār* (literally "House Arab") is a man who owns sheep as well as camels. In the fall he leads his flocks out into the desert after the fashion of the transhumant, from whom he differs in that he does no planting.[3] His summer camp is located near a town or city, where he can avail himself of its permanent water; he may also own a town house which he occupies during the season, and visits at other times.

The Shawaiya, who are the shepherd tribes proper, are highly specialized people. In the northwest they include principally the Sharar̄at; in the northeast Colonel Dickson identifies three separate groups, belonging to the Muntafiq confederation.[4] The shepherd tribes spend the summer at permanent water and in winter take their

[3] There seems to be a little confusion between Musil and Dickson in the classification of sheep raisers. Musil used the word Shawaiya to designate the kind of people Dickson calls ʿArabdar (properly al-ʿArab ud-Dār), and classifies the shepherd tribes, such as the Shararat, as Bedawin of inferior status. See Musil, *Manners and Customs of the Rwala Bedouins,* Monographs of the American Geographical Society, No. 6 (New York, 1928), pp. 603-605, and Dickson, *The Arab of the Desert,* pp. 108-113. Some if not all of this difficulty may be explained by the fact that Musil wrote about the northwestern and Dickson the northeastern nomadic area. Dickson's highly informal Arabic transliteration has been changed to conform with George Rentz' corrections in his review of Col. Dickson's book in *The Muslim World,* XLI, No. 1 (1951), 49-64.

[4] These are the Al bū Ṣalāh, the Ajwād, and the Beni Malik. Dickson, *op. cit.,* p. 545.

sheep to the usual places, riding mostly on asses. They are quite expert at their work and serve other tribes and townsmen in two ways: by taking out other people's sheep on contract and by acting as individually hired shepherds with tribes such as the ʿArab ud-Dār.

The second axis of the Badāwi's classificatory system is kinship. He divides all desert tribes into two groups: *ʿAsīlīn,* of pure origin and blood, descended from the patriarchs Qaḥtan and Ishmael; and all others. The pure of blood themselves represent two lines, the *ʿArab al ʿAraba* (Arab of the Arabs)[5] who go back to Yarab ibn Qaḥtan, who lived before Abraham, and the *ʿArab al-Mustaʿriba* (Arabs by Having Become Arabs), relative upstarts descended from Ishmael, son of Abraham and Hagar, the daughter of a king of Ḥijāz. The ʿArab al-Mustaʿriba include the tribe of Quraish, and hence the lineage of Muḥammad. About eighteen tribes or tribal confederations belong to this closed circle of ʿAsīlīn and these include the ʿAnaza with their famous branch the Ruwalla, the Shammar, the Āl Murra of the borders of the Empty Quarter, and the Bani Khālid.

As the inclusion of the Quraish indicates, desert residence and pure camel nomadism are not necessary qualifications. Most of the ʿAsīlīn are desert Bedawin because, away from the towns, it has been easier for these to keep their lines pure and because the concept of the pure family line is essential to their way of life. The townsman can be a success without a pure lineage—or can hire someone to fabricate it for him. Hundreds of thousands of Middle Eastern Muslims speak Arabic who are not, in this sense, Arabs.

The Aʿrab marries his father's brother's daughter, and if no such first cousin is available he will make sure that his wife is of equal status. Although the Badāwi marries and divorces several women either in a series or simultaneously or both, and a woman can expect to have several husbands, all mates are members of this closed corporation.

The ʿArab ud-Dār are not excluded from it, if they belong to the right tribes. In fact, in Kuwait if not elsewhere, it is common practice for well-to-do members of this group to receive their desert cousins in their town houses and to take the latter shopping, as well as to introduce them to the higher society of the city. Some of the permanently city-dwelling Arabs who hold high offices in the various governments also belong to the elite, as do most if not all Arab kings, and they are extremely proud of it. As a physical anthropologist I

[5] Also known as *ul-ʿArbā* and *ul-ʿArabiyya.*

have been called upon a number of times, in cities, to comment on the Bedawin-like features of my hosts and associates.

Arabs who are beyond the pale and who cannot mix genes with these aristocrats are much more numerous and as a rule worry as much or as little about it as do we Americans whose ancestors may not have come over on the *Mayflower*. These non-aristocratic people are far from homogenous. They include every category based on occupation which we have so far mentioned—camel nomads, shepherd tribes, ʿArab ud-Dār, transhumants, farmers, and traders. They also include three classes of people whom those just named would themselves refuse in marriage, Ṣulaba,[6] smiths, and slaves.

The Ṣulaba are members of a small ethnic community, living scattered in groups of one or two families usually attached to a camp of camel nomads. The Ṣulaba ride on asses and pitch small, threadbare tents just outside the camp. They serve as desert guides and are skilled hunters. They are also coppersmiths, repairing the Bedawins' vessels; woodworkers, charged with making wooden bowls and repairing well pulleys, saddles, and the like; and leatherworkers. Their women dance publicly and are said to be not above prostitution. (There is a story that in the summer, when the Bedawin are crowded about their wells and river banks, the Ṣulaba head for the open desert where they uncover secret sources of water and hold high jinks and a merry time. I cannot vouch for its truth.) Many Arabs are convinced that these people are descendants of the Crusaders, because some are said to be blond; to the anthropologist they and the shepherd tribes look like the oldest inhabitants of the desert.

The smiths (*Ṣunnaʿ*) are a group of ironworkers, who have their own kin and are reputed to be of partly Negro origin, although this is not always evident. A family of smiths is attached to each noble tribe, and calls itself Ṣunnaʿ al-Muṭair, or Smiths of the Muṭair, etc., just as some of the gypsy tinkers in England took the name of their protector and became Lees. They act as farriers, swordsmiths, and gunsmiths—shoeing the mares, repairing the weapons, beating out the tent stakes of their hosts and thus sparing the latter a trip to the town, and making it possible for them to keep on fighting in a critical moment. To the Badāwi at war, the smith is a vital member of his company.

The slaves are Negroes brought from Africa, and their descendants. Every princely household and the chief of every tribe have

[6] This plural is also rendered as *Sulubba* and *Slaib.*

them. The slave wears fine clothing, is fed of the best, even when his master goes hungry. He will fight for his master bravely and has much to do with the upbringing of his master's sons. He also is chief of protocol in the guest house or tent; the visitor from foreign parts will do well to keep in with the slaves. His master may set him free, and he may marry among the freedmen group in the towns, or the daughter of a smith.

The Badāwi splits his human world on still a third axis: whether or not the man and his group will fight. All of the ʿasīlīn tribes fall into the fighting class; if they fell out of it and became tribute payers to their erstwhile peers,[7] their blood would not avail them, and the chances are that it would soon be found in some way impure. Some of the non-ʿasīlīn Badw tribes are also fighters, as for example the Rashaida, hereditary retainers of the shaikhs of Kuwait and bitter foes of the Saʿūdi family. The wars between Rashīdi and Saʿūdi were unusually bloody, because the rules of chivalry which are followed in combats between two aristocratic outfits do not hold when one or both sides are outside the blood particular.

The nonaristocratic camel breeders who pay tribute instead of fighting perform a special service in the complex desert economy. They hire themselves out to the fighters as camel herders, leading the flock out to pasture, bringing it back, milking the she-camels, and going after water. Being noncombatants, no one will touch them, and their employers and the employers' slaves can spend their time guarding the flocks if danger is expected, guarding the animals sent for water, guarding the camp, and scouting for new pasture and for enemies.

The first-class Badāwi is thus more of a soldier and a policeman than a camel breeder. He has two other obligations of this order. One is protecting refugees from other tribes—those refugees who come to him in a prescribed ritual manner and who need shelter until they can get to safety outside the desert, or until compensation for their disturbance has been arranged and they can go home again. The other is giving travelers safe-conduct across the tribal territory, from border to border.

Both these obligations operate on the conceptual basis of *wejh* (face). A man's face is his honor. If his honor is clear and unques-

[7] Most or all have paid taxes at one time or another to one or more governments. This presumably does not count. Ibn Saʿūd, by calling his tax zakā, saves the tribesmen under his control the humiliation of tribute.

tioned, his face is white. If someone dishonors him, his face has been blackened and he must take steps to restore its color. The more important a free, fighting man, the greater his face. Weaker individuals or strangers who, though strong elsewhere, find themselves outside their home territory, have the privilege of demanding protection under the face of a great man, and were he to refuse it, no matter what the circumstances, his face would darken several shades. A traveler must ask permission to cross tribal territory. The shaikh who grants it assigns to the stranger an *akh* (brother), who accompanies him from border to border. The penalty for violation of protection, once granted, is death. The guest is sacred. This concept is of great importance in the development of caravan routes and trade. Without them, indeed, the deserts could not be crossed.

As to who will and will not fight, some of the sheepowners and shepherds fall in either category. Those who have driven their flocks down to Kuwait and Saʿudi territory in the fall from their homes in ʿIraq buy protection from ordinary raiding, but if war comes, weakening the authority of their protectors, the shepherds will drive their flocks back again out of season, provided they receive warning. If caught unawares, or warned too late, they will fight as desperately as anyone else, and they are armed with good rifles and carbines. The ʿArab ud-Dār sheepowners similarly try to avoid trouble, but they will fight to defend both their own property and that of their masters, the shaikhs of the towns where they live in summer.

Nor are all of the sedentary people pacifists. Some form parts of tribes which have settled on the land, and although they may not be sought out as bridegrooms for the camel nomads' daughters, they still retain their tribal organization and obey their shaikhs. If the desert tribes raid them, they will fight back, often with success. They count some noble blood, including that of the Shaʿlān, paramount chiefs of the Ruwalla. If the settled people live in a small oasis, however, they have little chance of resistance and usually become tributary to some camel-raising chief. If the oasis is larger the chief may establish his court there, and if he conquers other tribes he may establish himself there as a king.

It will be remembered that the sedentaries include merchants as well as farmers. We have already noted that in Oman merchants go out into the palm groves in season, to sell to the pickers. The same kind of enterprise is shown toward the camel breeders. The Badāwi cannot be expected to leave camp during the height of the season merely to ride back to the city on a shopping trip, nor can he be certain of buying a full season's supply each summer—during his visits to town, or from the dozens of tents set up near his camp by enterprising shopkeepers who pay for the privilege.

A certain class of shopkeepers even go out to the winter camps. These are the Kubaisāt, named after the town of al-Kubais on the Euphrates, whether they come from it or not. The Kubaisi leads a couple of camels, laden with merchandise, to a winter camp far out on the desert. He sets up a round white tent, easily distinguished (in case of trouble) from the black tents of the camp members. He pays the shaikh for the privilege of trading in the camp, and his gift may amount to one complete change of clothing. He sells small objects: bolts of cloth, braid, candles, sugar, and hardware, and will give the Bedawin credit at the modest rate of twenty-five per cent interest. The shaikh sees to it that debts are paid, for he does not want to lose his handy shop in the desert.

A much more high-powered kind of merchant is the ʿAqaili, the agent of one of the three or more big business houses, with offices in Baghdad, Basra, Damascus, Cairo, and elsewhere, who buys up camel futures. He is called an ʿAqaili because he is usually a member of the tribe of ʿAqail and comes from the town of al-Qāsim. He too comes out on the desert with his baggage animals, bringing cash and rifles as his stock-in-trade and taking in return priorities in camels. He too is protected by the shaikh, who gets a fee for every camel purchased. The ʿAqaili also pays off another clan member, whom he calls "brother." This brother is responsible for the care of the camels bought by the ʿAqaili, and their delivery at the beginning of summer. The ʿAqaili brands each camel bought with the mark of his firm and then moves on to the next camp.

Both the Kubaisi and the ʿAqaili belong to nonʿasīlīn tribes, and both are noncombatants. The same is true of the heads of the export-import houses for which the ʿAqailis work, who may send their sons to the American University of Beirut and to Oxford and who could buy out several shaikhs many times over. Of the people who may be found in a Bedawin camp, five classes—camel herds, Kubaisis, ʿAqailis, Ṣulaba, and smiths—are noncombatants. If a rival band raids a Bedawin camp early in the morning, only the shaikh, his male kin, and their slaves, are in danger, for they alone are fighters. The women will not be touched, nor the children. The smith will pound his anvil louder than ever, to make sure that no raider mistakes him, and the Ṣulabi camped in the nearby draw will come out cringing to offer his services to a new master. The Kubaisi will prepare his tent for the next stand, and if an ʿAqaili is present he will locate the brother who represents his firm among the raiding party, to make sure that of the captured camels about to be driven away, those with his company's brand will be delivered as previously contracted.

Thus life goes on, and the free Badāwi who follows the noblest of the professions—camel breeding, who belongs to the cream of the land, genealogically speaking, and who crowns his nobility by his willingness to fight with his peers over pasture and camels, pursues his stirring, eventful, and often brief career. His may seem a simple life, and in a sense it is, but it is also the keystone to a complicated arch, each stone of which may be equally simple.

In a country where nature itself has made life difficult and travel dangerous, the order of values placed upon human skills, competences, and specializations reflect these perils. Most honored of all is the possession of the best means of transport, the camel and the pampered mare, along with the ability to produce more of the same and the courage to fight off rivals and to protect travelers and the members of vital professions. No man can be a craftsman or trader, and a fighter too, else he would lose his immunity and his life, and the Badāwi his services and goods. The Badāwi is willing to risk his own life in battle to preserve a system which gives him a chance to survive. He is unwilling, however, to risk the lives of others whose absence would render his own life on the desert impossible. This delicate balance between the classes of people who make up the desert population, this system of calculated risks and laissez-faire, with glory to the brave and safety in humility, is the key to the social structure of the Middle East as a whole, which it mirrors on a smaller scale.

The third and largest piece of desert suitable for camel nomadism is the Sahara, and our third example of a nomad society is that of the People of the Veil, the Tuareg. Until 1920[8] when the French finally took this duty away from them, they policed the desert. Breeding camels and selling them to the caravan men, providing

[8] Henri Lhote, *Les Touaregs du Hoggar* (Paris, 1944), p. 377.

desert guides, fighting off rival bands, defending the caravans which paid for this service against their rivals, and providing forage for the merchants' camels, they made trade possible between the Sudan and North Africa.[9] To maintain themselves as specialists they too had to have a complicated set of service institutions protected by a number of fixed social attitudes governing their mutual relations, as in the case of the Bedawin.

West of the Tibesti, which houses another kind of people, the Shara contains four principal plateaus: the Azjer, Ahaggar, and Adrar Ahnet (reading from east to west), and in the south, the Aïr. Each of these contains sources of permanent water. The Adar Ahnet, which is the driest, has exactly thirty-three such sources. Each of the other three contain patches of land capable of cultivation, while the nearby fields of Abalessa provide the Adrar Ahnet people with cereals. Wheat, barley, and millet are the principal crops of these small but fruitful areas, along with onions, gourds, melons, and a few figs and grapes. Each of these four natural ecological areas also contains one or more uninhabited oases where the Tuareg go in season to harvest dates.

The domestic animals of this area are principally camels, asses, sheep, and goats, with some long-horned cattle in the Ahnet, and very few horses. The Tuareg seem even more skillful at camel riding than the Bedawin. They have developed a special breed of riding animals, and mounted on the females, they can maneuver them well enough to attack from the saddle with javelins. While the Arab leaps from camel to mare, and fights with a saber on horseback, the Tuareg jumps to the ground and duels on foot, protected by a huge, rectangular addax-hide shield, and fights with a one-handed, two-edged sword of Crusader type. The warriors practice this style of combat interminably. With their lean muscular bodies, and spider-long arms and legs, they develop great speed, mobility, and skill.

Each of these four natural regions is the home of a separate Tuareg confederation. A confederation is a group of noble tribes with their various dependents and protegés. Each tribe has its own government which, Berber style, consists of a council, ruled by a chief, the *amghar*. The paramount chief of the confederation is known by the title *amenokal;* his authority does not prevent the tribes under him

[9] E. W. Bovill, *Caravans of the Old Sahara* (London, 1933), p. 25.

from mutual raiding in times when no danger threatens all. As with the Bedawin, the amenokal must come from a certain family and be of pure noble blood.

On the north the Tuareg are separated from the fertile regions of North Africa by mountains and by relatively barren stretches of desert. The Atlas ranges are steep and dry on their southeastern faces. Contact with sedentary Berbers and Arabs, then, is inhibited by geography and is limited to the inhabitants of well-watered regions, like Mzab, Tuat, and Tidikelt, which are too large to raid—beside which plundering them would be killing the golden goose. On the south, the desert gradually shifts to grassland, and the grassland to park land, and eventually forest.

This is the Sudan. It is rich in grain, rich in cattle, and rich in people. The latter are mainly Hausa Negroes, some Muslim and some pagan. In their country there are several cities in which Arabs also dwell, and the Negroes are organized into a number of kingdoms. The rulers of these kingdoms tax their subjects and raid the more distant tribes for goods and for slaves. Here the great trans-Saharan caravans are organized, and here the Tuareg come to trade. They also come to raid in the open villages between cities—or so it was at the time the Tuareg were still functioning, up to the latter part of the nineteenth century.

The eyes of the Tuareg, then, were turned to the rich and open south, and their backs toward the land of their closest kin, the Senhajan Berbers of the Middle Atlas. Being warriors, the Tuareg had no time for handicrafts. They outfitted themselves almost entirely with the products of the Sudan—blue cloth for their clothing; the skillfully woven black veils worn, like the Arab's kufīya, to protect their lungs from fine particles of sand; all kinds of metalwork and leatherwork, including lances, swords, daggers, shields, saddles, and bags; wooden boxes; cereals including durra and rice; salt and dried cheeses. From the northern oases their purchases were limited mostly to dates, tobacco, tea, and sugar, with now and then fine weapons. Firearms, of course, also came from the north.

In return for these products the Tuareg gave livestock, ghee, and trade objects from the opposite side of the desert, including, of course, goods received as fees for their services, and cash. While the Tuareg used slaves and sold a few, they were not primarily in the slave business. Their trading in human as in other forms of merchandise was essentially for their own consumption, and they did not compete with the merchants whose caravans they protected.

The Tuareg themselves are divided into two hereditary classes, *Ihaggaren,* or Nobles, and *Imghad,* or Vassals.[10] This division is as old as the camel nomad heritage of the Tuareg themselves—sixteen centuries at the most. The Ihaggaren trace their descent from a woman named Tin Hinan, who came from Tafilelt and was buried at the confluence of the Wad Tit and the Wad Abalessa, in the Ahaggar.[11] The Imghad go back to Takamat, Tin Hinan's serving-woman, who first came with her and was buried near her. Both were Tuareg, both were white Berbers. The Ihaggaren, to whom it is particularly important, have memorized their genealogies and can recite them, like the noble tribesmen in Arabia. They trace their descent through their mothers, for theirs is a matrilineal society. The Tuareg women, who have little work to do because of the abundance of domestic help, amuse themselves by singing and reciting poetry and by writing the same in *tifinagh,* their curious archaic alphabet, a relic of the old Libyan unciform script. These noble dames take great pains to raise their children to have good manners and to teach them, especially the girls, to make music and to read and write.

The relationship between the noble tribe and its vassals is not quite the same as that in Arabia between warrior and tributary tribes, nor is it identical among all Tuaregs. The Imghad, who are much more numerous than their masters, are encouraged to pasture their camels in the best land; their masters want them to get rich. In the tribes of the Ahaggar confederation, apparently each noble has his individual vassals within the opposite number of his tribe's Imghad, and the tribute is paid from person to person.

Apparently the reason for this difference is that the Ihaggaren see their Imghad at close quarters twice a year. In the winter the nobles are out on the caravan road, at their stations. In the summer they are living in the high plateaus, feeding off their agricultural tenants. In fall and spring they camp among their Imghad and consume the products of their herds, while replacing their riding and baggage camels with new stock.

Among the Adrar Ahnet tribes, which are Arab-Tuareg hybrids

[10] A much more accurate translation than the usually rendered serf.

[11] This historic monument was dug up by an archaeological expedition in the 1920's and the bones of Tin Hinan removed.

of other ways as well, an elder of the noble tribe collects from the Imghad tribe as a whole. Each tent of Imghad pays one unit of tribute, in some cases in dates, per year to the nobles collectively. If they have been unable to send their yearly caravan to the oasis that year to harvest them, then the entire tribe pays a fee of twelve camels, or ten Negro slaves.

Ordinarily the Imghad do not initiate warfare on their own, but have been known to raid when placed in tempting situations. Their primary job is one of supply, but they too have slaves to do much of the detailed work. The Ihaggaren take Imghad with them to fight on big expeditions, and the nobles are obliged to protect their vassals at the cost of their own lives. The Imghad, however, will not sit meekly by; they also know how to defend themselves.

Also requiring protection are the agricultural serfs who provide vegetable food for their masters and for the Imghad. These people are Negro *Ḥarāṭīn,* part of the general oasis population of the Sahara, brought to the plateau by the Tuareg landowners and lodged in adobe houses and straw beehive huts. Like the hired help among the Berbers to the north, they receive a fifth share of the produce for themselves. Some of them are also skilled welldiggers, whom the Tuareg employ to maintain the permanent water supply.

In the Ahnet country a further complication is caused by the presence of two small tribes of Arabs, specialists in caravan work, who pay the nobles a small fee in dates and cloth. This permits them to camp among the Ahnet, who will defend them, and it gives them full protection on the caravan road which the warriors of this confederation police. In the eastern confederations specialists of another kind receive protection from all tribes, for no one will harm them. These are the families of *murabiṭīn,* or holy men, whose ancestors had obtained their hereditary *baraḳa,* or magical power, in some miraculous way. The murabiṭīn can read and write Arabic and recite the Qur'ān. They draw around them small companies of junior murabiṭīn, who travel with them, studying whatever branches of medieval Arab learning the master can teach. These men go from camp to camp, teaching the children the elementary knowledge usual in the Muslim *ḳuttāb* elsewhere, writing charms, healing, and conducting ritual. They are the equivalents of the sayyids among the Baluchis. No one will lay a hand on their holy persons, and when trouble arises between tribes and confederations, they hie to the tents of the leaders and to the councils, to offer their advice and services as peacemakers. (According to our authorities, their efforts at times were successful.)

So far we have discussed Ihaggaren, Imghad,[12] agricultural serfs, Arab tribes, and holy men. Two other categories remain, slaves and smiths. The Tuareg were in an excellent position to select the best slaves that passed through their hands for their own use. Each noble woman had one or more female slaves for the drudgery of cooking and cleaning, fetching water, baby sitting, and collecting wild vegetable food. They waited on their mistresses hand and foot. Male slaves tended the flocks for nobles and Imghad alike and served as guards in the camp. Occasionally a noble had one favorite slave in whom he placed full confidence, sending him out as messenger, arming him, and taking him into batttle. Such slaves usually repaid this attention by great loyalty and ferocity in combat.[13]

From among the available female slaves the young noble would pick one notable for her comeliness, strength, and good disposition. She would become his concubine, traveling with him wherever he went on the long and weary expeditions and offering him the comfort of her "cool" black skin. Sooner or later he would marry a woman of his own class and hue and would give her the children needed to perpetuate her line. This, however, was an expensive undertaking, and under the circumstances it could wait until the young noble reached his late twenties or even thirties, when he could afford to spend longer intervals in the home encampment. Meanwhile any children born to his concubine would rate as slaves, for "the belly holds the child," as the Tuareg say. He might set them free, but they would have no rank.

The blacksmiths hold exactly the same position among the Tuareg as in Arabia. They set up their movable anvils and forges in the camp of noble or Imghad, collect their due, and move on when they wish to serve a new client. They are partly Negroid, but not black like the slaves. They will not fight, nor will any one harm them. They marry their own kind, and no one else wants their daughters.

[12] There were also a few small tribes of *Irajenaten,* of half-noble, half-Imghad origin, exempt from tribute but shorn of a voice in the government. These are only casually mentioned and were not essential to the system; if anything, the reverse.

[13] The French, who have replaced the Tuareg, use their Senegalese troops for the same purpose.

The Tuareg system is just as complicated as those of Baluchi and Bedawin, but different from both, just as the two first described differ from each other in emphasis and detail. In all three, however, we find a noble, dashing group, whose members spend their time in martial games, the chase, and war, protecting their sources of food and equipment and raiding each other's, relegating to slaves and servants the drudgery of material existence, and policing the roads. Each in his own fashion provides for the perpetuation of his own inbred and highly specialized branch of the Mediterranean race. One detail in particular is common to all three. The maker and mender of arms and tools, the basic artifacts on which both warfare and all material culture depend, has an international passport. He is so low in popular esteem that no one will touch him, and his reward is bare subsistence. But he does his job as well, in his own cultural situation, as the lords of steel in ours, who sit at high table in the banquet of the West.

13 GREENER PASTURES

THE SECOND KIND of landscape in which nomadism is possible is the combination of high mountain meadow with lowlands, providing alternately summer and winter pasture. During the winter heavy snows make the summer pastures uninhabitable, while the melt-off provides lush grass for several months before autumn. Summer is the principal grazing time, the season of lambing and milking and fattening and growth of new wool. Winter is a time of relative quiet, with more dependence on agricultural products. Three ranges of mountains in the Middle East provide the conditions necessary for this kind of nomadism: the Atlas, the Zagros, and the Sulaimaniya ranges of Afghanistan.

Two sets of tribes use the Atlas summer pasture: the Ait ʿAtta and their neighbors, the Ait Yafelman, who winter in the Sahara—they cross the passes of the Grand Atlas northward in the spring and return in the fall; and the Zayan, Zemmur, Beni Mgild, and others who summer in the Middle Atlas and winter on the northern slopes near Meknes. The Ait ʿAtta[1] were the last tribe in North Africa to submit to the French, which they did only in 1936, after a ferocious and desperate resistance. They form a confederation of five groups of tribes, called *k̨homs,* or fifths. Each fifth is composed of a number of separate tribes, and each tribe is made up of a number of clans called in Berber *ik̨hsān,* or bones. The homeland of these tribes is the Jebel Saghro, a range of mountains running up to three thousand feet in height, deeply eroded, full of ravines, and surrounded by a steppe-covered plateau. The plateau in turn is delimited on all sides by seasonal watercourses, marked by oases.

The agricultural inhabitants of these oases are of two classes, *Ḥarrar* who are Arabs and Berbers, and Ḥarātīn, Negro serfs. These farmers are called *ik̨hemesen,* or "fifthers," since they are obliged to give the bulk of their crops to their landlords, keeping one fifth for themselves. In one oasis, Tezarin, lives a family of holy murabiṭīn who claim descent from the Prophet, and hence the title of sharīf.

[1] Based largely on Captain G. Spillmann, *Les Ait Atta du Sahara* (Rabat, 1936).

They own their land and are inviolate. Eighteen other seats of holy men are listed in the winter territory of the Ait ʿAtta. Six are Ṣūfi chapters, catering to the sedentaries; the nomads do not join brotherhoods. The rest are residences of branches of the murabitic family of Mūlai ʿAbdallah bin Ḥusayn, who died in 1568 and who founded the line.

These murabiṭīn are credited by the Ait ʿAtta with three main services of continuous protection: keeping them free of the central government of Morocco and of syphilis and protecting them from attack by their neighbors and rivals when they cross the pass of Tizi Mkorn on their way to their summer pasture, and return. The murabiṭīn also act as judges in disputes and receive an annual fee from all the tribes. In the old days the Ait ʿAtta recognized still a higher spiritual authority, that of the sharīf of Tamesloht in the Marrakesh district over the Atlas. Each year they sent him an offering, part of which he passed on to the sultan. The sultan reciprocated with a cash gift for the Ait ʿAtta, in recognition of their office as guardians of the Saharan marches. This was the only official relationship between the sultan and the confederation.

Besides oasis farmers of two categories, and sharīfs, another sedentary ethnic group appears: that of the Jewish settlement of Amzru, near Zagora. These Jews specialize in fine metalwork, including the manufacture of jewelry and daggers. Only the larger oases contain smiths, tanners, and millers, drawn from the Ḥarrar and Ḥaratīn elements. Since the oases can support only a limited population, it is the practice of many of their young men to go north to seek work in Fez and other cities, in which they form part of the ethnic mosaic.

A few of the Ait ʿAtta themselves have settled on the land; these are parts of the two oldest tribes of the confederation, the Ait Waḥlim and the Ait Yazza, inhabiting the fortified village (*qsār*) of Igherm Amazder. This stronghold is the spiritual heart of the confederation. In it they kept their red banner, which the Ait Yazza had the hereditary right to carry into battle. The inhabitants of this village are specialists in traditional law, the supreme court.[2] When a question has arisen which the shaikhs and councils of the tribe cannot settle, and even when the murabiṭ of Tezarin has rendered an unwelcome decision, the parties to the dispute take their case to Igherm

[2] The Berbers do not follow the sharīʿa.

Amazder. There a number of the men of the two ancient tribes will ponder and send back their word.

While many of the tribes and bones own tillage, and camp near it during part if not all of the winter, and while some of the older and more prominent men and their families stay there all the year, they usually live in tents, outside the villages. Each family owns a *tighremt,* or stronghold. These are tall, turreted fortresses of mud and stone, often three or four stories high, placed in a defensible position in the winter territory. Their principal function is that of storehouse and granary, but they also serve for defense in time of war. The Ait ʿAtta do not like to live in them, preferring to camp out in their tents nearby, or even in the courtyard.

In the wintertime the tribes pasture their sheep and goats in the herbage of the plateau around the Saghro and on the mountain itself when it is not too cold. In the spring each tribe sends a delegation to a council of the whole confederation, and there they elect a *shaiḵh al-ʿām,* or chief of the year. The sharīf of Tezarin ceremonially inducts him to office by placing a handful of grass under his turban and over his forehead. (The symbolism of this must be clear.) Then the families who will spend the summer in high pastures assemble; in some tribes they are always the same ones, in others they are chosen in rotation. Apparently most of the younger men go with their wives and children. The shaikh al-ʿām assigns each group its grazing land in the high meadows once they are over the Tizi Mkorn; he maintains order among them, visiting camp after camp, and when the summer is over, he brings them home. A shaikh al-ʿām may not be chosen from the same tribe for two consecutive years; another tribe must have its turn first. Some tribes have more turns than others, and some have none. The protocol is complicated, being determined by historical events.

The shaikh al-ʿām has a deputy in each tribe to act as go-between and to carry out his orders; there is also a special law man, elected with the shaikh al-ʿām, who attends all deliberations involving legal cases, and goes to Igherm Amazder when necessary. The shaikh al-ʿām himself is responsible for the resolution of internal quarrels, allotting the pastures of each tribe, handling negotiations with neighbors, watching the defenses, and keeping up communications between tribal contingents and between the people in the summer pasture and those below.

The Ait ʿAtta carry trade goods over the Atlas, delivering dates, henna, tamarisk galls, skins, and hides from the oases to the markets north of the mountains, and bringing back cereals and manufactured goods. In their own territory they have two markets, both on Wednesday; outside they trade in a dozen others, including those over the mountains. By using these out-of-door marts, they can avoid going to cities. Some of the markets are in the government territory, but the tribesmen who come on business are not as a rule molested.

Their way of life is less complicated than that of the camel nomads. Each year the Ait ʿAtta make but two moves of any consequence, and some of them do not move at all. Like the Tuareg they obtain much of their vegetable food from tenants and serfs in the oases, but their internal social system is simpler. They make no distinctions between grades of nomads. No artisans or traders of other nations go out into their camps with them, for they are nearly always in reach of a market. Their most critical situation is guiding and protecting the flocks on the two annual moves and keeping order in the summer pasture away from the established authorities of the sharīfs, the settled lawgivers, and the old men of the tribe huddled around their tighremts. They meet this situation by electing a strong man as leader each year and by giving him the deputies needed to delegate his authority.

The tribes that live permanently on the northwestern side of the Atlas produce the beautiful hooked or tufted rugs, in geometric designs, which Americans like to buy in the markets of Fez and Marrakesh; they go so well with modern houses and furniture. These rugs are known by the names of the tribes whose women make them; Beni Mgild, Zayan, Beni Mtir. These people obtain an excess of wool from their flocks, and wool brings in more cash and trade goods in the form of rugs than raw. Each tent has a horizontal loom built into the framework of its supporting poles.

These tribes are in between pastoralism and agriculture, following what the French call a life of *transhumance*.[3] Each has its headquarters, like that of the Ait ʿAtta in the Jebel Saghro. Each leaves some of its members at home during the season of pasturing the sheep elsewhere, like the Ait ʿAtta. Unlike the Ait ʿAtta, however, the tribesmen themselves cultivate the soil. Some live up in the mountains and send their flocks to the lowlands in winter. Others

[3] J. Bourilly, *Eléments de l'ethnographie marocaine* (Paris, 1932), pp. 154-172.

live on the lower flanks of the mountains and send their sheep up, like the Ait ʿAtta, in summer. Still others live in the middle and send them in both directions, up in summer and down in winter, thus permitting the shepherds to do some of the farm work in spring and fall. The social systems of these tribes are even less complicated since they have no serfs nor tenants, and no resident artisans nor traders. They patronize weekly markets and sometimes go to town. In some tribes most people go with the sheep, while in others only a few shepherds care for the combined flock, as in the villages described earlier. The rest vary between these extremes, and so does the need for authority and supervision in migration and pasture.

The transition from village life to sheep nomadism is a gradual one, completely dependent on subtle variations in the environment where political considerations do not interfere. Various stages in this transition characterize tribal peoples all the way across North Africa wherever there are seasonally available mountain pastures, and over into western Asia. By far the largest area of high-valley and mountaintop pastoralism in the Middle East is that of the Zagros chain in Iran, Turkey, and ʿIraq, and especially in Iran. Four principal groups of hardy mountaineers are concerned: the Kurds, the Lurs, the Bakhtiari, and the Qashqai.

Like the Berbers, the Kurds are a complete people in that they include farmers, citydwellers, and nomads and carry on a variety of occupations. Their home is the Zagros chain north of Kermanshah, as far as and beyond the Soviet border. Flanking the mountains on either side is a row of Kurdish towns, notably Sulaimaniya and Rowanduz on the ʿIraq side, and Sanandaj, Saqqiz, and Mahabad on the Iranian. Kirkuk, the oil center, is also largely Kurdish, and many Kurds live in Kermanshah. North of Mahabad the towns flanking the Zagros—such as Rezaiyeh or Shahpur—are inhabited largely by Azerbaijani Turks, Assyrians, and Armenians, but they serve as Kurdish shopping centers.

Most of the Kurds are farmers. Those who live on the slopes of the mountains usually send their flocks to the mountaintop pastures in the summer, under the care of some of their young people. In the winter when the snow is deep they stable them in caves. These caves are known by the number of sheep they can contain; for example, the cave of Tamtama in the Shikak country which I excavated in 1949 was a four hundred-sheep cave. Another in the hills south of Rezaiyeh was rated at three thousand. The famous Hazar Merd cave in the Sulaimaniya district on the 'Iraqi side, excavated by Dr. Dorothy Garrod, is named for the number of men it can hold—one thousand.

Some of the Kurds do not own villages on the slopes. The whole tribe summers on the upland grassland and then migrates en masse in the fall. He who travels the Kermanshah-Baghdad highway in the first week of November will see a most colorful sight along the road from Kermanshah to the border. On November 3, 1949, we counted roughly three thousand people, men, women, and children, walking, riding on horseback, mounted on cattle, and bobbing in cradles on their mothers' backs. Every animal able to carry a load bore one. Sheep covered the road and left behind them a half-inch layer of droppings which, under the impact of truck and bus tires, soon turned to a temporary and slippery macadam.

Every two or three miles we would see a group of men, two to five in number, unobtrusively carrying rifles and sitting on their horses, peering around corners in the rocky wall of the canyon, alert for trouble. These were the leader of the tribe and his men, policing the migration, seeing that no two- or four-legged creature should be left behind or get into trouble. Early every afternoon the advance guard would choose a camping place and unload their animals. piling the packs into semicircular enclosures and building fires. By dark most of the stragglers would be in. Animals and men usually could withstand the rigors and fatigue of this journey, except for the dogs. Even in the middle of the day they plodded along, glassy-eyed, their tongues hanging. By midafternoon some were riding.

These Kurds winter in the stubble of the fields of farmers who till the border of the Tigris plain, and on the grass which winter rains bring to the desert border. They make arrangements with these farmers, who may be Arabs, Assyrians, or Kurds like themselves, as they do with the villagers near whose homes they camp on the roads up and back. As a rule they do not own their winter pasture, but lease it. They do own the land of their summer pasture, however, and this they consider their home.

Economically, they produce an excess of wool, skins, milk, and mutton. Some of them are able to grow a little grain during the short summer season and to harvest a little fruit and pick some pistachio nuts, which they can also use in trade. The towns are so located relative to the mountain pastures that if a Kurd wants to trade during the summer he can usually reach a market within a six or seven hour's ride. He will start at three or four in the morning and may be back late the same night. He can obtain his tea and sugar, shiny brocaded cloth, knives and axes, and whatever else he needs in the town. Even if the sale of firearms is prohibited, he usually knows where to find them.

However, he may not be obliged to leave his upland meadow at all, for itinerant peddlers move from camp to camp with their wares. Some are Kurds, nontribal or from distant groups, selling sugar, tea, candles, matches, cigarettes, needles, and thread—the usual wares of the small peddler in any land. Others are Mongoloid wanderers from the cities of Russian and Chinese Turkestan; they specialize in repairing broken porcelain dishes with wire. These two, the Kurds and the Turkis, come as single men. A third group joins the summer herders with entire families, and these are the Qarach, or gypsies, riding on mules and donkeys and driving with them a few cows and sometimes sheep.

Like gypsies everywhere, they are viewed wtih suspicion. The women, who wear bright-colored clothing as in Hungary and Spain, tell fortunes and sell semiprecious stones guaranteed to bring lovers and babies. Like the Kurdish chapmen the male gypsies peddle small wares, but they also sharpen knives and sickles, repair pots and pans, and mend shoes. Along with goods and services they bring the Kurds amusement, putting on acrobatic shows with tightrope walking, and making monkeys dance and turn to the beat of the drum.

Politically the nomadic Kurds have one need: a strong authority—to assign the grazing, to police the critical three or four days of migration, and to deal with the owners of the warm lands where the tribe winters. This authority is furnished by the regular tribal mechanism of a division between nobles and commoners, chiefs and retainers, which all Kurds who live in the mountains, be they farmers or herdsmen, both need and possess. We shall consider this stratification later.

To the southeast is the country of the Lurs, or Lur-i-Kuchek. (The Lur-i-Buzurg are the Bakhtiari.) These people are subdivided into many small tribes with no over-all authority and apparently a multitude of different combinations of pasturage and tillage. I have found no competent work on either their economy or their social structure.

Beyond them is the country of the Bakhtiari, often described,[4] and magnificently depicted in the documentary film, *Grass,* by Cooper and Schoedsack. In summer they live in the valleys of the Upper Karun and its tributaries, including the headwaters of the Ab-i-Diz. Here the Zagros forms two ranges, an outer and an inner, with seven- to eight-thousand-foot alpine valleys between. The outer range is pierced in places for the tumultuous passage of the rivers into the Lower Karun, which crosses the plain of Ahwaz, the ancient land of Elam, to join the Shaṭṭ al-ʿArab. The valleys and their borders are forested with oak, elm, tamarisk, willow, apple, pear, cherry, plum, walnut, almond, and most of the other temperate fruits and decorative trees and shrubs that are elsewhere cultivated. There is especially an abundance of sweet acorns, which the mountaineers eat raw and make into flour.

The Bakhtiari, who inhabit this paradise in summer, are divided into two moieties, the Haft Lang and Chahar Lang, or Seven and Four tribes, on the basis of traditional ancestry from two brothers, one of whom had seven and the other four male offspring. Each tribe is further divided into clans, or camping units, consisting of a number of related families who always migrate together. Over each clan is a *ḳetchudā* (or katkhodā), whose office is elective, although some may contrive to make it hereditary. He is responsible for the conduct of his contingent on the long and arduous route of march, and he makes certain that his people take up their proper position in the great camp during tribal assemblies and also keep their sheep within their own pasture.

At the head of each tribe is a khan, whose office is strictly hereditary; over him are the *Ilḳhani,* the paramount chief of the Bakhtiari, and his deputy, the *Ilbegi.* Both these offices are elective from certain highly placed families and subject to confirmation by the shah, whose representative the Ilkhani becomes. Like that of provincial governors, his office is subject to revision every year. During most of the known history of this confederation the two top posts have been held within the Haft Lang, as at present, but the Chahar Lang also has had its day. The ruling family sends some of its sons to Tehran and else-

[4] Mrs. Isabella Bishop, *Journeys in Persia and Kurdistan.* Sir A. H. Layard, *Early Adventures in Persia, Susiana, and Babylonia,* 2 vols. M. C. Cooper and E. B. Schoedsack, *Grass* (New York, 1925), also their film of the same name. See also a novel by Youel Mirza, *Stripling* (New York, 1940). The tribe in which this story is set is not named.

where to be educated. A daughter is ex-Queen Suraya of Iran.

The Ilkhani has a summer capital at Shalamzar,[5] a village of 1400 people with a bazaar; its inhabitants farm and weave rugs. Near it the Ilkhani owns an experimental orchard. Among other villages in his summer pasture land are those of the Chahar Mahals, or Four Districts,[6] mostly inhabited by Armenians and Persianized Georgian Muslims. During the summer he holds court not only at Shalamzar but also at two other villages, Ardal and Auragun. At Auragun, which wears an air of hoary antiquity, a sacred stone stands under a grove of giant walnut trees: this stone, like the Stone of Scone, is well worn by the buttocks of kings. On it the Ilkhani sits as he hears compaints and renders justice.

While the Lurs (Lur-i-Kuchek) make many separate tribal migrations and consequently have many separate tribal governments, the Bakhtiari of all eleven tribes migrate twice a year as a single unit, since there is but one practicable way up and down between winter and summer pastures and only one short period each season when it is profitable to take it. The steep, snowy slopes, and the rushing waters of the Upper Karun, which must be crossed on rafts of inflated skins, are difficult enough for anyone; without expert organization and firm control, a migration of so many animals and people over such a trail could end only in rout.

The Bakhtiari obtain their food from their flocks and from the agricultural efforts of the villagers under their control, not only in the Chahar Mahals but in their winter pasture (garmsir) as well. Even in the summer pasture (sardsir) they grow a little grain and collect wild fruits. The proximity of the villages in summer, and of towns in winter, gives them a chance to trade, an opportunity of which the nearby Armenians take full advantage.

The Qashqai, who live east of the Bakhtiari along the Zagros chain and speak Turkic, are also organized as a unit, since they too must make a single migration twice yearly. Their garmsir is not contiguous with their sardsir, and they like some of the Kurds are obliged to pass through the territory of other peoples. They are ruled by a family of brothers, one of whom lives in Shiraz and another in Tehran, and who are Western-educated. Their organization is quite strict and efficient, and they are a powerful military force.

[5] A picture of an old palace may be found in Layard, *op. cit.*, I, 364.

[6] Lar, Khya, Mizak, and Gandaman. Bishop, *op. cit.* p. 31.

[7] *Ibid.*, p. 294.

These examples should suffice to illustrate the rationale of the second kind of nomadism, that of high alpine pastures and sheep. It requires tight organization of all who migrate together, while the number of different kinds of people needing each other's services is relatively small. Between herding and agriculture one sees many gradual stages, like a four-footed animal learning to walk. Camel nomadism, on the other hand, is an all-out shift, like a man-child leaving his mother's fingers and taking his first step.

Our third kind of nomadism is only marginal in the Middle East, being limited to the sea-level plain north of the Elburz in northeastern Iran and northwestern Afghanistan. It belongs to the vast grasslands of central Asia, from the Don past the Caspian to China, broken by deserts and watered by mountains. It is the ancient and barbarously magnificent horse culture of the Scythians of Herodotus, of Attila the Hun, of Jenghiz Khan, and of his grandson Hulagu, who gave the caliph of Baghdad gold to eat and whose name still brings shivers and black looks when mentioned in some countries of the Middle East.

It is a way of life built around the possession of the standard domestic animals on a vast grassy steppe. Horses, which must be hand-fed on the deserts, graze here at will. Cattle, which need the stubble of irrigated fields for their sustenance in more arid lands, graze with the horses, while sheep, which can live where any of the others can (except for camels), are also at home on the steppe, led and herded by their brighter cousin, the goat. Camels too are raised on the grassy plains, but they are the heavier-boned, warmer-coated bactrians to be seen all the way across Mongolia to China. The ass, the prime short-haul burden-bearer of most of the Middle East, is missing, for he cannot stand the cold; his small hoofs sink quickly through the snow which chills his scantily covered vitals.

The horse, which is the key animal of this nomadic complex, receives quite different treatment at the hands of the Turko-Mongol peoples of the steppes from that lavished on him by the Arab of the desert. To the Arab the horse is an expensive luxury, to be ridden only in the last dash of battle and in ceremonial procession. It cannot be milked, flayed, or eaten, or hitched to a cart. It is a symbol of its owner's high place in his relations with his fellows and a critical means of retaining that place in moments of life and death.

To the plainsmen a horse is one of many animals to be herded and grazed. A single man may own not merely a share in one horse but in many horses, and he need not be a chief. He rides a horse not only in battle but also, and much more frequently, on his daily business. His wife milks his mares and from the milk ferments his favorite drink. He will butcher a fat young stallion for its meat and tan its skin for his saddle. He too loves his favorite mount and cares for it tenderly. When a man dies, if his people are not too strictly Muslim, they will kill his favorite mount and bury it with him beneath a mound, so that in the green pastures of the afterworld he will not have to walk.

Although this grasslands horse culture is not the property of any one race or linguistic group, in the Middle East (as defined for the purposes of this book) it belongs almost exclusively to a single people, the Turkomans or Turkmen. Many more of these people live in the U.S.S.R. than in Iran and Afghanistan. They are the masters of Merv Oasis and also inhabit Khiva, on a branch of the Amu Darya River. It should be noted that their country does not consist of continuously habitable terrain; to the north it consists of an oasis and a river valley, and to the south, a plain watered by the runoff of the Elburz Mountains. In between are deserts which can only be crossed caravanwise.

The Turkomans who concern us are those living on the northern Elburz slopes and plain, from the eastern shore of the Caspian to the point where the Amu Darya enters Soviet territory. Even these are spatially separated. The Turkomans divide themselves into five main confederations or groups of tribes: the Salu in the Sarrakhs region,[8] Saruk at Merv, the Tekke in the Ashkabad country, the Goklan to their west, and the Yamut on the Gurgan plain, just east of the Caspian Sea. The Yamut live chiefly in Iranian territory, although they graze their animals on both sides of the border, which is the Atrek River. Or so they did until the Russians fortified the boundary and forbade crossings.

The country of the Yamuts is dotted with mounds, some as symmetrical as cupcakes and extending up to eighty feet in height. The tallest of these, Tureng Tepe, yielded twenty-two vessels of gold to treasure hunters in the early nineteenth century. Some of the mounds are the remains of villages, but others are the tombs of the kings and chieftains of an unknown Bronze Age people, or succession of

[8] Baron C. A. de Bode, "On the Yamud and Gokland Tribes of Turkomania," *Journal of the Ethnological Society of London*, I (Edinburgh, 1848), 60-78.

peoples, comparable to the royal tombs of the Scyths in the Nikopol region of Russia, near the bend of the lower Volga. These ancient warriors buried their important dead in their winter quarters, and the modern Turkomans use the same mounds as cemeteries.

The Yamuts, who number forty to fifty thousand families, are divided into five tribes, each of which is subdivided into from five to ten *shafts,* or camping units. These tribes are said to be descended from five brothers, whose father, Yamud, founded the nation. They are further divided into two categories on the basis of means of livelihood, and these categories—Chomur and Chorva—cut across tribes.

The Chomur live entirely in Iran, from the Gurgan River to a small stream called the Qarassu (Black Water) and up to Tureng Tepe. Although they own and graze animals, they are primarily farmers, raising wheat and melons and vegetables, and some rice in favored spots. Some live in houses, but most of them still occupy yurts.

A word about the yurt. It is to the steppes what the black tent is to the deserts and mountain pastures. All of the Turko-Mongol peoples use the yurt, from the Kalmuk Steppe of southern Russia to Manchuria. It consists of a portable frame and a covering material. The frame includes three principal parts: a doorway, side walls and roof. The doorway includes a frame of threshold, lintel, and sides, all undemountable, and the door itself, while the side walls are made of thin strips of beechwood set diagonally in two tiers and jointed. This frame will thus expand and collapse, and can be taken apart. Made fast to the doorframe at each end, it produces a circular wall in the form of a grille of diamond-shaped openings, some twelve feet in diameter. The roof is in two parts, a fixed wheel for the peak, and shafts to join the wheel to the top of the grille. All are lashed together, and the frame is braced by a band of hair webbing around the center, horizontally. Then the Turkomans lay sheets of black felt over the roof and make them fast; they cover the walls with the same material in winter, and with latticed bamboo in summer. A forked stake to windward holds a guy rope, and all is ready.

These movable houses are better than tents in their own environment because they are warm in winter. They are heavier and bulkier to move, but the Turkomans have carts on which to carry them. The circular space inside is divided into conventional areas, for the shrine, for the master and his wife, for the children, for guests, and so on. The furniture is built with curved backs, and everything is tidy and orderly. So much of Turkoman family behavior is regulated in terms of the spatial arrangements of this round house that they prefer living in it even when they are sedentary.

The Chorvas, whose home is the Atrek River country, are not farmers. They migrate northward in summer to the Balkhan hills, just west of Krasnovodsk and north of the Russian Transcaspian Railway. Here an altitude of more than five thousand feet provides moisture, a little summer precipitation, and grass. In the fall they return to the Atrek. (Such was the case, at least, before the Russian occupation, and the closing of the border. Now camps of these Chorvas are to be seen on the north bank of the Gurgan.)

The Chomurs are usually at peace with the Iranian government. They go regularly to the market at Gurgan where they sell their felt carpets and so-called "Bukhara" rugs, wheat, barley, butter, and sheep and horses, and buy manufactured goods, including cutlery and cloth. One village of Chomurs less than a mile beyond Tureng Tepe is called Gamish-li, or Water Buffalo People, who specialize in herding these animals. In 1949 a Persian farmer from Tureng Tepe village by mistake shot a water buffalo belonging to a widow of Gamish-Li, and great was the agitation which followed. While he had admitted at first that he had taken it for a gazelle, within twenty-four hours the story had changed; the water buffalo had been a notorious trampler of crops and had had to be put out of the way. Incidents like this cause trouble along the border, but no more than the system will take.

The Chorvas, however, were rarely at peace. They raided each other as well as Persian villages far into settled country. Even down at Khunik in the southern reaches of Khorasan, we were told of Turkoman raids as late as the turn of the century. These raids were for animals and other movable property, and especially for slaves. Until the Russian occupation there was an insatiable demand for Persian slaves in the khanates of Turkestan. One hundred years ago a young man would bring one hundred and fifty dollars and a young woman three hundred dollars, in the dollar-equivalent currency of the time. When the Russians took Khiva in 1864, they liberated forty thousand slaves, nearly all of whom were Persians.[9] This represented an investment of about ten million dollars. Slave raiding was big business.

[9] W. Jochelson, *Peoples of Asiatic Russia* (New York, 1928), p. 95.

As with the Tuareg, not all the slaves reach the market. Many of the more desirable young women remained in the yurts of their captors as wives or concubines. Again as with the Tuareg, a class distinction arose between the offspring of Turkoman mothers and the progeny of these captives. Only the former were considered noble. Since a racial distinction also obtained, the more Mongoloid type was the nobler.

Distinguished in another way, however, are those Turkoman families who claim Arab descent, not necessarily from the Prophet but from the first four caliphs, Abu Bakr, ʿOsman (as they call him), ʿUmar, and ʿAlī. The members of these shafts are holy men, like the murabiṭīn of North Africa and the Sahara. No one will harm them, and by virtue of this immunity, they have become caravan men and traveling merchants. It is they who conduct the camel caravans across the deserts between the Elburz slopes and the oases and who provide goods to outlying camps of Chorvas.

Blacksmithing is an honorable profession among the Turks of all kinds, as among Europeans. There are specialists in this work among the Turkomans themselves. Copper and brass vessels can easily be purchased at the bazaars of Gurgan, Sarrakhs, and the oasis towns, and the nonferrous metal work undoubtedly is done by Persian craftsmen or by Turks trained in the Persian techniques.

In this system of nomadism, then, we find first the distinction between sedentaries and nomads. This is not a sharp line, for if a man loses his flocks he may settle down as a farmer, while a rich agriculturist may buy flocks and set out as a nomad with some of his kin already living in that fashion. In the old days a Chorva could grow rich raiding; his Chomur kin might conceal him but would not dare join him. From the Chomurs the Chorva get vegetable food. A second distinction is between nobles and second-class citizens, based on blood lines, which are important since kinship forms the basis of the political institution. A third is between other Turkomans and the members of holy families, and this serves to keep the lines of transport and communication open across the desert. This is a system of moderate complexity, suited to its needs.

At the beginning of this chapter it was pointed out that different environments suited to grazing placed special priorities on different animals. So far we have studied those based on the camel, the sheep, and the horse. Another interesting animal, which has been mentioned only in passing, is the water buffalo. Wherever it is wet enough, wherever there are rivers and pools in which they can wallow, these animals may usually be seen. Inevitably they are in the charge of small children, whom the huge and often ferocious beasts will obey.

Among the Kurds of the foothills west of Lake Urmiya, and the Azerbaijani Turks and Assyrians, these animals are part of the usual barnyard population, and boys take them out in summer to graze and swim. Among the Turkomans, of course, a special group of villages have become water buffalo people, profiting from the milk and meat. In southern ʿIraq also, there are whole camps of water buffalo folk who rent pasture from the farmers and who shift their tunnel-like tents of straw matting a half mile or so at a time, as the fields they occupy come into cultivation. Since the water buffalo folk, whatever their nationality, always live in settled country and near markets, they lead their lives on a village level of simplicity.

14 TOWN AND CITY

THE VILLAGE AND THE NOMAD CAMP are the smallest, most integral units of community life found in the Middle East. They need each other, for the nomads must have vegetable food, while the villagers must receive processed goods from outside on the backs of the animals which the nomads raise. This exchange, however, is seldom direct. Villagers and campers barter products through the intermediacy of town and city traders. Both are dependent on town and city for manufactured goods and for socially necessary "luxuries" such as sugar, tea, and coffee.

A town is a community of traders and processors which has grown up around an outdoor market or through the expansion of a village handily situated for commerce. It also may have grown down, through the decay of a city. The difference between a town and a village is this: although the villagers include a few specialists, such as a carpenter, midwife, and bath-keeper, they care for the needs of the people of that village alone. The specialists in the town serve not only their fellow burghers but also the people of the surrounding camps and villages. The town is like the nucleus of a cell which includes all the villages dependent on it. Unless it has some local specialty it deals only in second-class merchandise, such as candles, matches, needles, thread, trade cloth, and hardware, and in foodstuffs.

Such a town, for example, is ʿAfaq (locally pronounced ʿAfej), in south-central ʿIraq, near the massive ruins of ancient Nippur. Housing some three thousand persons, ʿAfaq is located on a canal between the Tigris and Euphrates. Before the days of trucking and while it was still navigable, this canal provided the principal channel of communication with the rest of the country, as well as water. One bridge crosses it. On the west bank stand a number of relatively large buildings, widely spaced. These, the property of the central government, include the residence and offices of the *qāʾim-maqām,* who is district chief, deputy to the *mutaṣarrif* or governor of the province, located in Diwaniya. The judge also holds his court here; the police chief has his office and barracks, as well as the recruiting officer. A school, under the national Ministry of Education, provides primary instruction to the children of the town; a doctor from Baghdad operates a small hospital and clinic, and an irrigation officer has his headquarters here also. The smallest of these buildings is the "club," where the white-collar workers on this side of the canal convene to listen to the radio, to read magazines, and to play checkers.

This side of the canal, then, is given over to the activities of the government officials, whose duties were to administer the entire district, of which, in 1948, not one of them was a native. The qā'im-maqām and the judge were Shī'a Muslims from larger centers; the chief of police was a Sunni from the north; and the recruiting officer was a Christian Arab. The doctor and irrigation officer were both Jews. (I am not sure about the schoolteachers, of whom there were several.) These gentlemen of different sects and faiths all got along nicely together, dining and entertaining each other, and us,[1] in complete harmony.

The east side of the canal is the town itself. The road from Diwaniya leads directly across the government part of the town to the bridge, and beyond the canal it becomes the main *sūq,* or market, of 'Afaq. Here the road is a covered street some twenty feet wide, with booths on both sides. About fifty yards down it is crossed by another street parallel to the canal. The cross made by these two thoroughfares forms the basis of the structure of the town. To the south, three widely spaced streets run parallel to the main sūq; to the north, one can count five through streets and two dead-end alleys, while another dead end is a short covered market off the intersection in the first block north of the main sūq.

Beyond the fifth street to the north is the town refuse area, a haunt of yellow dogs and black and white magpies, who soon dispose of the more noisome offal dumped there. At the far corner of the third canal-side block, going south, one may see a number of gay plaid cloths waving in the breeze; these are towels drying, and they reveal the location of the *ḥammām,* or steam bath. A bit beyond the ḥammām is a walled enclosure, used during the summer as a market for the country people, who seek the shelter of the covered sūqs in the chill and rain of winter. Beyond the summer market is another haunt of scavenging dogs and magpies, the town slaughterhouse,

1 The members of the Nippur expedition, a joint enterprise of the Universities of Pennsylvania and of Chicago, led by Dr. Donald McCown.

where early in the morning the butchers perform their grisly task at a suitable distance from human habitation. Beyond this is a quiet and well-proportioned little dome, standing in the center of an enclosure and bedecked with shreds of colored cloth and a string of blue beads. This is a shrine. It marks the place where a sayyid's body was once washed before being carried to Karbala for burial. Inside is a small altar, patinated by the same hands which have tinted the walls of the doorway with henna.

The town is divided into four wards along the axes of the two main thoroughfares. Each ward is headed by an official called the *mukhtār,* appointed by the qā'im-maqām and approved by his constituents. His duties include acting as imām in the mosque of the ward; each has one, and all are Imāmi Shī'a. Over the four mukhtārs is the *ra'īs baladiya,* or town mayor, similarly appointed and confirmed. Besides acting as chief in interward affairs, he is the provost of the market and in charge of public works, such as keeping the street lights lighted and in order.

The townspeople include farmers who go out to their fields by the day, craftsmen, traders, and specialists in transportation. Butchers, dyers, weavers, grain merchants, cloth merchants, small grocers (*baql*-keepers), greengrocers, blacksmiths, tinsmiths, hardware merchants, tobacconists, tailors, shoemakers, barbers, bath attendants, gasoline and oil vendors, automobile mechanics, taxi-men, truck drivers, donkeymen, camelmen, and sailors—this is the list, as completely as Dr. Maḥmūd al-Amīn and I could make it in the time at our disposal. To it may be added the proprietors and personnel of two cafés, and of one small restaurant specializing in delicious shish-kababs.

Most of the craftsmen and shopkeepers apparently were natives of the town, but such was not the case with the specialists in transport. All of the truck drivers were outsiders, and so were most of the taxi-men, although some local youths had begun to take up driving and automobile repairing. The donkeymen included a few locals, but most of them belonged to a separate donkey people, whose village stood outside, and who specialized in the sale of charcoal as well as in transport. The camelmen were Bedawin. The sailors, whose business has fallen off because of the competition of the truckers and the silting of the canal, had their homes and families in the town and their *balams,* boats of Sumerian design, moored in the canal outside. It was their practice to go up to Hilla and down to Bedair with passengers and cargo. In the days of the first Nippur expedition, in the 1880's, this was the principal means of transportation to and from ʿAfaq, and of moving supplies and specimens.

When we walked into the covered sūq, we were usually greeted by the ra'īs baladiya, who escorted us to the shops, supervised the sales, and motioned back the crowd. It was winter, and the country people sat about the main intersection, displaying their wares on reed mats. As usual, some days were best for certain kinds of merchandise—early on a Thursday morning, for example, might be the time for mats. Some commodities were on sale every day, including water buffalo butter, which came in on the heads of the water buffalo womenfolk quite early, in time for breakfast. Outside the town one could see where these people came from: on the way to the site one passes a farming village, a camp of water buffalo people, a camp of Bedawin, several more villages, and a power-driven grist mill. Each of these aggregations had its role in the economy of the town and in the ecology of the district of which the town is the nucleus.

This leads to the next distinction: what is the difference between a town and a city? The city is larger. It is the seat of a more highly ranking government official. It handles a greater volume of trade. These are quantitative differences. What we are seeking is something qualitative, and as usual it appears out of a combination of quantitative changes. What is new about a city is that its craftsmen are superlatively skillful, making one or more kinds of de luxe objects which have a national, if not world-wide, reputation.

The reason for this is that the region is naturally endowed with a large quantity of some special kind of raw materials and that the number of craftsmen is so great that they exchange ideas, stimulating each other to greater effort and production of goods of increasingly finer quality. (It is like a large department in a university. The instructors and research men can talk over each other's ideas and together forge them into something new and sound, while the one-man department in another university has trouble even keeping up with the literature.)

In the Middle East the same thing happened. Fez, as we shall see shortly, was supreme in leather. Nablus made tamarindi, the carob sweet, the Arab predecessor of our cola drinks. The inhabitants of Sarmin, near Homs, manufactured brick soap, perfumed and unperfumed, red and yellow. Nasibin in northern ʿIraq produced rose water, Malaga turned out gilded pottery, while Wezzan wove fine tufted woolens. Baalbek craftsmen specialized in wooden plates and spoons, in sets of ten plates which fitted inside each other, and ten graded spoons to occupy the hollow space in the middle, the whole to be carried in a leather case.[2] These products moved from one end of the Middle East to the other, and beyond.

Like those in the town, the traders of the city are divided into two recognized classes, the *tājirs,* or wholesale export-import merchants, and the *baqqāls,* or retail shopkeepers. In the city the tājirs handle a variety of kinds of merchandise, while in a town like ʿAfaq they are confined to handling cloth and cereals. In the town most of the people aside from the government officials are of the same religion, while in the city one usually finds members of several Muslim sects and also Jews and Christians, although this is not invariable.

These are all real differences, but they are not sufficiently clear-cut to form the basis of a definition. Just as the village becomes a town under certain circumstances, so is there a threshold between town and city. In my opinion this threshold is the presence or absence of guilds. In the town the mukhtārs or their equivalents care for the domestic organization of the citizens, as members of wards, while the ra'īs baladiya or his equivalent controls their relations as manufacturers and traders. When the town grows and the number of individuals engaged in each craft or kind of trade increases beyond a certain point, the market provost and his deputies are unable to cope with the situations that arise between the members of a single craft and between crafts. Then the members of each craft organize as separate institutions, each with its head under the over-all guidance of the provost. The town has become a city.

In all the Middle East (as defined in Chapter 1) there must be at least fifty thousand villages and several thousand towns. The cities, however, may be numbered only in the hundreds. Of these hundreds some thirty or forty come to mind immediately: Marrakesh, Meknes, Tangier, Fez, Tlemsen, Algiers, Constantine, Qairawan, Tunis, Tripoli, Alexandria, Cairo, Tanta, Istambul, Izmir, Aden, Ṣanʿā, Mekka, al-Madina, Masqat, Kuwait, Basra, Baghdad, Jerusalem, Beirut, Damascus, Ḥoms, Ḥama, Aleppo, Mosul, Tabriz, Hamadam, Isfahan, Shiraz, Ahwaz, Tehran, Mashhad, Herat, and Kabul. These do not include Casablanca and Oran, which were small ports before

[2] For Nablus, Sarmin, Nasibin, Malaga, and Baalbek, see Ibn Baṭṭūṭa, *Travels in Asia and Africa, 1325–1354,* pp. 57, 61, 103, 314, and 64.

the French occupation, nor Dhahran and Abadan, which amounted to little before the days of oil.

Of these thirty or forty, about nine are historically and geographically paramount, and of these, two are ports of two other cities. In my opinion, these key cities of the old Muslim Middle East are Fez, Tunis, Cairo, Istambul, Damascus, Baghdad, Isfahan, Tabriz, and Mashhad.[3] Cairo and Alexandria, and the Baghdad-Basra combination are the nuclei of the two great exotic river valleys. Fez is the crossroads between the north-south caravan road from Tangier, and hence Europe, to the Sudan, and the east-west Sultan's Road (*Ṭarīq es-Sulṭān*), which ties the fertile Atlantic plain of Morocco to the rest of the world of Islam. Tunis, a few miles from ancient Carthage, is the natural port and center for the grain-rich intermontane valleys at the eastern end of the Atlas ridges. Damascus is at another crossroads: there meet the caravan route from the Yemen and the east-west road around the desert and down the Nahr al-Kebīr Valley to the Mediterranean. Tabriz became the principal trading center for ʿIraq and Iran after the destruction of Baghdad by the Mongols. It is a gateway to central Asia and China. Mashhad is the center of rich Khorasan, and the jumping-off point for caravans which swung eastward along the narrow road between the Elburz and the Dasht-i-Kavir, into the khanates of central Asia, and across Afghanistan into India.

Each of these cities forms the center of a rich agricultural area, and this is necessary to feed its inhabitants, who ran into the hundreds of thousands even in the earlier periods, while one or two, such as Cairo, have topped the million mark. Writing in the thirteenth century, Ibn Baṭṭūṭa lists among Cairo's inhabitants twelve thousand camel-using water carriers, thirty thousand mule and donkey renters, and the crews of thirty-six thousand Nile boats.[4] Several hundred thousand city people produce great quantities of manufactured goods, and the same large rural population which feeds them is needed to buy their products. Such large rural populations are the exception in the Middle East. The numerous inhabitants of a city also need to drink, to wash, and to use water for a number of industrial purposes such as milling grain, tanning hides, and scouring wool. Their water supply must far exceed that needed for a village or town, and it must be perennial and seasonally constant. Few places in the Middle

[3] I omit Tehran from this list because its greatness is modern.

[4] Ibn Baṭṭūṭa, *op. cit.,* p. 50.

East meet these requirements. Those which do, when favorably located for trade, are the sites of the cities in which we are interested.

Our nine selected cities are provided with water from two sources, exotic rivers and mountain streams. Cairo, Alexandria, Baghdad, and Basra have river water, abundant but muddy. Although some drink this water as it comes out of the stream, most prefer it filtered; huge porous clay jars were used for this purpose long before the erection of the filtration plants which now serve these cities. (Baghdad water tastes exactly like that of Philadelphia.) Tunis, Tabriz, and Mashhad are all watered by streams coming from neighboring mountains. Damascus is particularly favored by a whole river of cold, clear water which leaps out of a natural tunnel in the limestone hills some twenty miles west of the city, while Fez, built in the fold of a limestone plateau, receives a similar supply which rises near the upper end of the city.

If the town is the nucleus of a cell, the city is a nucleus of the next magnitude, about which a number of cells of lower density cluster. In the universe of the Middle East, these giant cells or cell clusters are spatially so arranged that a mutual relationship between all of them is apparent. At the risk of carrying this cytological simile too far, it might be said that the city itself has a cell-like structure with its own nucleus, its own mechanisms for withstanding shocks from within and without, and its own ways of absorbing and sloughing off foreign materials.

Although many people know the structure of many Middle Eastern cities, few have recorded their knowledge in a methodical fashion. Furthermore, in most Middle Eastern countries modernization has produced its maximum effect in the cities, and while it is simple to find an "unspoiled" village, or even town, a comparable city is rare. Hama may be such, and Ṣanʿā certainly was before the recent Jewish exodus, but neither has been carefully studied. Only one suitable city has been studied and documented in detail, and this is Fez. French sociologists and geographers, trained in the functional school of Durkheim and the Arabist tradition of Levi-Provençal, have pinned down the workings of this city to the smallest detail. Their work is a triumph of organization and method.

In 1911 General Moinier led a column of French troops into Fez. Like earlier visitors, they found it unchanged, a perfect and intact medieval city. The merchants of Fez were not unaware of the modern world; France and Britain had consulates there, and European schools had even been opened.[5] Colonies of Fāsis (natives of Fez) lived in Manchester and Marseilles, and one tājir had an English wife. The people of Fez, however, had managed to incorporate foreign trade into their lives without affecting the physical appearance of their city or the social structure of its inhabitants. Struck by its white and delicate beauty, Marechal Lyautey decreed that Fez should suffer no alteration. He planned, instead, a modern city to be built on the shoulder of the pass, some three miles to the west. Although hard times have come, and the streets of Fez are not as crowded as they were in 1911, the old city is still there, as any tourist can see, and as many have so done.

Fez is off center, being located at one corner of the Middle Eastern world, and it is small, with just under one hundred thousand population, although at its peak it must have reached two hundred thousand. It is, however, quite typical, and it is as much the cultural capital of its country as Cairo, Baghdad, or Damascus. In the total Middle Eastern picture, it might be compared to Boston in America. What is true of Fez is also true in a general way of every Muslim city, and the knowledge obtained by these outstanding studies can be applied widely elsewhere.

The first essential about Fez is its water. The Wed Fās flows through the city. It has been diverted into a number of channels, mostly underground, which provide nearly every large household in the main part of the city with a private source, while public fountains in the streets take care of the less privileged. Thus there is less work for the water carriers with their cups and goatskin bags than in most cities. Water carriers, however, do offer drinks to the thirsty in the market district; this service is paid for by a religious foundation. Unlike many oriental cities where the water is at the same time a source and a sewer, Fez has a separate drainage system, into which many toilet holes empty. The system emerges at the foot of the city into the river bed. It is said to have been built by a French renegade in the 1780's.

This water flows equally all the year around. It provides two hundred and eighty-six gallons a day per person (as compared to about 143 gallons in New York City). Hence the Fāsis are able to flush the streets on hot days and to sprinkle the markets; rich householders

[5] R. Le Tourneau, *La Ville de Fès avant le Protectorat* (Casablanca, 1949), p. 471.

can cool their gardens with fountains which spurt to a height of five feet and more, owing to the water drop of two hundred and fifty feet in less than a mile. This drop also provides power for the row of grist and tanbark mills, and for the hydroelectric power plant built in 1920, which provides electric light for nearly every house in the city and power for a number of factories outside.

The city itself was founded in 808 A.D. by Mūlai Idrīs II, a holy sharīf (as descendants of the Prophet are called in Morocco) and ancestor of the whole class of Idrīsite *shōrfa* (Moroccan Arabic plural of sharīf) who inhabit the city today. The land previously had been occupied by a small number of Christians, Jews, and "fire worshipers," who probably used it as a market center for the surrounding tribes. Refugee craftsmen from Cordova settled on the south bank and founded the Adwat al-Andalūsiyin, or Andalusian Quarter. Merchants from Qairawan, in Tunisia, settled the north bank, forming the Adwat al-Qarawiyin, which included a small Jewish section called Funduq al-Yahūdi (Jew's Hostel). At first these two quarters functioned as separate cities, but in 1070 A.D. Yūsuf ibn Tashfīn, the founder of Marrakesh, tore down the walls between them and added a third quarter, Adwat al-Lemtiyin, to the west, upstream. Like modern cities in Iran, Fez was growing upstream. In 1274 the Sultan Abu Yūsuf Yaʿqūb built a whole new section, Fās Jadīd (New Fez) still farther upstream. This included the royal palace and its grounds, a quarter for Muslims who were not of local descent, a *Millāḥ* or Jewish quarter, to which those Jews willing to leave Funduq al-Yahūdi moved, and a *qaṣba,* or fortified stronghold, the keep of the city. Although nearly eight hundred years old, Fās Jadīd is still the "new" city, still inhabited by government officials, Jews, parvenus, and outsiders. Some of the Jews refused to leave their mansions in the Funduq al-Yahūdi, preferring conversion; many of the wealthiest and most renowned Muslim families of Old Fez are their descendants.

The great period of Fez extended from the eleventh through the fifteenth centuries, the fourteenth being the peak. It was the political capital of the Maghrib, a center of manufacture, world trade, and education. Its universities were especially famous and drew students even from Europe to study astronomy, mathematics, geography, chemistry, anatomy, and medicine. History, law, and theology appealed to the orthodox. As late as 1613 its university libraries contained more than thirty-two thousand volumes, which would be difficult to find today.

About the time of the settlement of America and the formation of the great companies of the Indies among the Christian nations to the north, Fez began to slip back into dignified decay (for reasons to be discussed later). Cut off from the rest of the Muslim world by distance and desert, it was preserved in a comparative vacuum until the life span of men now living.

What made Fez great? For one thing, people of high quality. Mūlai Idrīs and his followers were no untutored Bedawin. They were city men from Ḥijāz and al-Yemen, firm in the faith, high-principled, and learned. Intermarriage with the Berber tribes on either side, but particularly to the north, brought in a hardy strain, while absorption of part of the early Jewish settlement added elements long versed in community living, crafts, trade, and the law. The Andalusians brought high skills, the Qairawan men experience in business. The blending of these elements produced the Fāsi, a special breed of men, especially trained. Fez is their city. Muslims from other regions may enter by day to work in the tanneries and other industrial enterprises, Jews to open their shops, but at night these perpetual strangers leave, and the gates are closed and locked.

For another thing, natural resources. To an abundance of clean, swift water may be added the presence of excellent limestone on the very edges of the city, long quarried for building material. A few hours' walk outside is a source of gypsum, needed for plaster, and even nearer is a deposit of clay to serve the potters. Around the city stand thousands of olive trees, furnishing quantities of oil for export, as well as for food, lamps, and soapmaking. Tanbark moves down on donkey back from the oak forests of the Riffian foothills and the Middle Atlas, while pit-sawn timbers of thuya and cedar supply the carpenters and cabinetmakers with material. Loads of charcoal come also from the forests.

The principal gateway to Fez is the Bab Bu Jlūd, from the west, the top of the rise. Through this gate one walks down along the course of the Wed Fās, much of which is covered over, while the street itself is shaded by a lattice work. On the left is the Bab Gīsa, the Tangier gate, which is also the gate of the Riffians, some of whom, in their yellow turbans and brown jellabas, can usually be seen resting in its shade. To the south is the Bab Ftuḥ, the Tafilelt gate. To the east, the Bab el Khok (Gate of Peaches) opens into a sprawling section of wealthy residences set in gardens; here the cream of Fez society summers.

Where the street descending from the Bu Jlūd gate meets the cross streets from the Bab Gīsa and the Bab Ftuḥ, there is the heart of the city. In it are the Qaiṣariya, or business section; the principal funduqs in which auctions are held; the principal universities; the mosque of the Qarawiyin; and, center of all and greatest shrine, the *zawiya* of Mūlaī Idrīs. This section is not only the heart of Fez; it is also the heart of the Qarawiyin quarter. The ʿAndalūsiyin has its own center with its great mosque and market place, for it was once a separate town, but these have been dwarfed. It is estimated that the Qarawiyin holds fifty-two thousand inhabitants to twenty-six thousand and five hundred for the ʿAndalūsiyin. It has twelve wards as against six, seventeen steam baths as against six, and ninety-two primary Qur'ānic schools as against twenty-four.[6]

The selling area is laid out by sūqs, one for each commodity. Those which concern fashion—such as silk, cotton print materials, and slippers—are crowded together in the Qaiṣariya, and their entrances are closed to animal traffic by highly polished poles over which one must step. The markets for less fashionable commodities spread around this center. Some have their own funduqs, large buildings of several stories built around a court and entered by a gate. The funduq is the center of a certain trade, and its guildhall, as for example the Najjārin or Carpenters' Funduq.[7] Some have as many as a hundred rooms, in which business may be carried out and tea drunk. They are stock exchanges for commodities. In the court wares are spread out and scales set up for weighing. Clerks sit by the doors to record transactions.

Tanneries and grain mills are located along the stream, for the water. Processing establishments are scattered where the rent is cheap. Weavers and shoemakers, who ply silent trades, often share business space for each others' company. Residences are located away from the center of town, with bakeries and baqqāls to provide bread and the small merchandise one finds in a village.

Prosper Ricard, writing in 1924,[8] named and described one hun-

[6] *Ibid.*, p. 136.

[7] Other funduqs are combination inns and boarding stables.

[8] "Les Métiers manuels à Fès," *Hesperis,* IV (1924), 205-224.

dred and five different hand skills concerned with processing alone, each with its body of specialists. To this he adds twenty-one kinds of specialists engaged in personal services, making one hundred and twenty-six. At least twenty kinds of traders and merchants can be identified, ten categories of political officers and staff, five for religion, and three for education aside from religion. Thus we reach a total of one hundred and sixty-four, which is probably a low estimate. This is truly a considerable division of labor.

For the town of ʿAfaq, Dr. al-Āmīn and I counted twenty to compare with these one hundred and sixty-four processors and traders, leaving out automobile men and the like who are also omitted from the Fez list. In Fez there is one trade or profession for about every six hundred and seventy persons. If we consider that omitting officials, holy men, housewives, children, slaves, servants, and old people, at least one out of four works at a trade, the average number of individual per trade would be about one hundred and sixty. This is enough to need organization. It is probably greater than the total of craftsmen and tradesmen in ʿAfaq. This alone illustrates the basic difference between town and city.

Space forbids reproduction of Ricard's list. However, the reader may wish to examine a few sections in detail, to get an idea of the degree of complexity involved. Under "Cereals" Ricard names: farmers who go outside the city to work on properties owned by rich citizens; mule drivers who carry grain, most of which is stored in pits just inside Bab Gīsa; the operators of two hundred-odd turbine grist mills; custom millers, number unspecified, who grind grain furnished by clients for a percentage; female kuskus rollers, who moisten semolina in baskets and roll it with the palms of their hands; bread kneaders, who produce some one hundred thousand loaves a day; bakers; makers of *sfenj,* a kind of doughnut cooked in deep fat; pastry cooks who specialize in a sweetmeat called "gazelle-horn"; female pastry cooks who specialize in the *paḳlava* or *mille-feuille* type of confection.

When a man wishes to build a house and has gone through the complications of establishing ownership of the land, and rights to roof over a section of a street, to use adjoining walls, and the like, he calls in a master mason, a master carpenter, and a master tiler. They study the project together, take measurements, and agree on a division of work. The owner buys the materials and pays off the three masters and their employees. Those hired by the master mason include five kinds of stonemasons, five kinds of lime workers,[9] and four kinds of plasterers. The master tiler deals with four kinds of specialists, the master carpenter with six. The total is twenty-three, skipping one for duplication.[10]

With such a fine division of labor among men who start learning their specialities in childhood, it is no wonder that a high level of technical perfection is achieved. I remember watching an old craftsman from Fez, one of the *zuwwāq,* or plaster carvers, with his helpers, working on a wall in the palace built in Tangier by the Honorable Maxwell Blake. The old man penciled out polygonal and floral designs on fine plaster at least two inches thick. His journeymen painstakingly chiseled them out, and the old man put on the finishing touches. The result was a decoration of extreme delicacy, a work of art.

All of the industry of Fez is hand work, except for milling. Including milling, each operation can be done by a team of a master, two or three journeymen, and the same number of apprentices, at the most. Hence each profession consists of a number of such parallel teams, organized into a guild. Of the many studies which have been made of these industries, that of the tanners is particularly suitable to consider as an example,[11] since tanning is the largest single industry in Fez, and its product, the city's most famous and most widely traded. The tanner's guild goes back to the founding of the city. Master tanners gathered here, to enjoy the abundance of water, hides, and tanbark, from Cordova, Qairawan, and Iran. Fez leather was once exported as far away as Baghdad, and shoes went to Egypt until the present century. Today many American women carry handbags made of Fez leather, although they may not know it. This is the famous Morocco leather, a trade name in bookbinding. At peak production these craftsmen tanned as many as four hundred and eighty thousand skins a year.

We might break down the subject of the tanning industry into four principal headings: *equipment, personnel,* the *actions* of the personnel with the equipment and with each other, and the *institu-*

[9] There is a duplication here between the quarriers who extract the building stone and those who cut out the lime for burning.

[10] See n. 9, above.

[11] R. Le Tourneau, L. Paye, and R. Guyot, "La Corporation des tanneurs et l'industrie de la tannerie à Fès," *Hesperis,* XXI (1935), 167-240, fasc. i-ii.

tions which these actions and interactions create. Equipment includes real estate, special installations on the same, movable equipment which is nonexpendable, and expendable materials. There are four tanneries in Fez in which one hundred and sixty-one master tanners, with their journeymen and apprentices, work, and one special plant, with sixty-six masters, in which wool is removed from sheepskins. This wool can be sold to the textile industry. Other animals do not present this problem. Their skins can go directly to the four tanneries. Over a dozen establishments provide the tanners with materials. These include four funduqs in which they buy raw goat- and cowskins, and semiprocessed sheepskins, three sūqs in which they buy alum, dyestuffs, pomegranate husks, and salt; four tan mills for tan and galls; and several grain mills which furnish bran, a by-product of flour milling.

In four mosques the tanners carry on ritual as members of their profession; three are special to them, like that of Sidi Yaʿqūb ad-Dubāghi (St. Jacob the Tanner); the fourth is the central zawiya of Mūlai Idrīs, which serves all crafts and professions. The zawiyas of five Ṣūfi brotherhoods care for their mystical needs, while the headquarters of three rifle companies furnish them with diversion outside the tan vats, as do the baths, teahouses, and their homes.

In the tanneries and sheepskin plant one can see roofed workshops, lime pits and platforms, round vats, tanning trenches, fixed mortars for crushing pomegranate husks, horizontal poles on which to hang skins, roofs on which to dry them, walls and open spaces, and in the corners, private chapels. The tanners' funduqs each contain booths, a paved courtyard, and a tearoom; the markets contain booths, the mills have their stones. These are all permanent installations on real estate, built for special purposes.

Portable but equally nonexpendable are the slanting poles on which the tanners scrape their skins, the pestles that go with the fixed mortars, semilunar knives, curved drawknives, lunate fleshers to be pressed by the tanner's chest, blocks of wood, graining irons, and cordage. At the mills are baskets and hammers.

Expendable materials may be divided into primary and secondary. Primary are the skins of goats, sheep, cows, and camels to be processed; secondary, the ingredients with which this is done; water, salt, lime, pigeon droppings, bran, tamarisk galls, alum, pomegranate husks, tartaric acid, and dyestuffs. In some very fine tanning fig syrup is also used.

The principal personnel are the full-time processors, who may be subdivided into four specialties, tanning proper, half-processing sheepskins, milling tanbark, and cutting tamarisk galls. The tanners and sheepskin men have their journeymen and apprentices. Other people involved in one way or another in the tanning business are hide sellers, ingredient sellers, gall brokers, auctioneers, leather buyers, hair buyers, sūq merchants, and the students who collect the droppings of the pigeons so thoughtfully fed by a religious foundation (ḥabūs). This list also includes the owners of the tanneries and funduqs, who are private businessmen, a corporation of holy men, officials of other corporations, and trustees for property owners. It also includes twenty political officers; thirteen clerks or notaries public who record transactions, an *amīn* or chief of each of the three tanners' guilds and one for the sheepskin men, the market provost (muḥtasib), the assistant provost (*ṣāḥib al-muḥtasib*), and the *pasha* of the city. One may also include certain religious officials: the staff of each mosque which tanners attend, including their private chapels, the shaikhs of their Ṣūfi lodges, and so on. In one way or another, the tanning industry involves everyone in the city, and many more outside it, although to most it is largely a matter of wearing shoes.

Now we have the places, the objects, the materials, and the people. Who does what with what to whom? (*Actions.*) This will fall into four categories: *obtaining, processing, getting rid of equipment and materials,* and *maintaining equilibrium* among the persons so occupied. The individual tanners obtain their use of the premises from their owners by paying rent. These owners are many and varied. One establishment is owned by three separate ḥabūs. One is the property of a number of private owners, some of whom call separately for their rent, while others employ a trustee to collect for the group. In 1924 rent cost each master tanner about seven to seven and a half francs per month, and the number of tanners per tannery ranged from six to eighty-seven.

The permanent installations, such as warehouses, vats, fixed mortars, and poles, may belong to different owners from the real estate itself; this is called *zīna* property. The tanner pays the zīna owner for the use of his equipment, and the zīna owner pays the owner or owners of the real estate a rental for the privileges of keeping these installations on the grounds and of renting them to the tanners. However, the master tanners own their own movable equipment, which they buy directly from the carpenters and smiths who make it. The master also buys his raw materials, of both categories, with his own capital. Donkeymen bring lime to the tanneries, and students carry in their pigeon droppings, but the tanner must walk to the auctions, the sūqs, and the mills for his other materials. This takes away part of his working time and prevents overexertion. The apprentices and the younger journeymen can stay behind to jump about in the cold, slimy pits.

The master obtains the services of his apprentices as follows: he takes on a beginner for an indefinite period, depending on how quickly he learns, usually two to five years. For a while the master gives the apprentice a few presents in lieu of pay, then three or four francs a week, and then two or three francs a day. When in the master's opinion the boy knows his trade, the master loans him enough money to buy six skins, lets him tan them with the others, and keep the profit. The young man is now a journeyman.

Three or four journeymen work for each master. They may be hired by the day, or on an oral contract which lets them stay as long as they maintain good behavior and as long as there is work to be done. The water is cold, the exertion considerable. A wise journeyman rests two or three days each week to save his strength. He earns between twenty-five and forty-five francs a week, 1935 exchange.[12] He is not a well-paid man, usually he is illiterate, and the work is hard, which may explain why more than half of his offspring seek other trades.

The master makes considerably more, but only one out of each four or five tanners becomes a master. He must be a good buyer, a good seller, and a good saver. One of ten masters is forced to borrow from sleeping partners to keep going. The partner may be a wealthier tanner, a city merchant, or a Jew. Instead of interest the master gives his partner a share of his profits. As soon as and if he can, he pays off the loan. In 1935 a master out of debt cleared about two thousand francs a year, or eighty dollars, no more than some of the journeymen, but more than the average. In past centuries, when Fez leather was selling in Cairo as the common material for good shoes, he presumably did better.

Besides journeymen and apprentices, the master must pay off the special hair scrapers, dyers, and curriers. Furthermore, part of his

[12] $1.00 to $1.80, 1935 standard, purchasing value much greater in Morocco than in the U.S. This would be more or less the equivalent of $25 to $45 a week, 1958 U.S. rate.

gross income goes to the funduq owners, who collect a commission for every skin traded to the auctioneers, and to the government clerks, who sit at the gate and in the funduq and levy both a gate tax and a sales tax on raw and tanned skins alike. From the eighteenth to the nineteenth century an additional tax was imposed, the *maks*, a market duty. It had no basis in the sharīʿa, and the tanners in particular disliked it. In 1873 the new sultan, Mulai al-Ḥasan, abolished it, but his collector continued exacting it, thinking to keep on with it until the end of his fiscal period. The tanners then revolted, seizing the qaṣba.[13] Although this revolt was put down, the fact that they dared to defy the government shows their local strength and importance.

Processing skins (and we shall omit the special techniques of the sheepskin people) requires twenty consecutive operations. In summer this sequence takes two months for the large skins and six weeks for the small. In winter the minimum for any size is three months. Thirteen of these twenty operations are usually performed by the master and his journeymen and apprentices. Seven usually require subspecialists, as follows: removing the hair from the skin by scraping it over a diagonal pole at a certain point in the sequence of events—this takes special men with much muscle; dyeing cowhides and camelskins—the regular tanners dye only sheep- and goatskins; finishing the skins, that is, carrying out the final five steps. This last is the job of curriers, who stretch, scrape, grain, rub with wood, and rub with iron. The basic tasks of slaking, tawing, tanning, fleshing, and softening are done by the regular tanners, the hardest job (scraping off the hair) and the most skilled (dyeing heavy skins and currying) by subspecialists. Most of these tasks require only one man. Some need two to hold and one to process, and here apprentices come in. Treading skins in the vats is done by several men together, for company and rhythm. The hair removers, dyers, and curriers work separately.

Of the four funduqs selling raw skins to the tanners, one receives the processed leather for disposal. This is the Sbitriyin funduq; in it raw goatskins change hands from nine to eleven in the morning, and in the afternoon auctioneers sell sheep leather from two to three, cow leather from three to four, and goat from four to six. This is a regular stockbroker's market. Buyers and sellers repair to the second-

[13] Le Tourneau, *La Ville de Fès avant le Protectorat*, p. 89.

floor café to drink tea and coffee, while they bargain over deals. Meanwhile the professional auctioneers are walking back and forth briskly, exhibiting skins and crying out the figure of the last price bid. They sometimes leave the funduq to pace through the sūqs on the chance that some slipper seller, or even a passer-by, will raise the bid. When the price has risen to a reasonable level, the auctioneer will return and ask the tanner if this latest offer is acceptable or if he must go on crying. The masters also sell the hair scraped from the hides to two special brokers, who retail some of it to Berber women who make it into cordage and export the rest to Europe. The sheepskin processors sell the short wool which they obtain as a by-product in a special market.

Obviously with as many as eighty-seven different teams of tanners working in the same premises and with the same fixed installations, buying their materials in four funduqs and a number of markets, selling through the intermediacy of a number of auctioneers, and paying off several kinds of taxes, there is ample room for trouble to arise. Since the basic economic institution of a master and his journeymen and apprentices is small, little of it will be labor trouble in the Western sense, but most will be trouble between small and independent equals. Hence the mechanisms for the maintenance of order and tranquillity in the tanning industry and its associated specialties take on special forms.

Within the industry, if two men sharing a tannery get in each other's way or on each other's nerves, they go to the amīn of that tannery for help, if the latter has not already heard of the trouble and intervened. In cases too serious for the amīn to settle, or in incidents between tanneries, tanners and funduq keepers, or tanners and merchants, the parties go before the assistant market provost's (ṣāḥib al-muḥtasib's) court. Above that, appeal may be made to the provost himself, and finally to the pasha of the city.

These are legal channels to resolve differences. A number of ritual actions serve to reduce the nervous strain, unite the tanners spiritually, and lessen the chances of trouble. One is attending the tannery mosque together for prayers. A second is giving feasts to mark the transition of a boy from apprentice to journeyman, a true Rite of Passage in which all his fellows join. A third is visiting the bedsides of sick fellow tanners and contributing money to help them; in many cases this is followed by attending their funerals. A fourth, once a year the tanners as a whole make a spectacular parade to the shrine of Mūlai Idrīs, where they consummate a special sacrifice which reenforces their solidarity as a powerful and worthy craft.

Another way of keeping out of trouble is for each man to spend some of his spare time in the company of other men who belong to the same general class stratum and level of sophistication but who are not tanners. A change of scene and of fellowship eases strain. If the tanner is a sportsman he can join a rifle company, organized by quarters, and make an annual hunting trip to the nearby mountains; on his return he can tan the trophies of the hunt, if the hunters have been lucky. If he has a philosophical turn of mind, he can join a brotherhood, partake in their ecstatic breathing exercises, and unite with the infinite in a state of hyperventilation. This will occupy his spare nervous energy and keep him out of quarrels.

These various activities create and feed the following kinds of institutions: two hundred and twenty-seven small economic institutions consisting of a tanner or sheepskin processor and his journeymen and apprentices; three guilds[14] of tanners, with one for each tannery except the smallest whose members joined the guild of the largest; one guild of sheepskin men, who worked in a single establishment; one guild of auctioneers; three rifle companies organized by quarters of the city, to which butchers, dyers, and shoemakers also belonged; chapters of five Ṣūfi brotherhoods; and four mosques to which others were free to come, as well as the chapels inside each tannery. The organization of all these institutions is of the simplest nature. Each is so small that everyone can know everyone else, and there are intermediaries between the leader and his followers. So far, then, the organization of the city seems to consist of a large number of simple, interlocking institutions.

What is true of the tanners goes for the other trades as well. Each has its amīn or number of amīns, its special shrines, and its membership in brotherhoods. Not all, however, are equal in wealth and social esteem. Social levels are graded informally, more as in our society than in the formal, labeled European fashion. These levels are found among the bulk of the population, that is among Muslims who earn their living in craft and trade. Four can easily be distinguished.

[14] The French writers call them corporations. Gibb and Bowen (*Islamic Society and the West,* I, Pt. I, 281), while initially labeling them *craft corporations*, use the word *guild* thereafter.

At the top is the class of tājirs, the big wholesale export-import merchants. They deal in cereals, wool, and other raw materials going out, and cloth, tea, sugar, sewing machines, and various kinds of hardware coming in. They belong to twenty or thirty old families, the Fāsis, Qanunis, Tazis, Baradas, Gususes, ʿAmranis, Sibsis, and others. They marry among themselves, and they consider international trade the most honorable of professions. Years ago their ancestors made large fortunes, and their money is kept in rigid trust, so that some live wholly on the income of their estates. Much of it is invested in lower class or even slum real estate, from which their agents collect rent. From these paramount families are recruited government officials and scholars.

The tājir's office is a tiny room in a downtown funduq. He displays no vulgar sign. Everyone knows where it is. His office furniture consists of a small table, a strongbox, and a telephone. Every now and then the phone rings, and he carries on a brief conversation, mostly in monosyllables. Self-effacing individuals enter, hand him papers, receive replies or wait for signatures, and depart quietly. Attendants from a nearby shop bring him steaming glasses of mint tea, which he holds gingerly by the heel and rim. He may rise to his feet, brush off his jellaba, and pick up his crimson felt prayer rug; he is off to the mosque or to the local chapter of his brotherhood. He will pray faithfully and correctly and even recite the litany of his order, but he will not jump and leap or hyperventilate his system. His devotions will be performed in the company of equals, with whom he will later do business. He will go home at noon to a hearty lunch and return to the office after a siesta.

The tājir lives in a large house, built around a garden, in which orange trees furnish color and jasmine provides perfume, wafted in on the spray of the fountain. In the center rear of the ground floor a single long and narrow room, running parallel to the axis of the street outside, is his chamber for entertaining guests. The back wall is double, the roof is at least twice the room's breadth, and the front is pierced by a large pointed arch, Persian style. This is screened by a curtain and may be closed in bad weather by a huge and ornate double door. The floor is covered with machine-made carpets from Manchester—the tājir sells Berber rugs but considers them crude. In the background stands at least one huge brass bed with many pillows, and several grandfather clocks chime frequently, set at staggered intervals.

From time to time the tājir gives a party. He calls in an outside cook with his squad of caterers to provide delicacies on a scale larger than the household facilities normally permit. He hires musicians, and also a team of *shaikhāt,* or female entertainers comparable to Japanese geisha. They are singers and *diseuses;* they know how to wring the hearts of their audiences with traditional Andalusian melodies and words made up for the moment; the guests vie with each other to paste coins on the shaikhāt's foreheads and stick folded bills under their headdresses.

The shaikhāt are dressed in the height of fashion. Like expensive Paris and Fifth Avenue models, they introduce new patterns of brocades and other textile materials to these parties. The women of the household, peering over the balconies and peeking around the corners, glimpse these ravishing costumes and later invite the shaikhāt to their quarters on a number of excuses. If a new style takes, there is a Saturday morning rush to the Qaiṣariya, and merchants are made and broken, and business-suited manufacturers in Lancashire and Lyon put on night shifts to supply orders.

Such parties are not limited to Fez. In Cairo, in Baghdad, in Tehran, even in Ṣan'ā, and throughout our section of the Middle Eastern world, the wealthy enjoy themselves. Now and then they forget what the Qur'ān said about the fruit of the vine, and feel as badly the next morning as any patron of a New York, London, or Paris night club. They are only Children of Adam, like the rest of us.

Before leaving the subject of the tājir it may be pertinent to note that unless he is in the foreign trade (like the 'Amranis and the Sibsi brothers) he may have trouble raising large sums of cash quickly because of the Prophet's repugnance to usury, and hence banking. The tājir's capital is largely in real estate, and he collects this in small bits. The same principle is true of his merchandise; a hundred shopkeepers may owe him money. He can send his agents around the Qaiṣariya quickly with storm signals raised, but if really in a hurry he has recourse to the Jews, whose religion places no restrictions on banking. Herein lies one of the sources of disequilibrium in Islam. Muḥammad could not have foreseen the rise of modern complex economic institutions, and he was quite specific about details, leaving few loopholes for change. In independent Muslim nations such as Egypt, 'Iraq, and Iran, banks owned and run by Muslims have arisen, but only as a part of the general process of Westernization. Many of the clerks who cash one's checks turn out to be Armenians.

Second of the four classes, in Fez as elsewhere, is that of the retail merchants. Like the tājirs they are literate, and many of them belong to first families. Some, in fact, are sons of tājirs who take a fling at the retail trade before they settle down. In their public lives they seem scarcely mobile; they climb into their shops in the morning, sit in a space small enough to enable reaching any article of merchandise without raising their buttocks, and emerge twice a day to go home. They appear to take as little exercise as any class of human beings, and as little exposure to the sun.

These appearances of immobility are not entirely true. In Fez the upper middle class shopkeeper prays regularly, and this requires exercise, as noted in Chapter 8. He usually belongs to a brotherhood, whose ritual may be a bit more athletic than those of the tājirs, but less so than those to which the tanners go, and probably less so than that of the Raḥmaniyas described in Chapter 9. If we jump from Fez to Iran, his Persian opposite number may belong to a zurkhané, or gymnasium, whose members meet at night, do push-ups to the music of the *Shahnama,* whirl, and exercise with heavy shields and bows. In any case it is easy for the stranger walking through the sūq to distinguish the soft, white-faced, and myopic shopkeeper, with his tender fingers, from the bronzed Badāwi or mountain man, with his bent-knee gait and his far-sighted squint against the nonexistent glare. The Middle East breeds these differences and sharpens them to a degree unknown in the Western world.

The third class in Fez is that of the master artisans, such as the tanners, shoemakers, masons, and so on, who like the merchants are organized into guilds. The fourth is composed of the poorer journeymen and unskilled laborers, such as the men who sit in a row in the open space by the Carpenter's Guildhall, holding baskets, and offering to carry home the purchases of shoppers. Donkey drivers, street cleaners, privy cleaners, and the like, fill out this bottom layer. Members of class four usually live in Fās Jadīd and are not considered Fāsis at all, but resident strangers.

At first glance these four classes would seem to be based on wealth and to a certain extent this is true. Education, however, is also important. The merchants of both classes are literate; they can read the Qur'ān and other works in classical Arabic. They can read the newspapers, printed in what to them is an artificial language. They converse among themselves in a dialect noted for its conservatism and classical refinement, but know the vulgar speech of the outside world as well. Some of them can read and speak European languages, particularly French. The third class, that of the skilled craftsmen, is nearly illiterate. Many of the masters have been to the *maktab,* or Qur'ānic school, and know the alphabet; they can spell out the holy chapters, but the newspapers defeat most of them. They also know whatever arithmetic is needed in their business. Class four is completely illiterate.

Neither wealth nor education tells the whole story. The mosaic of family lines and places of birth is as evident here as elsewhere. The tājir class is virtually a closed corporation. Now and then an extremely bright young outsider bursts inside the charmed circle of old families. To insure the perpetuation of his new status he usually finds some way of discovering an illustrious ancestor somewhere down the line, and adopts a suitable surname. The second class is the ethnic base on which the tājir class stands, including junior and poorer members of the same group of old families, and a few others which though ancient and honorable have never reached the top.

The third class is quite different, since only rarely does it feed the second. Some of the craftsmen are traditionally outsiders, like the sheepskin processors, who are Marrakshis, and the cowhide bagmakers, who are from Taghzuth in the Senhaja Srair to the north. Most of the master processors, however, are descended from craftsmen from Spain, Tunisia, and even Iran, and form a group apart. It was found that forty-five per cent of the master tanners' sons followed their fathers' trade. Since a man may be expected to have two sons, this ratio is high enough to insure that ordinarily only a native-born Fāsi tanner can rise from apprenticeship through journeyman status to the rank of master, and that the permanent journeymen are men from other cities.

This third class is the most numerous of the four and comprises well over half the city's population. It, as well as its divisions, the guilds, has a strong esprit de corps, and this has been noted of other cities throughout the Middle East. The fourth class is composed almost entirely of outsiders who live in New Fez and who, if they are lucky, make their way back to their native villages, camps, and oases to die.

The pattern of the mosaic comes out into sharper focus when one considers special groups based on race, religion, or other accidents of birth. The first of these particularly concerns the role of the Negro. Before the French occupation Fez had an open slave market, in which the bodies which had survived the Saharan caravans and had not been sold on the way were auctioned off. This auction convened every day in the wool market, just before sundown. Before the suppression of the caravans (until 1880 or 1890) Negroes were plentiful. A rich man who felt shy about bargaining in the open could have slaves brought to his house for inspection and negotiation. Between the 1880's and 1912 the market declined and shifted from Negroes to Berber girls taken from their parents in the far south. After 1912 the trade went on, clandestinely. How many slaves were bought in 1950, if any, I do not know (any more than I know how many illegal cockfights were held within a ten-mile radius of my home).

A rich man used to have a mule slave, to hold his stirrup while he mounted, to run ahead crying *"Bālaḳ!"* to clear the path, and to take the mule to a funduq while his master was in a place of business. Another male Negro guarded his door and kept track of those who entered and departed. An indulgent tājir might buy his pubescent son a Negro bed slave to keep him out of trouble until a suitable marriage could be arranged; this form of paternal solicitude is not without parallel in our own hemisphere. A young lady would also be given a female dowry slave whom she would bring to her husband's house as confidante, ally, and private detective. Other female slaves in the household served as cooks, waitresses, and housemaids, and while the mule slave and door slave might have wives among them, others were available to the male members of the household, particularly the growing sons.

Slave women lead, on the whole, happy lives. Some of them receive good musical educations. All are well fed and well dressed. They get out of doors much more often than their mistresses and can circulate between households as messengers and go-betweens. Their lives are freer, and their opportunities for interaction greater. If they are clever, as many of them are, they may soon jockey themselves into a position where they can control events in the household.

As the reader may by now have recognized, this household is the standard oriental domestic institution. It is or was found in China, in India, in ancient Egypt and Babylon, and in Old Testament descriptions. It is an extended patrilineal and patriarchal family, with plural marriages, concubines, servants, and slaves, a complete economic as well as familial institution. Although the slaves are still found openly only in Arabia itself, and although polygyny has been officially abolished in Turkey and made difficult in Iran, such a household is still basic, in one form or another, in most of the cities of the Middle East. It will continue to be so until hand labor has been replaced by modern power machinery not only in industry but in the home. Even the archaeologists need large households. They must have cooks and waiters and laundresses and gardeners and drivers. They can not spend their time cooking over charcoal pits and primus stoves, pumping and boiling drinking water, running errands, and shopping for hours at a time before each meal, and do their digging, too.

The only group based on the possession of a private religion is, of course, the Jewish colony. Although Jews have lived in Fez longer than Arabs, their numbers have been supplemented from time to time by fresh immigration, as, most notably, by the influx from Spain following the events of 1492. Until fifty years ago Spanish was spoken domestically in the Millaḥ of Fez, as it is still in the Tangier colony. Entering the Fez Millaḥ after a stiff walk uphill from the old city, the visitor may pause for more than his breath. He has the feeling of having been plucked bodily out of Morocco and set down in an old section of Lisbon. The streets are narrow, crowded, and noisy. Bare-faced women, dressed in gay colors, sit on chairs and on narrow doorsteps, talking with neighbors, while children dart between people's legs. The twang of guitar music vibrates out of the windows, and the smell of fish simmering in oil joins the underlying piquancy of frankincense, musk, and spices.

In the morning the Jewish artisans and merchants leave the Millaḥ and go to their work in the old city or the new. At night, if they feel tired, they hire the dilapidated carossas, derelict Victorias which once rolled smoothly down the Mall or the Boulevard des Italiens, to bring them home. These Jews specialize in ironworking, cobbling, goldsmithing, and banking, all of which involve imported materials or foreign connections; they are windows to the outside world. They themselves have their own internal social stratification, which parallels that of their Muslim neighbors. They too have their first families, some of whom bear Spanish names. Some of these are also borne within the closed circle of tājirs. They have their own cemetery and their own saints' tombs, some of which are located in the Madina and antedate the move from the Funduq al-Yahūdi to the Millaḥ Today many of them live in the Ville Nouvelle, and read French newspapers with their morning coffee. Others have moved to Casablanca, to Paris, and to New York, where it would be difficult to distinguish their unmosaicized children from others of Mediterranean origin.

The Jews are the only non-Muslim group which has survived the thirteen centuries of the city's existence. The "fire-worshipers" who anciently inhabited the Wed Fās have vanished without trace. There has been no continuous Christian community, although there have always been Christians, as slaves, renegades, or ambassadors. These Christians have been important in crafts and trade, in urban architecture—particularly the great walls and gates—and in government service. As stated earlier, a French renegade built the water system. A hired military instructor who kept his Christianity is still remembered, and members of his family still live in Tangier. He was the Qā'id (Kaid) MacLean, who wore a red fez and a plaid jellaba cut of the predominantly green MacLean tartan.

Another community owes its existence and way of life to its birth, in combination with religion. This is the family corporation of the three hundred-odd Idrīsite shorfa. In Morocco as in other lands distant from Mekka, descendants of the Prophet are numerous and occupy every level of society and income bracket. In Fez one can find many lines so descended, but only one ranks: those descended not only from Muḥammad but also from Mūlai Idrīs II, the founder of the city. They do not work. They pay no taxes. Paradise is guaranteed them. When otherwise unoccupied, a sharīf may sit outside his door, receiving persons who come to him for advice and help. He takes part in the rituals smoothing over the main crises of life recognized by the anthropologists; birth, marriage, death, and intermediate steps such as circumcision.[15] It is he who closes the deal between the fathers of a boy and girl slated for marriage—after the preliminary scouting by slave women and shaikhāt, the intermediate looking-over by the mothers, and the semifinal bargaining by male go-betweens.

The Idrīsite shorfa fulfill the same function as the pirs among the Baluchi, the murabiṭ tribesmen among the Tuareg and the individual holy men among the Ait ʿAtta. They are comparable to the holy top class of priests in ancient Marib of the Yemen, while in many ways

[15] Puberty as such is treated with the same prudery in their society as in ours.

their functions parallel those of the Brahmins of India. They are holy and cannot be touched in violence; they cannot fight or be fought. Their presence insures tranquillity, holy sanction, and peace.

A group of persons as important as this in the maintenance of equilibrium within a city, and as highly specialized, must have some means of support which will let them live in dignity, if not in the luxury of the wealthiest tājirs. Their center, the zawiya of Mūlai Idrīs, like the ziggurat in Nippur, constitutes the holy nucleus and symbol of all the mutual relations and seething activities of the people who fill the buildings and streets of the city. Once a month the trustees of the religious foundation which supports the shorfa opens the big alms box inside the holy building. Set under a silver-lined hole in the wall, this box has long received the offerings of the pious and grateful who pass it. These offerings are distributed to the individual male shorfa, according to the number of their children.

Although local, the feast of Mūlai Idrīs is the most colorful ritual of the year. Each guild marches through the streets to the tomb, bearing gifts, to the shrill of the shaum and the beat of drums. The silk merchants carry in open display, like a float in our parades, a fine new silk covering for the tomb. The shorfa remove last year's old cover, cut it in small pieces, and distribute these patches to rich friends, who give them substantial presents in return for these *baraka*[16]-laden tokens. Other guilds bring animals. The tanners lead in a fine fat bull, succulent and unblemished. After the sacrifice, potential steaks and roasts are cut into small cubes, which the shorfa distribute like the silk patches, with the same result.

Aside from the collection box and the increase of annual gifts, the family ḥabūs owns real estate, including shares in the tanneries, which yield rent. A sharīf may also acquire a rich father-in-law by marrying a tājir's daughter. His own daughters, who have no dowries (since their remittances cease once they leave the caste), are not in much demand. Unless they marry within their own family circle, many of them become spinsters. For these, however, the family corporation has also made provision. About two hundred of them live within the holy precincts (*ḥurm*) of Mūlai Idrīs, in a building called Dār Qitūn, the House of the Tent, since it marks the spot where their ancestor pitched his tent when laying out the city. The women receive a loaf of bread per day, plus other gifts. They take in and

[16] *Baraka* is the spiritual power or emanation of the holy men, like the medieval "touch," and the "mana" of Oceanic peoples.

protect wives who have run away from their husbands, for the Dār Qitūn, like the rest of the ḥurm, is sanctuary. The shaikhāt come there to be blessed and shower the holy ladies with attention in return for their baraka. Procuresses have also been known to come there to fill orders for their clients.

If for the moment we ignore the fact that the citizens of Fez are Muslims of the Malikite rite, governed by the sharī'a[17] and dutiful in their observance of the five pillars of the faith, and examine their ritual beliefs and practices from a sociological point of view, we will see that the cap fits the head, the symbol matches its referent institution. Each guild has its patron saint. Sīdī 'Alī bu Ghālib, for example, is the saint of barbers and surgeons. Each morning in heaven (if you believe the storytellers at the Bab Gīsa) he shaves the heads of dead murabiṭin, after which he flits down to the open place in front of the Carpenter's Guildhall, where he chats with the spirit of Mūlai Idrīs himself in the sweet odor of cedar chips mingled with the tart spices from the nearby Sūq al 'Aṭṭarīn (Perfumers' Market). This explanatory myth, which educated Fāsis believe as much as you do, illustrates a point. The barbers have their symbol, which is linked in some way with the symbol of the city as a whole. So it is for all the other guilds. Only the Idrīsite shorfa are different. They have but one patron, Mūlai Idrīs himself, to whom they are linked by physical descent and whose divine qualities and powers they share in dilution through the mechanism of their baraka.

Spiritually and physically, the center of the city is the area which surrounds the sanctuary of Mūlai Idrīs and includes the mosques of the Andalusians and the Qairawanis, as well as the Qaiṣariya. The mosques need officials, the shorfa need executives for their family trust, the merchants need education, and the Moroccan government needs able and intelligent young men for its civil service, and venerable and learned professors, the 'ulamā, to confirm the choice of a new sultan, to advise his majesty, and to view the moon at the beginning of Ramaḍān. Hence the heart of the city holds another institution, centered in the Qarawiyin mosque—the university.

In the Muslim world as a whole, many renowned universities may be found, of which the most famous today is that of al-Azhar in Cairo, rivaled in pregodless days by its sister institution at Bukhara. Muslims endowed universities while Oxford was still a market

[17] *Shra'a* in Morocco, spelled *chraa* by the French.

town. Their universities taught Aristotle when classical learning had disappeared north of the Mediterranean, and they rekindled the torch at the beginning of the Renaissance. While Rome in all her grandeur had no university, the Muslims gave us the model on which those of western Europe and America are based.

Although al-Azhar has kept pace with the times to the extent suited to an essentially theological institution, the University of Fez, cut off from the rest of Islam, remained wholly medieval until the beginning of the present century. The curriculum was primarily religious. Courses were still given in the unity of God, the ḥadīth, the sources of law, the law, juridical practice, logic, grammar, prose composition, versification, literature, and mathematics. Religion and law were considered primary; language, literature, and science secondary subjects. In former days it was also possible to receive instruction in astronomy, geography, medicine, lexicography, philology, metaphysics, Sūfi mysticism, and possibly history. Alchemy, considered irreligious, was said to be in the hands of the Jews.

The curriculum was organized under the qāḍī of Fez. He had the power to nominate professors for the approval of the sultan and was responsible for their doctrinal rectitude, although otherwise they had complete academic freedom. Being head of all the religious foundations of Fez, he thus could influence the ḥabūs of the Qarawiyin mosque, which financed this higher education, and he controlled the academic budget.

A scholar became a professor in the following manner. Having completed a satisfactory term of study with an established professor, he received an *ijāza,* or certificate. Several other professors might sign this later. This paper entitled him to teach. He took an unoccupied corner of the Qarawiyin mosque, drew a certain number of students about him, and asked them what they wanted to learn. Usually he started with one of the "secondary" subjects and gradually worked his way to the top, which was the law. He taught without pay, earning his living by outside activities.

After he had achieved some following and success, he wrote a petition to the sultan, and sent with it affidavits from some of the ʿulamā. If he had a friend in court, he could be sure of getting his request to his majesty within a reasonable time. Otherwise he would send it to one of the viziers, with a flattering verse of his own composition. If the sultan so chose he would issue a *ẓāhir* (proclamation) to the qāḍī, commanding the latter to put the teacher on the payroll.

There were five grades, and the newcomer usually started at the bottom.

The pay was not great in 1900, since the scale had not been changed to accommodate successive devaluations of the currency. A professor of the lowest grade received about ten cents a month, the highest the equivalent of $14.20. However, each faculty member was also given between ten and sixty measures (*mudd*) of grain each year, two jars of olive oil, some butter, and a bull from whose flesh to make *ḳhlī,* or preserved beef. At each of the three great religious feasts the sultan also gave each professor a cash present of from one to four dollars. The ḥabūs provided quarters or cash for rent if no space was available, while a change of garments was also provided three times a year. On the side a professor could extract fees of up to one hundred dollars from his clients for legal advice, and he could earn money preaching and leading the prayer in the mosque. Since almost inevitably a professor of the top rank was a member of one of the first families of Fez, he would also own some real estate which would provide further income.

Although not prescribed by formal rules, the professor was supposed to live in Fez and to give one class a day. He could teach whatever subject he chose provided the students wanted it. In 1904 there were seventeen *ʿulamā al-ḳbār,* or first-grade professors, out of a faculty of about forty-one. Theoretically each had a chair, but only nine were actually available, and of these only six were in use, because the other three ʿulamā did not consider themselves worthy to use them. Using a chair meant actually sitting in it while teaching, and this had great symbolic importance. The other professors sat on rugs or mats. The professors had no guild or other formal organization; as in all universities they formed ephemeral cliques and developed mutual grudges. They appeared in a body only when they met to confirm the election of a new sultan, or when the sultan summoned them to decide some grave legal matter. The big ʿulamā were held in great respect as wise men and moral leaders, for they were the interpreters of revealed knowldge.

There was no scholastic year. Many students came in the fall, after the harvest, but any time was acceptable. No tuition was charged. There were no fixed courses; a student got his paper when the professor thought that he knew enough about a subject. Occasionally, however, a professor would come to the end of a text, and then the students would hold a celebration, carrying him to their quarters on their shoulders and feasting him. During Ramaḍān, ḥadīth-reading replaced regular classes, and during the months of Ṣafar and Rabiʿ Awwal, the *qāḍī* of Fez took over one of the lecture hours to comment on the "Ḥamziya," a poem commemorating the deeds of Muḥammad's warlike uncle, Ḥamza. The students and faculty had three weeks off at each of the three lunar feasts, Mulūd, ʿAid el-Kabīr, and ʿAid aṣ-Ṣaghīr, and several other short holidays, including one day on the Julian calendar, June 24, the ʿAnṣra. Thursdays and Friday afternoons were free, except for classes in versification. The students also had one month off in the spring, during which they held a festival. There were six classes a day, from sunup until the hour of midafternoon prayer, the length of each class depending on the time of year.

In 1900 the student body numbered some four hundred, having dropped off from a peak of about one thousand. Of these, two categories could be distinguished, the Fāsis themselves, who lived at home, and the strangers who lived in the *madrasas,* or colleges.[18] The Fāsi students all came from the upper classes, except for a few sons of artisans or small shopkeepers, who were considered to be bright boys and who were being given a chance to improve their status. The strangers were chiefly poor young men who wanted to obtain certificates so that each could return to his village and become the local *fqiḥ*—who is a combination imām of the local mosque, elementary schoolmaster, and clerk—or else secretary to a *qāḍī* or *qāʾid*. The wealthier strangers found private lodgings and thus emulated the Fāsis. The six madrasas each accommodated from sixty to one hundred and fifty students. City boys from Tangier and elsewhere in the north occupied the ʿAṭṭarīn; this was the most fashionable. Riffians, Algerians, and boys from Tafilelt lived in the Sharratin, and so on. One was located in Fās Jadīd, and this served as a cramming school for students who need further preparation before they could enter the classes at the Qarawiyin.

Each of these "colleges" was a two- or three-story building with galleries opening onto a courtyard. Off the galleries were the students' cubicles, supposedly single, but usually occupied by two or even three. When the student arrived he brought with him, if his family could afford it, a mule load of staple food, including dry kuskus and preserved meat, dried apricots, and the like. He found

[18] The word *madrasa* is also translated as university, but in Fez, at least, this rendering would be misleading.

at the college an official called the *muqaddam*—a combined proctor, porter, and janitor, who occupied a room near the door. This muqaddam had to be a bachelor; he received a small salary from the qāḍī's office. The students also gave him presents and special tips for calling them to their prayers. Each student bought the key to his room from a departing predecessor, and these keys ranged in price with the esteem of the particular madrasa, from twenty to two hundred dollars. It is no wonder, then, that few could afford a single room, if indeed they wanted to. The muqaddam distributed drinking water and a loaf of bread per student per day, at the expense of the ḥabūs. The students cooked, studied, slept, and chatted in their rooms. Some would make the rounds of wealthy houses, eating free meals served in the courtyard, while others would earn money copying books in the library, collecting pigeon droppings for the tanners, and even begging. In the old days, before 1900, some of the professors took their classes on walking tours in the country during the summertime to avoid the heat—living off the villages for a few days at a time, moving on to avoid imposing too heavy a burden on the country people. The latter, in turn, profited by these visits by having their legal papers copied and amulets written.

Every year in the spring the students held their great celebration, the feast of the Sultan of the Students. Beginning in mid-April the nonresident students began collecting money, writing out false receipts in the sultan's name. They accumulated camping equipment and set up a tent village outside the town. Then they elected a sultan, who chose a complete court, duplicating that of the government. The real sultan sent the pseudosultan all the essential trappings of royalty, including a parasol, a fly switch, and a bodyguard of soldiers. On the appointed Friday the students paraded with music through the town and out to the tomb of the patron saint of students, then moving on to their camping place. The sultan sent them a gift of cash and livestock, and the Jewish community sent them a burlesque gift of cats and mice in cages. On the sixth day the sultan came, and the two courts faced each other. The student's courtiers mocked their opposite numbers, and the latter had to take this in good grace. Then the mock sultan asked a favor of the real sultan, which was granted; this might take the form of releasing some political prisoner from jail. On the last night the mock sultan escaped quietly if he could, but if he failed to reach his quarters undetected his fellows hazed him.

The life of a student obviously was an agreeable one, and many were loath to leave. Since the student received no over-all diploma, and since so much was free, many were tempted to continue their studies. Some became perpetual students, traveling from Fez to Qairawan and Tunis, then to Cairo, Baghdad, Mekka, and even Bukhara, or down to the Yemen. The reader will remember that the founders of Sūfi brotherhoods usually were men who had traveled widely and studied under many masters, such as Sayyid Muḥammad ibn ʿAlī as-Sanūsi. To what extent this peripatetic educational system helped unify the world of Islam is self-evident.

Before discussing the city government it will be well to review the other institutions, to consider to what extent they provide structure and stability to the over-all group of citizens. The family is a large patriarchal household, with a considerable staff of domestics, and capable of handling most of the needs of its members in preparing food and clothing and in bringing up children. The neighborhood bake oven, the steam bath, and the corner grocery take care of more elaborate needs. The household itself is large enough, and the sexes sufficiently separated, so that it takes on the aspect of a formal institution, with age grading and great deference shown by the son to his father. Polygyny, with several filial lines, fosters this remoteness. There is no clan organization, although kinship is greatly prized for prestige. Among poorer people one wife is normal, with strong ties between boys and their paternal uncles, particularly if the family comes from another place.

Economic institutions are no larger nor more complicated than families. The technological factors which keep the former relatively large also keep the latter small. Religious institutions are also simple, for the mosque has only one muqaddam and two or three assistants. With all this unitary simplicity and this multiplicity of small institutions, Fez society is divided horizontally into four major social classes and vertically into three quarters and eighteen wards. What holds the fabric together is a proliferation of associations and a wealth of attached ritual. These associations are of two kinds, the first including the guilds, the Sūfi brotherhoods, the hunting companies organized by quarters, and most of the religious foundations. These are the stiffening elements in segments of the population, holding together the people by classes and by quarters, keeping them busy, redressing wrongs, caring for the sick and the poor, and satisfying the need of the average man to belong to a group. This is the kind of association which cares for a segment of the population. The second type of association consists of the ʿulamā, and the ḥabūs of Mūlai Idrīs, with its association of holy kinsmen, supported by all the Muslims, sealing all critical transactions, and assuring the propriety and rectitude of legal human relations. They are a priesthood in the ancient sense, complete with shrine and inviolable sanctuary. All classes and all trades are their concern.

This urban society is so well organized, containing within its framework so many nonpolitical mechanisms for the maintenance of equilibrium, that it needs but a minimum of government, which is provided by three main officials and their staffs. These are the pasha, the qāḍī, and the muḥtasib. The pasha[19] is appointed by the sultan and usually is not a Fāsi. He and his assistant (khalīfa) have a court in the city where they hear criminal cases. His staff includes a body of police under a *shaush* and the personnel of a jail and a madhouse, as well as a tax collector. The qāḍī[20] has charge of the administration of sharīʿa law, the foundations, and the university. Under the old regime he was *qāḍī al-quyūḍ* or chief qāḍī of the empire, appointing and controlling all the other qāḍīs in the territory submitted to the central government. Under him are about three hundred *ʿadls* (plural *ʿudūl*) or notaries public. The muḥtasib, it will be remembered, is the market provost. Aside from the administrative functions of these three officials, it may be noted that the heads of wards have their own night patrols who tramp through the streets after the gates are closed, that the Jews have a separate administration, and that resident qā'ids, like the Marnisi, care for the needs of Riffian and other unsubmitted tribesmen when they come to town.

Half Paris and half Fez, with streetcars jangling through one section while veiled figures thread their ways through another, modern Middle Eastern cities present administrative problems which only a knowledge of both prototypes can solve. To this must be added an acquaintance with problems of the country people, villagers, and dwellers in tents and yurts, who come to the city to shop and see the sights and who still jump at the blast of a taxi horn.

[19] In earlier days the governor of Fez was called *ʿāmil.* The Turkish term *pasha* seeped in from Algeria with the French administration. Le Tourneau, *La Ville de Fès avant le Protectorat,* p. 211.

[20] There was only one in Fez until about 1850 when a second was added. *Ibid.,* p. 214.

15 SHAHS AND SULTANS

AT THIS POINT we might examine a brace of ancient and obvious facts—so ancient and so obvious that both politicians and public are wont to ignore them. These are: race and language are not the same thing; neither race nor language, nor any combination of the two, is necessarily equivalent to nationality. Any nation of any size and importance in the world includes among its citizens members of several races, or variants of a single race, who speak more than one language. Obviously the reason is that the historical forces which determine the transmission of race, speech, and nationality are not identical.

We know that race is acquired from the pleasure of one's parents, through the mechanism of twenty-four pair of microscopic ribbons known as chromosomes. Language is acquired from one's schoolmates and playmates and nurses (which is why Muḥammad deemed himself fortunate to have been brought up in the desert by the Bani Saʿd of golden accents). Nationality may be acquired in more than one way: by a person's having been born in a certain place; by the boundaries of a nation moving, so as to encompass him; by his own voluntary or involuntary motion from one political realm to another.

In our society nationality is a matter of geography and the possessions of certain rights—to vote, to pay taxes, to be tried by a jury of one's peers, and to obtain a passport. These things are not true of all societies, however, nor have they always been true of ours. In some of the world's countries slavery still exists. In others, free minorities are denied a vote. In still others, voting has not yet been heard of. The mockery of election, in which everyone is forced to vote "yes" on a one-party slate, may be a modern manifestation of the continued existence of his satanic majesty, the Devil, whom the Middle Easterners know well under the name *Iblīs.*

The old Middle Eastern concept is quite different from ours, and even more different from Communist Statism. Two kinds of nationality are recognized, one's People and one's Government. This has already been touched in chapters 1 and 6, but it would be well to crystallize this concept now.

People who belong to non-Muslim minorities, such as Jews, Armenians, Assyrians, Zoroastrians, Greeks, and Copts (as well as Americans and western Europeans who have been resident in Middle Eastern countries for two or three generations), consider themselves not Egyptians, Lebanese, ʿIraqis, and Persians, but Jews, Armenians, Assyrians, Zoroastrians, etc., etc. Their primary loyalty is to their own "nation," as they conceive the term. I have heard Assyrians ask: "Why doesn't the President of the United States move the Assyrian nation to America and give us a valley in California? We are good people." It is difficult to explain that a president is not a pre-parliamentary shah, with power to move nations, and that the practice of building up nationalities within nationalities cannot succeed in a modern, unified, industrial state.

The second concept of nationality, the State, is modified in the Middle East by the first concept, in that "nations" of the first order are international. It is still further modified by the possession of a common majority religion, Islam, by the common use of the language of that religion, Arabic, by the passage of pilgrims from country to country, by the web of Sūfi brotherhoods crossing over political boundaries, by the pre-Fulbright internationalism of students, and, from time to time, by the religious concept of the caliphate. When Ibn Baṭṭūṭa traveled from Tangier to China, and a stranger asked what he was, it is unlikely he would reply, "a Moroccan," or even "a Tangerine." It is probable that he answered, "a Muslim."

Pure geographical determinists will tell you that the boundaries of the state are drawn by a combination of geographical features and economic use. Egypt is the valley of the Nile; the Yemen is the agricultural plateau of southern Arabia, with its coast. But geography alone does not explain Afghanistan or Israel, any more than it tells us why parts of Delaware, Maryland, and Virginia occupy one peninsula, or why West Virginia looks like a submarine struck by a depth charge. History, including a record of the impact of outside peoples and nations, is the principal missing ingredient.

In general the state has some geographical unity. Time has a way of rounding off the corners and removing unassimilated pieces. Geographical unity usually implies diversity as well, the mutual and compensatory relationships of cities, towns, villages, and nomad camps, each of which needs the others, and which between them occupy a diversity of terrain. Another element which influences the size and shape of the state is the ratio between distance and available means of travel, since there is a limit to the time-space unit that any government, however efficient, can handle. America is three thousand miles wide, the U.S.S.R. six thousand. If, for the sake of argument, we grant that American public transport is five times as efficient as the Russian, then Leningrad and Vladivostok are ten times as far apart as Boston and San Francisco. One hundred years ago Boston and San Francisco were at least twenty times as far apart as they are now; without the transcontinental railroad, California might have become a separate nation. Before the advent of the bus, truck, and plane, Mashhad and Tabriz were weeks of travel apart; Baghdad was farther from Cairo than it now is from Chicago. The partitionment of the Middle Eastern landscape into its medieval political units made sense.

Even within these units it took a long time to move an army, by foot and horse, from one part of a country to another. Furthermore, men and horses must eat, and unless the expedition passed through inhabited country the food had to be taken along—which meant more animals. Men and animals need water, and in the Middle East water is scarce. Armies are handicapped on deserts, as the Romans found when they tried to invade Arabia. Armies from the lowlands are at a great disadvantage in mountains, particularly if the mountains are inhabited by warlike natives, as is usually the case. Xenophon found this out, and he did well to evacuate a fraction of his ten thousand Greeks through the defiles of Kurdistan to the Black Sea. Only an occasional military genius like Alexander the Great can defy these barriers and succeed. The names of such conquerors are still on the lips of men, embellished with epithets like "Dhu 'l-Qarnain" (the Possessor of the Two Horns) and linked with marvelous deeds.

The village is the nucleus of its supporting fields and pasturage, the town of its villages, the city of its area. Usually several cities which serve as centers of contiguous or associated areas will be combined as the focal points of a nation. In this case one city will serve as a capital and grow larger than the others, or the government will shift seasonally from city to city and will thus have several capitals.

In between the capitals and settled agricultural regions of two nations, one usually finds some wild and rugged border country. This is exactly comparable to the uninhabited land between two villages, where members of both may go to seek firewood and to hunt animals. The state, however, must have a boundary. Often this is a boundary in depth. In entering ʿIraq across the pipeline road from Jordan, the traveler shows his passport on the very border, gets a passport and customs check at Rutba Wells, and has his baggage inspected at Ramadi or sealed for the customs of Baghdad Airport. The border is a long one, and border posts are easy to walk around.

Furthermore the periodic movements of nomads require them to cross political boundaries on the way to their pastures. Camelmen and shepherds pass between ʿIraq, Saʿudi Arabia, and Kuwait. Kurds who summer in Iran may winter in ʿIraq. A wholesale inspection of baggage and passports would be difficult in these instances. Hence the old-fashioned Near Eastern governments were prepared for these movements, which to our concept of nationality seem irregular, and permitted them through the mechanism of the boundary in depth. If the nomad wanted to go beyond his winter pasture and visit the city, he was free to walk about the bazaars, no matter what the political status of his tribe, as long as he was unarmed. If he brought goods to trade, as was usually the case, he would pass customs just outside the city, rather than at the boundary of the state, where it would be difficult to distinguish between goods intended for sale and supplies earmarked for consumption, and whence it would be also hard for the government agents to return the receipts to the city.

Thus it is apparent why most of the old-fashioned Middle Eastern countries were divided into zones of degrees of authority. In the cities and lowland or flatland villages, the government ruled. Out on the deserts, or up in the mountains, authority lay in the hands of the tribes themselves. In some countries a political mechanism arose linking tribe to government, as for example the annual appointment of the Ilkhani of the Bakhtiari by the shah. In others the sultan held prestige and a shred of power through the channel of his religious primacy, as among the Ait ʿAtta.

In Morocco these two zones, the closely and the loosely governed, or the centrally governed and the free, are known by the names of *Bled el-Makhzen* and *Bled eṣ-Ṣibāʿ*,[1] meaning literally "Government

[1] The exact etymology of this word is uncertain. Three roots are possible: *sayyaba,* to be free; *ṣaʿaba,* to be difficult (and hence to revolt); and *ṣabaʿa,* to point the finger at in scorn (and hence to be insolent). In my opinion the third is the most interesting in translation.

Land" and "Land of Insolence." The insolence, of course, is judged from the point of view of the central government, which, conversely, regards its own domain as the "Land of Order." In three countries, Morocco, Iran, and Afghanistan, these zones can be seen most clearly and most typically. In one country, Egypt, they have not existed at all since the days when the fabulous Menes united the two kingdoms. The reason is clear: Egypt has no mountains, no habitable deserts, and few tribes. Every mile of the Nile Valley below Aswan is within easy reach of the mighty arm of Pharaoh, khedive, or king. The expansion of the Egyptian government into the Sudan in the nineteenth century was a European-style colonial venture with European riverboats, weapons, and to a certain extent personnel.

There are three main points on the scale of balance between the Bled el-Makhzen and the Bled eṣ-Ṣibāʿ, and from time to time all three have been reached. At one end the tribes are on the rampage. They swoop down out of the mountains or off the desert, looting villages, cutting roads, holding up caravans, and even sacking cities. They may go so far as to take over the government and establish dynasties which themselves decay and are overthrown. At the other end the government is in the control of a strong man, who rules the land with such an iron hand that you may leave a gold watch in the middle of the street in any town or city and return an hour later and find it still there. On the same street you will see a number of stump-wristed beggars whose hands have been cut off for stealing. (If your ears are attuned to the right wave length, you will hear mumblings, and if you have trained the rods of your eyes to pick up images from the side, you will catch furtive glances.)

Neither of these extremes represents a political institution in a state of equilibrium. Both, luckily, have been rare. At its best the old-fashioned Middle Eastern government is built on the same principles as the structure of the village or of the city, but on a larger scale. It is composed of a number of individual units each of which has its own life and its own internal equilibrium, held together by a common need for trade and mutual defense, in a loose system of give and take. So many nonpolitical mechanisms help maintain this structure that the government shows its sinews only in times of stress, when over-all command is imperative. At such a time, as for example when the sultan declares a *jihād,* or holy war, the mountain and desert men will come to town to enlist. In periods of equilibrium mountaineers and nomads come to town freely, their fastnesses are left alone, and they let the caravans of travelers, traders, and pilgrims cross the "Land of Insolence" without hindrance or inconvenience over and above the normal rigors of travel.

Today some thirteen independent governments and five protectorates, colonies, or overseas dominions of European powers share the territory of the Middle East as we have bounded it. Before the Muslim expansion of the eighth and following centuries, many other governments had existed, including the imperial powers of the Assyrians, Persians, Alexandrian Greeks, Romans, and Byzantines. In the countries which the Arabs conquered they encountered populations already habituated to rather complicated systems of government. From these populations it was easy to recruit whole staffs of clerks, as well as intelligent advisers and officials. Hence the erection of a new state, in accordance with the divine orders and precepts recorded in the sunna, was a rapid and relatively painless process.

Before Islam the Arabs of the Ḥijāz had had little or no experience in governing units larger than a small to medium-sized city. The Yemenis, on the other hand, had possessed formally organized states, each with four classes capped by an hereditary priesthood, almost the exact prototype of the structure of Fez. Hence it is little wonder that in the histories of the foundation of new states outside Arabia, Yemenite names are frequently seen. Yet even the Yemenis had never ruled extensive kingdoms. During most of their pre-Islamic history their country had been parceled out between four governments, centered on stations on the northerly caravan route. Only for a few centuries were they united under the Sabaean regime.

Although more suited than the Ḥijāzis for the erection of kingdoms, the Yemenis lacked the experience to govern the empires awaiting them outside in the lands more fertile and more varied, and blocked out on a wider scale than the natural regions of Arabia. Furthermore, their whole social attitude, and particularly their admirable habit of judging and dealing with their fellow human beings as individuals rather than as anonymous numbers, slowed down administration. An Arab king holds court nearly every waking hour of the day; both the late Imām Yaḥya of al-Yemen and the late King ʻAbd ul-ʻAzīz Al Saʻūd showed enormous patience and physical strength in making themselves available to their subjects and manifesting their wisdom on the most trivial as well as the gravest subjects. Like King Saul in the shade of his tamarisk tree, they gave and give their lives to their subjects. Obviously there is a threshold of population size beyond which this practice cannot be carried. When the seventh-century Arabs moved out of Arabia, that threshold was reached and left far behind. Purely Arab governments exist only in Arabia.

The government which Muḥammad's immediate followers set up in the richer lands outside the peninsula began as a religious state, doomed from the start to fragmentation and secularization. It was doomed to split up because the countries which the early Muslims conquered were so far apart and because no new means of transport or communication had been invented since the introduction of the camel, nor was any in the offing. It was doomed to secularization for the opposite geographical reason. While the distances were too great for the survival of a single government, they were small enough to permit trade rivalries, territorial conflicts, and war. They were also varied enough in type of terrain so that each, with a few exceptions, would have its Land of Insolence, which in dry years also meant war.

War requires a secular government. The priest deals in symbols, the warrior in swords. Modern Tibet and Incaic Peru are the best-known and most sharply focused examples of theocracies. Both these bodies politic existed in geographical isolation. In their effective periods, nature defeated their human enemies—equipped below a certain technological level—before the latter reached them. There was no need for a Foreign Office or for more of an army than internal security required. The crises to which these whole peoples were subjected came not from man but from nature.

A divine king in Tibet, Peru, or elsewhere can so order events among his people as to brace them to survive storms and wintry seasons, and he can tell them, on the basis of supernatural revelation, when to prepare the fields for sowing. In time of crop failure a divine king will say who shall eat and who shall die of starvation, lest all the food be gobbled up at once and everyone perish before the next harvest. In Micronesia, where tidal waves and typhoons periodically reduce the food supply below the critical level, divine chiefs are on hand ready for this crisis.[2] Through the exercise of his royal taboo or sanction, such a king can accomplish this extraordinary feat of discipline more efficiently and more quietly than any amount of legislation or any number of policemen. The priest-king can stop his

[2] I am indebted to my colleague Dr. Ward Goodenough for this analysis and interpretation.

own people in their tracks because they believe in him. He cannot stop the enemy who worship other gods or the concept of godlessness (as the Dalai Lama found when his chill eyrie was invaded by Chinese Communists).

The early Muslim state was a theocracy, based partly on the pattern of al-Yemen, a plateau country comparable to Tibet. The concept of foreign relations, of a peaceful nation carrying on mutual business with its equals, seems not to have occurred to the early caliphs. The world was divided into *Dār ul-Islām* and the *Dār ul-Ḥarb,* the House of Submission and the House of War. The House of Submission was the Arab state. The House of War was the world outside, subdivided into the lands occupied by the People of the Book, and those of the Heathen. The People of the Book should be conquered and made to pay a tax; the Heathen converted or put to the sword.

This concept was obviously unrealistic, but so continuous was the early Muslim expansion that no conflict with foreign powers was serious enough to modify it. The break came rather within the Islamic community itself, as the House of Submission split into several dwellings. War between them was fitful and unimportant, compared to wars of today. More important was the division within dwellings into lands of Submission and of Insolence. Although converted, the tribesmen often made more trouble within the realm than the Heathen outside in the House of War. Hence a peculiar situation arose; military power was a constant need, and yet the theocratic concept had its value too. Through the agency of holy men who shared a portion of his surpassing sanctity, the caliph or sultan could, from time to time, keep the tribes at bay. Most Muslim governments took the form of a compromise. Their rulers recognized the international character of the House of Peace as a whole, and let traders, pilgrims, Ṣūfi brothers, and scholars pass at will. The same rulers assumed command of the army in time of war, either against the infidels and ungodly, with whom they were never technically at peace, or against their own rebellious subjects whose resistance they hoped to soften to a certain extent through their holy power.

This anomalous system of government has persisted only on the fringes of the Muslim world. In the cultural as well as the geographical center, other things evolved. Muslim scholars, if not all Muslims, generally agree that the true caliphate of a united Islam ended with the death of 'Uthmān, the last of the three pertinent members of Muḥammad's own generation. While the ʿAbbasid caliphate of Baghdad which followed was perhaps, in the eyes of the majority, the legitimate line, its head was not the Commander of all the Faithful. After this dynasty had been brought to a close (to the off-stage noises of Hulagu's grim laughter), something new was needed. Luckily it was at hand—the rising power of the young Ottoman Empire, growing to the northwest in the better-watered land of Anatolia. The new government which gradually took over the Muslim states from Albania to the border of Iran was a mixture of many ingredients of variable vintage. Byzantine Greeks, Persians, and Arabs all added their share to the Turkish nucleus. To discover which element contributed which piece is a scholarly work beyond the range of this book; it will here suffice to show how it worked. This demonstration is made possible by the timely publication of the first volume of a more erudite study[3] to which the reader is recommended for further details and from which the material for the next dozen pages will be almost exclusively drawn.

During the six and a half centuries of its existence, the Imperial Ottoman government underwent many changes in size, strength, and form. Unable to follow each component institution through its proper cycle, we shall try to represent the total picture as of the period between the conquest of the western banks of the Bosphorus in 1453 A.D. and the end of what Gibb and Bowen call its best period, in 1767 A.D., with excursions on both sides of this chronological zone. A period of exploration and colonization in other parts of the world by western Europeans, this time span lay between the Arab Middle Ages and the beginning of the Industrial Revolution, which was to strike the Middle East as the Ottoman power fell apart.

Having designated a time locus broadly and vaguely, we can be a bit more specific about geography. The Ottoman Empire was centered about the Bosphorus. Its two richest and most popular regions were Rumelia and Anatolia, otherwise known as the Balkans—including at one time Hungary, and Asia Minor. These lands have much more rain than the regions with which this book is concerned, and are also more populous. Their inhabitants were and are various categories of Christians, including Armenians, Greeks, Albanians, Bulgarians, Rumanians, Serbs, Croats, and Hungarians, and various other categories of Muslims, including several varieties of Turks,

[3] Gibb and Bowen, *Islamic Society and the West,* Vol. I, Pt. I and Pt. II (Pt. II came out in 1956).

Kurds, and converts from Christianity. The Christians were mostly Greek Orthodox, with religious headquarters in Istanbul, the Ottoman capital. The Muslims were almost entirely Sunni, with the same headquarters once the sultans had assumed the title of caliph. Both Roman Catholics and Shīʿa were religious as well as political outsiders living on the flanks of empire, and their bordering presence gave Greek and Muslim a certain unity.

The Turks, who began as shamanistic pagans, had their choice between Islam and Christianity. Their historical route from central Asia into Anatolia and Rumelia took them through Muslim lands, and it was the Muslim civilization to which they were more thoroughly exposed. Yet in the fertile center of their domain, the Balkan-Anatolian nucleus, their culture grew as the rule of a Muslim Turkish landed aristocracy over settled populations of both religions, with the Christians initially in the majority. As the Turks extended their rule into the Arab-speaking lands, they tempered the exercise of this aristocratic privilege with a special indulgence for the people who spoke the language of the Qur'ān, and from whose members the Prophet had come. At the same time they set up forms of government which the Prophet could not have foreseen and which have survived in modified form until this day.

The personnel with whom the Sultans ruled an empire reaching from Algeria to ʿIraq and from the Crimea to the Yemen were a selected group of Muslims and Christians, among whom Arabs were rarely to be seen, except perhaps in the religious branches. This personnel was rigidly divided into clear-cut ranks, each with its special trappings, titles, and privileges. From Central Asia they had brought two military symbols, the yak-tail banner and the drum. Perhaps because of the scarcity of yaks, the tails of horses were substituted. These tails were called *ṭughs*. Officials of various grades rated from five to one ṭughs in descending order of rank, while the sultan himself went about with seven or nine waving from a pole, surmounted by a golden ball. The drum grew into a military band, to be played outside an official's residence twice a day, at the hours of midafternoon and evening prayer, and the number of pieces in the band was again a symbol of rank, like the number of bagpipers the chief of a Scottish or Irish clan is allowed to have march before him. Again as in Celtic usage, officials of various ranks were allowed fixed numbers of ornately dressed guards in their entourages.

Of the various titles in different languages from which they had to choose, the Turks selected vizir, pasha, and bey (Arabic, Persian, and Turkish, respectively) as special designations of rank. The Grand Vizir sported five ṭughs, other vizirs three. Pashas were in two levels, of three and two ṭughs, while beys rated one apiece. Music and guards varied accordingly. Although the Ottoman Empire passed into history before the birth of most of our readers, these titles are still to be seen in the daily press. One reads that a certain pasha has been elected prime minister of Egypt or that Naji Bey al-ʿAsīl, Director General of Antiquities in ʿIraq, has announced a new archaeological discovery from his office in Baghdad. The retention of these titles reminds us of the influence the Turkish Empire has had on the formation of the modern governments of the Arab lands once under its control.

The Ottoman Turks were able to keep pace with the growth of the Christian European nations because they had developed a division of labor in government which was capable of expansion into a complex bureaucracy, because they employed large numbers of European personnel, and because, like the Europeans, they developed the use of cavalry, firearms, and a navy. Like the Europeans again, they were able to capture noncontiguous countries from the sea. It was not from competition principally that the Ottoman power fell apart while that of the Christian nations grew, but from internal decay. This decay was a function of the inflexibility of its system, and a demonstration of the principle that absolute power corrupts. Like all totalitarian regimes it could flourish only when expanding. To understand the whys and wherefores of this, we must outline its form.

Two conspicuous conceptual differences set the Ottoman system apart from that of the Arabs: the concept of the attitude and duties of the caliph, and that of slavery. An Arab shaikh is a judicial officer. His function is to settle arguments among his own people and between them and others. He makes no laws, and he may not even be a war leader. Muḥammad took on legislative powers, in fact producing the basis of a whole legal system, the sharīʿa. He also became an executive. Yet he remained accessible to all his people, even when the number of his companions rose to the tens of thousands.

Although the Turkish sultan followed the sharīʿa which Muḥammad had instituted, he delegated its administration to a body of religious officials, the ʿulamā. He also gave up lay judicial efforts, turning them over to a system of civil courts, and concentrated on the executive duties of his office. As an executive he retired more and more into seclusion so that his people rarely saw him, and governed through intermediaries by decrees known as *qanūns.*

Among the Arabs slaves were never numerous. They were mostly household servants of African origin, with whom and with whose descendants a freeman would never marry. The Turks, to the contrary, considered as slaves all conquered infidels and all Christians who resisted. To them a slave was not merely a servant, but a person capable of education, refinement, and responsibility, a woman suitable to become the mother of one's heirs, or a loyal male whom one could trust against one's brothers and other jealous kin. Such a slave was a logical candidate for high office, with accompanying rank complete with music and horses' tails—in fact the highest below the throne itself, which could be and usually was occupied by a slave's son. The Turkish government became a slave government, in that the sultan in his harem was surrounded by female slaves, including his own mother, guarded by emasculated male slaves, and waited on by slave pages and valets, who brought him messages from slave officials. Being a slave implied social inferiority to no one but the sovereign himself.

From where did all these slaves come? Most of them came from the countries of southeastern and central Europe into which the Ottoman Empire expanded. As Imām of the Faithful, the sultan was entitled to one fifth of all the booty, and much of it was human. His officials selected hundreds of strong, handsome, bright-looking boys, young enough for complete indoctrination, and sent them to the capital to join the ranks of Gate Slaves. After the limits of conquest had been reached the Turks continued to recruit these boys by a special levy. By the eighteenth century, however, the Christians had found ways of buying off their sons, while the Turks also had found ways of getting theirs into the Gate Slave training schools, and hence into high offices. It was then that the whole principle of the system was undone, its discipline slackened, and its efficiency destroyed.

Once the boys reached Istanbul they were carefully screened by their future instructors, who divided them into two groups, the *Ich Oghlans* or Pages, and the *ʿAjemī Oghlans* or Foreign Boys. The former were selected for their intelligence, the latter for their physique and energy. Separately trained, both were given a stiff regime. The pages went to an old palace, where they were taught

Arabic, Persian, the Qur'ān, sharī'a law, archery, musketry, horsemanship, javelin throwing, military tactics, and music, by a staff of expert instructors including white eunuchs and religious specialists; no one received a better education except possibly the Muslims of good family who were trained in the universities to become 'ulamā, and these lacked the military instruction. After graduation the pages worked up the scale from domestic service in the palace to positions where they could attend the sultan personally and thence, according to their ability and favor, into high government positions, including the governorship of provinces and even the post of Grand Vizir.

The foreign boys were sent to barracks, and then divided into those who spoke Turkish and those who did not. The latter were farmed out to fief holders until they learned the language, and all were again screened for assignment into six *ojaqs,* or corps. Most of them went into the Gardeners, Woodcutters, Armorers, Navy, or Infantry. The last, under the name of Janissaries, is the most famous and was the most numerous. The boys who turned out to be stupid or intractable, or both, were relegated to a corps of laborers to be put out to hire.

Three other classes of slaves filled special roles. Christian males captured when fully grown were considered too old to train and too bitter to trust; they were given to the navy as galley slaves, along with criminals. Christian females captured or bought when young became inmates of the harem, where they were taught all the ladylike virtues, including music and sewing. A few hundreds of male slaves caught before puberty were castrated. These eunuchs were of two kinds, white and black. The former came mostly from the Caucasus, while the latter were Sudanese Negroes provided by the governors of Egypt. The castration of the latter was done by Coptic Christians—the sharī'a forbids a Muslim to perform this mutilation.

This dependence on slaves for the personnel of government had not been brought as such by the Turks out of central Asia, although its germs may be seen in earlier nomadic political systems. It arose with the rapid expansion of the Ottoman Empire in accordance with the letter if not the spirit of sharī'a law. The Turks who began these conquests were relatively few in number, and all warriors. Although by-passed for high office by the development of the new system, they did not go unrewarded. The sultans granted them conquered lands on which to settle, some as herdsmen and cultivators of new or depopulated tracts, others as feudal lords over indigenous peasantry. Both classes were required to provide men at arms, including themselves, in time of war, but both were free for their agricultural tasks in time of peace. This very favor placed them at a second disadvantage when compared to the slaves. Not only were they too prone to jealousy to be trusted as political officers, but they also were too attached to their lands to be mustered as permanent guards.

Jealousy was also a problem within the palace. In order to do away with disturbances at the moment of succession, Meḥmed II, the Conqueror of Constantinople (1451-1481 A.D.), issued a qanūn to the effect that whichever son of the late sultan should get the throne should kill all his brothers. Since the sultans had also abolished marriage and had begotten dozens of sons, each of whose mothers would have been happy to become mother of a sovereign, this concern of Meḥmed's can be understood. The time came, however, when the current candidates for extinction were able to have this rule changed. Instead, the sons of the reigning sultan were cooped up in private pavilions in the palace, each with his women, servants, pages, and eunuchs; his children were killed at birth. Upon succession one of the pampered prisoners saw the outside world for the first time. The expression "one of the prisoners" is used because the rule of succession was also changed. In 1617 A.D. when Aḥmed I died his sons were all minors, and hence his insane brother Muṣṭafā I was selected instead. From then on, by decree, the succession went to brothers, uncles and even cousins before sons. Since these collateral kinsmen had led extremely restricted lives, neither their education nor their experience had fitted them to rule, and a hereditary taint of insanity added to their incompetence. If the Gate Slave system had been kept up to its original form, it might not have mattered much who was sultan, but it too had begun to break down, and the combination furnished the bacteria of decay.

The government which these sultans headed was extremely formal and highly partitioned, and it grew to be inflexible. At the top was the Imperial Household, below which were the two main branches, the officials of which were known as People of the Pen and People of the Sword. The People of the Pen were free Muslims. They included the ʿulamā and qāḍīs, mullas and medical men, practitioners, and students of the learned professions and the Sacred Law. At their head was the Shaikh ul-Islam, who ranked with the ministers of the court. His emissaries, the qāḍīs, operated in every provincial capital. Their organization and duties followed the regular Muslim pattern already described.

Both the Imperial Household and the People of the Sword, however, were extremely complicated institutions, with a division of labor that defies all but the most general treatment in a nontechnical account, while stretching to the breaking point the competence of at least one anthropologist. Unlike the Arabs, the Turks produced a political institution as complex and as hierarchical as any in Europe in their own time, although quite different in pattern.

The Imperial Household consisted of the inhabitants of the Imperial Palace, in Istanbul, as well as the Old Palace, used largely for human discards. Serving both as a model for the lesser households of high officials and as a training school for officers of administration, it numbered several thousands of human beings of many ranks and of two and a half sexes, moving with varying degrees of freedom in three sections of the palace, known as the Harem, the Inner Court, and the Outer Court. The term Harem needs no explanation. The Inner Court was the sultan's chambers, and the Outer Court the area from which his private business with the outer world was conducted. Between the Inner Court and the Harem was a section called *Mabeyn,* or "in between," where imperial valets and barbers were allowed, and between the Inner and the Outer Courts lay the imperial Audience Chamber. Thus the ruler was strategically placed between his women and his fully male subjects.

Aside from captive kinsmen cooped in their pavilions, the inmates of the harem consisted of women, their young children, and eunuchs. Since after Meḥmed the Conqueror the sultans had given up marriage, the women were all technically concubines, graded in four ranks. At the top were the *qadins,* never more than four at a time, and subgraded from first to fourth. These ladies had private apartments, private baths, and private eunuchs. Next came the body of *gedik̲lis,* privileged ladies from whom the four qadins of the moment were chosen. Third were the *shāgird,* girls who were learning to make music, to dance, to sew and to embroider, to read, and to write. They were raw material on the way to becoming privileged ladies. These three ranks were thus in part age grades. In a noncareer category were the rest of the women, simple servants.

Before Meḥmed the Conqueror's death the sultans had married

both Muslim and Christian princesses, but after his time the harem ladies were all slaves and foreigners—chiefly European until the seventeenth century when the supply thinned out, and after that Caucasians. Despite their youth on arrival, these females brought an inestimable amount of European cultural influence into the court. They were also able to spread it outside; most of the women who entered the harem were eventually freed and given as favors to ambitious officials eager to penetrate the Imperial Household through the agency of their wives, who retained a visiting privilege. Two women, however, of gedikli rank, remained permanently; they were the harem officers, a Lady Intendant and a Ladies' Treasurer. The sultan had his own quarters in the harem, where he retired to pray and to entertain his female relatives. On the way in he wore silver-soled slippers, and the clanking of metal on glaze warned the women to scamper and hide until he passed or until he called for them.

This he did through the agency of his eunuchs, who numbered over two hundred. Until about 1600 A.D. the harem eunuchs were white, after which their black counterparts took over, pushing their less pigmented rivals into the Inner Court. The chief of the Black Eunuchs bore the title "Agha of the House of Felicity." Of the sultan's subjects he ranked third in the empire after the grand vizir and the Shaikh ul-Islām, rated as a vizir, and was thus entitled to a banner of three horse tails. He had the valuable privilege of passing papers between the grand vizir and the sultan, and was also the administrator of the waqfs of the holy cities of Mekka and al-Madīna. Below him, and below his colleague the Harem Treasurer, the rest of the Black Eunuchs were divided into four grades, which might be reached by simple seniority.

The Inner Court was occupied by members of the Inside Service. These consisted of White Eunuchs and Pages. The white eunuchs, who were also graded, were commanded by an officer called "Agha of the Gate of Felicity," since he had direct charge of guarding the gate from the Inner Court to the Harem, through three or four squads of ten page boys, each in the charge of a white eunuch. The white eunuchs were permanent members of this service. So were a few mutes and dwarfs, the former useful as messengers incapable of describing the intimate scenes they had witnessed or of repeating conversations. The Pages, however, who were the brighter boys screened from the initial pool of Gate Slaves, were in the Inside Service to complete their education; after the age of twenty-five those of them who still showed promise would be given government posts elsewhere. Like all Gate Slaves they were obliged to postpone marriage until after the completion of their duties.

The Inside Service was divided into five departments: the Great and Little Chambers, the Larder, the Treasury, and the Privy Chamber. The Pages were first trained in a college at Galata, then sent to the Great and Little Chambers for graduate study. White Eunuchs, *khojas* (Turkish for mullas), and older members of their own group taught them. Then they were divided among the other three departments. The Larder was responsible for the sultan's meals, the Treasury for his private funds, and the Privy Chamber for his toilet, wardrobe, and general comfort. Two points should be noted: a distinction was made between the sultan's private funds and the Imperial Treasury, which was a return to the long-neglected practice of the early Caliphates; and the duties of shaving, feeding, and dressing the sultan were of extreme importance because they gave the young men so privileged the opportunity of attracting the imperial notice. These young men succeeded each other in rotation as their predecessors were promoted.

As its name implies, the Outside Service provided the details of the sultan's immediate relationship with the world outside the palace, exclusive of internal government and of foreign relations. It thus involved a considerable variety of services, each with its officers and special men. The officers were called Stirrup Aghas and numbered as many as seventeen, of whom nine were also generals. Four were permanent fixtures throughout Ottoman history. The Standard Bearer had charge of the sultan's standard with its six or more horse tails; he also distributed standards of different degree to newly elevated officials. He further managed the imperial military band and a corps of special messengers. The Great Master of the Horse cared for the imperial stables and pastures; the Little Master of the Horse was in charge of the burden animals and wheeled vehicles. The Intendant of Doorkeepers was responsible for the outside doors to the middle court of the Harem and also served as master of ceremonies at meetings of the Imperial Divan. A fifth Stirrup Agha was the chief Gardener, in charge of two thousand men recruited from the Foreign Boys, few of whom did gardening. Their duties included acting as bodyguards on occasion, policing the grounds of imperial properties, controlling ports and shipping, rowing the sultan in his barge, taking the responsibility for professional entertainers brought into the palace, and torturing and executing officials of whatever rank at the imperial order.

Below the Stirrup Aghas were five commissioners called *Emīns*. Four were in charge of the city, the Mint, the imperial kitchen, and the imperial stables and hence the grain supply for the city. A fifth was financial secretary to the Emīn of the Royal Kitchen. Under the Emīns ranked a number of special corps, including the woodcutters and four bodies of guards. The woodcutters performed such nonsylvan acts as helping the chief eunuch administer waqfs and guarding portions of the Old and New Palaces. Smaller bodies of men provided sheep for the celebration of the ʿĪd al-Kabīr (*Qurban* in Turkish) and served as palace tailors, cobblers, and mat plaiters.

The four guards outfits were the archers, in four companies of one hundred; the inner bodyguard of one hundred and fifty men; fifteen companies of forty-two *chavushes* each, who served as palace ushers; and so-called Noble Guard of *Muteferriqa,* two hundred specially chosen men wearing uniforms of the utmost splendor and mounted on magnificent horses. These guards, who never left the sultan's side when on campaign, were the sons of eminent former Gate Slaves, the very cream of the Pages, and a few sons of tributary rulers.

(A word about the chavushes. If you approach the gate of the American consulate general in Tangier, two or three portly Riffians in splendid costumes will arise from stuffed cushions and stand at attention. One of them will take your calling card ceremoniously from your hand and disappear. In a few moments he will return, announcing suavely, "Yes sah, Mr. X will see you, sah, follow me, sah." In Tangier these men are called *shaushes*. So far has the long arm of Ottoman culture reached.)

The palace was in Istanbul, far from the territories with which this book is concerned. Nevertheless its organization served as a model for other palaces elsewhere, especially in Egypt, and its Inside Service in particular was a training school for officials who, for varying periods up to half a millennium, were to govern most of the countries of the Arab world. With the help of the People of the Pen for whose offices the Prophet and his followers had earlier provided, it was governed by the People of the Sword, the upper levels of whom were palace products, through the agencies of the Army, the Navy, the Central Administration, and the provincial governments themselves.

The Army was divided into those outfits which were recruited among the recipients of land grants and those which, having no lands, were directly paid. The former were feudal fief holders, the latter slaves. Before we consider the former a few words must be said about the land-grant system, which concerned principally the type of ownership which Tannous calls mīri (see Chapter 11). As the Turks conquered agricultural territories they divided the land into units of three sizes, called *timar, ziʿāmet,* and *ḳhaṣṣ*. A timar yielded less than twenty thousand pieces of silver, a ziʿāmet from twenty to just under one hundred thousand, and a khaṣṣ from a hundred thousand up. The khaṣṣ holdings were either given to princesses or harem ladies, or reserved as sources of revenue for high officials in the provinces concerned. As the officials were changed, the lands remained the property of the office. The timar and ziʿāmet fiefs were, on the other hand, given to individuals in reward for military or other service. They were hereditary as long as an heir was available and the obligations of the rank met; otherwise they were reassigned.

The holder of a timar or ziʿamet was called a *sipahi* (from which the French *spahi* is derived, via Algeria and the English *sepoy,* via India). These sipahis were graded accordingly into two classes on the basis of the number of retainers each could bring in time of war, and on the amount and quality of equipment. In each *sanjaq,* or province, the governor was officially commanding officer of the sipahis, but since he was subject to change, they elected a permanent officer, called *Alay-beyi,* who held a ziʿāmet grant, a banner, and a drum. He was a regimental commander. Under him were a number of officers called *cheri-bashi,* who in peacetime served as police chiefs for the local qāḍīs within the fractions of a sanjaq. A number of others, one grade down, mustered the sipahis and policed them in the field. The number of sipahis varied from one hundred and forty thousand to two hundred thousand (according to different calculations).

Other militia units were formed by the Turkish tribesmen settled in Anatolia and Rumelia. These included some seasonally nomadic Turkomans. They were organized in teams of four men, in which one served while the others supported him, or in teams of thirty, with five going out at a time. The Bulgarians, Christian and Muslim alike, furnished two special units, of grooms and hawkers, who raised horses and falcons for the court; a body of twenty to fifty thousand Rumelian scouts raided ahead of the army with the *droit de pillage,* like the French Foreign Legion; and three separate groups of berserk-like desperadoes called Bachelors, Soul-Stakers, and Madmen, cast confusion into all quarters. The services of the Turkish tribesmen were most useful in the earlier days of the empire. As the body of Gate Slaves increased, the services of the tribesmen became less needed, and these bodies faded into the role of labor battalions. With the conquest of Crimea, the Crimean Tatars took over the position of scouts.

Of the permanent troops, in contrast to the militia, the most numerous and famous were the Janissaries, an ojaq or corps composed of one hundred and ninety-six *ortas,* or companies of fifty men each in the early period, and of one hundred later. Each orta was commanded by a *chorbaji* with six deputies and a number of subofficers, probably equivalent to noncommissioned officers in European armies. The company also had its clerk and its chaplain, an imām. They were graded into three classes, of which the eldest consisted of retired and married pensioners, with the other two on active service. Their pay and rations were similarly graded.

Originally organized as the sultan's guard, they were later divided and stationed partly in the capital and partly in the provinces. Each company had its barracks and its large campaign tent, decorated with its private totemic symbol. A number of artisans, such as bootmakers and tailors, was attached to each company. One special company had eight Bektashi dervishes officially assigned to it; while on parade these marched ahead of the Chief of the Janissaries, dressed in green and shouting rhythmically *Kerīm Allāh!* (Bountiful is God!) to which the Janissaries responded *Hū!* (He is!).

The Janissaries were divided into three subcorps of which the commanding officer, the Agha of Janissaries, directly controlled one. The commanders of the other two were second-grade officers. Some company officers with special staff duties, a secretary, and the chief officer of the Foreign Boys in Istanbul from whom the Janissaries were recruited, were officers of the third grade. The members of the three grades made up the *divān* or council of the corps. Officers of the fourth rank were the regular company commanders. While in Istanbul the Agha of Janissaries served as chief of police with two special squads of detectives; he attended the Imperial Divāns and outranked all ministers below the rank of vizir.

Early in the fifteenth century firearms were introduced into the Ottoman Empire, initially, as in Europe, in the form of cannon. Trained in an archer's tradition as old as the Scythians, the Janissaries did not take kindly to this new and noisy medium. For it three new corps were created, recruited from a younger corp of Foreign Boys: the Gunners, Gun-carriage haulers, and Armorers, totaling forty-four hundred men. Seven hundred Armorers made the cannon and the ammunition, and kept the ordnance in repair. Three thousand carriage men got them to the battlefield, and seven hundred gunners discharged them. The Chief of Gunners also commanded the arsenals and powder magazines, each of which included on its staff an independent government inspector.

The rest of the standing army was the cavalry, which included six divisions. Two were drawn from the Pages and Janissaries, two others were Muslims from outside the empire, and two were sipahis, apparently on permanent duty or rotation. One of each of these three classes was posted at the sultan's right, the other three at his left. Each man, whether free or slave, had to take along two armed and mounted slaves at his own expense; the pay was enough to permit this. The cavalrymen wore fancy dress and had special privileges, as befitted an elite. Their station was not in the city, but in the villages outside, where they could graze and exercise their horses. The commander of each division, under whom served four general officers, was a member of the Outside Service of the Imperial Household.

While the Turks had a long tradition of warfare on land, naval activity was something for which they were unprepared. Yet they needed a navy to defeat the Crusaders and the Venetians, to conquer the islands of the Aegean, the eastern Mediterranean, and the Adriatic, to travel quickly and comfortably to Egypt, and to control the Barbary Coast. They built a navy by commissioning the Genoese, whom they had allowed to stay at Galata, to outfit them, by employing Genoese ships' officers, and by manning the ships with Greek, Albanian, and Dalmatian crews. These ships, like those of their enemies used for naval warfare in the Mediterranean, were galleys. A galley required a large number of oarsmen, an equally large number of men at arms, but relatively few seamen. The oarsmen were adult slaves and criminals; the men at arms were drawn at various times from different branches of the army.

Turkish naval warfare began with privateering, and up to almost the time of steam, freebooters were still to be found in the eastern Mediterranean, along with regular naval units. The first naval successes of the Ottomans were in the Black Sea, which they cleared of rivals; then they ousted the Knights of St. John from Rhodes. In the early sixteenth century a hero named Khair ud-Dīn, better known as Barbarossa, took Algiers, of which he became governor, and Tunis. Later he was raised to the rank of Lord High Admiral in the court. It was he who allied the Turks to France and created the first foreign capitulations, which provided a formal mechanism for relations between Westerners and Muslims in the Middle East. Barbarossa and his successors sported three horse tails and were made governors of the lands by the sea, which meant an annual summer cruise for tax collection among the defenseless islands.

The Turks were not good sailors, but depended on foreigners to the end. The admirality was a luscious plum and as such fell to court favorites who knew little or nothing about sailing. No ocean washed the Ottoman shores, and hence there was little incentive to develop the kind of craft with which the Portuguese, the Spanish, the Dutch, and the British were sailing to the Americas and the Indies. The downfall of the navy was merely a facet of the general eventual corruption.

The Army and the Navy were concerned with foreign affairs of a hostile nature. They were much more important than foreign affairs of a peaceful nature, so much so that no proper Foreign Office was established until late in Ottoman history. After all, most of the Faithful of Sunni persuasion were subjects of the sultan, while Christian neighbors belonged to the House of War (Dār ul-Ḥarb) and were thus fair prey. Hence, truck with ambassadors was relegated to a corps of interpreters, usually renegade Christians, under the Chief Secretary of the Chancery (of whom more shortly).

The internal government of the empire was placed directly in the hands of an official of the highest rank, the grand vizir, who rated five horse tails. As the sultan's deputy he ruled over the People of the Sword while his opposite number, the Shaikh ul-Islām, ruled the People of the Pen under two chief qāḍīs. Below the grand vizir and the Shaikh ul-Islām, members of these two branches paralleled each other, and their officials balanced each other in each rank category. In general, leaders of subinstitutions in the Sword branch were called by the title Agha, in the Pen branch Effendi. These were general titles, implying neither specific rank nor numbers of tails, if any. Today the word Agha is still used widely in and beyond the former Ottoman domain as an equivalent of Mister or Monsieur, while Effendi has become a label for the Westernized white-collar class.

At the beginning the sultan made public appearances, led his troops in war, and had much to say about what went on. The grand vizir was then more of an assistant or master of protocol, but as time went on and the sultans retired more and more into their harems, the power of the grand vizir grew, and he communicated with the sultan chiefly through the agency of the chief of the Black Eunuchs. At first the vizirial office was held by Turkish noblemen, but it was not long before it became the top plum of the Pages' tree. As the sultans withdrew and as slaves took over, the office became increasingly precarious: a grand vizir could be executed and replaced at the whim of a harem favorite egged on by some outside rival through the agency of the latter's wife.

Starting in the Outside Service, the grand vizir's office was moved in 1654 A.D. to a special building called the *Bābi ʿAlī* or High Door (usually translated in European languages as the Sublime Porte). Here the grand vizir lived and worked. One needed an appointment to see him, except on his one public monthly appearance. Everyone who approached him had to kiss the hem of his robe, excepting only the Shaikh ul-Islām. In the name of the sultan and with the sultan's consent the grand vizir ruled through qanūns, decrees which once issued became law; he ruled everyone except the members of the Imperial Household and the People of the Pen.

Periodically he called together an assembly, the Imperial Divān, in the palace. The members, all of whom rated as vizirs, included heads of major departments and visiting provincial governors of top rank, as well as high-ranking generals. Protocol was rigid and formality frigid at these meetings, in which a stool was reserved for the presiding officer, while members of the first rank sat in the center and those of the second remained afoot in the arcades. Here business of the Sword category was conducted—meaning warfare and the internal administration of the home regions of Anatolia and Rumelia, and of the outlying provinces.

The bureaucracy was highly compartmentalized and complicated. The Army and Navy were under the administration of the grand vizir, as was the civil organization. Directly under the grand vizir and serving as his deputy was an official called *Kakhya-Bey,* who was in charge of a General Secretary and a Master of Ceremonies. These three, originally servants of the grand vizir, ate at a separate mess and were never invited to the high table. (Because he had much to do with the appointment of new governors, the Kakhya-Bey derived his income largely from "kickbacks.")

The officers next in rank were the *Bash Defterdār,* or chief Treasurer, and the *Nishanji,* or qanūn-issuer. The chief treasurer had charge of public funds. He had his own building, housing four major divisions and thirty-two departments, all hierarchically graded, even to the classes of clerks. These were highly specialized, including for example men who had charge of stationery, and coin weighers. The chief treasurer was privileged in that he could present petitions to the sultan in person and could use the royal seal to validate his financial documents. The nishanji also used the seal on qanūns. Before issuing a qanūn he had the right to alter its wording, since it was he who prepared the documents in their final form. This not only gave him much power but also may have prevented the publication of hasty and ill-advised decrees. The nishanji's power was limited, however, in that no qanūn could be issued until the grand mufti, head of the People of the Pen, had checked it for legality according to the sharīʿa. Since the nishanji was himself drawn from the ʿulamā, this made him in a sense dependent on the grand mufti, who ranked him. Thus did the system of checks and controls serve to preserve an interdepartmental balance of power.

Three other officials, ranking below the bash defterdār and the nishanji, were the Chief Secretary of Chancery, the Chief of Records, and the Chief of the Chavushes. The first of these kept a record of all qanūns, orders, and pensions; these duties required a staff of one hundred and fifty clerks, in three grades. The chief secretary of chancery was a ghost writer as well; he drafted all the messages intended for the sultan from the grand vizir. It was also under him, through his interpreters, that foreign affairs were handled. The records chief, with three branches and one hundred clerks, kept a register of titles for lands and fiefs, including public property, private property, and changes in both. This covered the entire empire. The head chavush originally was an usher, sitting in the law court, over which the grand vizir presided. He came to take over several duties.

One was briefing the arguments for the grand vizir's decision; another was the punishment of criminals convicted both by the grand vizir and by the ʿulamā in their separate courts.

During the Ottoman Empire the number of provinces reached its maximum, thirty-six, each with its own government under a viceroy. The provinces were graded by size and amount of revenue, as were their governors, who rated from one to three tails. A three-tailed governor was given the rank of vizir, and his province was called an *eyālet;* next came *beylerbeyi* with two tails. (The Arabic equivalent for beylerbeyi is *wālī;* hence the word *vilayet* (*waliyāt*) for his grade of province.) Below him was a one-tailed *Sanjaq-Bey,* whose province was a sanjaq, the Turkish word for province in general, or in Arabic, *līwā.* (In Arabic, Sanjaq-Bey is called Mutaṣarrif.) Of these there were two grades depending upon revenue.

At the beginning the governors were appointed for life or good behavior; later the term was cut to three years, and finally to one. Under the governor were eight officials: a musterer of feudal troops, a garrison commander, three recorders of sipahis, a treasurer, and a local head chavush. Janissaries served as police. They and the treasurer, with organizational chiefs in the capital, had split loyalties and hence served as mutual checks. The sanjaq itself was divided into districts or judgeships, called *qaḍā.* Each was run by a qāḍī, drawn from the People of the Pen, and his executive, a *subashi,* of the Sword. Under them the people of the villages and of the tribes were left alone for the most part, coming to the towns in which the qāḍīs presided when they needed to trade or when some intervillage dispute arose which they could settle neither among themselves nor through the intermediacy of their landlords or landlords' deputies.

Today foreign news reports contain much about landlords in the former Ottoman provinces, as in Iran. It must be remembered that during the height of the Ottoman power these capitalists were subject to curbs by the central government, and it was not until the eighteenth century when decay had set in that the landowners became virtually autonomous and began to acquire the local power which so vexes reformers of the twentieth century.

In the Arab provinces, it will be remembered, the Turks showed proper respect for their teachers in religion and gave them considerable freedom. They did, however, impose a rigid class system foreign to the Semitic tradition. *ʿAsḳeris,* or men at arms, were the rulers. They could ride horses and carry swords. Their income came from landed properties. Peasants tilled the soil and supported the ʿAskeris, as well as the government. Townsmen plied their crafts and trades and governed themselves within their guilds. Mobility was not encouraged. Under the Turks, the Middle Eastern mosaic system reached its most complicated and most crystallized form.

Landlords of non-Arab extraction, however, were not imposed on the inhabitants of Arabia proper; some parts of ʿIraq, including some of the judgeships of Baghdad province and the Basra government, also escaped, as did the Barbary dey-ships conquered by Barbarossa. In Egypt the system was different, as might be expected.

In the first place, the Ottomans found a class of professional soldiers already in occupation when they arrived. These were the Mamluks, descendants of Janissary-like slaves brought in by Saladin when he reconquered the Nile Valley for the ʿAbbasid caliphate in 1171. Twice the Mamluks managed to take over the rule in Egypt: in 1257, only to be repressed in 1517 with the Ottoman conquest; and in 1707, when they pushed the Sublime Porte's pashas out of power, to be reduced once more and finally by the French, under Napoleon, in 1802.

In the second place, all cultivable land which did not already belong to religious foundations was divided up among members of the conquering ojaqs, who were assigned the grants under the title of multazim, or tax collector. By the seventeenth century these collectorships had become hereditary, and by the eighteenth the multazims had come to own the land outright; they were now landlords and still are (as discussed in Chapter 11).

During the period when Egypt was ruled by a pasha, his powers were limited in a way unknown to other provinces. A dīvān met four times a week, to make administrative decisions. The president of the council was a *kakhya,* its other members high-ranking officials of Sword and Pen. The pasha did not belong and was not invited; he was the executive officer for the council. With the pasha so restricted, it is little wonder that Egypt broke away more than once from the authority of Istanbul.

Whoever was in charge, the bureaucracy remained constant, with special jobs for Coptic, Jewish, and Muslim personnel. The villagers had their shaikhs, the shaikhs dealt with the officers of government, as did the heads of guilds. The bulk of the people spent their lives in poverty, trying to keep fed and clothed; it made no difference to them whether their taxes went to pashas or Mamluks, or what went on in the palaces. What they wanted was stability; as a contemporary Muslim writer observed, they were so accustomed to oppression that they feared kindness as a sign of weakness. (Today the Western world is interested in what goes on in Egypt, as elsewhere in the Middle East; with increasing frequency another "expert" discovers the plight of the fellaḥīn anew. Whatever these experts may think, or however the Egyptian government may appear to the Western press, one must realize that the most valid way to evaluate a social situation is against the scale of time; the fellaḥīn *are* attaining some recognition as human beings, they *are* being taught to read and write, and their health *is* beginning to be cared for.)

So much, for the moment, for the Turkish government, and its extension into Arab lands. Only one of these wholly escaped: Morocco. It must be remembered that Morocco too has a long and varied history, with many changes of dynasties and certain alterations in her system of government,[4] far too complicated and detailed for mention here. The following several paragraphs will consider the government of the Sherifian Empire, as it is called, before the French protectorate, which ended in 1956, officially began in 1912. This description will apply only to the Bled al-Makhzen, or Government Land; the Bled eṣ-Ṣibā', or Land of Insolence, will be covered in the next chapter.

Although Morocco is an Arab state, it is also a Berber empire. Both Arabs and Berbers live side by side, with the latter in the majority; both have had their share in ruling. The present dynasty, the Filāli, follows the Maliki code, stricter than the Ḥanifi but less rigorous than the Ḥanbali of Sa'udi Arabia. The sultans are descended from the Prophet through Fāṭima and 'Alī, whence their name 'Alāwi Sharīfs. They are a newer house than the Idrīsites, whose supremacy in Fez they recognize and support. As imāms of all North Africa they hold a religious authority which exceeds their temporal boundaries and includes the right to call all Muslims as far as Tunis to the jihād, or holy war. (There has been talk of late of reviving the caliphate under the present sultan, Sīdī Muḥammad ben Yūsuf[5] who is certainly as good a candidate as any in the Mus-

[4] See Henri Terrasse, *Histoire du Maroc* (Casablanca, 1949–50), 2 vols.

[5] Moroccan sultans are called *Mūlai* (my lord) unless named Muḥammad, in which case they are called *Sīdī,* to prevent confusion with the Prophet, and hence sacrilege.

lim world.

We have already considered the social and political structure of the city of Fez in some detail and have seen that the aristocratic families of Fez, through the agency of the universities, provided an informal kind of civil service pool and training school. The sultans lived in considerable magnificence in their three palaces at Fez, Meknes, and Marrakesh which they visited in rotation. Fez and Marrakesh were the two most favored cities; in fact it is the bodies of ʿulamā from these two metropoles who have the right to confirm or reject a new sultan in power.

Unlike the Turks, the Moorish sultans continued to consider the Imperial Treasury their private property and to make no distinction between state and personal capital or income. Unlike the Turks again they kept their grand vizirs (called in Morocco variously *Wazīr al-Kabīr* and *al-Fqih al-Kabīr,* the Great Clerk) in the palace as part of their entourages. The sultan was more accessible than the Turkish head of state, but less so than Ibn Saʿūd or the Imām of al-Yemen. Aside from his concubines he limited himself to the orthodox four wives, who were free Muslim ladies. He combined the three offices of spiritual leader, generalissimo, and temporal ruler. His officials had no horse tails and no permanent rank; the title pasha came to mean no more and no less than mayor. More important still, the system of granting estates in fief and building up a class of landlords was unknown in Morocco, although certain tribes, known as Ghaish, were given public lands and exempted from taxation on the agreement that they should furnish a certain number of mounted soldiers at all times. In this they resembled the Turkish *Musellems.*

The Imperial Household included its harem with black eunuchs from Abyssinia and slave women from Istanbul, as well as some European women. In the harem a number of special matrons prepared the new arrivals for the pleasure of their master, who sometimes had them parade in the harem gardens on Thursdays so that he could select his favorite for the week end. The "inside service" was in the hands of Negro page boys. Sons and daughters of the sultan were educated in isolated sanctuaries, each prince with a Negro companion of his own age, whom he called "brother" and who served him for life. Once a year the sultan provided formal weddings for those of his offspring who were ready. His daughters married wealthy men, some of them officials. Other favorites received women from his harem. Among his many sons the sultan would designate one as his heir, subject to the approval of the ʿulamā of Fez and of Marrakesh and to the acquiescence of his brothers; this favorite was sent into the provinces as a governor or general, as indoctrination for the duties ahead.

Unlike the Ottoman potentates, the Moorish sultans were in the habit of constantly moving about. They made public appearances at least once a week, when they went to the mosque for Friday prayer; in addition there were the three annual treks between their capitals, and their virtually annual campaigns against rebels. These expeditions kept them out of doors much of the time, and brought them close enough to most of their subjects so that they could be seen and appealed to. The sultan was always accompanied by a special bodyguard of some two dozen men, including the royal parasol-bearer, who kept his master's head shaded from the sun, the wielder of the royal fly-switch, to flick insects off the royal integument, a bull-voiced master of ceremonies, a spearbearer, a gunbearer, a flogger, a beheader, a tent-pitcher, a head groom, a water-bearer, a teamaker, a standard-bearer, a slipper bearer, and so on down the line.

Until the middle of the nineteenth century when European drillmasters were hired, the army was all cavalry. At its core was the Black Guard, called the Bukhāris, after the distinguished author el-Bukhāri, a copy of whose book of Traditions was carried into battle as a talisman. These slaves were quartered outside the palaces and were issued uniforms, horses, and weapons. Other outfits had to provide their own gear. Mixing with white women, the Bukhāris gradually became lighter in skin color and less Negroid in feature, except when reinforced by new slaves. From their body some of the government officials were recruited, and in 1697 a decree was issued permitting them to own property.

Another special group was the Ghaish, already mentioned; a third was the ʿUdaya, an Arab tribe of Bedawin origin, whom the sultans quartered outside the gates of Fez, much to the annoyance of its inhabitants, and whose duty it was to prevent the revolt of the city, while protecting it against raids from the Berber tribes nearby. A halfhearted attempt was made to build up an artillery service, Turkish style, but without much success; in camp the cannon were pointed toward Mekka to indicate the direction of prayer, and, since they were considered sanctuary, refugees were in the habit of dashing up to the cannon and embracing them. Once a consignment of oil sent to Tangier to clean the cannon was eaten by the gunners, who otherwise used them principally to announce the break of fasting at Ramaḍān.

The wazīrs, or ministers of the government, were in constant attendance at the court. The titles of these dignitaries and their division of governmental duties must have varied from time to time; since different reliable authors give different listings.[6] There was always, however, a grand wazīr, a chief qāḍī, a Treasurer, a Superintendent of Religious Foundations (Ḥabūs), and a Superintendent of the Imperial Domains, including grounds and buildings. Besides these were the heads of the Army and Navy, the provincial governors, and the qā'ids of tribes. The appointment of these officials was extremely informal. Thomas Pellow of Penrhyn who was himself a qā'id under Mūlai Ismā'īl (1672-1727 A.D.) stated that "they have no commission, but receive their authority only by his saying: 'Go govern such a country, by my general or admiral.'"[7] Budgett Meakin, a keen observer who wrote in the 1890's, was struck by the informality of the meetings of the court, stating that he had been brought before the ministers of state who were sitting around out of doors on carpets.[8]

Foreign affairs merited little attention; sometimes there was a special minister, while other foreign affairs were under the grand wazīr or even under the navy. The Islamic state did not conceive of a nation flanked by equal nations and engaged in peaceful international relations. The navy was largely composed of the Sallee rovers, privateers who docked their ships behind the sea gate of Salē, raided as far as England, and brought thousands of Christian slaves to the auction block; there they even sold some of King Philip's Wampanoags from Plymouth county and Rhode Island.

The treasurer (according to Meakin) kept his funds in three buildings, at Marrakesh, Fez, and Meknes. The coffers could be opened only "by agreement between the local superintendent, the governor of the palace, a trusted eunuch, and the woman in charge of the harem."[9] The sultan governed by issuing decrees called

[6] For the most modern and most critical account, see H. Terrasse, *op. cit.*, Vol. II. He describes the Moorish government as it existed at different periods.

[7] Thomas Pellow, *The Adventures of Thomas Pellow of Penrhyn, Mariner*, ed. by Dr. Robert Brown (London, 1890), pp. 137-138.

[8] Budgett Meakin, *The Moorish Empire* (London, 1899), p. 207.

[9] *Ibid.*, p. 206.

ẓāhirs,[10] the equivalent of the qanūns of their Ottoman counterparts. A corps of secretaries wrote down instructions, drew up documents, and sealed them with the royal stamp. Copies of these announcements were ridden posthaste to the cities of the empire, where they were read in the mosques to the accompaniment of salvos of artillery. The messengers who carried them were members of special corps, called *musakhkharīn;* they spent their time out of the saddle serving as ushers at the court. This was a profitable occupation, since their services required emoluments to insure an audience.

The administration of justice was divided between the pasha's or qā'id's court, which dealt with crimes of violence and disturbances of the peace, and the qāḍī's court, which settled disputes which could be referred to sharīʿa law. The pasha's police were the *makhzaniya,* special men drawn from the Ghaish tribes, who wore pointed fezzes; the qāḍī's agents had no special uniform. In cases of capital punishment the sultan, the pasha, and the qāḍī were all involved; the pasha sent the judgment to the sultan for confirmation, who passed it to the qāḍī for approval, who returned it to the pasha for execution. Taxes were of several kinds: in addition to the zakā specified as the third pillar of Islam, the government imposed a gate tax, a market tax, and customs duties, as well as discovering special ways of squeezing the uninfluential rich. Jews paid the special poll tax for People of the Book (jizīya). They had their own religious government, under their chief rabbi, who was under the administration of the chief qāḍī.

Of the Arab states ruled by the Ottomans, those located in the Arabian peninsula felt the effects of the Turkish regime the least. Saʿudi Arabia in its present form is a modern development, dating from after World War I, and Ibn Saʿūd's conquest of the Ḥijāz. It owes its present position of importance largely to the wisdom and powerful personality of its ruler, helped by the advice over many years of one Shaikh ʿAbdullah (known to the outside world as Major H. St. John B. Philby) and financed by two of the world's most lucrative institutions, the annual pilgrimage to Mekka and the Arabian-American Oil Company. In his strictly Muslim state King ʿAbd ul-ʿAzīz Āl Saʿūd has created what at first glance appears to be something quite ancient; actually it is something new.

Quite the reverse is true of the Yemen. Perched on a chilly plateau,

[10] French spelling is *dahir.*

this hermit kingdom is nearly as isolated at Tibet and probably less known. The Turks ruled it under a bey, the last of whom, known as Qāḍī-Rāghib, is still there. This remarkable and talented old gentleman was once on the staff of the Turkish Embassy in St. Petersburg; he was later Prime Minister at San'ā, where he has remained since the end of World War I. When the Turks retired, he simply moved from the governorship to the prime ministry, while the imām, whose ancestors had ruled the Yemen long before the Turks had been heard of, moved into the palace, adding the role of administrator to his spiritual functions.

In 1933 Waldo Forbes and I had the rare privilege of paying a visit to the Imām Yaḥya in his audience chamber in the palace. Several secretaries in the outer halls served as a screen; once past them, however, all was quite simple. Although a throne graced the far end of the chamber, the imām sat on a cushion against the long wall, with his secretaries on either side. In deference to our Christian lack of squatting facets, two Sunday school chairs were placed in front of the imām for our use. This was an act of great courtesy, since it placed our heads higher than his. The Qāḍī Rāghib acted as interpreter, while a number of secretaries were busy writing.

The imām showed a keen interest in the outside world and asked many pertinent questions. Our conversation naturally turned to the possibilities of archaeological work in his kingdom. While not averse to scientific study, he expressed the opinion that it would be difficult for him to tell the sheep from the goats among foreign applicants, and also said that it would do no harm to leave a few treasures in the ground for future scholars equipped with better techniques to excavate. While his opinion was against my immediate interests I could not help agreeing with him. At the end of our conference a secretary handed him a document for approval; he poured some pink powder from a box lying with his writing materials and affixed his seal to it. The secretary blew the loose powder away, and the document was ready.

On another occasion I had the privilege of acting as his confidential secretary in helping him pay a premium for his life insurance, which I hope the present imām has collected. The kindly old gentleman was assassinated in 1948 by a group of young ruffians, including one of his sons, and his loyal eldest son, Aḥmad, now occupies the throne, having murdered rival brothers.

While other governments required many ministers, that of al-

Yemen functioned with two, Qāḍī ʿAbdullah ʿAmri, who died defending his master, and Qāḍī Rāghib Bey. It is an indication of the religious character of the Yemeni government that both these officials bear the title of qāḍī. Qāḍī ʿAbdullah (whose son is now a United Nations delegate) had charge of internal affairs and war, Qāḍī Rāghib of foreign affairs. Each had his council of notables, called *mustasharīn,* to help him, but all decisions came immediately before the imām.

Outside the capital the Yemen is divided into districts, each with a governor, directly appointed by the imām. The governor administers the provincial capital and levies soldiers and collects taxes in his territory. For tax collecting he has a special secretary called *Amīr aṣ-Ṣundūq,* or Commander of the Box. Parallel to and independent of the governor is the *ḥākim,* who is provincial qāḍī. Appointed directly by the imām as his spiritual representative—for the imām is his own chief qāḍī—the ḥākim is completely independent of the governor. Under him are a number of qāḍīs of lower rank, situated among the tribes. These qāḍīs are usually chosen from holy families of sayyid, which gives them personal sanction. The tribal leaders are the shaikhs, who are politically subordinate to the governor. Under tribal shaikhs are lesser shaikhs, commanding villages. These two grades of shaikhs are responsible for order and taxes and for furnishing men in time of war, whom many of them personally lead. As in Morocco the Jews form a separate community under their chief rabbi, who in turn reports to the court. The simplicity of the Yemeni political system and its informality are a function of its size and isolation, as well as a reminder of the essential simplicity and personal character of the early Islamic state.

Of the remaining Muslim nations, Iran is most conspicuous. The Persians have understood the machinery of government longer than Arabs, Berbers, or Turks, and they remained outside the Ottoman Empire. It is difficult, however, to find a suitable period for our survey, because Persian history is a record of alternate dynasties of local and foreign provenience, while the modern age affected the Iranian government over a long period and not all at once. We have already considered the ancient system in Chapter 5. Here it is only necessary to show in what respect that system withstood the blows of time and what adjustments were made to the adoption of Islam, particularly to the recognition of the Imāmi Shīʿa faith as a state religion.

The date 1906 marks the end of the preconstitutional period in Iran. At this time reforms were instituted, including the establishment of a parliament; in 1925 when Riza Shah Pahlavi assumed control, modernization began in earnest. Before 1906 the government resembled that of the ancient Persians in many details. This is understandable, since the landscape had not changed, other than perhaps through increased deforestation; agricultural techniques had not been improved, nor were means of transport much different. The shah was an absolute monarch, difficult to approach; he ruled with a council of state, drawn from twenty-seven vizirs who headed departments, and a few court officials without portfolio. The provinces were managed by governors appointed for short periods, and each governor was assisted by a vizir. Azerbaijan, the most prosperous and at the same time most dangerous province, was governed by the heir to the throne. Post-horse riders carried messages between the capital and the provinces.

In many details the Persian court resembled the Ottoman, and much of the resemblance was due no doubt to give and take in both directions. The original model, however, was the Persian. One way in which they differed profoundly was in the relationship of religious institution to state. Whereas the Turkish sultan considered himself caliph and delegated the office of upholder of the sharī'a to the grand mufti, the shah, like his Achaemenian predecessors, kept out of the religious hierarchy, leaving it to his mujtahids, who depended for their ultimate authority on their own superiors in Karbala. The power of the mujtahids waxed and waned during Persian history, and at one time they held power over both civil and religious courts, while drawing a large income from waqfs. Nadir Shah, in the middle of the eighteenth century, seized much of their property and reduced their power. Some of the more lucrative waqf, like that of the Imām Riza, passed into government control, while the smaller ones remained under the religious hierarchy, which though Arab in inspiration and in ritual details, was Persian in its function and its place in the over-all scheme.

In Afghanistan, on the other hand, where most of the people are Sunnis and where the Ḥanifi school is the official sharī'a law, the religious and the political institutions are not separated. Although the amīrs made no claim to the caliphate, like the Turks, nor based their religious position on descent from the Prophet, like the sultan of Morocco and the imām of al-Yemen, they still assumed spiritual leadership. Directly under the head of the state was a chief qāḍī, whose court was the principal legal vehicle of the nation.

Administratively Afghanistan was divided into five provinces: Kabul, Turkestan, Herat, Kandahar, and Badakshan, each ruled by a governor bearing the title *nā'ib* and appointed by the amīr. The royal council, called *durbar,* as in British India, was made up of three categories of leaders: *sardars* or hereditary nobles, khans elected by their tribes, and mullas to represent the religious fraternity. Despite the introduction of a more Westernized system, it may still be said that no modern Islamic nation depends more on its clergy for guidance than Afghanistan. Aided by nature through isolation on one of the eaves of the world, its mullas have preserved their country more or less intact as an anthopologist's paradise, where Pathans, Tajiks, Uzbegs, Hazaras, and so-called "Nuristanis" (Kafirs), still wear their old-fashioned clothing and have not become too self-conscious to let themselves be studied.

16 THE LAND OF INSOLENCE

THERE IS SOMETHING in the concept of a Land of Insolence that appeals to Americans. Perhaps it is because we had one ourselves not long ago, in the Wild West, and because, a century earlier than that, on the village green at Lexington, our forebears set foot on the path of insolence to achieve freedom. Geography permits independence, technology defeats it. This is why the idea of One World, into which technical science is forcing us, leaves some people uneasy. If the world is to be one, what place will there be in it for rebels, and without rebels, who will keep the rest of the world on its toes?

Which brings up the subject of a fifth kind of division of labor in the Middle East. We have seen the divisions between peoples, between communities specializing in regional products, between the inhabitants of villages, camps, and cities, and between members of crafts and professions. The fifth, between the tame and the insolent, the domestic and the independent, makes provision for the supply of rebels who, since the beginning of the Bronze Age, have kept the urban civilization of the Middle East refreshed and in motion. It will be remembered that Egypt has no habitable mountains or deserts on the periphery of its river valley. It has no Land of Insolence, and although the Egyptians were as civilized as the succession of peoples in ʿIraq, Egypt's contribution to the civilization of the rest of the world has been but a fraction of Mesopotamia's.

According to the layman's knowledge of ancient history, as one early civilization (except in Egypt) began to totter, another peoples came down from the hills or off the desert and took over, only to decay in turn. The cycle is said to have been what sustained Middle Eastern civilization. This conventional explanation falls short in two respects. It fails to explain the decay within the cities in the first place, and it misrepresents the process of replacement. Urban decay is neither a mystery nor a moral force. In most old-fashioned Middle Eastern cities the water supply is unsanitary and the methods of waste disposal inadequate. Food is expensive, since it must be brought from the country; much of it is highly processed. It takes a man a long time to learn a trade, and not until he has become at least a journeyman can he afford to marry. In a tribe or village the division of labor between the sexes makes early marriage necessary; in the city a single man can rent a room and eat in the sūqs. There are other diversions to make up for his lack of female companionship. His work keeps him in the shade and exercises only parts of his body. The death rate is high, the birth rate low.[1] Perhaps half the population must come from outside each generation.

If the cities were dependent on spectacular invasions for personnel replacement, they would all be in ruins, and small sites at that. Replacement is a continuous process. Individuals, families, and small groups of families come in each year to take on city life. Some go home, but others stay. These replacements come from two sources: villages in submitted territory and the tribes outside. A villager makes a good workman because he is accustomed to long hours, concentration on his work, and the frugal life. He is also accustomed to living in a small group and minding his own business as far as events outside the group are concerned. He is ready to fit into the mosaic of urban life, somewhere near the bottom.

The tribesman has several advantages over the docile villager. He has been brought up on a higher standard of living, with more animal products in his diet, and is more likely to be strong and healthy. Furthermore he has been trained in an entirely different school; he is the hawk to the villager's pigeon. Brought up on a tradition of feuding and fighting, he has learned to take calculated risks and prizes his honor and that of his family above life. Knowing how to evaluate tight situations and to make quick decisions, he is accustomed to discipline and knows how to command as well as to obey. In the city he can use his muscular strength and vigor by becoming a porter, like the Kurds in Baghdad, or if he is bright as well, he may even rise to a position of authority. The water carrier or the guardsman can become king.

[1] In the ancient town mound of Tepe Gawra in northern 'Iraq, 393 burials were found in Levels 8 to 13, inclusive, plus another section designated as Area A. Two hundred and thirteen, or 54%, were infants; 106, or 27%, children; and 74, or 19%, were adults. A. J. Tobler, *Excavations at Tepe Gawra,* Museum Monographs, II, Levels IX-XX (Philadelphia, 1950), 111. With only 19% adult, the females capable of procreation before death must have numbered about 10%. For each breeding couple to perpetuate itself would require the average woman to produce 20 offspring. Other ancient cities show the same general ratio. Infant mortality is still extremely high in Middle Eastern cities.

The run-of-the-mill cultural training of the free villager or mountaineer has produced in him the same useful and famous qualities which the ancient Persians developed in their noble youths through expensive and rigorous schooling, as Xenophon so carefully explained. The Ottoman Turks understood this and carried the same principle to success in their education and use of the Pages and Foreign Boys. It is entertaining to look upon the colorful tribesmen of the Middle East as something exciting and photogenic, prime targets for tourism and sentiment, but it is more practical to study them as what they have always been—a backlog of healthy, hardy, disciplined personnel, as valuable to shahs and sultans as they are hard to handle.

The boundaries of the Land of Insolence are forever fluctuating, depending on the strength or weakness of the central governments concerned. In general, however, they follow climatic and geological contours, which give the tribesmen the mountains and deserts. Mountains and deserts, it will be remembered, are often inhabited by nomads, but nomads are not the only self-governing tribal people. Some of the mountains are suited for agriculture, and farmers whose terraces are protected by geographical barriers are just as warlike and just as well fitted to provide a human backlog to urban civilization as their more mobile kin. When compared to desert nomads they are also more durable, because their livelihood does not depend on raising animals which trucks put out of business, and because, in the long run, mountains offer a safer refuge than deserts.

Mountain farmers live in villages, as do the tax-paying peasants of the open plain. Aside from the practice of agriculture, the resemblance ends there. Four major groups of mountaineers concern us: the North African Berbers, the Druzes and other schismatics of Syria, the Kurds, and the Pathans. Some of the Berbers who live in desert camps or frequent high pastures in the heat of the year have already fallen under our rapid scrutiny; we have also gone into the government of the Druzes and the Yezidis, and that of the Kafirs, Kurds, and Pathans, who have nomads among their tribes, has been mentioned as well. Agricultural Berbers, Kurds, and Pathans, concern us now. The first consideration is the village, as elsewhere the basic social unit.

If we were to fly over these various mountains, we might come to the conclusion that the villages were of two kinds. One is the tight little community, the compact cluster of roofs perched on the shoulder of a hill. It differs from the village on the plain only in its location. This is what the birdman will see in the Moroccan Grand Atlas, in the Kabyle country of Algeria, in the Aures Mountains, and in Kurdistan. The other kind is the sprawling village, which does not look like any village at all, but rather a string of houses, widely separated, along the side of a watercourse. If the birdman looks carefully he will see that some of these houses are fortified. Every man's home is his castle. If he checks the map he will see that he is over the Moroccan Rif, or the land of the Pathans. (If he has heard, and believed, the usual tales of how these people bury their prisoners up to the neck in ant hills, or how the women cut them in little strips with knives, he will pray to his God that his motors shall not fail.)

To work up to a consideration of the Riffians and Pathans, let us start with a Kurdish village, named Walash.[2] This aggregation of twelve households and ninety human beings lies in a fold of the western slopes of the Zagros Mountains, on the Rowanduz road, completed by the ʿIraqi government since the end of the British occupation. The houses of Walash stand in blocks, each occupied by a group of several related families. Since they cover ground too steep and rocky to be cultivated, their roofs are set at different levels. Rooms lower down are usually devoted to storage, while those above are inhabited. A few houses are two-storied, and in these outside ladders lead the nimble mountaineers upstairs. Stone and mud are the materials of the walls. These are built when needed by masons from the town. The roof beams, of hewn beech and oak, will look old and smoke-glazed even in a new house; being extremely valuable, the tenant takes them with him when he moves. In the middle of the room is the firepit, the place for cooking; no chimney leads the smoke outside. Smarting the eyes of the inhabitants, its wisps find its way through the interstices of the roof.

Several of these houses will present a different appearance. With glass windows and hinged doors, they look larger and in better condition, for they belong to the Agha, the landlord and chief of the village. If it is summer there is a leaf-shaded pergola near the Agha's house. Under it rugs and cushions provide a lounging place, and

[2] Selected for the obvious reason that it is the only Kurdish village that has received careful study by a trained anthropologist. See Leach, *Social and Economic Organization of the Rowanduz Kurds.*

the smell of coffee and cigarette smoke label it the guest house. In the winter, guests are entertained indoors.

The land outside the village looks as if it had been carved by a cosmic cubist, for although the main sweeps of the landscape are plainly diagonal, the actual surfaces are horizontal and vertical. Step after step, terrace after terrace, show the work of hundreds and thousands of patient men, generation after generation, whittling patchwork fields out of mountain. These terraces describe a whole palette of subtly graded shades of green, from the rich bluish-green of onion patches near the bottom of the valley to the pastel of young wheat stalks high on the sides. At the very bottom a line of shiny blue divides the slopes: water. This bed will be dry during irrigation time. When the grist mill is grinding, the stream will seem to start in the middle of its course, where it churns out from under the paddlewheels.

Four purposes are thus served by the water of this stream. It soaks the rimmed paddy wherein grows the Agha's rice, an aristocratic cereal which he likes to serve in his guest house. It waters the vegetable gardens, used by individual tenants, and their tobacco lands as well. It drives the grist mill. There is not enough water, however, to do all of these things at once. Tobacco is needed both for smoking and for trading. Power milling saves much female muscular energy, as well as time. Everyone needs vegetables. Someone must decide who shall use how much water and when. That someone is the Agha.

The Agha is the number-one man in charge of the eighty-nine other human beings in the village. Four of the twelve households in the village are occupied by his close kin, who make up forty-six persons, or forty per cent of the villagers. Most of the others are also related to him, to a more distant degree. Although he succeeded his father as Agha, he was not the eldest son. By some informal process he was chosen from among his brothers as the one most suited to command. In a neighboring village, Rayat, the Agha's elder brother has charge of the annual summer migration to high pasture, while the Agha himself stays at home.

The Walash people do not send flocks away in summer; they consign their animals to a single herdsman, who can find enough grass and other fodder for them near the village the year round. The elder brother of the Agha of Walash, then, has no special duties, although he may help the Agha in the management of the grist mill and other minor tasks. Two of the Agha's married sons have left home to become aghas of other villages, but two others, with their families, are still in residence. Twenty persons, wives, servants, and children, make up the Agha's own household, while those of his brother and sons, consisting of eight each, round out the aristocratic forty per cent of the population.

In general, aghas are polygynous while commoners are monogamous. In 1938, the date of Leach's survey, the Agha of Walash had fifteen surviving children, the progeny of nine wives, of whom he presumably had never had more than four at one time. The families of aghas increase, while those of commoners barely hold their own. While some of the upper level are killed off in feuds (or once were), and others take office in other villages, there still is a gradual downward mobility for the less successful survivors, while emigration may take care of some of the excess, presumably from the lower levels. The brothers and sons of the Agha are also called Agha out of courtesy, but this deference cannot last many generations.

This is why nearly everyone in the village is related to each other, particularly because marriage among all but the Agha's immediate family is endogamous. The preferred marriage among commoners is between a young man and his father's brother's daughter, as among Bedawin. If this cannot be arranged he may have to take a wife from his father's sister's, his mother's brother's, or even his mother's sister's offspring. The Agha is called upon to approve all the marriages in his village. His principal motive, of course, is to keep the group as close together as he can. He does not want any ties with other villages at a level below his own. He intends to handle all intervillage affairs himself, and he must have the undivided loyalty of his people. It is he who marries outside the village and obtains outside wives for his sons. In this way he cements the relations between the various divisions of the tribe. By the same token the Agha tries to marry off his daughters to his peers in other villages. This not only produces further cement but also refunds him, at least in part, for the considerable bride price he has had to pay for each of his sons' wives. Not all of his daughters, however, leave the village. Now and then a young man of lowly origin within the village distinguishes himself in warfare and in the leadership of men, and such a young hero may be offered the hand of a daughter of the Agha. Once married to her, he has risen to the upper class and may indeed become an Agha himself, if not killed sooner. Thus there is mobility upward as well as downward, and, exceptionally, inheritance of rank through the mother.[3]

The desire for alliances is not the only motive which impels the village Agha to take several wives into his household. Many hands are needed for the unusual amount of kitchen work involved in running the guest house, in which he not only entertains and feeds travelers but also provides his own men with the luxury of sugar-sweetened tea and coffee, which most of them could not afford to serve at home. They make up for this, however, by providing a goat now and then, a bowl of *most* (yoghurt), or a half-sack of grain. Honored guests, if they are both well bred and wise, bring presents to the Agha, and these should include most if not all of the tea, coffee, and sugar that the villagers consume.

Relations between the Agha and his villagers are usually amicable. Were they not, another Agha might take his place. Leach gives one example in which the Agha of Walash kicked a man who had stolen water for his tobacco seedlings, but the thief probably deserved it; if the Agha had not taken this action someone else might have bashed him over the head with a shovel.[4] No doubt the rest of the village approved. (As many arguments arise over water as they do in the army over jeeps. In November, 1949, when we were driving from Sulaimaniya to investigate one of the Hazar Merd caves, our road was blocked by a flood caused by an irrigation theft.) Regulating the water supply is probably the Agha's chief duty inside the village. His outside duty is maintaining the relations of his village with other villages within and without the tribe, and with the official government. The need for a man possessing the quality of leadership may be clearly seen.

In his own mind and in the minds of his people, the Agha owns the land, and the other farmers are his tenants. Theoretically he collects half the produce, but the actual ratio varies considerably. If he wants to, the Agha can put a man out of his house, in which case the tenant pulls down the roof and takes away his rafters. Actually, however, evictions are rare, and then only with general approval.

[3] This upward mobility is not discussed by Leach. I find it in my field notes on the social organization of the Shikak tribe, over the border in Iran.

[4] During the irrigation season the commonest injury treated in rural hospitals in western Iran is said to be cranial fracture and/or concussion.

When a man dies the Agha decides which son, or brother, if any, shall take over the house and land. The problem of fragmentation does not arise here.

The government has other ideas about who owns the land. It recognizes three kinds of tenure in the Kurdish hills: *mulk,* which is outright property; *mīri,* which is state-owned land, subject to the performance of certain duties by the holder, and hence alienable; and *tapu,* which is also state-owned but which involves registration in which the descendants of the original recipient are guaranteed tenure. In Turkish days it made little difference to the Kurds what the government thought about their land. Now that the ʿIraqi government has built a road and can get at them, they have begun to care. Most of the land is classed as mīri, while the aghas are in favor of a shift to the tapu category. Only in the towns, where the greater aghas own houses, is there any mulk.

Speaking of the town, that is of course where the villagers go to do their shopping and where they come in contact with Christians and Jews. It is not necessary to leave home at all, however, since other mechanisms for trading exist. One specialist, a weaver, produces the woolen cloth that they need in the village. Now and then a peddler comes around with his traveling shop, to sell matches, needles, cigarette papers, spices, kerosene, thread, sugar, tea, and coffee. In the summertime he will move on up to the high meadows to cater to the nomads. In Walash it is the common people who buy from him. The Agha either makes his purchases in the town or buys from special travelers representing Jewish or Armenian merchants. These plutocrats will advance him credit without interest, but at a high price. These Armenians and Jews are not the only People of the Book with whom the Kurds deal. Scattered throughout their territory are villages of Assyrians, Nestorian Christians whose main area of concentration lies on the western shores of Lake Urumiya. These Assyrians are not only splendid farmers but also skilled craftsmen, many being carpenters. Ordinarily they can come and go freely, hiring out their services to the Kurds. Today one finds many of them serving as ʿIraqi government policemen.

The Rowanduz Valley contains two tribes, each under a paramount Agha. These tribes are Soran, which has but a single clan, and Balik, with three. The paramount Agha of Balik is our friend, Shaikh Muḥammad, Agha of Walash. Balik has five aghas, and since two of these are Shaikh Muḥammad's sons, his family is in the majority. Two villages, however, differ from the others. These are holy villages, ruled by a pair of dervishes, uncle and nephew, who run hospices of the Sūfi order of Nakhshbandi, centered at Bukhara. Being holy, the inhabitants of these villages are immune from warfare, which gives them the protection necessary for travel. Travel they do, throughout the hills and valleys, trading with the tribesmen immured by feuds, and smuggling over the borders.

Technically speaking, a tribe is an aggregation of groups known in the singular as *ṭa'ifa,* here translated as clan. All its members supposedly are related in the male line. Apparently all the ṭa'ifas in the tribe need not be related; Leach, for example, states that the Agha of Sorak was trying to persuade one of the Balik ṭa'ifas to break away from its parent group, presumably to join him. The ṭa'ifa is again composed of a number of smaller groups called *tira,* or lineage, which of course include a number of households. A village may contain more than one tira, but all of its members presumably belong to the same ṭa'ifa.

With no annual migration to organize and police, why this elaborate organization? The answer is, of course, that each village is an economic unit, separate from and in rivalry with its neighbors. It would be simple for them to raid each other, especially in the early spring when granaries are empty and tempers short. The tribal system keeps the peace in sufficient measure to permit the entry of processed goods and the exit of raw materials, so that a metal-age standard of living can be maintained. It also provides for the rapid mobilization of several hundreds of warriors in case of invasion.

From the time of the old Assyrians and the Medes down to the present, the established governments on either side of the Zagros have tried to bring the Kurds into their political orbits. For the same length of time the Kurds have resisted conquest and assimilation. When one reads the annals of history, the record of what conquerors have done to these people is not calculated to make submission attractive. They, on the other hand, have rarely played the role of meek victims, having done their share of cattle rustling and raiding. Over the Iranian border they have been known to kill and loot in the villages of Azerbaijani Turks, who in turn have victimized the Assyrians, with whom the Kurds are usually on good terms. The tale of all the raids and feuds and wars in these mountains, even during the last twenty years, could never be told in its entirety. However, these deeds of daring, self-sacrifice, greed, and treachery form the subject matter for Kurdish epic songs, which the young warrior hears as he lies awake in his cradle. One cannot fail to be impressed by the thorough indoctrination in the heroics of blood-letting that young Kurds, among other mountaineers, undergo.

Moving on to another land of mountain villages we arrive in the Kabyle country of Algeria.[5] This is the most densely populated part of the country, with two hundred and fifty persons to the square mile, and as many as five hundred and thirty in the region of Fort National. From a hilltop near that town one can, on a clear day, count over a hundred villages, perched on crags and the shoulders of mountains, admirably situated for defense, but often some distance both from the dependent fields and from water. These sites were selected, of course, in the days when each village was a sovereign state, and hence military considerations were paramount. In many villages the women spend much time carrying water uphill, and a considerable reserve is kept in storage.

Depending on the amount of arable land available, the villages vary greatly in size from hamlets of a half-dozen roofs to communities of several hundred, housing more than a thousand people. Where one sees several hamlets situated within a few miles of each other, the chances are that they are collectively administered as parts of a single village, while a hamlet unique in its neighborhood will be part of the next full-sized community. The farmers in a village go down to work in their fields in the morning and return at night, leaving the plow in the furrow until the cultivation is finished. These men work in pairs or in groups. Many legal devices, Berber in tradition and at variance with Muslim law, serve as mechanisms for partnership. A man prefers to own shares in several oxen than one whole ox; the danger of loss is less. Many men work for others on the Persian system of receiving one fifth of the crop for labor. Some of the men work on ḥabūs land, which belongs to the mosque.

The villagers belong to the usual patriarchal extended families, all in one house or cluster of houses. These houses in turn are grouped in wards. Usually the ward members are related to each other. Two public buildings stand in the center of the village, near an open

[5] The literature of Kabyle culture is voluminous. The classic work, however, is A. Hanoteau and A. Letourneux, *La Kabylie et les coutumes ḳabyles* (2d ed.; Paris, 1893), 3 vols. For a brief and competent English account, see Glora Wysner, *The Kabyle People* (New York, 1945).

space. They are the mosque and the *jamā'a* or village hall. There is no bathhouse, as in the Persian village, although these can be found in the city. One may find, however, a number of specialists. A large village will include one Jewish family, distinguishable only from the other people in occupation and religion; clothing and speech are the same as for the rest. The Jew is a jeweler, supplying the silver and coral ornaments which every bride needs. He has his kin in other villages, and indeed there are a few exclusively Jewish villages in Kabylia, as in the Moroccan Atlas, the Yemen, and other mountainous regions.

Another specialist is the blacksmith, who is also an outsider. The villagers lend him a house, and each family pays him a fixed portion of his yearly salary in grain and other produce. In return he guarantees to keep their donkeys and mules shod and their tools in repair. Another man will be a barber; still another a tailor, who cuts and stitches the hooded capes worn by the men, and decorates them with colored silk braid. A professional seamstress sews for the women. For a long time these sartorial experts have been using Singer sewing machines, which greatly speed up their work. One wonders to what extent the machine has built up these specialties; in the mountains of northern Morocco, where sewing is still done by hand, students in the mosque tailor for the men and embroider for both sexes.

Certain other experts come seasonally, making the rounds of many villages. These include saddlemakers and wooden bowl carvers. The latter, arriving in pairs, buy a thick-butted tree from its owner or owners, fell it, saw it in sections, and carve these into bowls, suited for familial kuskus-eating. These bowls they then sell to the villagers. Still other specialists are to be found at the weekly markets (described in Chapter 11). These are butchers, weighers, and measurers, and various categories of peddlers. Shoemakers will come to market too, and also to the village. Dancers and singers, beating time on tambourines, also make the rounds, appearing during the holiday seasons. With all these specialists available there is little need for the Kabyle to go to town, other than to find work.

In addition to the Jewish villages, one can also find whole communities of holy men in the mountains; they are marabuṭs (murabiṭīn) and owe their possession of baraka to descent from some noted saint. Only rarely are they also descendants of the Prophet. Many villages contain single families of these peace-loving religious specialists, who make a living healing by faith cures and giving advice to the sick at heart and lovelorn. One of them, either resident or imported for the purpose, serves as imām of the village mosque, intoning the call to prayer and teaching at the village school, where some of the boys acquire orally the rudiments of Islamic doctrine and practice, technically of the Malikite school, as in Morocco.

Once a week every male member of the village who has arrived at puberty and who has fasted during three successive Ramaḍāns is required to attend the jamāʿa, or town meeting. If he fails to appear he will be fined. To insure attendance, the headman (*ṭamen*) of each ward calls the roll of his constituents. If the weather is good the meeting is held in the open square; if not, in the special meeting hall. An elderly gentleman of imposing mien calls the meeting to order. He is the *amīn,* to all extents and purposes the mayor. He presents the agenda and acts as moderator in the discussion. Most of the talking, however, is done by a number of other graybeards equally impressive looking. They are the *ʿaqāl,* literally the "brains" of the village, men of mature years and judgment, relatively wealthy, and prominent in their families, wards, and parties. With the amīn and the imām, they have usually resolved all the questions on the agenda in advance, and argue them over for the benefit of the junior members, before they all vote. Although the junior members have little or nothing to say, their opinion is important. To put any project into action, it is necessary for the amīn to obtain a unanimous vote, rendered by voice or show of hands. Sometimes the juniors upset the plans of their elders, who retire defeated.

Before the French conquest the jamāʿa was as autonomous as our Houses of Congress. It could issue qanūns as definitively as the Sultan of Turkey, and enforce them. It could levy taxes, administer the ḥabūs, declare war, make alliances, and negotiate peace treaties. The key institution in Kabylia was the village and not the tribe, as among the Kurds. No doubt one reason for this was the greater rainfall, which permitted the growth of large villages, while mechanisms already described[6] permitted their economic independence.

Returning to the jamāʿa, we find that its members preferred not to deal with private disputes between individuals. If two men were arguing over something that concerned themselves alone, as for example a farmer trampling someone else's grain to get at his own fruit tree, the jamāʿa would appoint one or more informal judge,

[6] Chap. 12, pp. 191 ff.

or masters in equity, to hear the case, under the presidency of the amīn and in the presence of the ʿaqāl.

Theoretically, a number of villages in a geographically united region—those villages, let us say, which together shared a cycle of weekly markets (although this was not always the criterion)—considered themselves members of a given tribe, and a number of contiguous tribes constituted a confederation. These were skeleton organizations. Rarely did the tribe come together as such, and even more rarely was the confederation convened. Only a major invasion, as at the arrival of Turks and Frenchmen, could bring them together and induce them to elect an amghar. Most intervillage relations were regulated through another mechanism, that of the *ṣof* or political party. The men of each village were divided nearly equally into two ṣofs, of which one was always the stronger in any particular village. The head of the ṣof in power was always the amīn. As with all moiety systems, these divisions provided a balance of power and a mechanism for mutual aid. A man was free to change his party, for membership was not hereditary and parties cut across wards. A single ṣof would run through many villages, giving them a stronger bond than the more overt and cumbersome mechanism of tribal councils and confederation meetings. There can be little doubt that the cross-village party system did much to preserve the peace and to reduce the isolation caused by the blood feud.

Pairs of ṣof-like parties are common in Muslim lands. In southern Arabia towns and tribes are divided into two confederations, based on genealogy: the Ghāfari and Hināwi. However they may have arisen, they help maintain a balance of power in a region weak or defective in central governmental control. Similar parties arose in Syria and Egypt in Ottoman times, and the organization of Ahl al-Futuwwa of Anotalia was even more similar since it too divided the community into two rival groups.

Another mechanism which did much to preserve equilibrium inside the village was a kind of sacrifice conducted by the amīn on the proceeds of fines. When enough money had been collected he would buy a sheep or an ox and have it butchered; he would then distribute the meat in equal shares to each person inside the village, sex, age, and degree of wealth being left out of consideration. Meat hunger must have impelled many of the poorer members of the jamāʿa to vote for a strict maintenance of order through the imposition of these profitable fines. While such a banquet might be provided at any time, the amīn usually saved for critical moments when the equilibrium of the village was tottering. When some important person died, he produced a feast. When drought was threatening the crops, he had an ox killed to accompany a prayer for rain, and the increase in protein intake no doubt helped build up his constituents' fortitude. He of course kept himself well informed of the temper of the people, through the agency of the ṭamens of the ward. When he died or decided to retire, the "little jamāʿa," consisting of the local political leaders and other prominent members of the community, conferred to nominate his successor. The jamāʿa then voted on the candidate. When they found a man of whom all approved, a committee went to his house to inform him. He usually made a play of refusal but eventually gave in, after imposing certain conditions. Here again approval of the jamāʿa was required, after which he took office.

This system is democracy. Many political scientists have studied it and admired it. They have compared it to the early city-states of Greece and Rome and to our New England town meeting system. By its means the Kabyles, and other mountain Berbers of North Africa, have maintained their freedom, with various interruptions, for millenniums. The Kabyle village is not a specialized community in an orbit of similar communities with a town as nucleus. It is a miniature nation, maintaining its relations with other nations by means of the weekly market (international trade), and international associations (the ṣof system).

Like other Berbers and Arabs as well, the Kabyles are eager to receive and entertain strangers. Some visitors go to private houses as guests, others to the jamāʿa or to the mosque, where they are fed for three days at public expense. Any outsider who seeks protection may obtain its assurance from an individual, a ward, a ṣof, or the whole community. This protection is called *ʿanaiya.* It is an obligation of the most sacred character. Any member of a group offering ʿanaiya who in turn harmed the protegé would be killed. This device consequently provides for the maximum of intergroup relations and cultural diffusion; by sheltering refugees from vengeful wrath at home, it preserves human life and helps restore peace. Furthermore it acts as a mechanism by which vigorous if unpopular members of the Land of Insolence can reach the government territory alive. Since providing the city with such personnel is one of the prime biological and cultural reasons for the existence of the Land of Insolence, this is an important concept.

Another channel of intervillage relations is provided by the Raḥmaniya Brotherhood (whose devotions have been described in Chapter 8). This brotherhood arose only in the late eighteenth century and flowered in the nineteenth. It was the Raḥmaniya order which spearheaded the revolts of 1857 and 1871 against the French, which reveals its role. If left to their own devices as a free people the Kaybles would have had no need for Ṣūfī mysticism. Berber culture makes its people realists, and it satisfies their emotional needs. The Raḥmaniya order arose as an expression of revolt against the Turkish government and continued as an anti-French movement. Students of the American Indian will find a close parallel in the Ghost Dance of our own Plains tribes, which arose at a time of confusion when the buffalo were disappearing and reservation life was approaching reality.

As far as we can tell now, the Berbers of the Moroccan Grand Atlas, who with their kinsmen of the Sus Valley constitute the most numerous and most homogenous bloc of Berbers in North Africa, lived about the year 1860 much as the Kabyles whose culture we have just outlined.[7] The valleys on both sides of the mountain chain were inhabited by members of free villages who governed themselves by means of popular assemblies, the most important unit being the inhabitants of a geographical unit, i.e., a valley or branch of the same. From time to time the assembly would elect a chief to guide them in their wars against their neighbors, or in resistance to the sultan's agents. This military officer, called amghar (elder), was elected for but a single year.

The social system was somewhat complicated. Between a fifth and a tenth of the population, varying regionally, called themselves murabiṭīn. Living in separate villages, they usually owned the most fruitful land. Their duties were the same as elsewhere in North Africa. Usually each tribe or confederation boasted one special and private saint, whose tomb served as their holiest place, and whose descendants were, in effect, their priesthood.

The bulk of the Shluḥ formed the second class, the villagers and tribesmen. A third was made up of the so-called Ḥarātīn, whom we

[7] This section is based on Robert Montagne's penetrating study, *Les Berbères et le makhzen dans le sud du Maroc* (Paris, 1930).

have already met among the Tuareg and Ait ʿAtta—Negroid slaves and agricultural serfs, encountered mostly in the foothills. In the mountain communities they were rare, except where individuals from their body served as local blacksmiths. Later on, as the system changed and great chiefs arose, these obedient slaves grew more numerous in the mountains. At the bottom of the scale in local esteem were the Jews, metalworkers, and traders, who possessed villages of their own. Tradition has it that they had formerly been much more numerous, and had, in fact, constituted warlike tribes, but that most of them had been absorbed into the Berber community through conversion.

In 1860 the Shluḥ country contained three kinds of community from the political point of view. Most accessible were the villages on the edge of the plain, in full reach of the agents of the sultan. Here a qāʾid was placed as ruler of each tribe; the qāʾid had a khalīfa for each fraction of a tribe; under the khalīfas were shaikhs; and under the shaikhs muqaddams of hamlets. The rule was authoritative and direct, from top to bottom, as among the subjects of the imperial government living on the open plain. About halfway up the deep valleys one found a second kind of community. Here the villages in a section of the valley had their own government, complete with *Ait Arbaʿin,* as the assembly was called. However, since a little tribute must be paid the sultan each year through the intermediacy of the qāʾid on the edge of the plain, they needed someone whom they could call a shaikh to deal with the outside world. This was actually a member of the assembly chosen annually or otherwise for that purpose.

Higher up and away from the passes, the third type of community, the standard Berber republic, survived in isolation. Some of them still did when the French took over, but not many. Two circumstances worked against the continued existence of this system. One was the introduction of European-manufactured goods, weakening home industry and increasing the demand for trade. The mountaineer had to sell more of his crop to obtain these articles, particularly factory-woven cotton goods and hardware. His financial security was weakened, and he was brought into closer relations with the outside world. The other was the fluctuating state of political affairs in the imperial government. The sultans and would-be sultans needed help and were willing to reward ambitious leaders from the hills. Some of the amghars of small tribes succeeded in obtaining absolute power, after which they would go to Marrakesh and have themselves appointed qā'id. With imperial sanction and modern rifles, they conquered tribe after tribe, dissolving the assemblies and setting out khalīfas and shaikhs in the neighboring valleys to carry out their orders.

These qā'ids settled down into three houses, those of the Glawi, Gundafi, and Mtugi, reading from east to west along the Atlas. (The family of the Glawi, in its third generation, was headed by the late and powerful el Ḥaji Thāmi [Tihāmi], pasha of Marrakesh.) These three absolute autocrats so crushed the mountaineers under their control that only the oldest remember the earlier system of government. Each of them has a huge fortress, strategically located near the crest of the divide, as for example that of Telwet, which is the Glawi's stronghold. Inside high walls are a number of castles, with an inner court. Great granaries hold the tribute brought by the farmers; dungeons hide the starving bodies of bandits captured on the roads. Mountain Jews and Negro retainers throng the courtyard, and privileged visitors (I was one in 1927) eat in the guest chambers.

Delegating power to the three great qā'ids was a way of ruling without effort. These men, controlling private armies, could make or break sultans, and they also figured in the politics of the French Protectorate in a fashion similar to the fabulously wealthy princes of India under the British. Robert Montaigne speaks with feeling when he states that Native Affairs officers were able to take over the direction of the small confederation of Ida U Tanan before the Mtugi could swallow it.

Ruling by delegating power to a local autocrat was something new in Morocco, but farther east it is an old system, which we have already seen in operation in western Asia; this is the way both Romans and Sassanian Persians controlled the Nabatean Arabs. This is also the way that the shahs of Iran (when they have been strong enough) have dealt with the Bakhtiari and other tribesmen. The Iranian tribesmen, however, have a reason for unity, the need for order in their annual migration. The Shluh need no more unity than they had in 1860, at the price they have paid for it. What the French thought of this system is not easy to discover.

By now the reader is ready to join me in entering the Rif, as I first did in 1926, the year of 'Abd el-Krīm's surrender. On the way into the tribe of Gzennaya we noticed that our dog was growing ill. He soon died. Someone had poisoned him, not out of malice but as part of a scientific experiment—to test a new batch of poison before using it on the intended human victim. This feeling for science is strong among the Riffians. Once in a local feud a warrior shot a hydrocephalic opponent, not because he was a dangerous foe but in order to see what was inside his head. At great risk of life the warrior crawled over an exposed bank to retrieve the body. With his kinsmen he carried it to the mosque, where the schoolmaster trephined the grotesque skull. Draining out some of the liquid, he tasted it with his finger. "It is a little salty," he said. Then they all went back to their fighting.

The village where this took place was hardly a village at all, since it consisted of only thirteen houses in 1926. These were scattered along both sides of the small but tumultuous mountain stream called the Water of Iherrushen, just above where it joined a larger river, the Bayu, which flowed swiftly out of a perpendicular-walled canyon. As one sees this country from above, the flattest ground is near the crest of the divide; consequently the villages are more frequent here than where it is steeper lower down. The upstream people also get the first use of the water, vital for irrigation.

If we look closely we will see that one of the houses is a mosque. It has no minaret, but a white flag flying from the roof peak proclaims its holy purpose, which the whitewash on the porch and around the outer rims of the windows confirms. Legend has it that the ancestor of the inhabitants of this village, one ʿAbd el-Mumin (in Arabic al-Mu'min, from whom they and the village derive their name, Ulad ʿAbd el-Mumin) walked up the waters of the Iherrushen one afternoon just as the sun was setting over the divide to the west, his wife and his cow and his dog wading with him. Silhouetted against the sunlight he saw this mosque, newly built and empty, its door open, standing before him. Faced with this miracle he scuffed off the grass sandals with which he had been protecting his feet from the sharp stones, and entered the holy place to pray. He and his sons hewed and walled terraces along the valley, felled some trees and planted others, and all lived peacefully until the valley was full and men fell to quarreling over fruit trees, women, and water.

The twelve houses which we saw held ten men with their thirteen wives, nineteen sons, and fifteen daughters. That three men had two wives at once is no wonder, since six out of nine of their fathers had died by the rifle, and many of their brothers as well. Some provision must be made for young widows and their helpless children. To the human population of fifty-seven was added an animal roster of one hundred and twenty-five head: 10 cows, 1 calf, 15 sheep, 80 goats, 1 donkey, 2 mules, and 16 dogs. Six of the men owned the goats, and one the sheep; three men had none. Each man, however, owned a cow, for all needed milk.

There were a total of 923 food-bearing trees—more than 16 to a person, or 92 to a family. These were divided as follows: almonds, 525; figs, 272; olives, 71; pomegranates, 33; apricots, 16; oranges, lemons, and walnuts, 2 of each. Every man owned at least 4 almond, 15 fig, and 3 olive trees. Dried almonds and figs are absolutely necessary to sustain life in late winter once the grain has been eaten, while olive oil is the essential fat. The other kinds of trees produce useful fruits, but the Riffians can get along without them.

In these high valleys arboriculture is the main business of the people, and they prune, water, graft, and fertilize their trees with extreme care. Compared to this activity the Riffian spends but little time in his fields; he owns enough tillage for only about four weeks' plowing time a year, with a range of from twenty to forty-five days among the ten men. Those who have little are hired to work for those who have more, on the ancient system of granting a fifth to the plowman. Work on the vegetable gardens rates a fourth, while he who cares for another man's trees receives a third of the fruit, aside from windfalls which are for women, children, and the poor.

Unfruitful trees have long ago been felled to make way for the silver-leaved olives and the lofty walnuts. Up high on the ridges to either side one can still cut cedar and even a few pine. Below the man-made tree line is a zone of brushy goat pasture, and below this, but still steep, the vineyards. Here the families gather in September to pick the grapes, which they dry into raisins to be eaten with the figs and almonds. Up the valley a way there are two public installations, a small turbine water mill of familiar appearance, which belongs to the grandsons of its builder, and an olive press, which serves several villages. This olive press is actually near the center of another village, inhabited by holy people who never fight. Their holiest member regulates the protocol of olive pressing, aside from serving as imām to lead the Friday prayer, in which the grown men of all the villages of that part of the valley participate.

Over two generations ago, the Ulad ʿAbd el-Mumin were exiled from their valley, but some of them returned. It is a long story;[8] a summary will suffice here.

It all started one chilly night when Amar the Scabhead shot a neighbor by mistake. Now the ʿAbd el-Mumin had and still have neighbors, twenty-six families who call themselves Beni Tadmut, after their ancestress who was one of old ʿAbd el-Mumin's daughters. It seems that the Ulad ʿAbd el-Mumin had contracted an alliance by marriage with another clan over the ridge in the next tribe, the great and powerful Beni Urriaghel (later to produce the world-famous and still very much alive ʿAbd el-Krīm). This Urriaghli clan was in trouble. Sorely pressed, it was besieged by a coalition of its neighbors, and hence sent a messenger with a goat over the ridge. This messenger sacrificed the goat on the sill of the mosque, so that blood spattered on its door, and this was a great shame compulsion, which no man of honor could refuse. Hence both the Ulad ʿAbd el-Mumin and the Beni Tadmut, who shared the ancient mosque, went to the rescue.

They lifted the siege, but the enemy did not depart. One of the Tadmutis, creeping out on a reconnaissance by dim moonlight, was spotted by the aforementioned Amar the Scabhead, who shot him dead. At this a rumpus arose. Shots were exchanged, and with four parties involved it was hard to know who was shooting at whom. Sī ʿAlī, the venerable and highly respected village schoolmaster, who served both clans as imām, was obviously the man to intervene, and he set forth from the huddled group of Ulad ʿAbd el-Mumin in the direction of the Beni Tadmut, only a score of yards away. Unable to control their wrath, the Tadmutis shot him. At this point a hush fell over the scene, and by daybreak the two squadrons of kinsmen had gone home separately, carrying their dead. The Urriaghlis, over whom this trouble had arisen in the first place, fearing to stay at home, went along with the Ulad ʿAbd el-Mumin who, outnumbered two to one, were glad of their company.

When the dead had been buried, the combatants found a half a hundred men gathered solemnly in council beneath their olive trees. These were the members of the *Asht Arbaʿin,* the councilors from all the villages up and down the valley, who had heard of trouble and hastened to the spot to keep it from spreading (while enjoying

[8] Told at length in Carleton S. Coon, *Flesh of the Wild Ox* (New York, 1932).

in anticipation the meat of the fines which they hoped to collect). The moderator of the council was M'allim Muḥammad, the wealthiest and most venerable of the Ulad 'Abd el-Mumin, whose position placed his newly made enemies at a disadvantage. This they pointed out immediately.

It was clear that the Beni Tadmut were the greater offenders. The council decided that both sides should pay blood money to each other, but the sum paid by the Tadmutis would be the greater. Both should pay a fine to the council for having made it necessary to call them together. The Tadmutis, however, demanded also that the Urriaghlis should be forced to leave. The amghar of the next valley, one Ḥajj Bukkeish (later to become an unsuccessful rival of 'Abd el-Krīm's in the war against Spain) agreed with the Tadmutis and swung the council to this opinion. The Ulad 'Abd el-Mumin, however, refused, pointing out that their kinsmen whom they were protecting had already had their houses burnt down and their trees felled, and might starve should they go home—if they were not shot first.

The meeting broke up without decision and without the collection of a fine. However, Bukkeish and the other leaders resolved to call together a greater meeting, a council of all five sections of the tribal confederation, each consisting of several valleys; thus three levels of deliberative bodies would be involved. The guests whom the Ulad 'Abd el-Mumin refused to eject were members of another and even more powerful confederation, and large-scale intertribal trouble might easily arise. Meanwhile, the day before the holy feast of el 'Aid el-Kabīr (when despite the trouble everyone was bustling around as we do on the day before Christmas) the schoolmaster of the Beni Tadmut appeared, unarmed, with a goat and two other unarmed men. Approaching the M'allim Muḥammad's house, he declared that he had come to make a truce, and invited the Ulad 'Abd el-Mumin to come to the mosque and swear an oath.

After much deliberation and with some misgivings, the M'allim Muḥammad agreed, and set out with two of his sons. The Tadmutis, as feared, had led them into an ambush. First the Tadmutis killed Amar the Scabhead, then the M'allim Muḥammad shot two of them and was shot in turn, through the head. One son, the Ḥajj Muḥammad, escaped, wounded in the foot. He crawled up on the mountain and hid behind a rock. The next day, as the Beni Tadmut left their houses all dressed in their new clothes, to go to the big mosque up the valley for prayer, he shot their schoolmaster and two others before his rifle jammed, and he wept.

Now the Tadmutis laid a shame compulsion on Bukkeish's men at the foot of the valley by slaughtering an ox on their mosque door, and more blood was shed, until finally the councilors convened from hill and valley, to sit like birds of prey at the scene of slaughter. Many angry words were said; finally a decision was made. The Ulad ʿAbd el-Mumin had committed sacrilege by killing men, however much they deserved to die, on the holy feast day which the Prophet had designated as the end of the pilgrimage. For sacrilege there was only one punishment, exile. Leading a few thin cows the women of the Ulad ʿAbd el-Mumin and the few men who remained alive climbed the path out of the valley, with the smoke of their houses rising behind them. One day they returned, but that is another story. In the meantime they lived in a village outside of Fez with other exiled Riffians, caring for the olive trees of rich Arabs and dreaming of revenge. Not all returned, and their children and grandchildren may be seen, blue eyed and yellow turbaned, near the Bab Gīsa in Fez.

This true story illustrates the Riffian system of government. The unit of society above the family is not the village, but the clan, which owing to the linear nature of the arable land, spread along narrow watercourses, may be housed in several separate clusters of houses. Each clan has its own schoolmaster, who is also registrar of deeds, since he is always literate. Many of the other men are also. While their spoken language is Berber, they write in Arabic, usually more classical than the daily speech of the Moroccan Arabs, which but few of them can understand. Each village also has a blacksmith, a Negroid whose home is in Targuist, the arsenal tribe of ʿAbd el-Krīm.

In each cluster one village stands out as the seat of a Friday mosque, usually maintained by a holy descendant of even holier saints, whose tombs adorn the landscape and serve as minor places of pilgrimage, especially by women. Up in the tribes of Beni Amart and Targuist several mutually related families of murabiṭīn, the Ikhemrijen, dwell in green-roofed edifices built by Spanish renegades.

The village needs no council because all the men are kin, and there are no wards or ṣofs to split them. Rarely do the men number more than two or three dozen. The schoolboys, sitting in the mosque, play at government, with a mock Asht Arbaʿin of their own. On minor points of difference, the men let them arbitrate and set fines of a few eggs or loaves of bread, for their own consumption. Having thus learned the routine of sitting in judgment and also some of the oral qanūns, the boys are ready for the serious business ahead.

Once a week, when the nearest market meets, the older men of the neighboring villages, corresponding to the "brains" of the Kabyles, meet in a house just off the grounds, or in good weather, under a tree. Over glasses of tea they settle any disputes which may come up in the market or which litigants may bring them. When more serious matters arise, such as the trouble between the Ulad ʿAbd el-Mumin and the Beni Tadmut, the councilors of a single geographical unit, consisting of several clans, come together. They must be fed, and it is in the interest of the feuding parties to make a speedy settlement, with fines and blood money. Fines go to the councilors, who eat part and divide the rest. Blood money goes to the kin of the wounded or dead. If these councilors cannot settle the problem, the "fifth" is invoked—the whole series of little valleys and watershed cantons which forms the next largest political unit. Some tribes have only one "fifth," but Gzennaya and Beni Urriaghel each have five. If the "fifth" cannot settle the dispute, and the bloodshed spreads, then all the fifths join in. If the whole tribe is embroiled, the councilors of another tribe may invade and catch them unawares, to their great loss. The longer the fight remains unsettled the greater the number of participants, each new and larger body trying to capitalize on the confusion of the partisans.

It can be readily seen that few troubles reach intertribal proportions. This device of government in depth works. Feuding keeps the population down, and the fear of interference keeps the feud isolated and within bounds. Chronic troublemakers, and those who break the rules, must go. On the other hand when some outside force threatens more than a small portion of the Rif, the mechanism is at hand for all to unite, forcefully if ephemerally. The elders of one clan perform a compulsion of shame on another, thus forcing them into alliance, called *lif,* as elsewhere. As the danger grows, so does the lif. In this manner ʿAbd el-Krīm (who had been educated by the Spaniards) set up a government of the whole Rif, which defeated Spain in two great battles in 1921 and 1924, and but for the use of aircraft and tanks by his enemy, might have held the French army indefinitely at bay. No sultan had ever been able to conquer this classic corner of the Land of Insolence, which is all the more remarkable since much of it is not mountain at all, but open rolling country.

The Riffians are tough fighters. They won Spain for Franco, on a promise of freedom given them on the Yellow Plain of Ktama. One of them, 'Abd el-Krīm's jailer, once told me that he gave the Christian prisoners dirt mixed in their bread; this is nothing to what the Christians have done to them, which, out of deference to the sensitivity of my readers, I shall not print here. Needless to say, the Riffians buried no one alive in anthills, nor have their women hacked any prisoners to shreds. Having more recently but more briefly visited the Pathans, I can make the same denial for them with a little less conviction, but until shown otherwise I shall continue to believe that these tales come out of the same volume of fiction.

Speaking about the Pathans, however, reminds me much of the Riffians, with a few differences. The Riffians live in wetter and more fertile country, with more vegetation, and, although good Muslims, make little display of their religious feelings. They keep the fast and all the main feasts, adding a few of their own. The older men refuse to smoke, and some even refuse tea. They confined Jews to a few coastal settlements, notably Bades and Melilla, while Christians were not admitted at all, before the days of 'Abd el-Krīm, who let in Gordon Canning, Vincent Sheehan, and a few others without demanding previous conversion. One is told that the Pathans are "fanatical," but this again may be a form of general xenophobia channeled through the symbolic mechanism of religion.

The Pathans also are organized in tribes, divided into subtribes, partitioned into sections, split into clans, which are made up of patrilineal extended families.[9] Each family, clan, section, and subtribe has its head man, who represents his group in the *jirga,* or representative council of the group just above him. Like the Asht Arba'in, these councils convene to attempt to settle matters of dispute between their constituent members. Irrigation quarrels and cattle rustling are the chief business of the smaller jirgas, while adultery and murder draw the full tribal council, presided over by its chief officer, the khan. Like the amīn of a Kabyle village, he is often no more than a moderator. In case of murder, the killer flees the tribal territory at

[9] See H. Hörhager, *Die Volkstumsgrundlagen der Indischen nordwest-grenz Provinz* (Heidelberg, 1943). M. Elphinstone, *An Account of the Kingdom of Caubul and Its Dependencies* (London, 1825). C. Collin Davies, *The Problem of the Northwest Frontier, 1890–1908.*

once. A mediator, chosen by the jirga for his good character and impartiality, tries to appease the anger of the victim's family and to persuade them to accept blood money. The murderer may return only when the victim's kin have been sufficiently pacified to express their willingness to accept payment.

Often, however, they will not be appeased. One of them will seek out the murderer and kill him in turn, and then a feud is in full swing. Like the Asht Arbaʿin of a Riffian tribe, the jirga descends on the feuders, and if still no settlement can be made, burns their houses and drives them away. Thus are the manners and customs of the warriors from the two ends of our Muslim World virtually identical. Riffians and Pathans, brave warriors all, bracket our field of effort with curved daggers and long rifles.

This chapter began as an extension of a treatise on government, to explain the relations between the central governments of countries which had Lands of Insolence, and the tribal areas. First it was necessary to understand how the tribes themselves functioned. Technologically and economically, there are four kinds of tribes: those who live by sedentary farming, camel nomadism, high pasture grazing, and horse breeding on the steppes. Much nonsense has been written in the past to the effect that farmers are less alert and less warlike than pastoralists. No better farmers could be found than the Riffians and Pathans—and no better warriors. It is not the practice of agriculture in itself which inhibits alertness and belligerence, but submission to and dependence on a larger and stronger institution, be it the central government or a tribe of well-mounted nomads.

Politically speaking, all of these tribal peoples are alike in that they are organized into a series of institutions of increasing size, from extended family to clan or kin, then through one or two intermediate steps to tribe, and finally to confederation. Of these institutions the clan or kin is usually the strongest. It is the "action" group, the unit of revenge, whose members stick together through life and death. The larger groups are skeleton organizations, to be used if needed.

In another sense the tribal peoples break down into two contrasting categories. On the one side stand the Arabs and Kurds, as well as the Baluchis, Bakhtiaris, and Qashqais. Among these peoples each unit of government, however great or small, is ruled by a single, omnipotent chief. On the other side are the Pathans and most of the Berbers, who govern themselves through councils and assemblies and who elect chiefs only when a particular crisis demands one.

How can we explain this difference? One explanation is that as the division of labor increases, the need for control likewise increases, and control can be exercised more rapidly and effectively by a mayor than by a town meeting. The peoples who have managed to keep their democratic system of government have a minimum of division of labor, ethnically or through a class system, or in both ways; while those who are ruled by individual shaikhs or khans, or a hierarchy of officers, live in more complicated societies.

This leads to another observation. Aside from desert oases and high mountains, the regions which contain the largest proportions of dissident agricultural tribesmen are situated at the extremities of our Muslim area, in Morocco and Afghanistan. This resemblance cannot have been caused by topography alone. The centers of urban cultural growth were ʿIraq and Egypt, and Middle Eastern civilization spread out from those foci. The essential basis of Middle Eastern civilization is a fivefold division of labor, and the pattern is most complicated near the center of origin and simplest on the peripheries. The Riffians and the Pathans preserve the oldest design for small communities, while the Kabyles keep that for larger ones. These are relics of a preurban time, when Middle Eastern society consisted of a mosaic of many pieces, but of a repetitive pattern, like a tribal rug—instead of the coordinated scheme of a city-made rug with border, background, and medallion. The Middle Eastern landscape of that time was probably divided into a myriad of independent communities, with the village as the largest unit of population, with toolmakers the only specialists, and with trading carried on in open-air markets between communities. (It is of interest to note that the method of stopping fights between neighbors employed by people on this level is closely parallel to the technique only recently adopted, on a global scale, by the United Nations.)

The relations between the various segments of the Land of Insolence and the central governments of the nations to which they are officially assigned have been to some extent covered in passing, since in many cases the structure of the tribal government is partly a function of its outside relations. Every government in the world is built to face two kinds of crises, those from within and those from without. Tribal governments form no exception.

The basic relationship between the central and tribal governments is one of balance, of two opposed segments of a system in equilibrium. This does not mean that either the shahs and sultans or the tribal chiefs and elders necessarily were aware of this relationship. Some of the Turkish sultans undoubtedly were, and we must grant the same perspicacity to such wise and powerful rulers as Cyrus the Great and Shah ʿAbbās. On the whole, however, like all successful systems, it functioned automatically. Every now and then something happened to throw it out of balance—some ruler became too powerful and too aggressive at the expense of the welfare of the tribes, or some tribe or confederation took advantage of a moment of imperial weakness to descend upon the towns and take over, only to start a new dynasty. Usually equilibrium was soon restored.

Simple antagonism, however, will not suffice to describe this relationship. It may be complicated by a number of other factors, as in Morocco where some of the tribesmen recognize the spiritual but not the temporal power of the sultan, or in Iran where whole tribes of Kurds have been transplanted from the Zagros to the Elburz to be dissident in a more useful location. In some cases the formality of recognition links the tame and the dissident, like the confirmation of the Bakhtiari Ilkhanis by the shahs, or the granting of titles by the sultan of Morocco to the three great chiefs of the Atlas. Everywhere in the Middle East any tribesman, however dissident, was free to come to the city to trade, as long as he was a Muslim and as long as no price had been placed on his individual head. Throughout the Middle East it has been an immemorial practice for the occupant of the throne to marry the daughters of tribal leaders, in order to build up a personal relationship between the two segments of the realm, while the practice of holding hostages is also as old as tribes and governments.

In no department of Middle Eastern civilization is the impact of Western culture more apparent than in the balance between government and tribes. In a sense this innovation is to the government's immediate advantage, since motor vehicles and airplanes can outrun camels and horses. The desert is no longer a refuge, nor are camels needed for transport. Hitherto impregnable mountain strongholds can be bombed as easily as villages on the plain. In other ways the government is at a disadvantage. Modern rifles, smuggled in by conniving powers, are more useful in tribal hands, habituated to the manipulation of firearms, than in those of hastily drilled peasants whose fingers are bent to the hoe. Western methods of communication expose the tribesmen to propaganda which his education has not equipped him to reject. It is not every tribesman who can understand, although many of their leaders do, that it is to their greater advantage to stand by the ancient and habitual enemy, the government, while keeping it at arm's length, than to sell out to some new "friend" from another league.

The European powers that once assumed political control in Middle Eastern countries devoted much time and effort in the consideration of this problem. The British have been noted for their advocacy of the status quo, particularly in what is now Pakistan and in those parts of Arabia which have been under their control. With the Pathans, for example, they drew a line—that of Durand, beyond which the tribesmen could murder each other as they saw fit, so long as they did not transgress on the other side of the fence. It is apparent from the writings of British political experts that they admire the Pathans as fighting men, just as they admire the Bedawin, whose internal business they have made as little as possible their own. In the same way they isolated the Ḥaḍramaut, leaving it to its internal feuds, until the Ḥaḍramis themselves requested intervention, and the Peace of Ingrams was arranged.

The French, on the other hand, have worked on the theory that the entire Land of Insolence must be brought to heel first and paternally administered afterward. This theory did not arise suddenly, however, for the conquest of Algeria taught the French lessons which they tried to apply in Tunisia and Morocco. Their first contact was with Arabs. As they moved inland they unwittingly Arabized the Berbers. Discovering that the Berbers were more useful to them than the Arabs, they tried to arrest this process, particularly when it became evident that a wedge between the two peoples would be of political advantage.

No nation has produced more or better functional anthropological studies of non-European peoples, with a design for political application, than the French. Without the work of such men as the Bassets, Bel, Duveyrier, Guyot, Hanoteau, Laoust, Le Tourneau, Letourneux, Montagne, Ricard, and Terrasse (who made much of this book possible), the French might not have succeeded as well as they did, and if the officers of administration had paid more attention to their experts, they might have known even greater success. Both the

British and the French are on the way out, and one wonders which theory, if either, will prove to have been the better.

Both the British and the French have had the idea of setting aside the Land of Insolence as their special zones of interest, and protecting it against the direct rule of shahs and sultans. With this protection having disappeared, or being in the process of disappearance, one wonders, what next? On this—the kind of adjustment the shahs and sultans will make between these two classes of subjects—shall depend much of their success in the world of the future.

17 THE SHIP AND THE CARAVAN

THE TRAVEL-LOVING READER may now ask: "Why have we had to wait so long to hear about transportation?" The answer is that transportation involves and serves the entire cast of our varied and colorful show, which must be dressed and put on the stage before it can be set in motion. Sunnis, Shīʿas, Nestorians, Armenians, Jews, Copts, White and Black Eunuchs, pashas of two horse tails, Kurdish aghas, Bedawin shaikhs, descendants of the Prophet in their white robes, grand muftis, Fezzi merchants coming home from Manchester laden with sterling, and the bodies of the faithful destined for burial at Kerbala—all must travel, by land and by sea, through the territories of different governments, across dazzling deserts, and over arrogant mountain passes crisp with snow. Only now are all hands crowded on the cluttered deck, all the patient pilgrims assembled by the rows of kneeling camels, and the guards mounted. We are off. Let's go!

Relatively few will be traveling by sea. Long ago the Muslims yielded the seaways of the Mediterranean to the Christians, and in the Atlantic the Sallee rovers have long since stacked their oars. Only in the Indian Ocean and its two fingers, the Persian Gulf and the Red Sea, and in the inland waterways of Egypt and ʿIraq, can the traveler still see numbers of lateen-rigged sails. Excluding the craft on the rivers and Mediterranean, we find that some two thousand dhows, as these ships are collectively called in English, were registered in deep-sea trade at the outbreak of World War II. It is easiest to see them in the ports of Aden and Basra, but Bushire, Bandar ʿAbbas, Mukalla, Hodaida, and all the harbors of East Africa from Massawa to below Zanzibar, will do. Kuwait, however, is the best for our purpose, because it is the principal shipbuilding and trading port on the Persian Gulf, and the home of sailors, while the Persian Gulf itself, the ancient abode of the Sealands people, including the ancestors of the Phoenicians, is the heart of the seafaring profession in the Muslim world.[1]

[1] The following description is derived almost entirely from two works of Alan Villiers: *Sons of Sinbad* (New York, 1940), and "Some Aspects of the

Kuwait has little to offer in the way of cargo. It produces shipwrights and seafaring men, however, who can pick up cargoes elsewhere. The shipwrights build vessels of from seventy-five to three hundred tons burden, averaging a hundred, and worth about three thousand dollars each in 1939. Although only one hundred and six ships were registered in Kuwait then, many hundreds of others had been built there. The wood used is teak, brought from India. No naval architects design the hulls; the shipwrights follow traditional patterns. Two main classes of ship are adzed and pegged in the ways of Kuwait, the *būm* and the *baghala*.[2]

The būm is a double-ended craft with two forward-leaning masts, the mainmast stepped approximately amidships, and a bowsprit. It carries two lateen-rigged sails, and a jib. The baghala has a projecting bow, a square stern, and again two masts, but the main is stepped a bit forward of amidships, and there is no bowsprit, nor a jib. The būm is cheaper to build and easier to handle, and hence more popular. The baghala, on the other hand, with its fancy carving on the sternpiece and its more cumbersome shape, is more expensive and more difficult to sail, with no appreciable advantage other than its impressive appearance. Both are roomy. In both, the unit of size is not the tonnage but the number of packages of dates the hold can carry, amounting to about twenty to a ship's ton. The crew is also calculated in dates, with one seaman for every hundred packages.

The forecastle deck, which is the seamen's domain, is rimmed with their sea chests, in which they carry small items of trade for private smuggling, and in front of which they roll their sleeping rugs, in some cases good Persians, which they hope to sell at a profit. Below is a cabin which belongs to the captain, and in the waist a water butt and a galley. The latter is simply a clay fireplace, partially roofed and sheltered on three sides with boards. The quarter-deck is the navigating area, complete with compass set in a box and old wheels taken off European sailing vessels (in the dhows I have visited).[3]

Although the number of seamen is calculated in packages of dates, it is also a function of the size of the ship, and hence of the

---

Arab Dhow Trade," *The Middle East Journal,* II, No. 4 (October, 1947), 399-416. See also G. F. Hourani, *Arab Seafaring in the Indian Ocean* (Princeton, 1951).

[2] Būm, which Villiers spells *boom,* means "owl," and *baghala* "mule."

[3] Villiers mentions other steering devices which I have not seen on ships of this size.

sails. Each mast carries a single triangular sail, lashed along the hypotenuse edge to a heavy yard. In setting sail or in coming about, this sail must be raised and lowered, which takes many hands on the halyards. The main is the largest sail; the jib is no problem. Villiers states that in nine months on the būm *Triumph of Righteousness* he only saw the sail lowered once to come about.[4] That was because they were riding the monsoons, as Arab ships usually do. On the short voyage I took in the sanbūq *Mansur* in 1933, up the Red Sea coast from Aden to Hodeida, we tacked frequently.[5] On the smaller craft, sailing only with the mainsail, it took all hands and the passengers to lower, carry the end of the yard around the mast, and raise again. These ships do not tack easily, but they ride beautifully before the wind. We easily left the local steamer in our wake.

The smaller vessels, the *sanbūqs* and *zārūks,* used more on the Red Sea where maneuverability is important, differ from the būms and baghalas in several ways. The zārūk has a single sail, the sanbūq two. The sanbūq, at least, is decked only forward and astern; amidships the crew sits on the cargo or on movable hatching. The galley is forward with the sailors' chests; it consists of nothing but a clay-lined herring barrel and a quern. The helmsman crouches aft, steering with a tiller instead of a wheel. The ship's "head" consists of a frame of light poles, rigged to the lee rail slightly aft of amidships, and is equipped with a tin can dangling on a string, to be dipped for ablutions. That the device was made for small men only I soon discovered, for the first time I tried to use it the "head" collapsed, dropping one Christian passenger, neatly boxed, overboard.

The personnel of an Arab ship may be divided into three classes, the *nākhudhā* (a Persian word) or captain, the seamen, and the passengers. The nākhudhās comes from a family of navigators in Kuwait city. They are prosperous people, and merchants will loan them money, knowing that if the ship founders, they are good for the loss. Although they may be wealthy, they will not put their money into trade, except in ships' lumber, cordage, and other chandlery, and in shipbuilding. When a boy of such a family finishes his brief religious education, and in so doing has learned to read and write, necessary for keeping ships' accounts, he is sent to sea. He does not serve as a

[4] Not counting the time he spent below decks after being knocked unconscious by falling rigging. Villiers, *Sons of Sinbad,* pp. 44-48.

[5] See Carleton S. Coon, *Measuring Ethiopia and Flight into Arabia* (Boston, 1935).

seaman, in fact he never touches the rigging, for he is there to learn to become a navigator. The ship is commanded by an uncle, older brother, or other kinsman. When the time comes he will have a ship of his own.

Although the ship has a compass, no officer shoots the sun, and while the nākhudhās know the stars it is not often that they must depend on celestial navigation, since the Kuwaiti nākhudhās keep their ships nearly always within sight of land. What the boy learns is the intimate details of every mile of the shore, every current, every sand bar, every hidden reef, and all the changes caused by the tides. Because the moon makes the tide, he watches this satellite carefully. When out of sight of land between Bahrain and the head of the gulf, he uses the leadline, and by the sand and shell that this brings up, he knows exactly where he is.

The second class of personnel, that of the seamen, is recruited from an entirely different level of society. Many of the sailors are Negroes or the mixed descendants of Negroes, freemen but socially equivalent to smiths. Others are Persians or of Persian descent.[6] The cook is often a full-blooded Negro. These are poor men, many of them unmarried, although favored with many female friends ashore. When in Kuwait town some of them, homeless, sleep in the sūqs, where they serve as peddlers or porters during the summer season, provided they have not gone pearling. The pearling season comes just when the southwest monsoon, blowing in all its fury, keeps shipping off the curve of the monsoon track, and the gulf ships stay inside.

These seamen sometimes rise in the world. One of them who learns to navigate as well as his nākhudhā, or better, and who has shown powers of leadership over his fellows, may become *serang*, or mate. He will get a larger share in the ship's profits than the others, and he may even become the skipper of a river vessel in the Shatt-al-ʿArab, a profitable position but one without social prestige. From the latter he is barred by birth. He can, however, take command of the ship between ports when the nākhudhā decides to stay behind for business reasons, or for a brief honeymoon, for some of them keep households in several ports.

While the ship is inside a harbor, the sailors do all the porterage. At sea, they rig and repair the sails, raise, set, and lower them, swarm

[6] My measurements of the crews of several of these ships in Aden harbor in 1933 bear out Villiers' statements fully.

the mast to free the halyards, pull in the canvas, or serve as lookout, and take the helm under the direction of the nākhudhā or serang. When becalmed they lower the longboat and wear the ship, using disk-ended paddles, or if the ship is small they may propel it with sweeps. Having no regular watches, they are ever on call. One of them usually handles a drum. When mustered for a task, they leap to the deck into a regular pattern and perform a rhythmic dance, to a chanted prayer. It is like the *ḥosa* which the workmen on a large archaeological dig perform when the work is flagging and someone needs to pep things up. A wise archaeologist pays the ḥosa leader well, and nākhudhās use every inducement to lure musician-poets aboard their ships.

At every mooring, passengers come aboard and leave, much to the distress of European passport and customs officials in the colonial ports. They bring their own food, some of it on the hoof, and prepare it themselves. No matter where they are going they pay a fixed fee. Some of them are given quarters in the cabin, but most of them sleep and live on the deck, under what would seem to a European to be crowded conditions. A būm of one hundred and fifty tons, with a crew of twenty-eight, a large longboat, a gig, and a half-built smaller ship on deck, carried between one hundred and twenty and one hundred and forty passengers, some of whom were merchants going to do private business in the ports of call. On one occasion Villiers' ship was called upon to carry a small tribe from Ḥaḍramaut to Africa.[7]

The big ships out of Kuwait spend the night at sea, but the sanbūqs often anchor in sheltered spots near the land. The ship I was on put in to allow the crew members to go ashore to collect firewood and to steal melons from nearby gardens. On all the ships the sailors do as much fishing as they can, to supplement a diet otherwise consisting almost exclusively of coarse bread made of sorghum, freshly baked on board. That is what we were served. On the date ships the cargo is perhaps too valuable to eat as daily rations.

The financial aspect of this Arab shipping business is complicated, particularly since the sharīʿa permits neither interest nor insurance. Even more highly placed in the Kuwaiti social scale than the families of skippers are the big families of tājirs, the rich merchants who finance the shipbuilding and ship purchasing and who send out the staple cargoes of dates on consignment. The merchants have no

[7] *Sons of Sinbad,* pp. 55 ff.

desire to own ships, preferring to loan their money to the nākhudhās and having them bear the risk.

In many instances the financier also owns date plantations up the river, and it is his own fruit he is shipping. This is not always the case; he may buy up dates by the package on the open market. The nākhudhā does not buy the dates from the merchant but delivers them to a resident agent of the merchant's business house, who is usually a younger relative. A powerful house will have agents in Bombay, Mukalla, Aden, and several African ports. If so arranged, however, the nākhudhā may sell some or all of the dates on the markets where no agent has been stationed. Much depends on the price, which in turn of course depends on supply and demand. An advantage of the sailing vessel over European steamships, as far as the date trade is concerned, is that the būm or baghala pays very low port dues, and since the sailors are paid by shares of the profit from the ship's voyage, no time factor is involved. The ship can lay over indefinitely until the market has eased. Meanwhile all hands, from skipper to crew and passengers, have time to indulge in private trading, which is everyone's privilege.

Ships like these have been sailing the Indian Ocean for several thousands of years, manned not only by Arabs but by Persians, Indians, and Indonesians. They have carried close relatives of the Polynesians to Madagascar, and such food plants as rice, taro, the coconut, and the banana to Negro Africa, as well as the humped cattle which form the livelihood, capital, and symbols of prestige of several East African tribes. There is little doubt that they supplied most of the critical metals, particularly tin, to the Middle Eastern urban peoples from Assyrian times onward, if not earlier, as well as the more romantic-sounding ivory, ebony, and frankincense, and slaves by the thousands. They carried the timbers for their own construction, and the fibers for their cordage, out of India. They carried thousands of Ḥaḍramaut men to the East Indies, where they converted the Javanese and Moros, among others, to Islam, while some of their numbers mixed with local peoples to form the Malay. They carried travelers like Ibn Baṭṭūṭa (of whom we have heard much and will soon hear more) as far as China, where a whole city of Arabs, complete with sūqs, mosques, qāḍīs, shaikh ul-Islām, and Sūfi brotherhoods, existed during the thirteenth century as part of what is now Amoy.[8] Ships like these have made possible not only the

[8] Ibn Baṭṭūṭa, *Travels in Asia and Africa, 1325-1354*, pp. 287 ff.

exchange of goods between the Middle East and other lands, and of personnel, but also the development and maintenance of the complex system of human relations within which Middle Eastern society operates.

These distinctions, however, the ship shares with its younger competitor, the camel. Although reduced in volume since the time of the Portuguese expansion, Arab shipping still goes on, as Villiers has shown. The camel caravans may also have lost some business through the diversion of trade to the sea route with European bottoms, but its real blow came only with motor vehicles. The traveler passing between Tehran and Mashhad will still see dozens of strings of camels carrying packages of merchandise east and west. In the Yemen hundreds of pad-footed beasts climb up and down the escarpment every day, between Ṣanʿā and Hodaida, and the trade is far from finished in North Africa—although the caravans that once marched along the beach to Tangier would now have a hard time hurdling the fences built out into the water by bathhouse proprietors. To study the caravan trade—one of the most fascinating aspects of Middle Eastern civilization—out of experience rather than books is still possible, and I hope some properly trained and vigorous young man will do it, while time is still less valuable than gasoline or money.

The routes over which camel caravans have been wont to travel are as numerous as they are long, and several volumes would be needed even to list them. However, a few outstanding ones may be mentioned. Crossing the Sahara from north to south, linking Muslim North Africa with the rich Sudan, are three principal roads, with several crossovers. This may be seen on Map 7, where one may also see the desert route from Fez to Cairo, which many pilgrims preferred to traveling through the more populous and more mountainous regions nearer the coast.

East of Egypt the same highways which had served the ancients gave passage to their Muslim descendants. From Mukalla and Aden on the Indian Ocean, tracks converged on the cities of al-Yemen, whence the high road inside the escarpment led to Mekka, al-Madina, and the Mediterranean. Around the rim of the desert the trail led to Damascus, Homs, Hama, Aleppo, Mosul, and Baghdad, the head of shipping, and also the terminus of the mountain passage to Hamadan, whence one could choose between the Tehran-Mashhad Turkestan-China and that to Yezd, Kerman, Zahidan, and on to

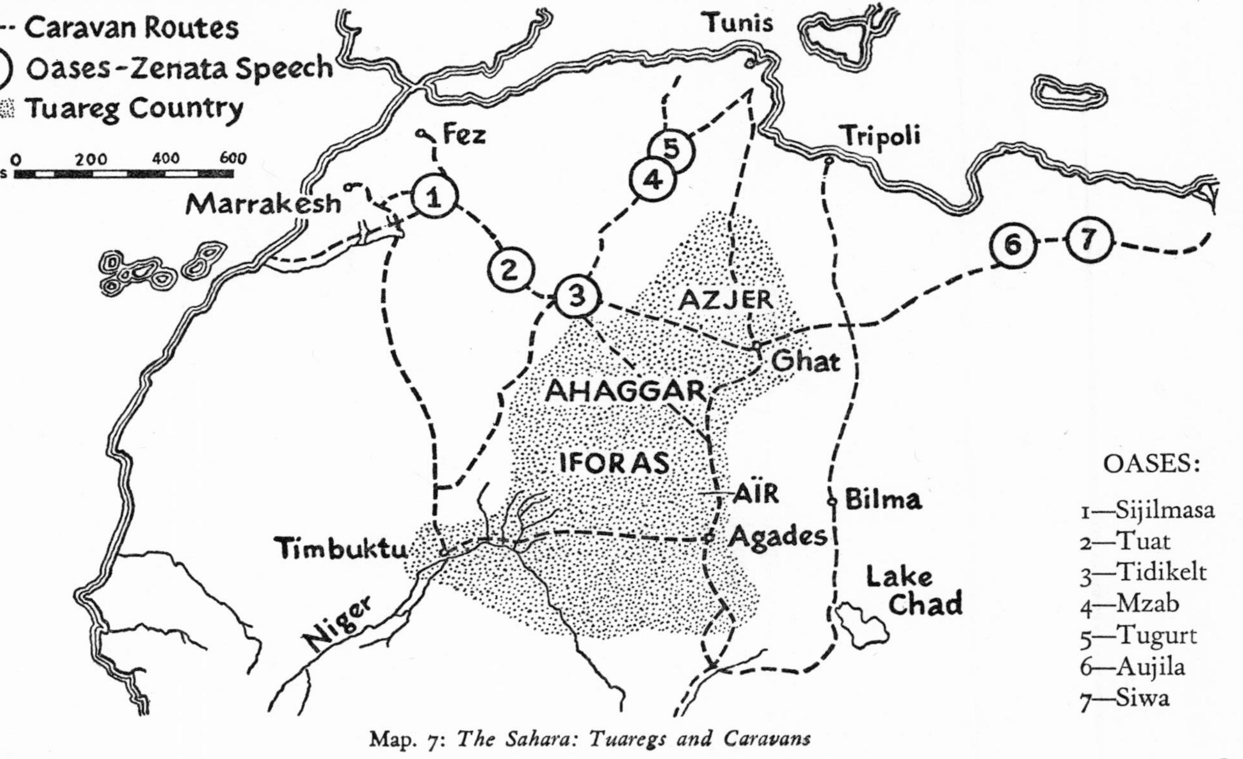

OASES:

1—Sijilmasa
2—Tuat
3—Tidikelt
4—Mzab
5—Tugurt
6—Aujila
7—Siwa

Map. 7: *The Sahara: Tuaregs and Caravans*

India. Another choice was Mosul-Tabriz-Qazvin, with branches to Armenia, Transcaucasia, and the shore of the Caspian Sea, whence one could travel through Muslim territory as far up the Volga as Kazan.

Whichever of these trails it might have been our traveler's lot to follow, he would have joined, in the old days, one of four different kinds of caravan. These were the military, religious, small commercial, and large commercial.[9] The first alone is possibly extinct, consisting as it did of pregasoline armies on the march. The expedition of the bey of Tripoli to Cyrenaica in 1817, for the purpose of putting down the revolt of his brother, will serve as an example.[10] The army was made up of the bey's regular troops, organized in the Turkish manner, plus levies from Bedawin tribes encountered along the way, before they had a chance to escape. Aside from the Bedawin, who presumably had their own beasts, every five or six soldiers pooled their wealth to buy a camel. This animal carried barley for their horses, barley meal for their own consumption, palm-leaf mats on which the soldiers could sleep, a waterskin, and a small wooden pail.

Equipped as simply as this they could travel light and fast. By threat, extortion, and plain robbery they lived off the land and were not afraid to wear out their camels; they could "liberate" others without much difficulty. At their halting places along the trail they had no fear of raiders, any possible body of whom they greatly outnumbered. Hence they camped by protocol rather than with an eye to defense, facing the direction to be taken on the next stage of the march. In the center of a semicircle the bey's batmen set his great tent. To either side stood the pavilions of his major-domo and chief physician, which in turn were flanked by the booths of the bey's Mamluk and Negro guards. Behind, in a deeper semicircle, were pitched the tents of his troops, and between the two horns of the

[9] W. D. Schorger, "The Caravan Trails of North Africa," senior honors thesis in anthropology (Peabody Museum Library, Harvard University, 1947). For source material I am using principally E. W. Bovill, *Caravans of the Old Sahara;* Captain J. Riley, *The Authentic Narrative of the Loss of the American Brig* Commerce (New York, 1918); Ibn Baṭṭūṭa, *op. cit.;* J. P. Ferrier, *Caravan Journeys and Wanderings in Persia, Afghanistan, Turkistan, and Beloochistan* (London, 1856); and Sir Richard Burton, *Personal Narrative of a Pilgrimage to Al-Madinah and Meccah* (London, 1893), 2 vols.

[10] Paolo della Cella, *Narrative of an Expedition from Tripoli in Barbary to the Western Frontier of Egypt,* trans. by A. Aufrère (London, 1822), pp. 9-11.

semicircle the bey's horses were picketed. This was also the station for the artillery and his standards. This is, actually, the Turko-Mongol style of camp,[11] carried over to Africa.

One of the chief difficulties of this kind of military expedition is that it must keep moving as it soon eats up the local supply of foodstuffs. In Morocco, where the sultans used to practice a similar technique in putting down rebellious tribes within their reach, the soldiers had to do nothing more than remain camped in a given spot for a few days before the local inhabitants would pay their back taxes to get rid of them, while neighboring tribesmen whose chances of resistance were slight hastened to pay up in order to forestall a visitation.[12]

The second type of caravan, the company of pilgrims, resembled the military in one principal respect: usually it was so large that its members were relatively safe. During part of their journey many of the pilgrims went by sea, in ships like those described earlier in this chapter,[13] as informally as other passengers. It is well known that a ship's company forms a separate and autonomous institution while the vessel is at sea. Like any other isolated group of people engaged on a common enterprise, they need a commanding officer, who in turn requires a staff. The same is true of companies of travelers on land. In the military caravan the officers and staff are provided by the military institution itself, but in a caravan of pilgrims the command and structure must be set up in some other way.

The great pilgrim caravan from ʿIraq which Ibn Baṭṭūṭa joined on its homeward journey on November 17, 1326 A.D., was financed by Sultan Abū Saʿīd, who had appointed a professional caravan commander to take charge, a man whose duties were as varied and whose authority was as necessary as those of the captain of an ocean liner. His chief concern was for the welfare of the poorer pilgrims. For their benefit he had brought along:

> . . . many draught camels for supplying the poorer pilgrims

[11] Michael Prawdin, *The Mongol Empire, Its Rise and Legacy* (New York, 1940), p. 84.

[12] Meakin cited, but was too canny to endorse, several instances in which Middle Atlas Berbers, in panic at the prospect of such an invasion, cut the throats of young women before the sultan's troops, in order to lay a shame compulsion on them and thus be spared. B. Meakin, *The Moorish Empire,* p. 221.

[13] See Burton, *op. cit.,* I, 186-206, chap. 10.

> with water, and other camels to carry the provisions issued as alms and the medicines, potions, and sugar required for any who fell ill. Whenever the caravan halted food was cooked in great brass cauldrons, and from these the needs of the poorer pilgrims and those who had no provisions were supplied. A number of spare camels accompanied it to carry those who were unable to walk. All those measures were due to the benefactions and generosity of the Sultan Abū Saʿīd.[14]

For the pilgrims who had money to spend, merchants who traveled with the caravan, like sandwich butchers on trains, set up their portable booths at each stop, creating a veritable daytime bazaar, since the caravan traveled at night, by torchlight. Hence everyone could eat, whether he had brought supplies or money, neither or both. Ibn Baṭṭūṭa, an old hand at wangling free rides, was given the use of a half of a camel litter all the way from Mekka to Baghdad. On a previous caravan out of Tunis he had been elected qāḍī to settle disputes between pilgrims. On this trip some other dignitary already must have been chosen.

The principal concern of the commander was water. At al-Madina he took on three days' supply, enough to get them to Wadi 'l-ʿArūs. Between there and the next station, al-ʿUsaila, was four days' march across part of the Najd Plateau. Here and at the next station, they took water from ancient tanks, but at the fourth they found the tanks dry, and they drew it from wells. For at least a thousand persons and an even larger number of animals to drain so much from a series of desert reservoirs must have created a critical local water shortage. Surely a political issue must have been raised; the caravan, we recall, was sponsored by the sultan of ʿIraq.

The local Bedawin, whether or not they were compensated in other ways, sold the pilgrims sheep, milk, and ghee, accepting in return only a special kind of coarse cloth brought along for the purpose. Halfway between Mekka and Baghdad the caravan reached a walled fortress named Fayd, where the solvent among the outgoing pilgrims had left a portion of their supplies, enough to provide for the last half of the trip back. Two sons of the amīr of the ruling tribe of that region awaited them, with armed men, to see that they picked up their belongings, to sell them camels and sheep, and to

[14] Ibn Baṭṭūṭa, *op. cit.*, p. 78.

shelter them from the demands of the horde of local people eager to beg and, if chance permitted, to pilfer.

Beggars are always partial to travelers, and pilgrims are natural targets for their attention. Even today one sees them hanging about bus stops, looking pathetic and impeding traffic. One reason for their presence at transport stations is, of course, that a traveler usually has a supply of ready cash and must bring it out into view. Another is that it is more profitable to approach a stranger than someone seen every day, for the shaking hand and faltering voice carry the most conviction the first time witnessed. While moneyed locals budget their zakā, the pilgrims, filled with the unworldly glow of a pious experience, are on a special fiscal regime and will probably never see the beggar a second time. From the standpoint of the community as a whole it is a fine thing to have its contributions to local charity swelled by funds from outside, but not to the point where the beggars break the peace or drive business away. Hence one reason for the armed escort.

Beggars, however, are at worst a petty nuisance; much more serious is the possibility of attack by Bedawin or hillmen. Without doubt these two sons of the amīr were on hand to grant the caravan safe-conduct through their father's territory, under the face of that great man. How much the leader of the caravan paid for this, in favors or in cash, we shall probably never know. Ibn Baṭṭūṭa also neglected to tell us whether or not the caravan included professional guards, and if not, who acted as police. Sir Richard Burton, traveling on a pilgrim caravan more than five centuries later, describes a body of five hundred tough Albanian cavalrymen who did their best to protect the travelers in their charge from the bullets of the impious and greedy.[15] Although in one encounter they managed to drive away their assailants, they succeeded only at the cost of twelve men. It is possible that the security of the caravan roads had fallen off between Ibn Baṭṭūṭa and Burton.

Within either caravan, however, a certain amount of trouble could easily have arisen to warrant the presence of police. In both we are told that pilgrims of many countries were included, speaking Persian, Pushtu, and Indian languages as well as Arabic, and insisting on their separate ways of prayer. Burton mentions the scorn of the Sunnis at the Persians for pronouncing five extra words of ritual;

[15] Burton, *op. cit.*, I, 272-274.

the way the Sunnis taunted the Shīʿa by pronouncing, over and over, the names of the first three caliphs; and the vow of a fellow pilgrim to plunge his knife into another at journey's end.

Returning to Ibn Baṭṭūṭa's caravan, we read that when they were twelve days out of al-Kūfa, at the tanks of Waqisa, the caravan commander met his most critical water problem, for he had to load enough for twelve days. Luckily it was near the end of the journey and most of the heavy and bulky supplies had been consumed. At Waqisa the pilgrims found merchants from al-Kūfa who had come out especially to meet them, bringing flour, bread, dates, and fruit, to give strength for the last lap of desert travel. This was not Ibn Baṭṭūṭa's sole pilgrim journey, but it was the only one he described in any detail. Burton and other travelers of the nineteenth century give us much more, but by then the golden days of Islam were far behind.

Much commoner are the small commercial caravans, the ordinary carriers on which most of the overland trade depends. These caravans are still being conducted and could easily be studied.[16] Such a caravan consists of a small group of merchants with their goods, or a single merchant, his servants, and his goods, moving from one trading center to another. Very often plain travelers, pilgrims or otherwise, will attach themselves to a merchant caravan or may form one of their own with guides and servants.

Less than fifty years ago groups of merchants and travelers would assemble in Moroccan cities, waiting until they were numerous enough and could hire enough guards, before starting out to another city, but that was in a period of relative anarchy. On the Sahara as on the edges of Asiatic deserts, it was standard procedure. In Morocco a number of Jewish merchants, not included in the caravan as full-fledged members, would ride on its outskirts on their donkeys, seeking protection. When the caravan came to a river in flood, it was a favorite trick to force one of these People of the Book out into the stream to test its depth and strength. If he got across, the Muslims followed.

In the case of a small caravan crossing the desert, the principal danger is not sandstorms nor desert marauders, but thirst, and hence the principal care is to carry and preserve enough water. Camels, therefore, are used to carry water, food, and merchandise; they are

[16] The best study of such a caravan to my knowledge is Owen Lattimore, *Desert Road to Turkestan* (Boston, 1929), pp. 121-126. Although lying outside our area, it is nevertheless pertinent.

not ridden unless absolutely necessary. The number of animals to be taken depends on the supplies needed, which in turn depends on the distance to be covered and the frequency of water holes. The personnel to be taken along depends on the nature of the country to be crossed and the actual kind of goods carried. It includes varying numbers of merchants with or without travelers, one or more guides, a number of camel drivers, and a body of professional soldiers or guards. One of the merchants is selected by his fellows to be leader, for someone must have the final authority. However, being a merchant and not a transport specialist like the leader of Ibn Baṭṭūṭa's caravan, he will exercise it as little as possible, leaving most of the decisions to the guides.

The camel drivers do the work on the road, loading and unloading, making and breaking camp, cooking, and waiting on their employers. The guides are hired locally, either for the entire journey or for portions of it in which they had special regional competence. Professional guides specialize in knowing a given area or a certain set of trails, piloting by landmarks by day and by stars at night. (Pellow's guide claimed to follow the trail by smell.) Marching at the head of the caravan, the guide sets the pace, usually between two and a half and three miles per hour. If a man is tired, he lies down and takes a nap, then runs after the caravan to catch up. Only if injured or exhausted is he allowed to ride. If the guide becomes hopelessly lost, or the waterskins run dry, then it is every man for himself, for the authority of the head merchant will not carry this far. Indeed this may be best from the survival standopint, for if all were to stay together the chances of someone getting through would be less. By the same token, a man who falls by the wayside is left. To stop the whole caravan and to try to care for him would endanger the lives of all.

On the trail the daily routine is rigidly maintained, because it is vital to cover a given distance. The travelers arise before daybreak, march a set number of hours, up to twelve, covering as many as twenty-five to thirty miles. On long marches they cook only twice a day, breakfast and supper, and eat a handful of dates, often without stopping, for lunch. They maintain this routine until the next water has been reached, but on short hauls they may rest to drink tea. When night has fallen and it is time to camp, the procedure depends on whether or not they suspect danger. If so they force the camels, hobbled, to lie in a circle, in the middle of which they heap their precious merchandise, supplies, and water. While wealthy and important merchants and travelers may sleep in tents, most of the people lie between the camels and the baggage, sheltering themselves from the wind and sand by the bales themselves, and by makeshift walls of brush. Soldiers are supposed to keep night watch, presumably in turns.

If there seems to be no danger and forage is at hand, the camels are allowed to graze during the night. Otherwise the drivers give them dates, all in a heap, and the most aggressive camel eats the most. Unless absolutely necessary, the drivers refuse to give the camels water out of the skins. In order to avoid this necessity they fatten the camels for a month or more before a long journey and train them to go without water for increasing periods. On the trail the camels follow the guide in a single line, and the drivers keep them moving by singing songs. Arab music, with its narrow intervals, finds in camels an appreciative audience.

Once arrived at their destination we presume that the members of the expedition find various means and excuses to see as little of each other as possible until the time has come to return or move on. Actually these caravans are constantly adding and losing personnel, which may well be a mercy.

The large commercial caravan is usually made up of a number of small caravans teamed together. Instead of electing one of their number as leader, they hire a professional shaikh of caravans, who makes all final decisions and to whom all members are responsible. We have seen that two special tribes of caravan men, of Arab descent, live among the Western Tuareg, to whom the former pay a nominal tribute, in return for full protection. Men who have inherited such special relationships with the masters of the desert are thus of particular value to trans-Saharan travelers. These shaikhs receive payment in the form of a percentage of each merchant's profit for the trip, much as the crew of a ship is paid, and without doubt they can carry on a little trading of their own.

Riley,[17] referring to the period between 1812 and 1815, describes a caravan of eight hundred men and three thousand camels which went from Wed Nun to Timbuktu, and another, of fifteen hundred men and four thousand camels, from Timbuktu to the Mediterranean coast. Enterprises of this size were big business. Apparently the traveling merchants from all the cities between Tripoli and Fez got

[17] Riley, *op. cit.*, p. 204.

together once a year for a single huge caravan to Timbuktu, bringing back on the return trip, gold, ivory, valuable gums, and as many as two thousand slaves. With the latter outnumbering their captors, and with so many people who might not only go astray but make trouble in the inhabited portions of the route, it was necessary for the shaikh to exercise an authority of military strictness, paying particular attention to the rationing of water and the use of forage. All of the men were armed with muskets and swords; with so large a group they were in a position to defend themselves without the need of special soldiers. On the other hand, so plump was the prize that they were always in danger of being attacked by some rival tribe too powerful for their Tuareg protectors to drive off. Sometimes bloody battles took place, and once, according to Riley, one of these caravans was lost in a sandstorm. When in a critical moment the shaikh ordered certain camels killed, the merchants revolted and murdered the shaikh. The caravan then broke up in fights and disintegrated into small groups, each of which had to work out its own survival.[18]

As might be expected, Ibn Baṭṭūṭa has his dinar's worth to add to this story. He too crossed the Sahara. He says that on the way southward, after his caravan had reached a certain watering place named Tisar, they sent out a special runner, a native from a tribe called Massufa, among whom this feat was a specialty. The runner went on to Walata, the nearest town in the Sudan, carrying letters from members of the caravan to their friends there, asking for lodging. Merchants who had no friends there learned the names of likely citizens, to whom they wrote, sight unseen. The recipients of the letters come out four nights' journey into the desert bearing water, which the caravan would sorely need, because its members could not carry enough to take them all the way in. These runners were known to have disappeared in the desert, in which case some or all of the caravan members perished.[19] That this was a regular practice on a much-traveled route I find a bit hard to credit.

Large commercial caravans on Asiatic soil operated in much the same fashion as African ones and experienced similar difficulties. Although many splendid accounts may be available, the two which I find most entertaining are the true account of Ferrier and the fictionalized version in *Hajji Baba of Isfahan,* which is so true to

[18] *Ibid.,* pp. 164-165.

[19] Ibn Baṭṭūṭa, *op. cit.,* p. 318.

life that many Persians, among whom it is widely read in translation, find it difficult to believe that the author was an Englishman.[20]

Ferrier and Hajji Baba were wont to spend the night in caravanserais, large buildings built around central courts and containing dozens of cubicles for the convenience of travelers. In Iran these are especially numerous, having been built, at reasonable stages, by several of the more powerful shahs, including the famous Shah ʿAbbās (1588-1629 A.D.). The caravanserai is a hotel for man and beast in which the traveler can eat his own food or buy it, as he pleases, and where he can meet other travelers and exchange information. Today enterprising Persian innkeepers are building a new kind of caravanserai, a motel with a courtyard, in which the traveler may park his truck or car safely overnight, and with rooms and food. Establishments similar to caravanserais are found in the settled parts of most Muslim countries, under different names: for example, funduq in North Africa, and *khān* in Turkish-speaking territory.

The most wonderful thing about travel in the most felicitous period of Islam, and to a certain extent at all periods, was the number of devices which made possible a maximum circulation of personnel. Free transport and free food on pilgrim caravans, free lodging in Ṣūfi chapters, houses of the Ahl al-Futuwwa, country mosques, travelers' aid from some of the religious foundations, the chance to make a living by trading along the way or by serving as scribe—all of these mechanisms which kept people moving about played a great role in homogenizing Muslim civilization. As part of this process travel promoted the circulation of goods, so that different cities, as well as different villages, could specialize in different products, with the certainty of large sales over a wide geographical coverage as a reward for the development of superior skills in processing locally abundant materials. Travel made it possible for the people of Nasibin in northern ʿIraq to make their rose water, for the inhabitants of Sarmin, to export their fine perfumed soap, and for the people of Baalbek to specialize in manufacturing their wooden plates and spoons.

In all the tales of early Muslim travel little is said about passports or customs inspections. Both were known and required in certain places and certain times. On the way out of Egypt while traveling toward Syria, Ibn Baṭṭūṭa stopped at a post called Qatya on what is now the Suez Canal, for a most modern kind of ordeal. He states

[20] Ferrier, *op. cit.* James J. Morier, *Hajji Baba of Isfahan* (New York, 1937).

that no one could enter Syria without a passport from Egypt, and vice versa. A large office staffed with officers, clerks, and notaries collected a thousand gold dinars a day in customs revenue. Aside from the desire for dinars, one reason advanced for these precautions was to keep spies out of ʿIraq. At night, when the border was closed, the local Bedawin, who were employed for this purpose, smoothed over the sand round about, and in the morning the governor looked for tracks. If he found any, he set his Bedawin on the trail. Having inevitably produced the lawbreaker, they turned him over to the governor, who could punish him in a manner of his own choosing. Despite the strictness of this control, the governor greeted Ibn Baṭṭūṭa with great courtesy and let him and his whole company pass without hindrance.[21]

Egypt is a naturally sealed country and, on its eastern approaches, easy to guard. In most of the Middle Eastern lands, however, borders are wide and can be crossed at ease, as they frequently are. I have seen Arabs from Jordan walk around the ʿIraqi border post on the pipeline road in the same spirit in which the passengers on Villiers' boat glided conveniently overboard. The Islamic community was a singularly unified world of its own, in which the whole trend was to permit free trade and free passage, without let or hindrance. In the common possession of that spirit lay one of the reasons for its greatness.

[21] Ibn Baṭṭūṭa, *op. cit.*, pp. 54-55.

18 A LESSON IN AUSTERITY

MY IMMEDIATE PURPOSE in writing this book was the overt one of trying to provide a background of geographical and cultural information, and hence of understanding, for Americans interested in the Middle East. It is therefore slanted directly at two classes of persons, those about to go out to any or all of the twenty-odd countries concerned, and those who, while remaining at home, want to know enough to be able to form intelligent opinions about the foreign relations of the United States in this area.

In trying to attain this objective I have avoided attempting to bring the picture up to date. Many other authors, far more versed in modern history and in current events than I, are doing this daily. Another potential pitfall which I have tried to by-pass is that of taking sides or playing favorites. So far as I am concerned, both the Sunni and Shīʿa dogmas are equally virtuous, while the troubles between the Israelis and the citizens of the Arab states are none of my business. What *is* my business is to point out—to those who are planning to build dams or who are estimating the costs and efficiency of local labor for factories in which they are thinking of placing investments—what the people, with whom they or their clients will be dealing, are really like.

It is also my business to show them how master craftsmen have managed to maintain such a high level of skill for thousands of years with a minimum of equipment; how the concept of hundreds of masters all doing the same thing, while organized into an autonomous guild, is quite different from the Western idea of a factory. This is only one item in the list of "practical" information which I have been trying to impart. Any intelligent person who is faced with workaday problems can dig out many others.

Another practical aspect of this study is that it shows how little the governments of Muslim nations in the past have interfered with the private lives of their citizens, whose mutual relationships have been channeled through many other kinds of structure, notably the religious. Such institutions as the Ṣūfi brotherhood, the religious foundation (waqf), the guild, the ṣof, the village council, and the concept of the great man's "face," are revealed as precious mechanisms which keep Muslim society on an even keel and which, in the dreary processes of mechanization, should be preserved and adapted to new uses rather than discouraged and destroyed.

A second purpose is to demonstrate the practicability of the techniques of applied anthropology in complex, literate civilizations as well as in simpler, preliterate cultures. The fact that the Middle East has the longest recorded history of all the areas in the world offered both a challenge and an advantage. The challenge has been accepted and the advantage, I hope, utilized. At least ground has been broken for others, to whom this kind of study should be less of a novelty.

Why it was a novelty is clear enough. Tickets to Kabul cost more than trips to Santa Fé. Before we needed regional experts, anthropological research programs were cut to the size of the Ph.D. thesis, and research on a society as complex as that of the Middle East would produce more information than was needed. It was easier, and quite good enough, to spend the summer on an Indian reservation debriefing a half-dozen tribal survivors, taking down their tales of the good old days before their memories should fail forever. Few of our universities offered linguistic training in modern Arabic, Persian, or Turkish, and in the Middle East languages are essential. Our country had too few interests in the Middle East to warrant special attention on the part of foundations, now fully alive to the need of scholars competent in the culture of that area.

We were taught, with full justification, that anthropologists should concentrate on the peoples about to disappear physically or culturally or both, and wring every possible drop of information from them before it was too late. However it may have distracted us from problems that now appear important, this preoccupation with the simplest cultures has been the key to the success of the anthropological method, since it has taught us to view each culture as a whole, instead of piecemeal. We cannot understand the economics, the family structure, the religious practices, or the government of a people unless we know the outline of its entire cultural story, on the dimensions of space and time. Since understanding is what we are seeking, this second purpose is a part of the first.

Understanding, the keynote to the third purpose, is a two-way process. We Americans are not trying to help the peoples of the Middle East attain a standard of living comparable to our own merely out of the kindness of our hearts, nor are we doing it, I hope, only for our own material advantage in building new markets, nor just to keep our rivals of the moment out of the oil fields, although both of these are valid reasons. If we are smart, we also are doing it in order to learn something of value to ourselves.

Christianity came out of the East, and so did its parent religion, Judaism. So also did the cereals with which we make our bread, and the domestic animals whose milk and flesh burden our lavish tables. So did our knowledge of the furnace with forced draft in which we smelt our ores, and the wheel on a rotating shaft with which we run our factories and our vehicles. And so did the written word.

Since the Middle East has given us so much already, perhaps it has some wisdom left over which we have not tapped or which we learned long ago and later forgot. It is easy to forget basic principles of human behavior at a time when technology is moving at a previously unheard of pace, and social devices are straining to keep up with it. At such a time the judgment of old men goes unheeded, for they are ignorant of the latest techniques. To refresh our knowledge of basic truths about man's relation to man, we must turn to a more stable society, the adjustment of which has long since been worked out and tested, before it too falls into the industrial whirlpool and starts floundering about even more desperately than our own.

The first lesson that we learn is this. In any human society all the good will and fine intentions in the world, all the most energetic efforts of the most gifted men the species can produce, will be utterly wasted if the system in which they live is wrong, and they fail to change it. On the other hand if the system is right, and its people refuse to let it be changed, individual members of that society can be as selfish, unpleasant, unwise, and generally antisocial as they like, and still the others will get along together without trouble.

What makes a system right or wrong? These are subjective words. Translated into more scientific terms, they mean systems which are built to stay in equilibrium, and those which can fall out of adjustment easily, through defective social mechanisms. The social mechanisms which keep societies that have them in order, so that their individual members enjoy the greatest possible measure of happiness, consist of paired balances and automatic controls which stop trouble in its tracks. When an individual is out of order so that his acts will endanger others, traditional sanctions are at once invoked against him, and the disorder contained. Witness the gathering of the clans when trouble arose between the Ulad 'Abd el-Mumin and the Beni Tadmut.

Old Middle Eastern society as I have tried to describe it was a system kept in equilibrium by a large number of these automatic controls. Prominent among them was the fivefold division of labor itself, which gave everyone a chance to specialize in one way or another, and thus to channel his energy, whether he realized it or not, into the most efficient utilization possible of the landscape by the greatest number of people, at a preindustrial level of technology. All of the personnel in the Middle East, from the Rif to the Pathan country which form its cultural frontiers, are as efficiently deployed in their various interlocking tasks as if some divine planner had picked them up, assigned them jobs according to blueprint, and set them down in their proper places.

How did this happen? Mechanists will say by trial and error. According to them no human mind planned it, it just worked itself out that way. Religious people will say that it is but another manifestation of the hand of God and His interests in human affairs. If we look through the world, we will see many societies, simple and complex alike, working according to complicated schemes of adjustment, just as the golden plover guides his yearly course by some means no man has fathomed. We will see other societies that human beings have planned, detail by detail, and in them people are not well adjusted or happy. In them systems of checks and balances are lacking. The tyrant cannot be killed to ease his people, the freeman cannot believe the word of his neighbor under oath, and no man dares admit that the knowledge of his country's experts may be incomplete, or that his ruler is fallible.

Other human beings have dictated ways of life that have worked and are still working. But their dictation has taken the form of the enunciation of broad, general principles, such as to love thy neighbor as thyself and not to covet thy neighbor's wife. These principles, which the three great religions of the Middle East have given us, have been enunciated not as the creations of the minds behind the mouths through which they issued, but as messages sent from God through His human vehicles. As the word of God, so ascribed by their utterers through an honest conviction that such wisdom lay beyond their own human capacities, these principles have carried more weight than if they had been immodestly presented as the word of man, alone and unaided.

Jesus Christ had nothing to say against the use of pork or wine, for His Message took only the broadest form and is as applicable in one place and time as in any other. Muḥammad's, however, like that of the Hebrew scriptures, was much more specific, as we have seen. If we study the details, item by item, we will soon see that these specifications limit the individual only in the direction of extravagance. Within the bounds of the knowledge of his time, Muḥammad set up a marvelously shatterproof scheme.

Analyzing it as objectively as possible, the keynote to the Islamic way of life is that it provided a maximum goodness of fit for a swarm of human beings, living in the environment of the Middle East, to a progressively deteriorating landscape. Take, for example, the dietary law against eating pork, which the Jews had possessed long before Muḥammad. All sorts of rationalizations have been offered to explain it, including the trichinosis theory and the idea that rich fat is not good for one in a hot climate. Neither of these holds much water. In the days of the Talmudic doctors, and of Muḥammad, no more was known about trichinosis than about tuberculosis or cancer. Furthermore it is not always hot in the Middle East, and on a cold day pork tastes as good, and is as easily digested, in Aleppo as in Alaska.

The pig is an animal which furnishes no by-products. All it has to offer is its flesh. Since it is hard to flay, its skin is not available for use. Other domestic animals furnish milk, wool, or transportation, or some combination of the three. All else equal, keeping swine is an extravagance. Now in an unexploited Mediterranean environment where large patches of oak and beech cover remain, it is easy to send a swineherd into the forest to watch his charges munch acorns and beechnuts and root for truffles. The pigs can be fed on materials not otherwise used. A sow will produce up to ten shoats a year, and the farmer and his family can eat fresh pork in the fall, while putting down hams, sausages, and sides of bacon for the winter. Economically the pig is a splendid thing.

Once the population has grown and the oaks have been cut down to make way for olive trees, there is no place to graze the pigs. If they are to be kept they must be fed on food which people need, and a pig eats more than several men. Any man who does so now will be making a show of his wealth; he will be disturbing the equilibrium of the group among whom he lives and preventing an equable distribution of foodstuffs. The pig must go. It went. The goat, its former companion in the forest, can eat the dried weeds and twigs in the waste land between villages and transfer this material, otherwise serviceable only as fuel, into milk, day after day. The goat helped the poor and landless to find sustenance, and the goat stayed.

As for wine, which was not forbidden among either Jews or Christians, we must remember that grapes will not grow in the Ḥijāz, Muḥammad's home. Wine, which must be imported, takes up valuable baggage space on camels' backs, and it is heavy. If the Ḥijāzi merchants drink it, they will spend money, while if they use this baggage allotment for merchandise in transit they will save money instead. Furthermore if the caravan men decide to drink wine on the trail, they may never reach their destination. Even more important probably was the social aspect of wine drinking. Muslims are very hospitable and always offer a guest a drink. If he must serve wine to all comers a man of moderate income will soon be impoverished. The accounts of Muslim historians are full of references to drinking, but only among schismatics living on chilly mountains and rich men in the cities. To the common man, the devout Muslim who has a family to support and who still enjoys the company of his friends, wine is an extravagance which his religion helps him do without and which he feels under no social pressure to produce for guests.

Another interesting item is the veil. In Iran women used to wear the *chuddar,* a semicircle of cloth which could be so draped as to cover the entire body, except for the eyes. Many still wear them. These chuddars all look more or less alike. An attractive young woman can go out in the streets in a chuddar without drawing attention which might lead to trouble for herself and her husband. Marital arrangements do not depend on chance meetings on the street, but upon careful negotiations between families. At the same time a middle-aged lady whose clothing is threadbare can appear in a similar chuddar and feel no shame, while a highly placed dame will have no chance to display her jewelry and excite envy. The chuddar is a great leveler, extremely useful in a land of overpopulation and potential social tension.

In Arab lands women disguise their figures in similar fashion, while wearing some kind of a special veil, about which Sir Richard Burton wrote:

> It is the most coquettish article of woman's attire. . . . It conceals coarse skin, fleshy noses, wide mouths, and vanishing

> chins, whilst it sets off to best advantage what in these lands is almost always lustrous and liquid—the eye.[1]

In attracting as in avoiding attention, then, Muslim usage is a great leveler of women, as of men. It also helps preserve the anonymity of the individual in a crowded place. Out in the country, and particularly among the tribes, one seldom sees veils. What is useful in the city is an encumbrance here. The country women need to work unhampered out of doors, and besides, everyone knows everyone else.

One more example of Muslim sagacity may be seen in their ability to live gracefully with little furniture. The old-fashioned Arab or Persian removes his shoes when he enters a room, leaving them at the door. He can do this simply and unostentatiously because his footgear has been designed for this purpose. Thus he will neither wear out the rugs nor trample them with mud. In a room enclosed by bare white walls and roofed by a lofty ceiling, an oriental rug is a thing of beauty. In a Western room, whose walls are covered with paper printed in loud designs, whose ceiling is low, and whose floor is cluttered with chairs, tables, radio cabinets, and bookcases, such a rug is wasted.

Wool is cheap in the Middle East and locally produced. Wood is expensive, and most of it must be imported. Rugs and hassocks, then, give rest to the weary, and chairs are not needed. One can be just as comfortable and just as dignified on the floor as in a chair. If the king or caliph sits on a rug, he is not doing anything which his humblest subject, equipped with a reed mat of his own plaiting, cannot also do. When the king or caliph prepares for a meal, he washes his hands first. This again is something that his humblest subject can afford to do, and in a society whose table manners were developed before the germ theory was known, it shows considerable wisdom. Once his hands are clean, the host can serve food to his guests with his fingers, with little fear of contamination. Performed in an atmosphere of warmth and dignity, this simple and personal act builds bonds between the men eating from a single bowl which can never be forged over the banquet table.

Returning to the subject of cleanliness, both Muslim and Jew are bound by rigid rules. The laws regarding the slaughtering of animals and handling of meat could hardly be improved for use

[1] Sir Richard Burton, *Pilgrimage to Al-Madinah and Meccah,* I, 229, n. 2.

in countries lacking refrigeration. Shaving areas of the body prone to infestation and infection, and washing both hands and intimate organs before and after use, are practices that many outside the Middle East could do well to emulate. Undoubtedly they have helped greatly in the war against germs, and are still useful in conjunction with the more potent battery of water purification and antisepsis.

These examples should be enough to demonstrate how Middle Easterners have adjusted themselves to the rigors of increasing population in the face of deforestation, soil erosion, a lowered water table, and other creeping misfortunes. Essentially their adjustment has taken on three aspects. The first is a clever use of local materials to achieve the maximum convenience in eating, in housing, in clothing, in transportation, and in all kinds of processing. The second is the adoption of standards of behavior which reduce to a minimum all possible sources of envy and friction between rich and poor, humble and wellborn. The third is the development of an athletic, repetitive, highly conditioning routine of religious devotion, which will make the observance of the other two aspects unquestioned and automatic.

At this point nearly enough has been said. The Islamic way of life, with which this book is chiefly concerned, has been described. It has made possible the optimum survival and happiness of millions of human beings in an increasingly impoverished environment over a fourteen-hundred-year period. The older Jewish way, which has been described so often and so well by others, has on the other hand preserved in both East and West a special corps of highly skilled and intellectual personnel, through centuries of alternate adversity and prosperity. In the East the Christian way has played a similar role, but in the West it has served as the guide to the behavior of people living in the comparative luxury of an environment with plenty of rainfall, fuel, and other natural advantages lacking in the East, which made possible our creation of the Industrial Age on the basis of Middle Eastern technical discoveries.

In the East a number of newly Westernized Muslim "intellectuals" are beginning to slack off in their religious devotion. In the West the sons of similar agnostics are beginning to go to church. Americans now realize that hard times lie ahead, that our resources are dwindling and our population growing. We have the burden of most of the world on our shoulders. We realize now that we need courage without sentimentality, faith without bigotry, and the opportunity to pursue all branches of scientific inquiry wherever they may lead, without letting science master us. It is a big job for which we are preparing. As part of our preparation we cannot afford to neglect the study of other civilizations, to learn what lessons we can which will be of use to us in the guidance of our own. Surely a knowledge of the most ancient of the world's civilizations, and how it worked during a similar period of trial and adversity, should help us.

That civilization strangely anticipated in many ways the One World for which so many two-legged mammals now yearn, a world in which the only passport that a human being needs is his quality of being human, in which both central and tribal governments exist only in order to keep the peace among a host of other institutions which cross international borders, in which travelers are welcomed and fed along their way, education is free, and the most honored and valuable possession which a man can attain is wisdom. If we can once more, in our own way and on a larger scale, achieve these things, we will have derived profit from a lesson in austerity.

19 SEVEN YEARS OF LITTLE WISDOM

IN THE FIRST EDITION of *Caravan* no attempt was made to bring the book up to date concerning current political happenings in the Middle East. The whole idea was background. At the time I was writing, the gradual Westernization of Egypt, particularly of the Turkish-speaking element in the upper social and political layer—the element from which Nasser's chief adherents have arisen—had been going on for more than a century. At the same time the Westernization of the Yemen was still embryonic. Other authors had chronicled the high points of the process of acculturation in various lands of the Middle East. As an anthropologist my job, as I saw it, was to describe and analyze the cultural bases from which these changes emerged.

Now that the Middle East is holding the center of the stage in world events, now that civilization seems fated to die in the very cradle in which it was nurtured, it is all the more necessary, if we are to understand the process of disintegration, rebirth, or whatever it may turn out to be, that we recognize the principles on which Middle Eastern civilization has a habit of operating. In its disharmonic Westernization, as in its earlier partial accommodations to the pattern of Rome and of Istanbul, it has followed traditional channels, and may be expected to sail within bounds of their buoys in the foreseeable future.

First of all, an ancient cleavage has reopened. The Arabic-speaking Muslims who govern their lives by the *shāri'a* code of Islamic law are behaving quite differently from the non-Arabic-speaking Muslims who have long followed their own indigenous and pre-Islamic *qanūns*. The Turks and Iranians have become Westernized in varying degrees with greater ease than the Muslim Arabs have done, because their basic concepts of human relations at family and community level are closer to those of Europeans. Like their ancient and medieval ancestors, they have also been able to set up and maintain stable governments. On the other hand the Berbers have revolted as they always do when the central government ruling them has grown weak enough to permit it. Today in North Africa the principal trouble spots are those that first witnessed revolts in Roman times.

At this moment of second writing, the news of the world is focused less on these non-Arabic Muslim areas than on the so-called Arab states, from Egypt to Iraq, and from Lebanon to Oman and the Yemen. In the center of the spotlight stand the Northern Arabs, descended partly from those who came north in early Islamic times and partly from their converts. These people have trouble with political independence. It may be recalled that they also had trouble shortly after the Prophet died. Almost at once Syria and Iraq split apart, and al-Ḥasan and al-Ḥusain were killed as quickly and in as cold blood as the late King Faisal of Iraq. Almost immediately Shīʿa and Kharajites broke off from the company of faithful to found faiths of their own, while within the Sunni ranks rival doctors founded the four existing schools of the *shārīʿa.*

Part of the current trouble in the Arab lands is that their centers of urban population are separated from each other by deserts, mountains, water, and foreign nations. Perhaps a greater barrier to unity is simply that, faced with independence, they have no traditional mechanism for unity, no framework for building up large political structures. Loyalty is to a man's father, uncles, and brothers. The preferred marriage is with the father's brother's daughter, and this keeps the lineage within narrow bounds. As kinship fans out under this system, the lines of cleavage grow stronger than the ties of loyalty.

Despite efforts to introduce western-style parliaments and bureaucracies, centuries of rule by Turks, and decades of rule by the British and French, have failed to alter the basic Arab system of human relations. We must remember that most of Colonel Nasser's fellow colonels, who have set up a framework for expansion, are not Arabs by tradition but Turks from that Ottoman elite of Cairo, with a century of Westernization behind them. Shishekli, the former dictator of Syria, is a Kurd, as was Saladin of the Crusades.

Another part of the trouble is the Arabs' failure to assimilate Western culture evenly. Like the Japanese, they clung to their old values while adopting our technology, and Western ideals and procedures differ widely from some of the basic concepts of Islamic civilization described in earlier chapters. For example, according to Islamic procedure special peoples like the Christians and Jews are welcome to live in Arab lands, except in the holy regions of the Ḥijāz, as long as they keep to themselves, mind their own business, and do not attempt to participate in government outside their own sheltered communities. The formation of the Jewish state of Israel in a part of Palestine, completely shattered that concept. Even earlier, the rise of the Christian half of the population in Lebanon, through superior education, migration of relatives to the West, and indeed nearly complete Westernization in many respects, placed the Muslim half at a disadvantage. No one could have expected Muslims to tolerate indefinitely a system which calls for a Christian president. So the modern emergence of the Jewish state of Israel and the predominantly Christian state of Lebanon have violated the basic concept of the role of special peoples in an Islamic world. These are very sore points which respond readily to needling from outside.

In the Islamic civilization of pre-Turkish times, the concept of nationality was always amorphous, and so it continued to be while the Ottoman Empire blanketed most of the Arab world. Citizenship in a state was, indeed, subordinate as an outlet of loyalty to religious affiliation. The important thing was not to be an Egyptian or a Syrian or a Moroccan, but to be a Muslim. Even today few Arabs can understand how citizens of different faiths can have equal status in nations like the United States and Great Britain. After the rise of Israel most of the Arab states refused to grant visas to American citizens of Jewish faith or origin except under most unusual circumstances.

This meant that Jewish archaeologists could no longer excavate, as they had previously, their old sites in Iraq or Syria, and that Jewish personnel were excluded from American installations in Sa'udi Arabia. This was, and remains a clear violation of our conception of international rights, but they have pointed out in reply that our exclusion of polygamists, with their wives, from America is equally uncalled for. However, despite all this Jewish women do not seem to matter. In several instances Jewish wives have accompanied their Christian husbands to their work in Arab lands. Muḥammad had one Christian wife; the religion of women is a matter of little importance.

A matter which is much more important in the present state of the world, and one which is little realized by Western policy-makers, apparently, is that, according to Arab belief, *the world is divided into two mutually hostile and irreconcilable portions, the Dar ul-Islam or House of Peace, and the Dar ul-Ḥarb or House of War*. The House of Peace is ruled by Believers, although special peoples such as Christians and Jews may reside inside it under circumstances stated earlier. The House of War is ruled by Unbelievers, and their lands and inhabitants are fair prey. Whenever possible, peace should be kept between the states and communities occupying the House of Peace. Whenever feasible or useful, war should be waged by the dwellers in the House of Peace against them who dwell in the House of War.

The so-called Arab nationalism of Colonel Nasser follows exactly these ancient lines. In smuggling arms to the Algerian rebels he is not, by this system of belief, violating the borders of modern states, so much as he is helping fellow Muslims of what was once part of the House of Peace to regain their former status. In broadcasting inflamatory propaganda over the Cairo radio to Kenya, Tanganyika, and Uganda, he is not so much fighting "colonialism" as he is following the old Muslim missionary spirit in trying to extend the House of Peace into the realm of Unbelievers, including some out-and-out heathen. However he himself may rationalize it, to other Muslims his movement is an attempt at Islamic expansion comparable to that of the early days of Islam. "Colonialism" and "nationalism" are western concepts that do not fit this situation, however much some Arabs may bandy these words around. We may be faced with something more serious than either, a much older concept which could become the principal ingredient of a modern-dress Crusade.

One may wonder why, in the height of trouble, oil keeps on flowing through pipelines and ships keep on steaming through the Suez Canal. Back in Sabaean times, caravans marched across hostile deserts and ships laden with merchandise sailed over troubled waters. Out on the desert, not long ago, blacksmiths, Ṣulaba, and merchants carried on their business without disturbance through the heat of battle. While warriors fight, trade must not cease. The ancient business of the Arabs is transportation, and trade, like the show, must go on, particularly when the movement of oil and ships brings in rich tolls. Before the lifelines are to be cut and substantial sources of income slashed with them, political trouble has to be more than critical.

In the old, traditional Islam, one of the principal sources of stability of the social order was the body of rules against boastful display and extravagance. The surfaces of houses facing the street were plain, and their entrances drab. Out on the street women covered their charms with amorphous garments and disfiguring veils. In the house they kept to their quarters when male guests were being entertained. The prohibition of wine made it possible for a poor man to entertain his friends in dignity. Clothing had to be plain, without silk or precious metal showing. Every man sat on the ground, eliminating the need of expensive furniture. The common man called his king by his given name. What has become of all this?

In Damascus, Baghdad, and Cairo modern houses are far from plain. Many women walk about in western clothing, with rudimentary veils. Drinking is common, some westernized Muslims even eat pork, and some fail to keep the holy fast of Ramaḍan. The fact that some men wear western clothing and others do not, emphasizes differences in wealth and status. Under Turkish influence titles became important, and government officials like to be addressed as So-and-so Bey. A doctor's degree is also vital for a man of political prominence. The greatest source of discord, perhaps, is the automobile. The owners of cars are clearly marked from the motorless and within the ranks of privilege the make of the car, its size, and age are also matters of high prestige. It is also *de rigeur* to drive as fast as possible and not to let anyone pass. Duels have been fought in Lebanon because one car passed another. Dust and accidents do little to endear the wheel-borne to the donkey riders and pedestrians, and a string of camels scattered by an automobile may take hours to reassemble and reload. Differences in behavior such as these can all be blamed on the West. Some kind of a revival movement should not come as a surprise.

In our own blundering way, and with the best of intentions, we have fostered these difficulties directly as well as indirectly. We have sent out to capitals of the Arab states hundreds of young Americans accompanied by wives and numerous children to serve as diplomats, foreign-aid personnel, information-service personnel, and purveyors of what used to be called technical knowledge but is now labelled know-how. Smiling ambassadors of good will, they have had to keep up their American standard of living for the sake of their families; they have taken over the best apartments, at enormous profit to the landlords; they drive the most expensive station wagons, keep their food in the most modern deepfreezes, and serve the most expensive drinks and hors d'oeuvres to hundreds of local inhabitants in an effort to spread kindness and understanding to our Middle Eastern friends—or at least until recently they did.

Because of financial inequalities, old-fashioned domestic arrangements, or other good reasons, many of the guests have failed to invite their hosts back. To many of the friendliest of Arabs, this inequality through unwitting display has caused embarrassment followed by resentment. In many instances our efforts at good will have backfired. Even worse, in some Middle Eastern capitals Americans have become so numerous that they have formed clubs, repeating one of the least popular aspects of colonialism.

The Arabs who have been able to ask us back, and those taken into our clubs as guests, are mostly the owners of vast tracts of land or men who for other reasons stand out among their fellows as reactionaries and plutocrats and serve as easy targets for Communist and Pan-Arab agitators. In times of flash revolutions, they are the men whose houses will be stoned and whose bodies will be found in the street.

With a few notable exceptions, our foreign-aid dealings have consisted of government-to-government loans or handouts, rather than business arrangements of mutual profit between private companies. Thus have we laid ourselves open to the charge of bolstering unpopular regimes.

Although the Russians have not been able to make themselves equally envied by conspicuous display, they have suffered more than us from their reputation of godlessness. While we are second-class People of the Book, they are out-and-out Unbelievers. This can, however, be temporarily condoned, because Nasser and other heads of state who have taken aid from them have done so in the belief that all's fair when dealing with Heathen; as the Arabs are brighter than the slow-witted Muscovites, the Arabs can outsmart them in the end. Several times I have heard this statement seriously made.

Nevertheless the Russians have appealed to the very class of men whose envy and hostility we excite, that of the impecunious intellectual who has lost his simple religious conviction, been educated in a Western or Western-inspired university, and been bitterly disappointed to find himself relegated to an underpaid subordinate government post. From the seat of his second-hand bicycle he views with baleful glances an American technician, with half his education, riding by in a splendid station wagon on his way to repair the air conditioner in an American emissary's rented villa. How, thinks the man on the bicycle, could Communism deal him a more bitter blow than this? When the stone-throwing starts in front of the hated embassy, he parks his bicycle in a safe spot and joins the mob.

All over Asia, from Taipei to Beirut, we have run into this kind of trouble during the last few years. Our degree of popularity can almost be predicted as a reciprocal of the number of our citizens that we send to each country. Never before in the history of mankind has the world's richest nation flooded poorer nations with hordes of emissaries bent on doing good but succeeding also in creating distaste and envy. This is a global problem which our government has to face; it is not my job to solve it here. For present purposes it is enough to say this has been happening in the Middle East as elsewhere.

Few people feel happy about being given something for nothing. In the Arab lands where bribes are as natural as handshakes, the bribes are given for services rendered. A handout, however, is viewed with suspicion, as being an advance payment for some unspecified and possibly embarrassing service in the future.

"If we take it," says the government official to himself, "what do they want in return? If they really want nothing back, then it must be tribute. They are acknowledging our natural superiority as Muslims and are paying off through weakness, as believers in inferior religions have always done."

Some Middle Eastern countries have refused foreign aid through pride, caution, or both. Others have refused it because the amount offered was less than that given a neighboring country. Our greatest success in Arab lands has been where we offered and received a clear *quid pro quo* without frills or nonsense.

The seven years that have passed since this book first appeared have been years of decline for the Western European powers in the Middle East, especially in the Arab countries. They have been also seven years of little wisdom for the United States, whose citizens seem singularly incapable of understanding and acting on basic differences in the cultures of the world, particularly in interpersonal relations and values. The Arabs have been following a traditional pattern of behavior all along the line, one easily predictable in its major lines of action. It is still predictable in the immediate future.

How we, as the strongest and richest nation living in our half of the House of War will act, should depend not only on what the leader of the other half of the House may do, and this is our principal obsession, but on our ability to think in terms of cultures other than our own—which change much more slowly underneath than they do on the surface—and to make and carry out long-term plans on this basis.

GLOSSARY

THIS APPENDIX is presented as a check list of the Arabic and other foreign terms, other than proper names, appearing in the text. In transliterating Arabic the standard Library of Congress system has been used, employing the following consonantal symbols: ' (hamza), b, t, th, j, ḥ, kh, d, dh, r, s, sh, ṣ, ḍ, ṭ, ẓ, ', gh, f, q, k, l, m, n, h, w, and y. Since their enunciation is rarely if ever perceptible, initial and final hamzas have been omitted. Macrons indicate vowels prolonged by alef, waw, and ya (ā, ī, ū). Except where it represents a final element of the root, as in qāḍī, terminal macrons have been omitted, as in ṣūfi. The inflectional endings -īyya and -īyyīn have in most cases been reduced to -iya and -iyin; for example, makhzaniya, Qaraqiyin.

For the reader unacquainted with Arabic pronunciation, a few simple rules will suffice to show how difficult this problem is. The consonants b, t, j, d, z, s, f, k, m, n, h, w, and y are pronounced more or less as in English; th as in "thing," dh like the soft th of "this." Kh is our old friend the ch of "loch"; r is trilled lightly; l approaches ly, as in German and Scandinavian languages. Q and the letters with dots under them are palatalized. For q, snap a k sound from the back of your oral cavity. For the others, throw out your chest, draw in your chin, draw your tongue into an arch to the rear of your oral cavity (as with q), and say slowly, enunciating each consonant distinctly, in as haughty a tone as possible: "Haw! Iz thot sso!" If successful, you may have achieved an ḥ, ẓ, ḍ, ṭ, and ṣ. Only three stumbling blocks remain: hamza, 'ain, and ghain. The hamza (') is a glottal stop, as in the Glasgow pronunciation of "wha' a lo' a li''le bo''les!" (What a lot of little bottles). The 'ain is a voiced fricative emerging from the region of the vocal cords. The ghain (gh) is an unvoiced sound made in the back of the palate, similar to but not identical with a French r. One more rule about consonants: where one of them is doubled, pronounce each of the two separately, like the two t's in flat-top. Vowels are as in Italian except where an approximation to a dialect sound has been attempted with e, o, or a diphthong.

Persian is relatively easy, with only three unfamiliar sounds. Of these kh and gh are as in Arabic, while jh is like the French j. Berber presents no further problems. Turkish is distinguished by a number of closed vowels which I personally cannot pronounce and have not tried to designate. Since accent, stress, and long vowels are not as important semantically in the other languages as in Arabic, I have not used macrons with them except in words taken from Arabic.

The following code indicates the language or group to which the word is thought to belong: A = Arabic; B = Berber; Bal. = Baluchi; I = Indic; K = Kurdish; M = Moroccan Arabic; P = Persian; Pu. = Pushtu; T = Turkish. All unmarked items are Arabic.

ʿāda (A), ʿādat (T)	customary law.
adhān	the Muslim call to prayer.
ʿadil, *pl.* ʿudūl	a legal clerk, notary public.
agha (T)	a title, originally military, now means anything from tribal chief to "Mister."
ahl al-futuwwa	People of Virtue, members of a special kind of religious association.
ʿaid . . .	*see* īd . . .
ait arbaʿin (B-A)	*see* asht arbaʿin.
ʿajemi oghlan (T-A)	"Foreign Boy"; a youthful slave from whose company the Janissaries and certain other Ottoman forces were recruited.
alay-beyi (T)	a high-ranking officer of sipahis.
amenokal (B)	the chief of a Tuareg confederation.
amghar (B)	leader, member of the tribal council.
ʿāmil	governor, agent.
amīn	official in a position of trust, as amīn aṣ-ṣandūq (treasurer); the executive officer of a Kabyle village.
amīr	prince, leader.
amīr ul-mu'minīn	Commander of the Faithful, a title given to the caliph.
ʿanaiya	truce, protection.
ankhan (K)	a Yezidi priest, fourth grade.
anṣār	*see* Naṣr.
ʿaqāl, *sing.* ʿāqil	lit. "brains"; leaders of a Kabyle village.
aʿrābi, *pl.* aʿrāb	Arabs of the desert, Bedawin.
al-ʿArab ud-Dār	lit. "House Arabs"; Arabs who summer near towns.
al-ʿArab ul-ʿArbā (ul-ʿAraba, ul-ʿArabiya)	pure, genuine Arabs.
al-ʿArab ul-Mustaʿriba	Arabs reputed to be remotely descended from arabized foreigners.
arbob (P)	landowner.
aṣḥāb	pl. of ṣāḥib; collectively, Companions of the Prophet.

asht arbaʿin (B-A)	the democratic council of the Berbers.
aṣilīn	Arabs considered to be of pure blood, i.e., descended from Qaḥtan or Ishmael.
ʿaskari (T ʿaskeri)	soldier.
bābi-ʿali (T-P-A)	the Sublime Porte, H.Q. of the Ottoman government.
badāwi, *pl.* al-badw	a nomad; *see* aʿrāb and bedawin.
baghala	a square-stemmed Arab sailing ship; lit. "a mule."
bairam (T)	*see* ʿīd ul-aḍḥā.
balam	an ʿIraqi river boat.
bandaka (P-old)	slaves, subjects.
baql	a retail shop, neighborhood grocery.
baqqāl	the proprietor of same.
baraka (M)	blessing; a supernatural quality said to be possessed by certain holy men.
bash-defterdar (T-P)	a high-ranking Ottoman finance officer.
bedawin (Eng.)	an incorrect but well-known plural of badāwi; it has become standard English.
beg, bek, bey (T)	originally, the chief of the oldest ulu in a Turkish tribe. Now variously used as a title.
beylerbeyi (T)	an officer of sipahis who was also a provincial governor and rated two horse tails.
bled el-makhzen (M)	territory controlled by the government.
bled eṣ-ṣibāʿ (M)	territory not controlled by the government; the Land of Insolence.
būm	a type of double-ended Arab sailing ship.
caliph (Eng.)	*see* khalīfa.
chapao (Bal.)	a raid.
chavush (T)	lit. "herald"; one of a corps of Ottoman officials who served as ushers, messengers, and guards.
cheri-bashi (T)	a sipahi officer of the second grade.
chomur (T)	a partly or wholly sedentary Turkoman.
chorbaji (T)	the commanding officer of an orta of Janissaries.
chorva (T)	a fully nomadic Turkoman.
chuddar (P)	a woman's cloak and veil; a tent.
dāhir (M)	*see* ẓāhir.
dār ul-ḥarb	the House of War; countries ruled by non-Muslims.
dār ul-islām	the House of Peace; countries ruled by Muslims.
darwish (P)	a member of a Ṣūfi brotherhood.
dehgan (P-old)	a Sassanian landowner's agent.
dehkan (P)	a Persian-speaking villager in Pakistani, Baluchistan.
dehwar (P)	*see* dehkan.
dervish (Eng.-P)	*see* darwish.
dhikr	the private ritual formula of a Ṣūfi brotherhood.
dhow (Swahili-Eng.)	a collective term for Arab sailing vessels.

dīnār (A-Greek)	a gold coin of one mithqāl's weight.
dirham (A-Greek)	a silver coin, originally shaped like a date stone.
divan (P-A)	*see* diwān.
diwān	a court; in S. 'Iraq, a reed building used as a shaikh's court and guest house.
diwān al-maẓālim	a supreme court seated in the entourage of a caliph.
durbar (P) (I)?	the Afghan royal council.
effendi (T)	a title granted to certain civilian officials.
emīn (T-A)	a commissioner; as of the city, mint, kitchen, etc.
eyālet (T)	the province of a governor rating three horse tails.
faqih, *pl.* fuquhā	a cleric; prayer leader and schoolmaster.
faqīr, *pl.* fuqarā	a poor man; technically one who owns too little property to require payment of the zakā.
fātiḥa	the opening sūra of the Qur'ān.
fatwa	a judicial decision.
fellaḥ, *pl.* fellaḥīn	a farmer, peasant.
funduq	an inn, serving many purposes.
garmsir (P)	winter pasture.
gavband (P)	a village ox owner.
gedikli (T)	one of a class of privileged female slaves in the imperial Ottoman harem.
ḥabūs (M)	an endowed religious foundation; a trust fund.
ḥadīth	a tradition concerning the Prophet.
hajj	the pilgrimage to Mekka, a pilgrim.
hajji	a pilgrim to Mekka.
ḥākim	judge, governor, ruler, umpire; in al-Yemen a provincial judge.
ḥāl	a state or condition, esp. that of ecstasy.
ḥalāl	ritually permissible.
ḥammām	a steam bath.
ḥanafi	one of the four principal schools of sunni law.
ḥanbali	another one of the four principal schools of sunni law.
haoma (P-old)	a ritual drink of the ancient Persians.
ḥarām	ritually forbidden.
ḥarātīn (properly Ḥarāthīn)	Negroid agricultural serfs of the Sahara.
hijra	Muḥammad's strategic withdrawal from Mekka to al-Madīna.
ḥikma	the "wisdom" inherent in the Prophet, believed to have given his words and actions, apart from revelation, the sanction of divine authority.

ḥosa ('Iraq, coll.)?	a chantey-dance performed by workmen to restore energy.
ḥurm	a sacred enclosure.
ibn ul-'amm	the father's brother's son; preferred mate for a young Arab lady.
ich oghlan (T)	lit. "Inside Boy"; a page.
'īd eṣ-ṣaghīr	*see* 'id ul-fiṭr.
'īd ul-aḍḥā	"the feast of sacrifice"; the feast of the tenth day of the month of pilgrimage.
'īd ul-fiṭr	"festival of fast-breaking"; end of Ramaḍān.
'īd ul-kabīr	*see* 'īd ul-aḍḥā.
Ihaggaren (B)	Tuareg nobles.
iḥrām	the special clothing worn by a male pilgrim to Mekka.
ījāza	a diploma permitting the holder to teach a specified subject.
ikhemesen (ikhummasen) (B-A)	agricultural laborers receiving one fifth of the cereal crop harvested.
ikhwān	brethren, as of a Ṣūfi brotherhood.
ilbegi (P-T)	deputy chief of the Bakhtiari.
ilkhani (P-T)	chief of the Bakhtiari.
imām	prayer leader, caliph, ruler of al-Yemen.
imazilen (B)	craftsmen, including blacksmiths, whose occupations are considered debased.
imghad (B)	Tuareg vassals.
īqāl (coll. 'aghāl)	a headband used to hold down the kufiya.
irajenaten (B)	half-noble Tuareg tribesmen.
iyāla	*see* eyālet.
izref (B)	*see* qanūn.
jamā'a (B-A)	a Berber council.
jangal (P)	forest, esp. that on the Caspian shore of Iran.
jann	*see* jinni.
jast (I)	a Kafiri elder.
jazīya (M)	*see* jizya.
jellaba (M)	a hooded, sleeved, pull-over cloak worn in North Africa.
jihād	holy war.
jinni, *pl.* jann, jinn, or jnūn	one of a class of supernatural beings.
jirga (Pu.)	the democratic council of the Pathans.
jizya	tribute, poll tax.
ka'ba	the sacred building in the center of the sacred enclosure in Mekka; its focal point, the Black Stone, serves as the geographical pole of Islam.
kāhin	shaman, soothsayer.

kakhya (T-P)	a president of the council in Egypt.
kakhya-bey (T-P-T)	a general lieutenant of the Ottoman Grand Vizir.
katkhodā (P)	the landowner's resident agent in a village.
kaum (Bal.-A)	camp, a unit of population.
kaval (K)	a third-grade Yezidi priest, executive officer of a shaikh.
ketchudā (katkhodā)	a tribal officer among the Bakhtiari.
khalīfa	the authoritative head of the Muslim community; the Prophet's successor.
khamsīn	a "fifty-day" summer wind.
khān (T)	an inn.
khan (T)	chief of a tribal confederation, an emperor.
khaṣṣ (T-A?)	a landed estate yielding at least 100,000 pieces of silver each year.
khawārij	Kharijites, a heterodox Muslim sect.
khawaṣṣ	the members of the inner circle of the Sanūsi.
khlī (M)	pickled chopped beef.
khoja (T)	a Muslim cleric.
koḥl	properly kuḥl, powdered antimony.
kufiya	a headcloth worn by Arabs to keep out dust.
kuttāb	*see* maktab.
lawash, lavash (P)	thin, unleavened bread.
liwā	lit. "flag, standard"; a province.
mabeyn (mabain) (T-A)	that part of an Ottoman sultan's palace between the inner courts and the harem.
madrasa	a college, in the English sense.
makhzani, *pl.* makhzaniya (M)	a government policeman.
maks	a market tax.
maktab	an elementary religious school.
māliki	one of the four principal schools of Sunni law.
mʿallim	*see* muʿallim.
manāt	a female idol in the pre-Islamic of Kaʿba.
marabout (Fr.-A)	*see* murabiṭ.
mashā	land owned by a village in common.
matrūka	land shared without allotment.
meḥalla	a military camp.
millaḥ (M)	a Jewish quarter.
mir (P-A)	a prince, leader, descendant of the Prophet.
mīri	state-owned land, leased on a long-term basis.
miskīn, *pl.* masākīn	a poor person, totally without property.
mithqāl	a measure of weight in gold; a coin of the same weight.
most (P)	yoghurt; a milk solid formed by bacterial action.
mu'adhdhin	the person who calls the Muslim faithful to prayer.
muʿallim, *pl.* muʿallimīn	a master craftsman.

mudd — a dry measure.
muezzin (Fr.-T-A) — *see* muʿadhdhin.
mufti — a lawyer who delivers a legal sentence; a qualified jurist.
muḥtasib — market provost, in charge of guilds.
mujtahid — a high-ranking Shīʿa cleric, comparable to a Grand Mufti.
mukhṭār — mayor of a village, ward leader of a city.
mulk — private land held in fee simple.
mulla (P-A) — a Muslim cleric, schoolmaster.
multazim — a provincial tax-farmer; in Egypt, landowner.
muntasibīn — illiterate lay members of the Sanūsi sect.
muqaddam — official in charge of a public building; a college porter.
murabiṭ — monk, member of a brotherhood living in a retreat; the tomb of such a person.
musakhkharīn — a special corps of messengers serving the sultans of Morocco.
musallam — a class of Ottoman soldiers granted tax-free lands.
mustasharīn — the council of notables assisting one of the two state ministers of al-Yemen.
mutafarriqa — one of several ojaqs recruited from the ʿAjemi Oghlans to form a special bodyguard for the Ottoman sultan.
mustaṣarrif — the governor of a liwā or province, in ʿIraq.

nā'ib — a provincial governor in Afghanistan.
nākhudā (A-P) — the captain of a ship.
naṣr, *pl.* anṣār — the men of al-Madīna who supported Muḥammad.
nāẓir — the executive officer of a waqf or ḥabūs.
nishanji (T) — an Ottoman official who traced the sultan's monogram on official documents.

ojaq (T) — lit. "hearth"; a corps.
orta (T) — lit. "center"; a company of soldiers, forming a subdivision of an ojaq.

paklava (?) — a Graeco-Turkish pastry.
pasha (T-P) — a Turkish title of high rank; mayor of a North African city.
pir (P) — old man, saint, head of a religious brotherhood.
pushtin (P) — a sheepskin coat with the wool inside.

qaḍā (T-A) — a district forming part of a sanjak.
qāḍī — a judge.
qāḍī ul-quyūḍ — chief judge of Morocco.

qadin (T) — lit. "woman"; a first-class consort of an Ottoman sultan after the abolition of royal marriage.

qā'id (kaid) (M) — a tribal chief.

qa'im-maqām (T-A) — Ottoman agha's lieutenant; in ʿIraq, governor of a subprovince.

qanat (P-?) — an irrigation tunnel.

qanūn — the unwritten law code of the Berbers (izref); a decree issued by an Ottoman sultan.

al-qaṣba (M) — the citadel or fortified refuge of a city; the old Muslim quarter of a modern mixed city.

qaṣr, *pl.* qṣār (M) — a fortress, similar to a tighremt.

qibla — the direction of Mekka from any given point, which a Muslim faces in prayer.

qiyās — analogy, a tool in religious law making.

Qur'ān — the Muslim scripture.

qurban (T) — *see* īd ul-aḍḥā.

rāʿi, *pl.* ruʿā'a — shepherds, pastoralists without camels.

ra'īs baladiya — headman of a village (Egypt) mayor of a town (ʿIraq).

ramaḍān — the month of fasting.

ribāṭ — a monastic retreat.

ṣāḥib, *pl.* aṣḥāb — companion, friend (*see* aṣḥāb).

ṣāḥib al-muḥtasib — the market provost's assistant.

ṣalā — prayer.

sanbūq — a small square-stemmed sailing vessel, esp. in the Red Sea.

ṣaniʿ, *pl.* ṣunnaʿ — debased artisans, blacksmiths.

sanjaq (T) — lit. "a standard"; a province, equivalent to Arabic liwā.

sardsir (P) — summer pasture.

ṣarrāf — money-changer.

ṣaum — fasting.

ṣayyād, *sing.* ṣā'id — hunter, fowler, esp. a group living on the banks of the lower Helmand.

sayyid, *pl.* asyād (among others) — a descendant of the Prophet through Fāṭima and ʿAlī. *See also* sharīf, mir.

serang (P) — mate on a sailing vessel.

sfenj (M) — lit. "sponge"; a doughnut.

shāfiʿi — one of the four principal schools of Sunni law.

shaft (T) — a Turkoman camping unit, five to ten of which form a tribe.

shagird (T) — a "pupil"; a newly arrived slave girl in the Ottoman harem.

shahāda — testimony, the first pillar of Islam.

shahīd — a village lawyer in Egypt.

shahnama (P) — Firdusi's epic poem, the *Book of Kings*.

shaikh	a leader, esp. of a tribe, or of a religious brotherhood.
shaikh al-balad	village headman, esp. in Egypt.
shaikh ul-islām	the chief qāḍī of a capital city.
shaikhāt	a female musical entertainer.
sharīʿa	Muslim law.
sharīf, *pl.* ashraf, shorfa (M)	a descendant of the Prophet.
sharqi (M)	a hot summer wind from the east.
shaush (M-T)	an usher; *see* chavush.
Shīʿa	the followers of ʿAlī, who reject the first three caliphs.
sipahi (spahi, sepoy)	a fief-holding Ottoman cavalryman.
sirdar (Bal.-?)	leader of a kaum or camp.
ṣof (B-A)	a political alliance joining segments of different villages.
subashi (T)	the executive officer of the qāḍī of a sanjaq.
ṣūfi	lit. "woolly"; a mystic, a member of a religious brotherhood.
ṣundūq	a large box; treasury.
sunna	the tradition; "a system of social and legal usages" —Gibb, *Mohammedanism* (1949), p. 73.
ṣunnāʿ	*see* ṣaniʿ.
sunni	one of the large sect of Muslims who acknowledge the first four caliphs, accept the six "authentic" books of tradition, and belong to any of the four accepted schools of jurisprudence.
sūq	a market.
sūra	a chapter, esp. of the Qur'ān.
ta'ifa (K-A)	a Kurdish clan.
tajik (P)?	a Persian villager living in Soviet or Afghan territory.
tājir	a wholesale merchant or trader.
ṭamen, *pl.* ṭemman (B-A)	assistant to the amīn of a Kabyle village; policeman, ward leader.
tapu (K?)	state-owned land which must be registered; descendants of the original recipient are guaranteed tenure.
taqiya	dissimulation; concealing one's true religious affiliation among strangers.
ṭarīqa	lit. "a way"; the special set of beliefs of a religious brotherhood.
tifinagh (B)	the Tuareg alphabet.
tighremt (B)	a castle granary of the Beraber or Shluḥ.
timar (T?)	a landed estate yielding less than 20,000 pieces of silver each year.
tira (K?)	a small Kurdish kinship group, lineage.

ṭugh (T)	a horse's (or yak's) tail, used as a symbol of rank.
tumandar (Bal.)	head of a tribal council and war leader.
ʿulamā	a committee of religious scholars located in a given Islamic capital city.
ulu (T)	a social unit; originally, the group of people who winter together.
ʿurf	the Persian common law code.
ʿūrfa (ʿIraq)	the poet who leads a ḥosa.
vezir, vizir (T-A)	*see* wazīr.
vilayet (T-A)	an Ottoman province.
wādi (M wed, Fr. oued)	a river, dry stream bed, valley.
walāya	*see* vilayet.
wālī	governor of a walāya or vilayet.
waqf	*see* ḥabūs.
waṣiya	seignoral land in Egypt, reserved for the multazim.
wazīr	a minister of state.
yaum an-naḥr	lit. "day of sacrifice"; *see* ʿid ul-aḍḥā.
ẓāhir (M)	a proclamation, decree.
zakā	alms, the third pillar of Islam.
zārūq	a small double-ended ship.
zawiya	the shrine serving as headquarters and school for a religious brotherhood.
ziʿāmet (T-A)	an Ottoman fief.
zikr	*see* dhikr.
zīna (M)	property consisting of fixed installations within buildings or enclosures.
zurkhané (P)	a gymnasium.
zuwwāq (M)	plaster carvers.

BIBLIOGRAPHY

Baṭṭūṭa, Ibn. *Travels in Asia and Africa, 1325-1354.* Translated by H. A. R. Gibb. New York, 1929.

Bel, Alfred. *La Religion musulmane en Berberie.* Vol. I. Paris, 1938.

Benhazera, Maurice. *Six mois chez les Touaregs du Ahaggar.* Algiers, 1911.

Birge, John Kingsley. *The Beḳtashi Order of Dervishes.* London, 1937.

Bishop, Mrs. Isabella (Bird). *Journeys in Persia and Kurdistan.* London, 1891.

Bissuel, H. *Les Touaregs de l'Ouest.* Algiers, 1888.

Blake, Robert P., and Frye, Richard N. *"History of the Nation of the Archers,* by Grigor of Akanc," *Harvard Journal of Asiatic Studies,* XII, Nos. 3, 4 (1949), 269-399 [1-131].

Blunt, Lady Anne. *Bedouin Tribes of the Euphrates.* New York, 1896.

Boas, Franz. *The Social Organization and the Secret Societies of the Kwaḳiutl Indians.* Report of the Smithsonian Institute. Washington, D.C., 1895.

Bode, Baron C. A. de. "On the Yamud and Gokland Tribes of Turkomania," *Journal of the Ethnological Society of London,* I (Edinburgh, 1848), 60-78.

Bourilly, Joseph. *Eléments de l'ethnographie marocaine,* Paris, 1932.

Boville, E. W. *Caravans of the Old Sahara.* London, 1933.

Bowen, Richard LeB., Jr. "Pearl Fisheries of the Persian Gulf," *The Middle East Journal,* V, No. 2 (1951), 161-180.

Brockelmann, Carl. *History of the Islamic Peoples.* Translated from the German by Joel Carmichael and Moshe Pearlmann. New York, 1947.

Browne, Edward G. *A Year amongst the Persians, 1887-1888.* London, 1950.

Brunel, René. *Essai sur la confrérie religieuse des 'Aissaoua au Maroc.* Paris, 1926.

Burton, Sir Richard. *Personal Narrative of a Pilgrimage to Al-Madinah and Meccah.* London, 1893. 2 vols.

Cameron, George C. *History of Early Iran.* Chicago, 1936.

———. *The Persepolis Treasury Tablets.* University of Chicago Oriental Institute Publications. Vol. LXV. Chicago, 1948.

Cella, Paolo della. *Narrative of an Expedition from Tripoli in Barbary to the Western Frontier of Egypt.* Translated by Anthony Aufrère. London, 1822.

Charles, Henri. *Les Tribus moutonnières du Moyen Euphrate.* Beirut, 1939.

Cline, Walter. *Notes on the People of Siwah and el Garah in the Libyan Desert.* General Series in Anthropology, No. 4. Menasha, Wisconsin, 1936.

Coon, Carleton S. *Cave Exploration in Iran, 1949.* Museum Monographs. Philadelphia, 1951.

———. *Flesh of the Wild Ox.* New York, 1932.

———. *Measuring Ethiopia and Flight into Arabia.* Boston, 1935.

———. "North Africa," in Ralph Linton, ed., *Most of the World*. New York, 1949. Pp. 405-461.

———. *The Races of Europe*. New York, 1939.

———, ed. *A Reader in General Anthropology*. New York, 1948.

———. *Southern Arabia, a Problem for the Future*. Peabody Museum Papers. XX. Cambridge, Massachusetts, 1943.

———. *Tribes of the Rif*. Harvard African Studies, Peabody Museum. Vol. IX. Cambridge, Massachusetts, 1931.

Cooper, Merian C. and Schoedsack, Ernest B. *Grass*. New York, 1925.

Davies, C. Collin. *The Problem of the Northwest Frontier, 1890-1908*. Cambridge, England, 1932.

Dennett, Daniel C., Jr. *Conversion and the Poll Tax in Early Islam*. Harvard Historical Monographs. Vol. XXII. Cambridge, Massachusetts, 1950.

Depont, Octave, and Coppolani, Xavier. *Les Confréries religieuses musulmanes*. Algiers, 1897.

Despois, Jean. *L'Afrique du Nord*. Vol. I. Paris, 1949.

———. *Le Djebel Nefousa*. Paris, 1935.

Dickson, Harold R. P. *The Arab of the Desert*. London, 1949.

Dougherty, R. P. *The Sealand of Ancient Arabia*. Yale Oriental Series, *Researches*. Vol. XIX. New Haven, 1932.

Duveyrier, Henri. *Les Touaregs du Nord*. Paris, 1864.

Elphinstone, Mountstuart. *An Account of the Kingdom of Caubul and Its Dependencies*. London, 1825.

Encyclopaedia of Islam. London and Leyden, 1913-38.

Erman, Adolf. *Aegypten und aegyptisches Leben im Altertum*. Translated by Hermann Ranke. Tübingen, 1923.

———. *Life in Ancient Egypt*. London, 1894.

Evans-Pritchard, E. E. *The Sanūsi of Cyrenaica*. Oxford, 1949.

Faris, Nabih Amin, ed. *The Arab Heritage*. Princeton, 1949.

Ferrier, J. P. *Caravan Journeys and Wanderings in Persia, Afghanistan, Turkistan, and Beloochistan*. London, 1856.

Field, Henry, and Glubb, J. B. *The Yezidis, Salubba, and Other Tribes of Iraq and Adjacent Regions*. General Series in Anthropology, No. 10. Menasha, Wisconsin, 1943.

Fisher, W. B. *The Middle East, a Physical, Social, and Regional Geography*. London, 1950.

Fraser-Tytler, W. K. *Afghanistan*. London, 1950.

Gautier, E. F. *Le Passé de l'Afrique du Nord*. Paris, 1942.

———. *Sahara, the Great Desert*. Translated by Dorothy Ford Mayhew. New York, 1935.

Gibb, H. A. R. *Mohammedanism*. London, 1949.

———, and Bowen, Harold. *Islamic Society and the West: Islamic Society in the Eighteenth Century*. Vol. I, Pt. 1. London, 1950.

Haas, William S. "The Zikr of the Raḥmaniya Order, a Psycho-physiological Analysis," *The Moslem World*, XXXIII, No. 1 (January, 1943).

Hanoteau, Adolphe, and Letourneux, A. *La Kabylie et les coutumes kabyles*. Paris, 1893; 2d ed. 3 vols. See *Wysner, Glora May,* for translation.

Harris, Walter B. *A Journey Through the Yemen*. London, 1893.

———. *Tafilelt.* London, 1895.
Hayden, L. J. "Living Standards in Rural Iran," *The Middle East Journal,* III, No. 2 (1949), 140-150.
Herodotus, *Historia.* Translated by George Rawlinson. Everyman's Library. London, 1910. 2 vols.
Hitti, Philip. *The Arabs, a Short History.* Princeton, 1943.
———. *History of the Arabs.* London, 1937, 4th ed., 1949.
———. *History of Syria.* New York, 1951.
Holme, H. C. "Palestine," in *The Middle East, a Political and Economic Survey.* London and New York, 1950.
Hörhager, Herbert. *Die Volkstumsgrundlagen der indischen Nordwest-Grenz Provinz.* Heidelberg, Magdeburg, and Berlin, 1943.
Hourani, A. H. "Syria and Lebanon," in *The Middle East, a Political and Economic Survey.*
Hourani, George F. *Arab Seafaring in the Indian Ocean.* Princeton Oriental Studies. Vol. XIII. Princeton, 1951.
Huart, Clement. *L'Evolution de l'humanité: La Perse antique.* Vol. XXV. Paris, 1925.
Hughes, Thomas Patrick. *Dictionary of Islam.* London, 1885.
Issawi, Charles. *An Arab Philosophy of History: Selections from the* Prolegomena *of Ibn Khaldun of Tunis (1332-1406).* London, 1950.
Jochelson, Waldemar. *Peoples of Asiatic Russia.* New York, 1928.
Koller, P. Ange. *Essai sur l'esprit du Berbère marocain.* Fribourg, 1949.
Lambton, A. K. S. "Iran," in *The Middle East, a Political and Economic Survey.*
Lammens, Henri. *Islam, Beliefs and Institutions.* Translated from the French by T. Denison Ross. London, 1929.
Lane, Edward William. *The Manners and Customs of the Modern Egyptians.* Everyman's Library. New York, n.d.
Laoust, E. *L'Habitation chez les transhumants du Maroc Central.* Paris, 1936.
Lattimore, Owen. *The Desert Road to Turkestan.* Boston, 1929.
Layard, Sir Austen Henry. *Early Adventures in Persia, Susiana, and Babylonia.* London, 1887. 2 vols.
Leach, E. R. *Social and Economic Organization of the Rowanduz Kurds.* London School of Economics and Political Science Monographs on Social Anthropology, No. 3. London, 1940.
Le Tourneau, Robert. *La Villa de Fès avant le Protectorat.* Casablanca, 1949.
———, Paye, L., and Guyot, R. "La Corporation des tanneurs et l'industrie de la tannerie à Fès," *Hesperis,* XXI (1935), 167-240, fasc. i-ii.
Lewis, Bernard. *The Arabs in History.* London, 1950.
Lhote, Henri. *Les Touaregs du Hoggar.* Paris, 1944.
Lloyd, Seton. "Iraq," in *The Middle East, a Political and Economic Survey.*
Lucas, A. *Ancient Egyptian Materials and Industries.* London, 1934; 2d ed.
Mackay, Ernest. *The Indus Civilization.* London, 1935.
Marvin, Charles. *Merv, or the Man-stealing Turcomans.* London, 1881.
Meakin, Budgett. *The Land of the Moors.* London, 1901.
———. *The Moorish Empire.* London, 1899.
———. *The Moors.* London, 1902.
Meissner, Bruno. *Babylonien und Assyrien.* Vol. I. Heidelberg, 1920.

Miles, S. B. *Countries and Tribes of the Persian Gulf*. London, 1919. 2 vols.

Mirza, Youel. *Stripling*. New York, 1940.

Montagne, Robert. *Les Berbères et le makhzen dans le sud du Maroc*. Paris, 1930.

———. *La Civilisation du désert*. Paris, 1947.

Morgenstierne, Georg. *Report on a Linguistic Mission to Afghanistan*. Institut für Sammenlignende Kulturforskning. Vol. I, Serie C-1-2. Oslo, 1926.

Morier, James J. *Hajji Baba of Isfahan*. Random House de Luxe Edition. New York, 1937.

Muir, Sir William. *The Caliphate*. Revised by T. H. Weir. Edinburgh, 1924.

———. *The Life of Mohammad*. Revised by T. H. Weir. Edinburgh, 1923.

Musil, Alois. *Manners and Customs of the Rwala Bedouins*. Monographs of the American Geographical Society, No. 6. New York, 1928.

Nielson, Ditlef, ed. *Handbuch der altarabischen Altertumskunde*. Vol. I. Copenhagen, 1927.

O'Donovan, Edmond. *The Merv Oasis*. New York, 1883. 2 vols.

Oliver, Douglas. *The Horomorun Concepts of Southern Bougainville*. Peabody Museum Papers. XX. Cambridge, Massachusetts, 1943. 50-65.

Opler, Morris, and Singh, Rudra Datt. "The Division of Labor in an Indian Village," in Carleton Coon, ed., *A Reader in General Anthropology*, pp. 464-495, chap. 17.

Oppenheim, Max Freiherr von. *Die Beduinen*. Leipzig, 1939-43. 2 vols.

Pellow, Thomas. *The Adventures of Thomas Pellow of Penrhyn, Mariner*. Edited by Dr. Robert Brown. London, 1890.

Philby, St. John B. *Arabia*. New York, 1930.

———. *Arabian Days*. London, 1948.

———. *The Empty Quarter*. London, 1933.

Pottinger, Henry. *Travels in Beloochistan and Sinde*. London, 1816.

Prawdin, Michael. *The Mongol Empire, Its Rise and Legacy*. Translated from the German by Eden and Cedar Paul. New York, 1940.

Ricard, Prosper. "Les Métiers manuels à Fès," *Hesperis*, IV (1924), 205-224.

Riley, Captain J. *The Authentic Narrative of the Loss of the American Brig* Commerce. New York, 1918.

Robertson, Sir George. "Kafiristan," *Encyclopaedia Britannica*, 13th ed. Vol. XV.

———. *The Kafirs of the Hindu Kush*. London, 1896.

Rodd, Francis R. *People of the Veil*. London, 1926.

Schorger, William D. "The Caravan Trails of North Africa." Senior honors thesis in anthropology. Peabody Museum Library, Harvard University, 1947.

Scott, Hugh. *In the High Yemen*. London, 1942; revised ed., 1947.

Şenyürek, Muzaffer Suleiman. *Fossil Man in Tangier*. Peabody Museum Papers. Vol. XVI, No. 3. Cambridge, Massachusetts, 1940.

Speiser, Ephraim A. *Mesopotamian Origins*. Philadelphia, 1930.

Spillmann, Georges. *Les Ait Atta du Sahara*. Rabat, 1936.

Stuhlmann, Franz. *Ein Kulturgeschichtlicher Ausflug im Aures*. Hamburg, 1912.

———. *Die Mazigh-volker*. Hamburg, 1914.

Sykes, Sir Percy. *A History of Persia.* Oxford, 1922.

"The Tale of the Shipwrecked Sailor," *Petersburg Papyrus* 1115.

Tannous, Afif I. "The Arab Village Community in the Middle East," *Smithsonian Report for 1943,* Pub. 3760 (Washington, D.C., 1944), pp. 523-544.

———. "Emigration, a Force of Social Change in an Arab Village," *Rural Sociology,* VII (1942), 62-74.

———. "Land Tenure in the Middle East," *Foreign Agriculture,* Office of Agricultural Relations, VII, No. 8 (August, 1943), 170-177.

Terrasse, Henri. *Histoire du Maroc.* Casablanca, 1949-50. 2 vols.

Tharaud, Jerome and Jean. *Fèz ou les bourgeois de l'Islam.* Paris, 1930.

———. *Marrakesh ou les seigneurs de l'Atlas.* Paris, 1920.

Thomas, Bertram. *Alarms and Excursions in Arabia.* London, 1931.

Tobler, A. J. *Excavations at Tepe Gawra.* Museum Monographs. Vol. II, Levels ix-xx. Philadelphia, 1950.

Tweedy, Owen. "Arabia and Egypt," in *The Middle East, a Political and Economic Survey.*

Ungnad, Arthur. *Zeitschrift für aegyptische Sprache.* Bd. 43 (1906), pp. 161-162.

Vida, Giorgio Levi della. "Pre-Islamic Arabia," in N. A. Faris, ed., *The Arab Heritage.*

Villiers, Alan. "Some Aspects of the Arab Dhow Trade," *The Middle East Journal,* II, No. 4 (October, 1947), 399-416.

———. *Sons of Sinbad.* New York, 1940.

Wilber, Donald L. *Iran, Past and Present.* Princeton, 1948.

Wilson, Sir Arnold. *The Persian Gulf.* London, 1928.

Wilson, S. G. *Persian Life and Customs.* New York, 1895.

Woolley, C. L. *Ur Excavations.* London and Philadelphia, 1934.

Wysner, Glora May. *The Kabyle People.* New York, 1945.

ADDENDUM TO BIBLIOGRAPHY

Allen, H. B. *Rural Education and Welfare in the Middle East,* London, 1946.

Ammar, Abbas M. *The People of Sharqiya,* Cairo, 1944, 2 vols.

———. *A Demographic Study of an Egyptian Province,* (Sharqiya) London, 1948.

Ammar, Hamed. *Growing Up In An Egyptian Village,* New York, 1954.

Anderson, J. N. D. *Recent Developments in Sharia Law,* The Muslim World, Vols. 40 1950—thru Vol. 42 1952.

Antonius, George. *The Arab Awakening,* Philadelphia, 1939.

Arkell, A. J. *The History of the Sudan up to 1821,* London, 1955.

Atlantic Monthly, Middle East Supplement, October 1956.

Ayrout, Henry Habib. *The Fellaheen,* Cairo, 1945.

Barth, F., *Principles of Social Organization in Southern Kurdistan,* Oslo, 1953.

Bent, Theodore & Mrs. *Southern Arabia,* London, 1900.

Birge, J. K. *A Guide to Turkish Area Study,* Washington, 1949.

Blackman, Winifred. *The Fellahin of Upper Egypt,* London, 1927.

Bonné, Alfred. *State and Economics in the Middle East,* London, 1948.

Boucheman, A. de. *Une Petite Cité Caravanière,* Sukne, Damascus, 1937.

Bowen, Richard LeB. *Arab Dhows of Eastern Arabia,* The American Neptune, IX 1949, pp. 87–132.
———. *The Dhow Sailor,* The American Neptune, XI 1951, pp. 161–202.
———. *Marine Industries of Eastern Arabia,* Geog. Rev. XLI 1951, pp. 384–400.
———. *Primitive Watercraft of Arabia,* The American Neptune, XII 1952, pp. 186–229.
Bray, Denys de S. *The Life History of a Brahui,* London, 1913.
———. *Ethnographic Survey of Baluchistan,* Bombay, 1913. 2 vols.
Bushakra, Amy. *I Married an Arab,* New York, 1951.
Caroe, Sir Olaf K. *Soviet Empire: The Turks of Central Asia and Stalinism,* London, 1953.
Charles, H. *Tribus Moutonnières du Moyen Euphrate,* Damascus, 1939.
Churchill, C. *The City of Beirut,* Beirut, 1954.
Cleland, Wendell. *The Population Problem in Egypt,* Lancaster, Pa., 1936.
Clerget, Marcel. *Le Caire,* Cairo, 1934.
Cooke, H. V. *Challenge and Response in the Middle East,* New York, 1952.
Corry, C. E. *The Blood Feud,* London, 1937.
Daghestani, K. *La Famille Musulmane Contemporaine en Syrie,* Paris, 1932.
Dames, M. L. *The Baloch Race.* London, 1904.
Donaldson, Bess A. *The Wild Rue,* London, 1938.
Donaldson, D. M. *The Shi'ite Religion,* London, 1933.
Doughty, C. M. *Travels in Arabia Deserta,* London, 1928.
El-'ali, Salih Ahmad. *Social and Economic Organization of Basra,* (in Arabic) Baghdad, 1953.
El-Hakin, Tewfik. *Maze of Justice,* Harvard Press, London, 1947.
Ellis, H. B. *Heritage of the Desert,* New York, 1956.
Elwell-Sutton, L. P. *Modern Iran,* London, 1941.
———. *A Guide to Iranian Area Study,* Ann Arbor, 1952.
Ethnographic Survey of India, *Anthropometric Data from Baluchistan,* Calcutta, 1908.
Faroughy, Abbas. *Introducing Yemen,* New York, 1947.
———. *The Bahrain Islands,* New York, 1951.
Frye, Richard N. *Iran,* New York, 1953.
Gaudefroy-Demonbynes, Maurice. *Muslim Institutions,* Allen and Unwin, London, 1950.
Ghirshman, R. *Iran, from the Earliest Times to the Islamic Conquest,* Penguin, London, 1954.
Glubb, J. B. *The Story of the Arab Legion,* London, 1948.
Granqvist, Hilma. *Birth and Childhood Among the Arabs,* Helsinki, 1947.
———. *Child Problems Among the Arabs,* Helsinki, 1951.
Groseclose, Elgin. *Introduction to Iran,* New York, 1947.
Guillaume, Alfred. *Islam,* Pelican, 1955.
Gulick, John. *Social Structure and Culture Change in a Lebanese Village,* New York, 1955.
Hart, David M. *An Ethnographic Survey of the Riffian Tribe of Aith Wuryaghil,* Tamuda, vol. 2, #1, 1954, pp. 51–86.
Hass, W. S. *Iran,* New York, 1946.

Hedgecock, S. E. (*Fulanain*) *The Marsh Arab: Hajji Rikkan,* Philadelphia, 1928.
Hourani, A. H. *Syria and Lebanon,* London, 1946.
———. *Minorities in the Arab World,* London, 1947.
Hudson, Alfred E. *Kazak Social Structure,* New Haven, 1938.
Hugronje, C. Snouck, *Mekka,* The Hague, 1888-89.
Hurewitz, J. C. *Middle East Dilemmas,* New York, 1953.
Hussein, Taha. *An Egyptian Childhood,* London, 1932.
Irgun, Orfa. *The Story of a Turkish Family,* New York, 1950.
Issawi, Charles. *Egypt at Midcentury,* London, 1954.
Khadduri, Majid. *Independent Iraq,* London, 1951.
———. Editor, *Jordan,* HRAF 26, New Haven, 1956.
Kkayyat, Jafar. *The Iraqi Village* (In Arabic) Beirut, 1950.
Kirk, George E. *A Short History of the Middle East,* New York, 1949. New Edition, London, 1956.
Krader, Laurence. *Handbook of Central Asia,* Subcontractor's Monograph, HRAF #49, 3 vols., New Haven, 1956.
Lampton, A. K. S. *Landlord & Peasant in Persia,* New York, 1953.
Laqueur, W. Z. *Communism and Nationalism in the Middle East,* New York, 1956.
Latron, Andre. *La Vie Rurale en Syrie et au Liban,* Beirut, 1936.
Lawrence, T. E. *Seven Pillars of Wisdom,* New York, 1936.
Lenczowski, George. *The Middle East in World Affairs,* Ithaca, 1952.
Levy, Ruben. *Sociology of Islam,* London, 1930–33, Revised 1957.
Lewis, G. L. *Turkey,* New York, 1955.
Makal, Mahmut. *A Village on Anatolia,* London, 1953.
Mashayekhi, M. B., and Guy S. Hayes. *Some Demographic and Health Characteristics of 173 Villages in a Rural Area of Iran,* New York, 1952.
Masse, Henri. *Croyances et Coutumes Persanes,* Paris, 1938.
Mehdevi, Anne S. *Persian Adventure,* New York, 1953.
Miner, Horace. *The Primitive City of Timbuctoo,* Princeton, 1953.
Murray, G. W. *Sons of Ishmael,* London, 1935.
Natirbov, Patricia, ed., The Coptic Church, *Christianity in Egypt,* Washington, 1955.
Nikitine, B. *Les Kurdes,* Paris, 1956.
Oppenheim, Max. *Die Beduinen,* vol. 3, Leipzig, 1952.
O'Shea, Raymond. *The Sand Kings of Oman,* London, 1947.
Patai, Rafael. *Israel Between East and West: A Study in Human Relations,* Philadelphia, 1953.
Patai, R. Editor, *Jordan,* HRAF #26, New Haven, 1956.
———. *Lebanon,* HRAF #46, New Haven, 1956.
———. *Syria,* HRAF #40, New Haven, 1956.
Philby, St. J. B. *Saudi Arabia,* London, 1955.
Picthall, Marmaduke. *Said the Fisherman,* New York, 1933.
Raswan, Carl R. *Black Tents of Arabia,* Boston, 1935.
Ross, Elizabeth N. *A Lady Doctor in Bakhtiariland,* London, 1921.

Royal Institute of International Affairs, *The Middle East, A Political and Economic Survey,* London, 1958.

Sanger, Richard. *The Arabian Peninsula,* Ithaca, 1954.

Sherabi, H. B. *Handbook on the Contemporary Middle East,* Washington, D. C., 1956.

Stirling, Paul. *The Social Structure of the Turkish Village,* Unpublished, microfilm available in Peabody Museum, Harvard University.

Thesiger, Wilfred. *The Ma'dan or Marsh Dwellers of Southern Iraq,* Roy. Cent. Asiatic Journal, Vol. 41, pp. 4–25, 1954.

Twitchell, K. S. *Saudi Arabia,* Princeton, 1953.

Van Ess, John. *Meet the Arab,* London, 1947.

Vidal, F. S. *Date Culture in the Oasis of al-Hasa,* Middle East Journal, Vol. 8, #4, pp. 416–428, 1954.

Villiers, Alan. *Monsoon Seas,* New York, 1952.

Warriner, Doreen. *Land and Poverty in the Middle East,* New York, 1948.

Weulersse, Jacques. *Paysans de Syrie et du Proche Orient,* Paris, 1946.

Wilber, Donald. *Afghanistan,* HRAF Pub., New Haven, 1956.

Wilber, Donald N. *Annotated Bibliography of Afghanistan,* HRAF, New Haven, 1956.

Ziadeh, Nicola. *Syria and Lebanon,* London, 1957.

INDEX

A. NAMES OF PLACES

(For names of persons, peoples, and deities, see page 382)

B. NAMES OF PERSONS, PEOPLES, AND DEITIES

(Europeans and Americans are included only if they have participated in Middle Eastern civilization thoroughly and over a long period, or if they are of Middle Eastern origin.)